BOOK 4 – CORPORATE FINANCE, PORTFOLIO MANAGEMENT, AND EQUITY INVESTMENTS

SCHWESERNOTES™ 2013 CFA LEVEL I BOOK 4: CORPORATE FINANCE, PORTFOLIO MANAGEMENT, AND EQUITY INVESTMENTS

©2012 Kaplan, Inc. All rights reserved.

Published in 2012 by Kaplan, Inc.

Printed in the United States of America.

ISBN: 978-1-4277-4266-7 / 1-4277-4266-9

PPN: 3200-2847

READING ASSIGNMENTS AND LEARNING OUTCOME STATEMENTS

The following material is a review of the Corporate Finance, Portfolio Management, and Equity Investments principles designed to address the learning outcome statements set forth by CFA Institute.

STUDY SESSION 11

Reading Assignments

Corporate Finance, CFA Program 2013 Curriculum, Volume 4 (CFA Institute, 2012)

STUDY SESSION 12

Reading Assignments

Portfolio Management, CFA Program 2013 Curriculum, Volume 4 (CFA Institute, 2012)

STUDY SESSION 13

Reading Assignments

Equity: Market Organization, Market Indices, and Market Efficiency, CFA Program 2013 Curriculum, Volume 5 (CFA Institute, 2012)

STUDY SESSION 14

Reading Assignments

Equity Analysis and Valuation, CFA Program 2013 Curriculum, Volume 5 (CFA Institute, 2012)

LEARNING OUTCOME STATEMENTS (LOS)

STUDY SESSION 11

The topical coverage corresponds with the following CFA Institute assigned reading:

36. Capital Budgeting

The candidate should be able to:

a. Describe the capital budgeting process, including the typical steps of the process, and distinguish among the various categories of capital projects. (page 11)

b. Describe the basic principles of capital budgeting, including cash flow estimation. (page 12)

c. Explain how the evaluation and selection of capital projects is affected by mutually exclusive projects, project sequencing, and capital rationing. (page 14)

d. Calculate and interpret the results using each of the following methods to evaluate a single capital project: net present value (NPV), internal rate of return (IRR), payback period, discounted payback period, and profitability index (PI). (page 14)

e. Explain the NPV profile, compare the NPV and IRR methods when evaluating independent and mutually exclusive projects, and describe the problems associated with each of the evaluation methods. (page 22)

f. Describe and account for the relative popularity of the various capital budgeting methods and explain the relation between NPV and company value and stock price. (page 25)

g. Describe the expected relations among an investment's NPV, company value, and share price. (page 25)

The topical coverage corresponds with the following CFA Institute assigned reading:

37. Cost of Capital

The candidate should be able to:

a. Calculate and interpret the weighted average cost of capital (WACC) of a company. (page 35)

b. Describe how taxes affect the cost of capital from different capital sources. (page 35)

c. Explain alternative methods of calculating the weights used in the WACC, including the use of the company's target capital structure. (page 37)

d. Explain how the marginal cost of capital and the investment opportunity schedule are used to determine the optimal capital budget. (page 38)

e. Explain the marginal cost of capital's role in determining the net present value of a project. (page 39)

f. Calculate and interpret the cost of fixed rate debt capital using the yield-to-maturity approach and the debt-rating approach. (page 39)

g. Calculate and interpret the cost of noncallable, nonconvertible preferred stock. (page 40)

h. Calculate and interpret the cost of equity capital using the capital asset pricing model approach, the dividend discount model approach, and the bond-yield-plus risk-premium approach. (page 41)

i. Calculate and interpret the beta and cost of capital for a project. (page 43)

j. Explain the country risk premium in the estimation of the cost of equity for a company located in a developing market. (page 45)

©2012 Kaplan, Inc.

k. Describe the marginal cost of capital schedule, explain why it may be upward-sloping with respect to additional capital, and calculate and interpret its breakpoints. (page 46)

l. Explain and demonstrate the correct treatment of flotation costs. (page 48)

The topical coverage corresponds with the following CFA Institute assigned reading:

38. Measures of Leverage

The candidate should be able to:

a. Define and explain leverage, business risk, sales risk, operating risk, and financial risk, and classify a risk, given a description. (page 60)

b. Calculate and interpret the degree of operating leverage, the degree of financial leverage, and the degree of total leverage. (page 61)

c. Describe the effect of financial leverage on a company's net income and return on equity. (page 64)

d. Calculate the breakeven quantity of sales and determine the company's net income at various sales levels. (page 66)

e. Calculate and interpret the operating breakeven quantity of sales. (page 66)

The topical coverage corresponds with the following CFA Institute assigned reading:

39. Dividends and Share Repurchases: Basics

The candidate should be able to:

a. Describe regular cash dividends, extra dividends, stock dividends, stock splits, and reverse stock splits, including their expected effect on a shareholder's wealth and a company's financial ratios. (page 75)

b. Describe dividend payment chronology, including the significance of declaration, holder-of-record, ex-dividend, and payment dates. (page 78)

c. Compare share repurchase methods. (page 79)

d. Calculate and compare the effects of a share repurchase on earnings per share when 1) the repurchase is financed with the company's excess cash and 2) the company uses funded debt to finance the repurchase. (page 79)

e. Calculate the effect of a share repurchase on book value per share. (page 82)

f. Explain why a cash dividend and a share repurchase of the same amount are equivalent in terms of the effect on shareholders' wealth, all else being equal. (page 82)

The topical coverage corresponds with the following CFA Institute assigned reading:

40. Working Capital Management

The candidate should be able to:

a. Describe primary and secondary sources of liquidity and factors that influence a company's liquidity position. (page 89)

b. Compare a company's liquidity measures with those of peer companies. (page 90)

c. Evaluate working capital effectiveness of a company based on its operating and cash conversion cycles, and compare the company's effectiveness with that of peer companies. (page 92)

d. Explain the effect of different types of cash flows on a company's net daily cash position. (page 92)

e. Calculate and interpret comparable yields on various securities, compare portfolio returns against a standard benchmark, and evaluate a company's short-term investment policy guidelines. (page 93)

    f.   Evaluate a company's management of accounts receivable, inventory, and accounts payable over time and compared to peer companies. (page 95)

    g.   Evaluate the choices of short-term funding available to a company and recommend a financing method. (page 98)

The topical coverage corresponds with the following CFA Institute assigned reading:
41. The Corporate Governance of Listed Companies: A Manual for Investors
The candidate should be able to:

    a.   Define corporate governance. (page 105)

    b.   Describe practices related to board and committee independence, experience, compensation, external consultants, and frequency of elections, and determine whether they are supportive of shareowner protection. (page 106)

    c.   Describe board independence and explain the importance of independent board members in corporate governance. (page 107)

    d.   Identify factors that an analyst should consider when evaluating the qualifications of board members. (page 107)

    e.   Describe the responsibilities of the audit, compensation, and nominations committees and identify factors an investor should consider when evaluating the quality of each committee. (page 108)

    f.   Explain the provisions that should be included in a strong corporate code of ethics. (page 110)

    g.   Evaluate, from a shareowner's perspective, company policies related to voting rules, shareowner sponsored proposals, common stock classes, and takeover defenses. (page 111)

STUDY SESSION 12

The topical coverage corresponds with the following CFA Institute assigned reading:
42. Portfolio Management: An Overview
The candidate should be able to:

    a.   Describe the portfolio approach to investing. (page 125)

    b.   Describe types of investors and distinctive characteristics and needs of each. (page 126)

    c.   Describe the steps in the portfolio management process. (page 127)

    d.   Describe mutual funds and compare them with other pooled investment products. (page 128)

The topical coverage corresponds with the following CFA Institute assigned reading:
43. Portfolio Risk and Return: Part I
The candidate should be able to:

    a.   Calculate and interpret major return measures and describe their appropriate uses. (page 136)

    b.   Calculate and interpret the mean, variance, and covariance (or correlation) of asset returns based on historical data. (page 139)

    c.   Describe the characteristics of the major asset classes that investors consider in forming portfolios. (page 142)

    d.   Explain risk aversion and its implications for portfolio selection. (page 143)

    e.   Calculate and interpret portfolio standard deviation. (page 144)

    f.   Describe the effect on a portfolio's risk of investing in assets that are less than perfectly correlated. (page 145)

   g. Describe and interpret the minimum-variance and efficient frontiers of risky assets and the global minimum-variance portfolio. (page 147)

   h. Discuss the selection of an optimal portfolio, given an investor's utility (or risk aversion) and the capital allocation line. (page 148)

The topical coverage corresponds with the following CFA Institute assigned reading:

44. Portfolio Risk and Return: Part II

The candidate should be able to:

   a. Describe the implications of combining a risk-free asset with a portfolio of risky assets. (page 159)

   b. Explain the capital allocation line (CAL) and the capital market line (CML). (page 160)

   c. Explain systematic and nonsystematic risk, including why an investor should not expect to receive additional return for bearing nonsystematic risk. (page 164)

   d. Explain return generating models (including the market model) and their uses. (page 166)

   e. Calculate and interpret beta. (page 167)

   f. Explain the capital asset pricing model (CAPM), including the required assumptions, and the security market line (SML). (page 169)

   g. Calculate and interpret the expected return of an asset using the CAPM. (page 173)

   h. Describe and demonstrate applications of the CAPM and the SML. (page 174)

The topical coverage corresponds with the following CFA Institute assigned reading:

45. Basics of Portfolio Planning and Construction

The candidate should be able to:

   a. Describe the reasons for a written investment policy statement (IPS). (page 184)

   b. Describe the major components of an IPS. (page 184)

   c. Describe risk and return objectives and how they may be developed for a client. (page 185)

   d. Distinguish between the willingness and the ability (capacity) to take risk in analyzing an investor's financial risk tolerance. (page 186)

   e. Describe the investment constraints of liquidity, time horizon, tax concerns, legal and regulatory factors, and unique circumstances and their implications for the choice of portfolio assets. (page 186)

   f. Explain the specification of asset classes in relation to asset allocation. (page 188)

   g. Discuss the principles of portfolio construction and the role of asset allocation in relation to the IPS. (page 189)

STUDY SESSION 13

The topical coverage corresponds with the following CFA Institute assigned reading:

46. Market Organization and Structure

The candidate should be able to:

   a. Explain the main functions of the financial system. (page 198)

   b. Describe classifications of assets and markets. (page 200)

   c. Describe the major types of securities, currencies, contracts, commodities, and real assets that trade in organized markets, including their distinguishing characteristics and major subtypes. (page 201)

d.   Describe types of financial intermediaries and services that they provide. (page 204)
e.   Compare positions an investor can take in an asset. (page 207)
f.   Calculate and interpret the leverage ratio, the rate of return on a margin transaction, and the security price at which the investor would receive a margin call. (page 209)
g.   Compare execution, validity, and clearing instructions. (page 210)
h.   Compare market orders with limit orders. (page 210)
i.   Define primary and secondary markets and explain how secondary markets support primary markets. (page 213)
j.   Describe how securities, contracts, and currencies are traded in quote-driven, order-driven, and brokered markets. (page 215)
k.   Describe characteristics of a well-functioning financial system. (page 217)
l.   Describe objectives of market regulation. (page 218)

The topical coverage corresponds with the following CFA Institute assigned reading:
47.   **Security Market Indices**
The candidate should be able to:
a.   Describe a security market index. (page 226)
b.   Calculate and interpret the value, price return, and total return of an index. (page 226)
c.   Describe the choices and issues in index construction and management. (page 227)
d.   Compare the different weighting methods used in index construction. (page 227)
e.   Calculate and analyze the value and return of an index on the basis of its weighting method. (page 229)
f.   Describe rebalancing and reconstitution of an index. (page 233)
g.   Describe uses of security market indices. (page 234)
h.   Describe types of equity indices. (page 234)
i.   Describe types of fixed-income indices. (page 235)
j.   Describe indices representing alternative investments. (page 236)
k.   Compare types of security market indices. (page 237)

The topical coverage corresponds with the following CFA Institute assigned reading:
48.   **Market Efficiency**
The candidate should be able to:
a.   Describe market efficiency and related concepts, including their importance to investment practitioners. (page 245)
b.   Distinguish between market value and intrinsic value. (page 246)
c.   Explain factors that affect a market's efficiency. (page 246)
d.   Contrast weak-form, semi-strong-form, and strong-form market efficiency. (page 247)
e.   Explain the implications of each form of market efficiency for fundamental analysis, technical analysis, and the choice between active and passive portfolio management. (page 248)
f.   Describe selected market anomalies. (page 249)
g.   Contrast the behavioral finance view of investor behavior to that of traditional finance. (page 252)

STUDY SESSION 14

The topical coverage corresponds with the following CFA Institute assigned reading:

49. Overview of Equity Securities

The candidate should be able to:

a. Describe characteristics of types of equity securities. (page 258)

b. Describe differences in voting rights and other ownership characteristics among different equity classes. (page 259)

c. Distinguish between public and private equity securities. (page 260)

d. Describe methods for investing in non-domestic equity securities. (page 261)

e. Compare the risk and return characteristics of types of equity securities. (page 262)

f. Explain the role of equity securities in the financing of a company's assets. (page 263)

g. Distinguish between the market value and book value of equity securities. (page 263)

h. Compare a company's cost of equity, its (accounting) return on equity, and investors' required rates of return. (page 264)

The topical coverage corresponds with the following CFA Institute assigned reading:

50. Introduction to Industry and Company Analysis

The candidate should be able to:

a. Explain the uses of industry analysis and the relation of industry analysis to company analysis. (page 271)

b. Compare methods by which companies can be grouped, current industry classification systems, and classify a company, given a description of its activities and the classification system. (page 271)

c. Explain the factors that affect the sensitivity of a company to the business cycle and the uses and limitations of industry and company descriptors such as "growth," "defensive," and "cyclical". (page 274)

d. Explain the relation of "peer group," as used in equity valuation, to a company's industry classification. (page 275)

e. Describe the elements that need to be covered in a thorough industry analysis. (page 276)

f. Describe the principles of strategic analysis of an industry. (page 276)

g. Explain the effects of barriers to entry, industry concentration, industry capacity, and market share stability on pricing power and return on capital. (page 278)

h. Describe product and industry life cycle models, classify an industry as to life cycle phase (e.g., embryonic, growth, shakeout, maturity, and decline) based on a description of it, and describe the limitations of the life-cycle concept in forecasting industry performance. (page 280)

i. Compare characteristics of representative industries from the various economic sectors. (page 282)

j. Describe demographic, governmental, social and technological influences on industry growth, profitability and risk. (page 282)

k. Describe the elements that should be covered in a thorough company analysis. (page 283)

The topical coverage corresponds with the following CFA Institute assigned reading:

51. Equity Valuation: Concepts and Basic Tools

The candidate should be able to:

a. Evaluate whether a security, given its current market price and a value estimate, is overvalued, fairly valued, or undervalued by the market. (page 291)

b. Describe major categories of equity valuation models. (page 292)

c. Explain the rationale for using present-value of cash flow models to value equity and describe the dividend discount and free-cash-flow-to-equity models. (page 293)

d. Calculate the intrinsic value of a non-callable, non-convertible preferred stock. (page 296)

e. Calculate and interpret the intrinsic value of an equity security based on the Gordon (constant) growth dividend discount model or a two-stage dividend discount model, as appropriate. (page 297)

f. Identify companies for which the constant growth or a multistage dividend discount model is appropriate. (page 302)

g. Explain the rationale for using price multiples to value equity and distinguish between multiples based on comparables versus multiples based on fundamentals. (page 303)

h. Calculate and interpret the following multiples: price to earnings, price to an estimate of operating cash flow, price to sales, and price to book value. (page 303)

i. Explain the use of enterprise value multiples in equity valuation and demonstrate the use of enterprise value multiples to estimate equity value. (page 308)

j. Explain asset-based valuation models and demonstrate the use of asset-based models to calculate equity value. (page 309)

k. Explain advantages and disadvantages of each category of valuation model. (page 311)

CAPITAL BUDGETING

EXAM FOCUS

If you recollect little from your basic financial management course in college (or if you didn't take one), you will need to spend some time on this review and go through the examples quite carefully. To be prepared for the exam, you need to know how to calculate all of the measures used to evaluate capital projects and the decision rules associated with them. Be sure you can interpret an NPV profile; one could be given as part of a question. Finally, know the reasoning behind the facts that (1) IRR and NPV give the same accept/reject decision for a single project and (2) IRR and NPV can give conflicting rankings for mutually exclusive projects.

LOS 36.a: Describe the capital budgeting process, including the typical steps of the process, and distinguish among the various categories of capital projects.

CFA® Program Curriculum, Volume 4, page 6

The **capital budgeting process** is the process of identifying and evaluating capital projects, that is, projects where the cash flow to the firm will be received over a period longer than a year. Any corporate decisions with an impact on future earnings can be examined using this framework. Decisions about whether to buy a new machine, expand business in another geographic area, move the corporate headquarters to Cleveland, or replace a delivery truck, to name a few, can be examined using a capital budgeting analysis.

For a number of good reasons, capital budgeting may be the most important responsibility that a financial manager has. First, because a capital budgeting decision often involves the purchase of costly long-term assets with lives of many years, the decisions made may determine the future success of the firm. Second, the principles underlying the capital budgeting process also apply to other corporate decisions, such as working capital management and making strategic mergers and acquisitions. Finally, making good capital budgeting decisions is consistent with management's primary goal of maximizing shareholder value.

The capital budgeting process has four administrative steps:

Step 1: *Idea generation.* The most important step in the capital budgeting process is generating good project ideas. Ideas can come from a number of sources including senior management, functional divisions, employees, or sources outside the company.

Step 2: *Analyzing project proposals.* Because the decision to accept or reject a capital project is based on the project's expected future cash flows, a cash flow forecast must be made for each product to determine its expected profitability.

Step 3: Create the firm-wide capital budget. Firms must prioritize profitable projects according to the timing of the project's cash flows, available company resources, and the company's overall strategic plan. Many projects that are attractive individually may not make sense strategically.

Step 4: Monitoring decisions and conducting a post-audit. It is important to follow up on all capital budgeting decisions. An analyst should compare the actual results to the projected results, and project managers should explain why projections did or did not match actual performance. Because the capital budgeting process is only as good as the estimates of the inputs into the model used to forecast cash flows, a post-audit should be used to identify systematic errors in the forecasting process and improve company operations.

Categories of Capital Budgeting Projects

Capital budgeting projects may be divided into the following categories:

- *Replacement projects to maintain the business* are normally made without detailed analysis. The only issues are whether the existing operations should continue and, if so, whether existing procedures or processes should be maintained.
- *Replacement projects for cost reduction* determine whether equipment that is obsolete, but still usable, should be replaced. A fairly detailed analysis is necessary in this case.
- *Expansion projects* are taken on to grow the business and involve a complex decision-making process because they require an explicit forecast of future demand. A very detailed analysis is required.
- *New product or market development* also entails a complex decision-making process that will require a detailed analysis due to the large amount of uncertainty involved.
- *Mandatory projects* may be required by a governmental agency or insurance company and typically involve safety-related or environmental concerns. These projects typically generate little to no revenue, but they accompany new revenue-producing projects undertaken by the company.
- *Other projects.* Some projects are not easily analyzed through the capital budgeting process. Such projects may include a pet project of senior management (e.g., corporate perks) or a high-risk endeavor that is difficult to analyze with typical capital budgeting assessment methods (e.g., research and development projects).

LOS 36.b: Describe the basic principles of capital budgeting, including cash flow estimation.

CFA® Program Curriculum, Volume 4, page 8

The capital budgeting process involves five key principles:

1. *Decisions are based on cash flows, not accounting income.* The relevant cash flows to consider as part of the capital budgeting process are **incremental cash flows**, the changes in cash flows that will occur if the project is undertaken.

    Sunk costs are costs that cannot be avoided, even if the project is not undertaken. Because these costs are not affected by the accept/reject decision, they should not be included in the analysis. An example of a sunk cost is a consulting fee paid to a marketing research firm to estimate demand for a new product prior to a decision on the project.

Externalities are the effects the acceptance of a project may have on other firm cash flows. The primary one is a negative externality called **cannibalization**, which occurs when a new project takes sales from an existing product. When considering externalities, the full implication of the new project (loss in sales of existing products) should be taken into account. An example of cannibalization is when a soft drink company introduces a diet version of an existing beverage. The analyst should subtract the lost sales of the existing beverage from the expected new sales of the diet version when estimated incremental project cash flows. A positive externality exists when doing the project would have a positive effect on sales of a firm's other product lines.

A project has a **conventional cash flow pattern** if the sign on the cash flows changes only once, with one or more cash outflows followed by one or more cash inflows. An **unconventional cash flow pattern** has more than one sign change. For example, a project might have an initial investment outflow, a series of cash inflows, and a cash outflow for asset retirement costs at the end of the project's life.

2. *Cash flows are based on opportunity costs.* **Opportunity costs** are cash flows that a firm will lose by undertaking the project under analysis. These are cash flows generated by an asset the firm already owns that would be forgone if the project under consideration is undertaken. Opportunity costs should be included in project costs. For example, when building a plant, even if the firm already owns the land, the cost of the land should be charged to the project because it could be sold if not used.

3. *The timing of cash flows is important.* Capital budgeting decisions account for the time value of money, which means that cash flows received earlier are worth more than cash flows to be received later.

4. *Cash flows are analyzed on an after-tax basis.* The impact of taxes must be considered when analyzing all capital budgeting projects. Firm value is based on cash flows they get to keep, not those they send to the government.

5. *Financing costs are reflected in the project's required rate of return.* Do not consider financing costs specific to the project when estimating incremental cash flows. The discount rate used in the capital budgeting analysis takes account of the firm's cost of capital. Only projects that are expected to return more than the cost of the capital needed to fund them will increase the value of the firm.

LOS 36.c: Explain how the evaluation and selection of capital projects is affected by mutually exclusive projects, project sequencing, and capital rationing.

CFA® Program Curriculum, Volume 4, page 9

Independent vs. Mutually Exclusive Projects

Independent projects are projects that are unrelated to each other and allow for each project to be evaluated based on its own profitability. For example, if projects A and B are independent, and both projects are profitable, then the firm could accept both projects. **Mutually exclusive** means that only one project in a set of possible projects can be accepted and that the projects compete with each other. If projects A and B were mutually exclusive, the firm could accept either Project A or Project B, but not both. A capital budgeting decision between two different stamping machines with different costs and output would be an example of choosing between two mutually exclusive projects.

Project Sequencing

Some projects must be undertaken in a certain order, or sequence, so that investing in a project today creates the opportunity to invest in other projects in the future. For example, if a project undertaken today is profitable, that may create the opportunity to invest in a second project a year from now. However, if the project undertaken today turns out to be unprofitable, the firm will not invest in the second project.

Unlimited Funds vs. Capital Rationing

If a firm has unlimited access to capital, the firm can undertake all projects with expected returns that exceed the cost of capital. Many firms have constraints on the amount of capital they can raise and must use *capital rationing*. If a firm's profitable project opportunities exceed the amount of funds available, the firm must ration, or prioritize, its capital expenditures with the goal of achieving the maximum increase in value for shareholders given its available capital.

LOS 36.d: Calculate and interpret the results using each of the following methods to evaluate a single capital project: net present value (NPV), internal rate of return (IRR), payback period, discounted payback period, and profitability index (PI).

CFA® Program Curriculum, Volume 4, page 10

Net Present Value (NPV)

We first examined the calculation of net present value (NPV) in Quantitative Methods. The NPV is the sum of the present values of all the expected incremental cash flows if a project is undertaken. The discount rate used is the firm's cost of capital, adjusted for the risk level of the project. For a normal project, with an initial cash outflow followed by a series of expected after-tax cash inflows, the NPV is the present value of the expected inflows minus the initial cost of the project.

$$NPV = CF_0 + \frac{CF_1}{(1+k)^1} + \frac{CF_2}{(1+k)^2} + \ldots + \frac{CF_n}{(1+k)^n} = \sum_{t=0}^{n} \frac{CF_t}{(1+k)^t}$$

where:
CF_0 = initial investment outlay (a negative cash flow)
CF_t = after-tax cash flow at time t
k = required rate of return for project

A positive NPV project is expected to increase shareholder wealth, a negative NPV project is expected to decrease shareholder wealth, and a zero NPV project has no expected effect on shareholder wealth.

For *independent* projects, the *NPV decision rule* is simply to accept any project with a positive NPV and to reject any project with a negative NPV.

Example: NPV analysis

Using the project cash flows presented in Table 1, compute the NPV of each project's cash flows and determine for each project whether it should be accepted or rejected. Assume that the cost of capital is 10%.

Table 1: Expected Net After-Tax Cash Flows

Year (t)	Project A	Project B
0	−$2,000	−$2,000
1	1,000	200
2	800	600
3	600	800
4	200	1,200

Answer:

$$NPV_A = -2,000 + \frac{1,000}{(1.1)^1} + \frac{800}{(1.1)^2} + \frac{600}{(1.1)^3} + \frac{200}{(1.1)^4} = \$157.64$$

$$NPV_B = -2,000 + \frac{200}{(1.1)^1} + \frac{600}{(1.1)^2} + \frac{800}{(1.1)^3} + \frac{1,200}{(1.1)^4} = \$98.36$$

Both Project A and Project B have positive NPVs, so both should be accepted.

You may calculate the NPV directly by using the cash flow (CF) keys on your calculator. The process is illustrated in Table 2 and Table 3 for Project A.

Table 2: Calculating NPV$_A$ With the TI Business Analyst II Plus

Key Strokes	Explanation	Display
[CF] [2nd] [CLR WORK]	Clear memory registers	CF0 = 0.00000
2,000 [+/−] [ENTER]	Initial cash outlay	CF0 = −2,000.00000
[↓] 1,000 [ENTER]	Period 1 cash flow	C01 = 1,000.00000
[↓]	Frequency of cash flow 1	F01 = 1.00000
[↓] 800 [ENTER]	Period 2 cash flow	C02 = 800.00000
[↓]	Frequency of cash flow 2	F02 = 1.00000
[↓] 600 [ENTER]	Period 3 cash flow	C03 = 600.00000
[↓]	Frequency of cash flow 3	F03 = 1.00000
[↓] 200 [ENTER]	Period 4 cash flow	C04 = 200.00000
[↓]	Frequency of cash flow 4	F04 = 1.00000
[NPV] 10 [ENTER]	10% discount rate	I = 10.00000
[↓] [CPT]	Calculate NPV	NPV = 157.63951

Table 3: Calculating NPV$_A$ With the HP12C

Key Strokes	Explanation	Display
[f]→[FIN] → [f] → [REG]	Clear memory registers	0.00000
[f] [5]	Display 5 decimals. You only need to do this once.	0.00000
2,000 [CHS] [g] [CF0]	Initial cash outlay	−2,000.00000
1,000 [g] [CFj]	Period 1 cash flow	1,000.00000
800 [g] [CFj]	Period 2 cash flow	800.00000
600 [g] [CFj]	Period 3 cash flow	600.00000
200 [g] [CFj]	Period 4 cash flow	200.00000
10 [i]	10% discount rate	10.00000
[f] [NPV]	Calculate NPV	157.63951

Internal Rate of Return (IRR)

For a normal project, the **internal rate of return** (IRR) is the discount rate that makes the present value of the expected incremental after-tax cash inflows just equal to the initial cost of the project. More generally, the IRR is the discount rate that makes the present values of a project's estimated cash inflows equal to the present value of the project's estimated cash outflows. That is, IRR is the discount rate that makes the following relationship hold:

PV (inflows) = PV (outflows)

The IRR is also the discount rate for which the NPV of a project is equal to zero:

$$NPV = 0 = CF_0 + \frac{CF_1}{(1+IRR)^1} + \frac{CF_2}{(1+IRR)^2} + \ldots + \frac{CF_n}{(1+IRR)^n} = \sum_{t=0}^{n} \frac{CF_t}{(1+IRR)^t}$$

To calculate the IRR, you may use the trial-and-error method. That is, just keep guessing IRRs until you get the right one, or you may use a financial calculator.

IRR decision rule: First, determine the required rate of return for a given project. This is usually the firm's cost of capital. Note that the required rate of return may be higher or lower than the firm's cost of capital to adjust for differences between project risk and the firm's average project risk.

If IRR > the required rate of return, accept the project.

If IRR < the required rate of return, reject the project.

Example: IRR

Continuing with the cash flows presented in Table 1 for projects A and B, compute the IRR for each project and determine whether to accept or reject each project under the assumptions that the projects are independent and that the required rate of return is 10%.

Answer:

$$\text{Project A: } 0 = -2,000 + \frac{1,000}{(1+IRR_A)^1} + \frac{800}{(1+IRR_A)^2} + \frac{600}{(1+IRR_A)^3} + \frac{200}{(1+IRR_A)^4}$$

$$\text{Project B: } 0 = -2,000 + \frac{200}{(1+IRR_B)^1} + \frac{600}{(1+IRR_B)^2} + \frac{800}{(1+IRR_B)^3} + \frac{1,200}{(1+IRR_B)^4}$$

The cash flows should be entered as in Table 2 and Table 3 (if you haven't changed them, they are still there from the calculation of NPV).

With the TI calculator, the IRR can be calculated with:

[IRR] [CPT] to get 14.4888(%) for Project A and 11.7906(%) for Project B.

With the HP12C, the IRR can be calculated with:

[f] [IRR]

Both projects should be accepted because their IRRs are greater than the 10% required rate of return.

Payback Period

The **payback period** (PBP) is the number of years it takes to recover the initial cost of an investment.

Example: Payback period

Calculate the payback periods for the two projects that have the cash flows presented in Table 1. Note the Year 0 cash flow represents the initial cost of each project.

Answer:

Note that the cumulative net cash flow (NCF) is just the running total of the cash flows at the end of each time period. Payback will occur when the cumulative NCF equals zero. To find the payback periods, construct Table 4.

Table 4: Cumulative Net Cash Flows

	Year (t)	0	1	2	3	4
Project A	Net cash flow	−2,000	1,000	800	600	200
	Cumulative NCF	−2,000	−1,000	−200	400	600
Project B	Net cash flow	−2,000	200	600	800	1,200
	Cumulative NCF	−2,000	−1,800	−1,200	−400	800

The payback period is determined from the cumulative net cash flow table as follows:

$$\text{payback period} = \text{full years until recovery} + \frac{\text{unrecovered cost at the beginning of last year}}{\text{cash flow during the last year}}$$

$$\text{payback period A} = 2 + \frac{200}{600} = 2.33 \text{ years}$$

$$\text{payback period B} = 3 + \frac{400}{1200} = 3.33 \text{ years}$$

Because the payback period is a measure of liquidity, for a firm with liquidity concerns, the shorter a project's payback period, the better. However, project decisions should not be made on the basis of their payback periods because of the method's drawbacks.

The main drawbacks of the payback period are that it does not take into account either the time value of money or cash flows beyond the payback period, which means terminal or salvage value wouldn't be considered. These drawbacks mean that the payback period is useless as a measure of profitability.

The main benefit of the payback period is that it is a good measure of project liquidity. Firms with limited access to additional liquidity often impose a maximum payback period and then use a measure of profitability, such as NPV or IRR, to evaluate projects that satisfy this maximum payback period constraint.

 Professor's Note: If you have the Professional model of the TI calculator, you can easily calculate the payback period and the discounted payback period (which follows). Once NPV is displayed, use the down arrow to scroll through NFV (net future value), to PB (payback), and DPB (discounted payback). You must use the compute key when "PB=" is displayed. If the annual net cash flows are equal, the payback period is simply project cost divided by the annual cash flow.

Discounted Payback Period

The **discounted payback period** uses the present values of the project's estimated cash flows. It is the number of years it takes a project to recover its initial investment in present value terms and, therefore, must be greater than the payback period without discounting.

Example: Discounted payback method

Compute the discounted payback period for projects A and B described in Table 5. Assume that the firm's cost of capital is 10% and the firm's maximum discounted payback period is four years.

Table 5: Cash Flows for Projects A and B

	Year (t)	0	1	2	3	4
Project A	Net Cash Flow	−2,000	1,000	800	600	200
	Discounted NCF	−2,000	910	661	451	137
	Cumulative DNCF	−2,000	−1,090	−429	22	159
Project B	Net Cash Flow	−2,000	200	600	800	1,200
	Discounted NCF	−2,000	182	496	601	820
	Cumulative DNCF	−2,000	−1,818	−1,322	−721	99

Answer:

$$\text{discounted payback A} = 2 + \frac{429}{451} = 2.95 \text{ years}$$

$$\text{discounted payback B} = 3 + \frac{721}{820} = 3.88 \text{ years}$$

The discounted payback period addresses one of the drawbacks of the payback period by discounting cash flows at the project's required rate of return. However, the discounted payback period still does not consider any cash flows beyond the payback period, which means that it is a poor measure of profitability. Again, its use is primarily as a measure of liquidity.

Profitability Index (PI)

The **profitability index** (PI) is the present value of a project's future cash flows divided by the initial cash outlay:

$$PI = \frac{PV \text{ of future cash flows}}{CF_0} = 1 + \frac{NPV}{CF_0}$$

The profitability index is related closely to net present value. The NPV is the difference between the present value of future cash flows and the initial cash outlay, and the PI is the ratio of the present value of future cash flows to the initial cash outlay.

If the NPV of a project is positive, the PI will be greater than one. If the NPV is negative, the PI will be less than one. It follows that the *decision rule* for the PI is:

If PI > 1.0, accept the project.

If PI < 1.0, reject the project.

Example: Profitability index

Going back to our original example, calculate the PI for projects A and B. Note that Table 1 has been reproduced as Table 6.

Table 6: Expected Net After-Tax Cash Flows

Year (t)	Project A	Project B
0	–$2,000	–$2,000
1	1,000	200
2	800	600
3	600	800
4	200	1,200

Answer:

$$\text{PV future cash flows}_A = \frac{1,000}{(1.1)^1} + \frac{800}{(1.1)^2} + \frac{600}{(1.1)^3} + \frac{200}{(1.1)^4} = \$2,157.64$$

$$PI_A = \frac{\$2,157.64}{\$2,000} = 1.079$$

$$\text{PV future cash flows}_B = \frac{200}{(1.1)^1} + \frac{600}{(1.1)^2} + \frac{800}{(1.1)^3} + \frac{1,200}{(1.1)^4} = \$2,098.36$$

$$PI_B = \frac{\$2,098.36}{\$2,000} = 1.049$$

Decision: If projects A and B are independent, accept both projects because PI > 1 for both projects.

Professor's Note: The accept/reject decision rule here is exactly equivalent to both the NPV and IRR decision rules. That is, if PI > 1, then the NPV must be positive, and the IRR must be greater than the discount rate. Note also that once you have the NPV, you can just add back the initial outlay to get the PV of the cash inflows used here. Recall that the NPV of Project B is $98.36 with an initial cost of $2,000. PI is simply (2,000 + 98.36) / 2000.

LOS 36.e: Explain the NPV profile, compare the NPV and IRR methods when evaluating independent and mutually exclusive projects, and describe the problems associated with each of the evaluation methods.

CFA® Program Curriculum, Volume 4, page 16

A project's **NPV profile** is a graph that shows a project's NPV for different discount rates. The NPV profiles for the two projects described in the previous example are presented in Figure 1. The project NPVs are summarized in the table below the graph. The discount rates are on the x-axis of the NPV profile, and the corresponding NPVs are plotted on the y-axis.

Figure 1: NPV Profiles

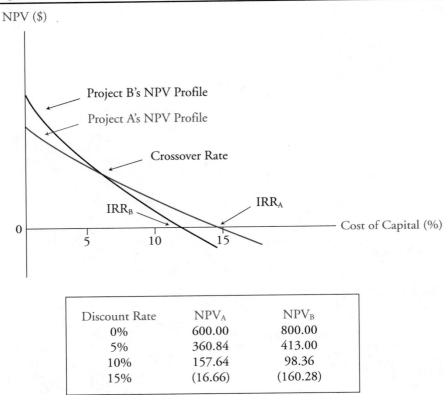

Discount Rate	NPV$_A$	NPV$_B$
0%	600.00	800.00
5%	360.84	413.00
10%	157.64	98.36
15%	(16.66)	(160.28)

Note that the projects' IRRs are the discount rates where the NPV profiles intersect the x-axis, because these are the discount rates for which NPV equals zero. Recall that the IRR is the discount rate that results in an NPV of zero.

Also notice in Figure 1 that the NPV profiles intersect. They intersect at the discount rate for which NPVs of the projects are equal, 7.2%. This rate at which the NPVs are equal is called the **crossover rate**. At discount rates below 7.2% (to the left of the intersection), Project B has the greater NPV, and at discount rates above 7.2%, Project A has a greater NPV. Clearly, the discount rate used in the analysis can determine which one of two mutually exclusive projects will be accepted.

The NPV profiles for projects A and B intersect because of a difference in the timing of the cash flows. Examining the cash flows for the projects (Table 1), we can see that the total cash inflows for Project B are greater ($2,800) than those of Project A ($2,600). Because they both have the same initial cost ($2,000) at a discount rate of zero, Project B has a greater NPV (2,800 – 2,000 = $800) than Project A (2,600 – 2000 = $600).

We can also see that the cash flows for Project B come later in the project's life. That's why the NPV of Project B falls faster than the NPV of Project A as the discount rate increases, and the NPVs are eventually equal at a discount rate of 7.2%. At discount rates above 7.2%, the fact that the total cash flows of Project B are greater in nominal dollars is overridden by the fact that Project B's cash flows come later in the project's life than those of Project A.

Example: Crossover rate

Two projects have the following cash flows:

	20X1	20X2	20X3	20X4
Project A	–550	150	300	450
Project B	–300	50	200	300

What is the crossover rate for Project A and Project B?

Answer:

The crossover rate is the discount rate that makes the NPVs of Projects A and B equal. That is, it makes the NPV of the *differences between* the two projects' cash flows equal zero.

To determine the crossover rate, subtract the cash flows of Project B from those of Project A and calculate the IRR of the differences.

	20X1	20X2	20X3	20X4
Project A – Project B	–250	100	100	150

CF0 = –250; CF1 = 100; CF2 = 100; CF3 = 150; CPT IRR = 17.5%

The Relative Advantages and Disadvantages of the NPV and IRR Methods

A **key advantage of NPV** is that it is a direct measure of the expected increase in the value of the firm. NPV is theoretically the best method. Its main weakness is that it does not include any consideration of the size of the project. For example, an NPV of $100 is great for a project costing $100 but not so great for a project costing $1 million.

A **key advantage of IRR** is that it measures profitability as a percentage, showing the return on each dollar invested. The IRR provides information on the margin of safety that the NPV does not. From the IRR, we can tell how much below the IRR (estimated return) the actual project return could fall, in percentage terms, before the project becomes uneconomic (has a negative NPV).

The *disadvantages* of the IRR method are (1) the possibility of producing rankings of mutually exclusive projects different from those from NPV analysis and (2) the possibility that a project has multiple IRRs or no IRR.

Conflicting Project Rankings

Consider two projects with an initial investment of €1,000 and a required rate of return of 10%. Project X will generate cash inflows of €500 at the end of each of the next five years. Project Y will generate a single cash flow of €4,000 at the end of the fifth year.

Year	Project X	Project Y
0	−€1,000	−€1,000
1	500	0
2	500	0
3	500	0
4	500	0
5	500	4,000
NPV	€895	€1,484
IRR	41.0%	32.0%

Project X has a higher IRR, but Project Y has a higher NPV. Which is the better project? If Project X is selected, the firm will be worth €895 more because the PV of the expected cash flows is €895 more than the initial cost of the project. Project Y, however, is expected to increase the value of the firm by €1,484. Project Y is the better project. Because NPV measures the expected increase in wealth from undertaking a project, NPV is the only acceptable criterion when ranking projects.

Another reason, besides cash flow timing differences, that NPV and IRR may give conflicting project rankings is differences in project size. Consider two projects, one with an initial outlay of $100,000, and one with an initial outlay of $1 million. The smaller project may have a higher IRR, but the increase in firm value (NPV) may be small compared to the increase in firm value (NPV) of the larger project, even though its IRR is lower.

It is sometimes said that the NPV method implicitly assumes that project cash flows can be reinvested at the discount rate used to calculate NPV. This is a realistic assumption, because it is reasonable to assume that project cash flows could be used to reduce the firm's capital requirements. Any funds that are used to reduce the firm's capital requirements allow the firm to avoid the cost of capital on those funds. Just by reducing its equity capital and debt, the firm could "earn" its cost of capital on funds used to reduce its capital requirements. If we were to rank projects by their IRRs, we would be implicitly assuming that project cash flows could be reinvested at the project's IRR. This is unrealistic and, strictly speaking, if the firm could earn that rate on invested funds, that rate should be the one used to discount project cash flows.

The "Multiple IRR" and "No IRR" Problems

If a project has cash outflows during its life or at the end of its life in addition to its initial cash outflow, the project is said to have an unconventional cash flow pattern. Projects with such cash flows may have more than one IRR (there may be more than one discount rate that will produce an NPV equal to zero).

It is also possible to have a project where there is no discount rate that results in a zero NPV, that is, the project does not have an IRR. A project with no IRR may actually be a profitable project. The lack of an IRR results from the project having unconventional cash flows, where mathematically, no IRR exists. NPV does not have this problem and produces theoretically correct decisions for projects with unconventional cash flow patterns.

Neither of these problems can arise with the NPV method. If a project has non-normal cash flows, the NPV method will give the appropriate accept/reject decision.

LOS 36.f: Describe and account for the relative popularity of the various capital budgeting methods and explain the relation between NPV and company value and stock price.

LOS 36.g: Describe the expected relations among an investment's NPV, company value, and share price.

CFA® Program Curriculum, Volume 4, page 25

Despite the superiority of NPV and IRR methods for evaluating projects, surveys of corporate financial managers show that a variety of methods are used. The surveys show that the capital budgeting method used by a company varied according to four general criteria:

1. **Location.** European countries tended to use the payback period method as much or more than the IRR and NPV methods.

2. **Size of the company.** The larger the company, the more likely it was to use discounted cash flow techniques such as the NPV and IRR methods.

3. **Public vs. private.** Private companies used the payback period more often than public companies. Public companies tended to prefer discounted cash flow methods.

4. **Management education.** The higher the level of education (i.e., MBA), the more likely the company was to use discounted cash flow techniques, such as the NPV and IRR methods.

The Relationship Between NPV and Stock Price

Because the NPV method is a direct measure of the expected change in firm value from undertaking a capital project, it is also the criterion most related to stock prices. In theory, a positive NPV project should cause a proportionate increase in a company's stock price.

Example: Relationship between NPV and stock price

Presstech is investing $500 million in new printing equipment. The present value of the future after-tax cash flows resulting from the equipment is $750 million. Presstech currently has 100 million shares outstanding, with a current market price of $45 per share. Assuming that this project is new information and is independent of other expectations about the company, calculate the effect of the new equipment on the value of the company and the effect on Presstech's stock price.

Answer:

NPV of the new printing equipment project = $750 million – $500 million = $250 million.

Value of company prior to new equipment project = 100 million shares × $45 per share = $4.5 billion.

Value of company after new equipment project = $4.5 billion + $250 million = $4.75 billion.

Price per share after new equipment project = $4.75 billion / 100 million shares = $47.50.

The stock price should increase from $45.00 per share to $47.50 per share as a result of the project.

In reality, the impact of a project on the company's stock price is more complicated than the previous example. A company's stock price is a function of the present value of its expected future earnings stream. As a result, changes in the stock price will result more from changes in *expectations* about a firm's positive NPV projects. If a company announces a project for which managers expect a positive NPV but analysts expect a lower level of profitability from the project than the company does (e.g., an acquisition), the stock price may actually drop on the announcement. As another example, a project announcement may be taken as a signal about other future capital projects, raising expectations and resulting in a stock price increase that is much greater than what the NPV of the announced project would justify.

KEY CONCEPTS

LOS 36.a

Capital budgeting is the process of evaluating capital projects, projects with cash flows over more than one year.

The four steps of the capital budgeting process are: (1) Generate investment ideas; (2) Analyze project ideas; (3) Create firm-wide capital budget; and (4) Monitor decisions and conduct a post-audit.

Categories of capital projects include: (1) Replacement projects for maintaining the business or for cost reduction; (2) Expansion projects; (3) New product or market development; (4) Mandatory projects to meet environmental or regulatory requirements; (5) Other projects, such as research and development or pet projects of senior management.

LOS 36.b

Capital budgeting decisions should be based on incremental after-tax cash flows, the expected differences in after-tax cash flows if a project is undertaken. Sunk (already incurred) costs are not considered, but externalities and cash opportunity costs must be included in project cash flows.

LOS 36.c

Acceptable independent projects can all be undertaken, while a firm must choose between or among mutually exclusive projects.

Project sequencing concerns the opportunities for future capital projects that may be created by undertaking a current project.

If a firm cannot undertake all profitable projects because of limited ability to raise capital, the firm should choose that group of fundable positive NPV projects with the highest total NPV.

LOS 36.d

NPV is the sum of the present values of a project's expected cash flows and represents the increase in firm value from undertaking a project. Positive NPV projects should be undertaken, but negative NPV projects are expected to decrease the value of the firm.

The IRR is the discount rate that equates the present values of the project's expected cash inflows and outflows and, thus, is the discount rate for which the NPV of a project is zero. A project for which the IRR is greater (less) than the discount rate will have an NPV that is positive (negative) and should be accepted (not be accepted).

The payback (discounted payback) period is the number of years required to recover the original cost of the project (original cost of the project in present value terms).

The profitability index is the ratio of the present value of a project's future cash flows to its initial cash outlay and is greater than one when a project's NPV is positive.

LOS 36.e

An NPV profile plots a project's NPV as a function of the discount rate, and it intersects the horizontal axis (NPV = 0) at its IRR. If two NPV profiles intersect at some discount rate, that is the crossover rate, and different projects are preferred at discount rates higher and lower than the crossover rate.

For projects with conventional cash flow patterns, the NPV and IRR methods produce the same accept/reject decision, but projects with unconventional cash flow patterns can produce multiple IRRs or no IRR.

Mutually exclusive projects can be ranked based on their NPVs, but rankings based on other methods will not necessarily maximize the value of the firm.

LOS 36.f

Small companies, private companies, and companies outside the United States are more likely to use techniques simpler than NPV, such as payback period.

LOS 36.g

The NPV method is a measure of the expected change in company value from undertaking a project. A firm's stock price may be affected to the extent that engaging in a project with that NPV was previously unanticipated by investors.

CONCEPT CHECKERS

1. Which of the following statements concerning the principles underlying the capital budgeting process is *most accurate*?
   A. Cash flows should be based on opportunity costs.
   B. Financing costs should be reflected in a project's incremental cash flows.
   C. The net income for a project is essential for making a correct capital budgeting decision.

2. Which of the following statements about the payback period method is *least accurate*? The payback period:
   A. provides a rough measure of a project's liquidity.
   B. considers all cash flows throughout the entire life of a project.
   C. is the number of years it takes to recover the original cost of the investment.

3. Which of the following statements about NPV and IRR is *least accurate*?
   A. The IRR is the discount rate that equates the present value of the cash inflows with the present value of outflows.
   B. For mutually exclusive projects, if the NPV method and the IRR method give conflicting rankings, the analyst should use the IRRs to select the project.
   C. The NPV method assumes that cash flows will be reinvested at the cost of capital, while IRR rankings implicitly assume that cash flows are reinvested at the IRR.

4. Which of the following statements is *least accurate*? The discounted payback period:
   A. frequently ignores terminal values.
   B. is generally shorter than the regular payback.
   C. is the time it takes for the present value of the project's cash inflows to equal the initial cost of the investment.

5. Which of the following statements about NPV and IRR is *least accurate*?
   A. The IRR can be positive even if the NPV is negative.
   B. When the IRR is equal to the cost of capital, the NPV will be zero.
   C. The NPV will be positive if the IRR is less than the cost of capital.

Use the following data to answer Questions 6 through 10.

A company is considering the purchase of a copier that costs $5,000. Assume a required rate of return of 10% and the following cash flow schedule:

- Year 1: $3,000.
- Year 2: $2,000.
- Year 3: $2,000.

6. What is the project's payback period?
   A. 1.5 years.
   B. 2.0 years.
   C. 2.5 years.

7. The project's discounted payback period is *closest* to:
   A. 1.4 years.
   B. 2.0 years.
   C. 2.4 years.

8. What is the project's NPV?
   A. −$309.
   B. +$883.
   C. +$1,523.

9. The project's IRR is *closest* to:
   A. 10%.
   B. 15%.
   C. 20%.

10. What is the project's profitability index (PI)?
    A. 0.72.
    B. 1.18.
    C. 1.72.

11. An analyst has gathered the following information about a project:
    - Cost $10,000
    - Annual cash inflow $4,000
    - Life   4 years
    - Cost of capital   12%

    Which of the following statements about the project is *least accurate*?
    A. The discounted payback period is 3.5 years.
    B. The IRR of the project is 21.9%; accept the project.
    C. The NPV of the project is +$2,149; accept the project.

Use the following data for Questions 12 and 13.

An analyst has gathered the following data about two projects, each with a 12% required rate of return.

	Project A	Project B
Initial cost	$15,000	$20,000
Life	5 years	4 years
Cash inflows	$5,000/year	$7,500/year

12. If the projects are independent, the company should:
    A. accept Project A and reject Project B.
    B. reject Project A and accept Project B.
    C. accept both projects.

13. If the projects are mutually exclusive, the company should:
    A. reject both projects.
    B. accept Project A and reject Project B.
    C. reject Project A and accept Project B.

14. The NPV profiles of two projects will intersect:
    A. at their internal rates of return.
    B. if they have different discount rates.
    C. at the discount rate that makes their net present values equal.

15. The post-audit is used to:
    A. improve cash flow forecasts and stimulate management to improve operations and bring results into line with forecasts.
    B. improve cash flow forecasts and eliminate potentially profitable but risky projects.
    C. stimulate management to improve operations, bring results into line with forecasts, and eliminate potentially profitable but risky projects.

16. Based on surveys of comparable firms, which of the following firms would be *most likely* to use NPV as its preferred method for evaluating capital projects?
   A. A small public industrial company located in France.
   B. A private company located in the United States.
   C. A large public company located in the United States.

17. Fullen Machinery is investing $400 million in new industrial equipment. The present value of the future after-tax cash flows resulting from the equipment is $700 million. Fullen currently has 200 million shares of common stock outstanding, with a current market price of $36 per share. Assuming that this project is new information and is independent of other expectations about the company, what is the theoretical effect of the new equipment on Fullen's stock price? The stock price will:
   A. decrease to $33.50.
   B. increase to $37.50.
   C. increase to $39.50.

©2012 Kaplan, Inc.

ANSWERS – CONCEPT CHECKERS

1. **A**   Cash flows are based on opportunity costs. Financing costs are recognized in the project's required rate of return. Accounting net income, which includes non-cash expenses, is irrelevant; incremental cash flows are essential for making correct capital budgeting decisions.

2. **B**   The payback period ignores cash flows that go beyond the payback period.

3. **B**   NPV should always be used if NPV and IRR give conflicting decisions.

4. **B**   The discounted payback is longer than the regular payback because cash flows are discounted to their present value.

5. **C**   If IRR is less than the cost of capital, the result will be a negative NPV.

6. **B**   Cash flow (CF) after year 2 = –5,000 + 3,000 + 2,000 = 0. Cost of copier is paid back in the first two years.

7. **C**   Year 1 discounted cash flow = 3,000 / 1.10 = 2,727; year 2 DCF = 2,000 / 1.10^2 = 1,653; year 3 DCF = 2,000 / 1.10^3 = 1,503. CF required after year 2 = –5,000 + 2,727 +1,653 = –\$620, 620 / year 3 DCF = 620 / 1,503 = 0.41, for a discounted payback of 2.4 years.

   Using a financial calculator:
   Year 1: I = 10%; FV = 3,000; N = 1; PMT = 0; CPT → PV = –2,727
   Year 2: N = 2; FV = 2,000; CPT → PV = –1,653
   Year 3: N = 3; CPT → PV = –1,503
   5,000 – (2,727 + 1,653) = 620, 620 / 1,503 = 0.413, so discounted payback = 2 + 0.4 = 2.4.

8. **B**   NPV = CF_0 + (discounted cash flows years 0 to 3 calculated in Question 7) = –5,000 + (2,727 + 1,653 + 1,503) = –5,000 + 5,833 = \$883.

9. **C**   From the information given, you know the NPV is positive, so the IRR must be greater than 10%. You only have two choices, 15% and 20%. Pick one and solve the NPV; if it's not close to zero, you guessed wrong—pick the other one. Alternatively, you can solve directly for the IRR as CF_0 = –5,000, CF_1 = 3,000, CF_2 = 2,000, CF_3 = 2,000. IRR = 20.64%.

10. **B**   PI = PV of future cash flows / CF_0 (discounted cash flows years 0 to 3 calculated in Question 7). PI = (2,727 + 1,653 + 1,503) / 5,000 = 1.177.

11. **A**   The discounted payback period of 3.15 is calculated as follows:

$$CF_0 = -10,000; \quad PVCF_1 = \frac{4,000}{1.12} = 3,571; \quad PVCF_2 = \frac{4,000}{1.12^2} = 3,189; \quad PVCF_3 = \frac{4,000}{1.12^3} = 2,847;$$

$$\text{and } PVCF_4 = \frac{4,000}{1.12^4} = 2,542. \quad \text{CF after year 3} = -10,000 + 3,571 + 3,189 + 2,847 = -393$$

$$\frac{393}{\text{year 4 DCF}} = \frac{393}{2,542} = 0.15, \text{ for a discounted payback period of 3.15 years.}$$

12. **C**   Independent projects accept all with positive NPVs or IRRs greater than cost of capital. NPV computation is easy—treat cash flows as an annuity.

Project A: N = 5; I = 12; PMT = 5,000; FV = 0; CPT → PV = –18,024
NPV_A = 18,024 – 15,000 = $3,024

Project B: N = 4; I = 12; PMT = 7,500; FV = 0; CPT → PV = –22,780
NPV_B = 22,780 – 20,000 = $2,780

13. **B**   Accept the project with the highest NPV.

14. **C**   The crossover rate for the NPV profiles of two projects occurs at the discount rate that results in both projects having equal NPVs.

15. **A**   A post-audit identifies what went right and what went wrong. It is used to improve forecasting and operations.

16. **C**   According to survey results, large companies, public companies, U.S. companies, and companies managed by a corporate manager with an advanced degree are more likely to use discounted cash flow techniques like NPV to evaluate capital projects.

17. **B**   The NPV of the new equipment is $700 million – $400 million = $300 million. The value of this project is added to Fullen's current market value. On a per-share basis, the addition is worth $300 million / 200 million shares, for a net addition to the share price of $1.50. $36.00 + $1.50 = $37.50.

COST OF CAPITAL

EXAM FOCUS

The firm must decide how to raise the capital to fund its business or finance its growth, dividing it among common equity, debt, and preferred stock. The mix that produces the minimum overall cost of capital will maximize the value of the firm (share price). From this topic review, you must understand weighted average cost of capital and its calculation and be ready to calculate the costs of retained earnings, new common stock, preferred stock, and the after-tax cost of debt. Don't worry about choosing among the methods for calculating the cost of retained earnings; the information given in the question will make it clear which one to use. You must know all these methods and understand why the marginal cost of capital increases as greater amounts of capital are raised over a given period (usually taken to be a year).

LOS 37.a: Calculate and interpret the weighted average cost of capital (WACC) of a company.

LOS 37.b: Describe how taxes affect the cost of capital from different capital sources.

CFA® Program Curriculum, Volume 4, page 36

The capital budgeting process involves discounted cash flow analysis. To conduct such analysis, you must know the firm's proper discount rate. This topic review discusses how, as an analyst, you can determine the proper rate at which to discount the cash flows associated with a capital budgeting project. This discount rate is the firm's **weighted average cost of capital** (WACC) and is also referred to as the **marginal cost of capital** (MCC).

Basic definitions. On the right (liability) side of a firm's balance sheet, we have debt, preferred stock, and common equity. These are normally referred to as the *capital components* of the firm. Any increase in a firm's total assets will have to be financed through an increase in at least one of these capital accounts. The cost of each of these components is called the *component cost* of capital.

Throughout this review, we focus on the following capital components and their component costs:

k_d The rate at which the firm can issue new debt. This is the yield to maturity on existing debt. This is also called the before-tax component cost of debt.

$k_d(1 - t)$ The after-tax cost of debt. Here, *t* is the firm's marginal tax rate. The after-tax component cost of debt, $k_d(1 - t)$, is used to calculate the WACC.

k_{ps} The cost of preferred stock.

k_{ce} The cost of common equity. It is the required rate of return on common stock and is generally difficult to estimate.

In many countries, the interest paid on corporate debt is tax deductible. Because we are interested in the after-tax cost of capital, we adjust the cost of debt, k_d, for the firm's marginal tax rate, t. Because there is typically no tax deduction allowed for payments to common or preferred stockholders, there is no equivalent deduction to k_{ps} or k_{ce}.

How a company raises capital and how it budgets or invests it are considered independently. Most companies have separate departments for the two tasks. The financing department is responsible for keeping costs low and using a balance of funding sources: common equity, preferred stock, and debt. Generally, it is necessary to raise each type of capital in large sums. The large sums may temporarily overweight the most recently issued capital, but in the long run, the firm will adhere to target weights. Because of these and other financing considerations, each investment decision must be made assuming a WACC, which includes each of the different sources of capital and is based on the long-run target weights. A company creates value by producing a return on assets that is higher than the required rate of return on the capital needed to fund those assets.

The WACC, as we have described it, is the cost of financing firm assets. We can view this cost as an opportunity cost. Consider how a company could reduce its costs if it found a way to produce its output using fewer assets, like less working capital. If we need less working capital, we can use the funds freed up to buy back our debt and equity securities in a mix that just matches our target capital structure. Our after-tax savings would be the WACC based on our target capital structure multiplied by the total value of the securities that are no longer outstanding.

For these reasons, any time we are considering a project that requires expenditures, comparing the return on those expenditures to the WACC is the appropriate way to determine whether undertaking that project will increase the value of the firm. This is the essence of the capital budgeting decision. Because a firm's WACC reflects the average risk of the projects that make up the firm, it is not appropriate for evaluating all new projects. It should be adjusted upward for projects with greater-than-average risk and downward for projects with less-than-average risk.

The weights in the calculation of a firm's WACC are the proportions of each source of capital in a firm's capital structure.

Calculating a Company's Weighted Average Cost of Capital

The WACC is given by:

$$\text{WACC} = (w_d)[k_d(1 - t)] + (w_{ps})(k_{ps}) + (w_{ce})(k_{ce})$$

where:
w_d = percentage of debt in the capital structure
w_{ps} = percentage of preferred stock in the capital structure
w_{ce} = percentage of common stock in the capital structure

Example: Computing WACC

Suppose Dexter, Inc.'s target capital structure is as follows:

$w_d = 0.45$, $w_{ps} = 0.05$, and $w_{ce} = 0.50$

Its before-tax cost of debt is 8%, its cost of equity is 12%, its cost of preferred stock is 8.4%, and its marginal tax rate is 40%. Calculate Dexter's WACC.

Answer:

Dexter's WACC will be:

$$WACC = (w_d)(k_d)(1 - t) + (w_{ps})(k_{ps}) + (w_{ce})(k_{ce})$$

$$WACC = (0.45)(0.08)(0.6) + (0.05)(0.084) + (0.50)(0.12) = 0.0858 \cong 8.6\%$$

LOS 37.c: Explain alternative methods of calculating the weights used in the WACC, including the use of the company's target capital structure.

CFA® Program Curriculum, Volume 4, page 38

The weights in the calculation of WACC should be based on the firm's target capital structure; that is, the proportions (based on market values) of debt, preferred stock, and equity that the firm expects to achieve over time. In the absence of any explicit information about a firm's target capital structure from the firm itself, an analyst may simply use the firm's current capital structure (based on market values) as the best indication of its target capital structure. If there has been a noticeable trend in the firm's capital structure, the analyst may want to incorporate this trend into his estimate of the firm's target capital structure. For example, if a firm has been reducing its proportion of debt financing each year for two or three years, the analyst may wish to use a weight on debt that is lower than the firm's current weight on debt in constructing the firm's target capital structure.

Alternatively, an analyst may wish to use the industry average capital structure as the target capital structure for a firm under analysis.

Example: Determining target capital structure weights

The market values of a firm's capital are as follows:

- Debt outstanding: $8 million
- Preferred stock outstanding: $2 million
- Common stock outstanding: $10 million
- Total capital: $20 million

What is the firm's target capital structure based on its existing capital structure?

Answer:

debt 40%, $w_d = 0.40$

preferred stock 10%, $w_{ps} = 0.10$

common stock 50%, $w_{ce} = 0.50$

For the industry average approach, we would simply use the arithmetic average of the current market weights (for each capital source) from a sample of industry firms.

LOS 37.d: Explain how the marginal cost of capital and the investment opportunity schedule are used to determine the optimal capital budget.

CFA® Program Curriculum, Volume 4, page 40

A company increases its value and creates wealth for its shareholders by earning more on its investment in assets than is required by those who provide the capital for the firm. A firm's WACC may increase as larger amounts of capital are raised. Thus, its marginal cost of capital, the cost of raising additional capital, can increase as larger amounts are invested in new projects. This is illustrated by the upward-sloping **marginal cost of capital curve** in Figure 1. Given the expected returns (IRRs) on potential projects, we can order the expenditures on additional projects from highest to lowest IRR. This will allow us to construct a downward sloping **investment opportunity schedule**, such as that shown in Figure 1.

Figure 1: The Optimal Capital Budget

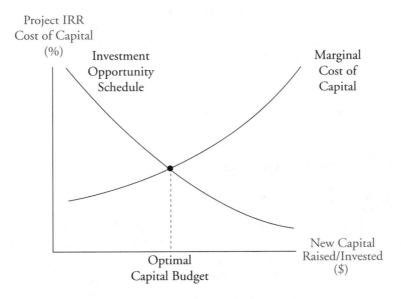

©2012 Kaplan, Inc.

The intersection of the investment opportunity schedule with the marginal cost of capital curve identifies the amount of the **optimal capital budget**. The intuition here is that the firm should undertake all those projects with IRRs greater than the cost of funds, the same criterion developed in the capital budgeting topic review. This will maximize the value created. At the same time, no projects with IRRs less than the marginal cost of the additional capital required to fund them should be undertaken, as they will erode the value created by the firm.

LOS 37.e: Explain the marginal cost of capital's role in determining the net present value of a project.

CFA® Program Curriculum, Volume 4, page 40

One cautionary note regarding the simple logic behind Figure 1 is in order. All projects do not have the same risk. The WACC is the appropriate discount rate for projects that have approximately the same level of risk as the firm's existing projects. This is because the component costs of capital used to calculate the firm's WACC are based on the existing level of firm risk. To evaluate a project with greater than (the firm's) average risk, a discount rate greater than the firm's existing WACC should be used. Projects with below-average risk should be evaluated using a discount rate less than the firm's WACC.

An additional issue to consider when using a firm's WACC (marginal cost of capital) to evaluate a specific project is that there is an implicit assumption that the capital structure of the firm will remain at the target capital structure over the life of the project.

These complexities aside, we can still conclude that the NPVs of potential projects of firm-average risk should be calculated using the marginal cost of capital for the firm. Projects for which the present value of the after-tax cash inflows is greater than the present value of the after-tax cash outflows should be undertaken by the firm.

LOS 37.f: Calculate and interpret the cost of fixed rate debt capital using the yield-to-maturity approach and the debt-rating approach.

CFA® Program Curriculum, Volume 4, page 42

The **after-tax cost of debt**, $k_d(1 - t)$, is used in computing the WACC. It is the interest rate at which firms can issue new debt (k_d) net of the tax savings from the tax deductibility of interest, $k_d(t)$:

after-tax cost of debt = interest rate – tax savings = $k_d - k_d(t) = k_d(1 - t)$

after-tax cost of debt = $k_d(1 - t)$

Example: Cost of debt

Dexter, Inc., is planning to issue new debt at an interest rate of 8%. Dexter has a 40% marginal federal-plus-state tax rate. What is Dexter's cost of debt capital?

Answer:

$$k_d(1 - t) = 8\%(1 - 0.4) = 4.8\%$$

Professor's Note: It is important that you realize that the cost of debt is the market interest rate (YTM) on new (marginal) debt, not the coupon rate on the firm's existing debt. CFA Institute may provide you with both rates, and you need to select the current market rate.

If a market YTM is not available because the firm's debt is not publicly traded, the analyst may use the rating and maturity of the firm's existing debt to estimate the before-tax cost of debt. If, for example, the firm's debt carries a single-A rating and has an average maturity of 15 years, the analyst can use the yield curve for single-A rated debt to determine the current market rate for debt with a 15-year maturity.

If any characteristics of the firm's anticipated debt would affect the yield (e.g., covenants or seniority), the analyst should make the appropriate adjustment to his estimated before-tax cost of debt. For firms that primarily employ floating-rate debt, the analyst should estimate the longer-term cost of the firm's debt using the current yield curve (term structure) for debt of the appropriate rating category.

LOS 37.g: Calculate and interpret the cost of noncallable, nonconvertible preferred stock.

CFA® Program Curriculum, Volume 4, page 44

The **cost of preferred stock** (k_{ps}) is:

$$k_{ps} = D_{ps} / P$$

where:
D_{ps} = preferred dividends
P = market price of preferred

Example: Cost of preferred stock

Suppose Dexter, Inc., has preferred stock that pays an $8 dividend per share and sells for $100 per share. What is Dexter's cost of preferred stock?

Answer:

$$k_{ps} = D_{ps} / P$$

$$k_{ps} = \$8 / \$100 = 0.08 = 8\%$$

Note that the equation $k_{ps} = D_{ps} / P$ is just a rearrangement of the preferred stock valuation model $P = D_{ps} / k_{ps}$, where P is the market price.

LOS 37.h: Calculate and interpret the cost of equity capital using the capital asset pricing model approach, the dividend discount model approach, and the bond-yield-plus risk-premium approach.

CFA® Program Curriculum, Volume 4, page 46

The opportunity **cost of equity capital** (k_{ce}) is the required rate of return on the firm's common stock. The rationale here is that the firm could avoid part of the cost of common stock outstanding by using retained earnings to buy back shares of its own stock. The cost of (i.e., the required return on) common equity can be estimated using one of the following three approaches:

1. **The capital asset pricing model approach.**
   Step 1: Estimate the risk-free rate, RFR. Yields on default risk-free debt such as U.S. Treasury notes are usually used. The most appropriate maturity to choose is one that is close to the useful life of the project.
   Step 2: Estimate the stock's beta, β. This is the stock's risk measure.
   Step 3: Estimate the expected rate of return on the market, $E(R_{mkt})$.
   Step 4: Use the capital asset pricing model (CAPM) equation to estimate the required rate of return:

$$k_{ce} = RFR + \beta[E(R_m) - RFR]$$

Example: Using CAPM to estimate k_{ce}

Suppose RFR = 6%, R_{mkt} = 11%, and Dexter has a beta of 1.1. Estimate Dexter's cost of equity.

Answer:

The required rate of return for Dexter's stock is:

$$k_{ce} = 6\% + 1.1(11\% - 6\%) = 11.5\%$$

Professor's Note: If you are unfamiliar with the capital asset pricing model, you can find more detail and the basic elements of its derivation in the Study Session on portfolio management.

2. **The dividend discount model approach.** If dividends are expected to grow at a constant rate, g, then the current value of the stock is given by the dividend growth model:

$$P_0 = \frac{D_1}{k_{ce} - g}$$

where:
D_1 = next year's dividend
k_{ce} = required rate of return on common equity
g = firm's expected constant growth rate

Rearranging the terms, you can solve for k_{ce}:

$$k_{ce} = \frac{D_1}{P_0} + g$$

In order to use $k_{ce} = \frac{D_1}{P_0} + g$, you have to estimate the expected growth rate, g. This can be done by:

- Using the growth rate as projected by security analysts.
- Using the following equation to estimate a firm's sustainable growth rate:

$$g = (\text{retention rate})(\text{return on equity}) = (1 - \text{payout rate})(ROE)$$

The difficulty with this model is estimating the firm's future growth rate.

Example: Estimating k_{ce} using the dividend discount model

Suppose Dexter's stock sells for $21, next year's dividend is expected to be $1, Dexter's expected ROE is 12%, and Dexter is expected to pay out 40% of its earnings. What is Dexter's cost of equity?

Answer:

$$g = (ROE)(\text{retention rate})$$

$$g = (0.12)(1 - 0.4) = 0.072 = 7.2\%$$

$$k_{ce} = (1 \, / \, 21) + 0.072 = 0.12 \text{ or } 12\%$$

---

3. **Bond yield plus risk premium approach.** Analysts often use an ad hoc approach to estimate the required rate of return. They add a risk premium (three to five percentage points) to the market yield on the firm's long-term debt.

$$k_{ce} = \text{bond yield} + \text{risk premium}$$

Example: Estimating k_{ce} with bond yields plus a risk premium

Dexter's interest rate on long-term debt is 8%. Suppose the risk premium is estimated to be 5%. Estimate Dexter's cost of equity.

Answer:

Dexter's estimated cost of equity is:

$$k_{ce} = 8\% + 5\% = 13\%$$

Note that the three models gave us three different estimates of k_{ce}. The CAPM estimate was 11.5%, the dividend discount model estimate was 12%, and the bond yield plus risk premium estimate was 13%. Analysts must use their judgment to decide which is most appropriate.

LOS 37.i: Calculate and interpret the beta and cost of capital for a project.

CFA® Program Curriculum, Volume 4, page 51

A **project's beta** is a measure of its systematic or market risk. Just as we can use a firm's beta to estimate its required return on equity, we can use a project's beta to adjust for differences between a specific project's risk and the average risk of a firm's projects.

Because a specific project is not represented by a publicly traded security, we typically cannot estimate a project's beta directly. One process that can be used is based on the equity beta of a publicly traded firm that is engaged in a business similar to, and with risk similar to, the project under consideration. This is referred to as the **pure-play method** because we begin with the beta of a company or group of companies that are *purely* engaged in a business similar to that of the project and are therefore comparable to the project. Thus, using the beta of a conglomerate that is engaged in the same business as the project would be inappropriate because its beta depends on its many different lines of business.

The beta of a firm is a function not only of the business risks of its projects (lines of business) but also of its financial structure. For a given set of projects, the greater a firm's reliance on debt financing, the greater its equity beta. For this reason, we must adjust the pure-play beta from a comparable company (or group of companies) for the company's leverage (unlever it) and then adjust it (re-lever it) based on the financial structure of the company evaluating the project. We can then use this equity beta to calculate the cost of equity to be used in evaluating the project.

To get the *asset beta* for a publicly traded firm, we use the following formula:

$$\beta_{ASSET} = \beta_{EQUITY} \left[\frac{1}{1 + \left((1-t)\dfrac{D}{E} \right)} \right]$$

where:

D/E = *comparable company's* debt-to-equity ratio and *t* is its marginal tax rate

To get the equity beta for the project, we use the *subject firm's* tax rate and debt-to-equity ratio:

$$\beta_{PROJECT} = \beta_{ASSET} \left[1 + \left((1-t)\frac{D}{E} \right) \right]$$

The following example illustrates this technique.

Example: Cost of capital for a project

Acme, Inc., is considering a project in the food distribution business. It has a D/E ratio of 2, a marginal tax rate of 40%, and its debt currently has a yield of 14%. Balfor, a publicly traded firm that operates only in the food distribution business, has a D/E ratio of 1.5, a marginal tax rate of 30%, and an equity beta of 0.9. The risk-free rate is 5%, and the expected return on the market portfolio is 12%. Calculate Balfor's asset beta, the project's equity beta, and the appropriate WACC to use in evaluating the project.

Answer:

Balfor's asset beta:

$$\beta_{ASSET} = 0.9 \left[\frac{1}{1 + (1 - 0.3)(1.5)} \right] = 0.439$$

Equity beta for the project:

$$\beta_{PROJECT} = 0.439[1 + (1 - 0.4)(2)] = 0.966$$

Project cost of equity = 5% + 0.966(12% − 5%) = 11.762%

To get the weights of debt and equity, use the D/E ratio and give equity a value of 1. Here, D/E = 2, so if E = 1, D = 2. The weight for debt, D/(D + E), is 2/(2 + 1) = 2/3, and the weight for equity, E/(D + E), is 1/(2 + 1) = 1/3. The appropriate WACC for the project is therefore:

$$\frac{1}{3}(11.762\%) + \frac{2}{3}(14\%)(1 - 0.4) = 9.52\%$$

While the method is theoretically correct, there are several challenging issues involved in estimating the beta of the comparable (or any) company's equity:

- Beta is estimated using historical returns data. The estimate is sensitive to the length of time used and the frequency (daily, weekly, etc.) of the data.
- The estimate is affected by which index is chosen to represent the market return.
- Betas are believed to revert toward 1 over time, and the estimate may need to be adjusted for this tendency.
- Estimates of beta for small-capitalization firms may need to be adjusted upward to reflect risk inherent in small firms that is not captured by the usual estimation methods.

LOS 37.j: Explain the country risk premium in the estimation of the cost of equity for a company located in a developing market.

CFA® Program Curriculum, Volume 4, page 58

Using the CAPM to estimate the cost of equity is problematic in developing countries because beta does not adequately capture country risk. To reflect the increased risk associated with investing in a developing country, a **country risk premium** is added to the market risk premium when using the CAPM.

The general risk of the developing country is reflected in its **sovereign yield spread**. This is the difference in yields between the developing country's government bonds (denominated in the developed market's currency) and Treasury bonds of a similar maturity. To estimate an equity risk premium for the country, adjust the sovereign yield spread by the ratio of volatility between the country's equity market and its government bond market (for bonds denominated in the developed market's currency). A more volatile equity market increases the country risk premium, other things equal.

The revised CAPM equation is stated as:

$$k_{ce} = R_F + \beta \left[E(R_{MKT}) - R_F + CRP \right]$$

where:
CRP = country risk premium

The country risk premium can be calculated as:

$$CRP = \text{sovereign yield spread} \times \left(\frac{\text{annualized standard deviation of equity index of developing country}}{\text{annualized standard deviation of sovereign bond market in terms of the developed market currency}} \right)$$

where:
sovereign yield spread = difference between the yields of government bonds in the developing country and Treasury bonds of similar maturities

Example: Country risk premium

Robert Rodriguez, an analyst with Omni Corporation, is estimating a country risk premium to include in his estimate of the cost of equity for a project Omni is starting in Venezuela. Rodriguez has compiled the following information for his analysis:

- Venezuelan U.S. dollar-denominated 10-year government bond yield = 8.6%.
- 10-year U.S. Treasury bond yield = 4.8%.
- Annualized standard deviation of Venezuelan stock index = 32%.
- Annualized standard deviation of Venezuelan U.S. dollar-denominated 10-year government bond = 22%.
- Project beta = 1.25.
- Expected market return = 10.4%.
- Risk-free rate = 4.2%.

Calculate the country risk premium and the cost of equity for Omni's Venezuelan project.

Answer:

Country risk premium:

$$CRP = (0.086 - 0.048)\left(\frac{0.32}{0.22}\right) = 0.038\left(\frac{0.32}{0.22}\right) = 0.0553, \text{ or } 5.53\%$$

Cost of equity:

$$\begin{aligned}
k_{ce} &= R_F + \beta\big[E(R_{MKT}) - R_F + CRP\big] \\
&= 0.042 + 1.25\big[0.104 - 0.042 + 0.0553\big] \\
&= 0.042 + 1.25\big[0.1173\big] \\
&= 0.1886, \text{ or } 18.86\%
\end{aligned}$$

LOS 37.k: Describe the marginal cost of capital schedule, explain why it may be upward-sloping with respect to additional capital, and calculate and interpret its break-points.

CFA® Program Curriculum, Volume 4, page 59

The **marginal cost of capital** (MCC) is the cost of the last new dollar of capital a firm raises. As a firm raises more and more capital, the costs of different sources of financing will increase. For example, as a firm raises additional debt, the cost of debt will rise to account for the additional financial risk. This will occur, for example, if bond covenants in the firm's existing senior debt agreement prohibit the firm from issuing additional debt with the same seniority as the existing debt. Therefore, the company will have to issue more expensive subordinated bonds at a higher cost of debt, which increases the marginal cost of capital.

Also, issuing new equity is more expensive than using retained earnings due to flotation costs (which are discussed in more detail in the next LOS). The bottom line is that raising additional capital results in an increase in the WACC.

The **marginal cost of capital schedule** shows the WACC for different amounts of financing. Typically, the MCC is shown as a graph. Because different sources of financing become more expensive as the firm raises more capital, the MCC schedule typically has an upward slope.

Break points occur any time the cost of one of the components of the company's WACC changes. A break point is calculated as:

$$\text{break point} = \frac{\text{amount of capital at which the component's cost of capital changes}}{\text{weight of the component in the capital structure}}$$

Example: Calculating break points

The Omni Corporation has a target capital structure of 60% equity and 40% debt. The schedule of financing costs for the Omni Corporation is shown in the figure below.

Schedule of Capital Costs for Omni

Amount of New Debt (in millions)	After-Tax Cost of Debt	Amount of New Equity (in millions)	Cost of Equity
$0 to $99	4.2%	$0 to $199	6.5%
$100 to $199	4.6%	$200 to $399	8.0%
$200 to $299	5.0%	$400 to $599	9.5%

Calculate the break points for Omni Corporation and graph the marginal cost of capital schedule.

Answer:

Omni will have a break point each time a component cost of capital changes, for a total of four break points.

$$\text{break point}_{\text{debt} > \$100mm} = \frac{\$100 \text{ million}}{0.4} = \$250 \text{ million}$$

$$\text{break point}_{\text{debt} > \$200mm} = \frac{\$200 \text{ million}}{0.4} = \$500 \text{ million}$$

$$\text{break point}_{\text{equity} > \$200mm} = \frac{\$200 \text{ million}}{0.6} = \$333 \text{ million}$$

$$\text{break point}_{\text{equity} > \$400mm} = \frac{\$400 \text{ million}}{0.6} = \$667 \text{ million}$$

The following figure shows Omni Corporation's WACC for the different break points.

WACC for Alternative Levels of Financing

Capital (in millions)	Equity (60%)	Cost of Equity	Debt (40%)	Cost of Debt	WACC
$50	$30	6.5%	$20	4.2%	5.58%
$250	$150	6.5%	$100	4.6%	5.74%
$333	$200	8.0%	$133	4.6%	6.64%
$500	$300	8.0%	$200	5.0%	6.80%
$667	$400	9.5%	$267	5.0%	7.70%

The following figure is a graph of the marginal cost of capital schedule given in the previous figure. Notice the upward slope of the line due to the increased financing costs as more financing is needed.

Marginal Cost of Capital Schedule for Omni Corporation

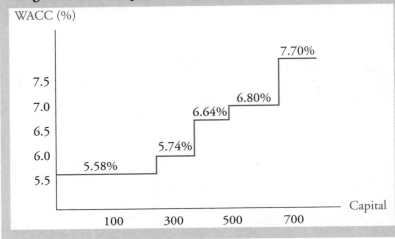

LOS 37.l: Explain and demonstrate the correct treatment of flotation costs.

CFA® Program Curriculum, Volume 4, page 62

Flotation costs are the fees charged by investment bankers when a company raises external equity capital. Flotation costs can be substantial and often amount to between 2% and 7% of the total amount of equity capital raised, depending on the type of offering.

Incorrect Treatment of Flotation Costs

Because the LOS asks for the "correct treatment of flotation costs," that implies that there is an incorrect treatment. Many financial textbooks incorporate flotation costs directly into the cost of capital by increasing the cost of external equity. For example, if a company has a dividend of $1.50 per share, a current price of $30 per share, and an expected growth rate of 6%, the cost of equity without flotation costs would be:

$$r_e = \left(\frac{\$1.50(1+0.06)}{\$30} \right) + 0.06 = 0.1130, \text{ or } 11.30\%$$

 Professor's Note: Here we're using the constant growth model, rather than the CAPM, to estimate the cost of equity.

If we incorporate flotation costs of 4.5% directly into the cost of equity computation, the cost of equity increases:

$$r_e = \left[\frac{\$1.50(1+0.06)}{\$30(1-0.045)} \right] + 0.06 = 0.1155, \text{ or } 11.55\%$$

Correct Treatment of Flotation Costs

In the incorrect treatment we have just seen, flotation costs effectively increase the WACC by a fixed percentage and will be a factor for the duration of the project because future project cash flows are discounted at this higher WACC to determine project NPV. The problem with this approach is that flotation costs are not an ongoing expense for the firm. Flotation costs are a cash outflow that occurs at the initiation of a project and affect the project NPV by increasing the initial cash outflow. Therefore, *the correct way to account for flotation costs is to adjust the initial project cost.* An analyst should calculate the dollar amount of the flotation cost attributable to the project and increase the initial cash outflow for the project.

Example: Correctly accounting for flotation costs

Omni Corporation is considering a project that requires a $400,000 cash outlay and is expected to produce cash flows of $150,000 per year for the next four years. Omni's tax rate is 35%, and the before-tax cost of debt is 6.5%. The current share price for Omni's stock is $36 per share, and the expected dividend next year is $2 per share. Omni's expected growth rate is 5%. Assume that Omni finances the project with 50% debt and 50% equity capital and that flotation costs for equity are 4.5%. The appropriate discount rate for the project is the WACC.

Calculate the NPV of the project using the correct treatment of flotation costs and discuss how the result of this method differs from the result obtained from the incorrect treatment of flotation costs.

Answer:

after-tax cost of debt $= 6.5\% \, (1 - 0.35) = 4.23\%$

cost of equity $= \left(\dfrac{\$2}{\$36}\right) + 0.05 = 0.1055$, or 10.55%

WACC $= 0.50(0.0423) + 0.50(0.1055) = 7.39\%$

Because the project is financed with 50% equity, the amount of equity capital raised is $0.50 \times \$400{,}000 = \$200{,}000$.

Flotation costs are 4.5%, which equates to a dollar cost of $\$200{,}000 \times 0.045 = \$9{,}000$.

$$NPV = -\$400{,}000 - \$9{,}000 + \frac{\$150{,}000}{1.0739} + \frac{\$150{,}000}{(1.0739)^2} + \frac{\$150{,}000}{(1.0739)^3} + \frac{\$150{,}000}{(1.0739)^4}$$

$$= \$94{,}640$$

For comparison, if we would have adjusted the cost of equity for flotation costs, the cost of equity would have increased to 10.82% $\left(= \dfrac{\$2.00}{\$36(1 - 0.045)} + 0.05\right)$, which would have increased the WACC to 7.53%. Using this method, the NPV of the project would have been:

$$NPV = -\$400{,}000 + \frac{\$150{,}000}{1.0753} + \frac{\$150{,}000}{(1.0753)^2} + \frac{\$150{,}000}{(1.0753)^3} + \frac{\$150{,}000}{(1.0753)^4} = \$102{,}061$$

The two methods result in significantly different estimates for the project NPV. Adjusting the initial outflow for the dollar amount of the flotation costs is the correct approach because it provides the most accurate assessment of the project's value once all costs are considered.

Note that flotation costs may be tax-deductible for some firms. In that case, the initial cash flow of the project should be adjusted by the after-tax flotation cost. In this example, Omni would have an after-tax flotation cost of $\$9{,}000(1 - 0.35) = \$5{,}850$ and the project NPV would be $\$97{,}790$.

KEY CONCEPTS

LOS 37.a

$$WACC = (w_d)(k_d)(1-t) + (w_{ps})(k_{ps}) + (w_{ce})(k_{ce})$$

The weighted average cost of capital, or WACC, is calculated using weights based on the market values of each component of a firm's capital structure and is the correct discount rate to use to discount the cash flows of projects with risk equal to the average risk of a firm's projects.

LOS 37.b

Interest expense on a firm's debt is tax deductible, so the pre-tax cost of debt must be reduced by the firm's marginal tax rate to get an after-tax cost of debt capital:

after-tax cost of debt = k_d (1 – firm's marginal tax rate)

The pre-tax and after-tax capital costs are equal for both preferred stock and common equity because dividends paid by the firm are not tax deductible.

LOS 37.c

WACC should be calculated based on a firm's target capital structure weights.

If information on a firm's target capital structure is not available, an analyst can use the firm's current capital structure, based on market values, or the average capital structure in the firm's industry as estimates of the target capital structure.

LOS 37.d

A firm's marginal cost of capital (WACC at each level of capital investment) increases as it needs to raise larger amounts of capital. This is shown by an upward-sloping marginal cost of capital curve.

An investment opportunity schedule shows the IRRs of (in decreasing order), and the initial investment amounts for, a firm's potential projects.

The intersection of a firm's investment opportunity schedule with its marginal cost of capital curve indicates the optimal amount of capital expenditure, the amount of investment required to undertake all positive NPV projects.

LOS 37.e

The marginal cost of capital (the WACC for additional units of capital) should be used as the discount rate when calculating project NPVs for capital budgeting decisions.

Adjustments to the cost of capital are necessary when a project differs in risk from the average risk of a firm's existing projects. The discount rate should be adjusted upward for higher-risk projects and downward for lower-risk projects.

LOS 37.f
The before-tax cost of fixed-rate debt capital, k_d, is the rate at which the firm can issue new debt.
- The yield-to-maturity approach assumes the before-tax cost of debt capital is the YTM on the firm's existing publicly traded debt.
- If a market YTM is not available, the analyst can use the debt rating approach, estimating the before-tax cost of debt capital based on market yields for debt with the same rating and average maturity as the firm's existing debt.

LOS 37.g
The cost (and yield) of noncallable, nonconvertible preferred stock is simply the annual dividend divided by the market price of preferred shares.

LOS 37.h
The cost of equity capital, k_{ce}, is the required rate of return on the firm's common stock.

There are three approaches to estimating k_{ce}:
- CAPM approach: $k_{ce} = RFR + \beta[E(R_{mkt}) - RFR]$.
- Dividend discount model approach: $k_{ce} = (D_1/P_0) + g$.
- Bond yield plus risk premium approach: add a risk premium of 3% to 5% to the market yield on the firm's long-term debt.

LOS 37.i
When a project's risk differs from that of the firm's average project, we can use the beta of a company or group of companies that are exclusively in the same business as the project to calculate the project's required return. This *pure-play method* involves the following steps:

1. Estimate the beta for a comparable company or companies.

2. Unlever the beta to get the asset beta using the marginal tax rate and debt-to-equity ratio for the comparable company:

$$\beta_{ASSET} = \beta_{EQUITY} \left\{ \frac{1}{1 + \left[(1-t)\dfrac{D}{E} \right]} \right\}$$

3. Re-lever the beta using the marginal tax rate and debt-to-equity ratio for the firm considering the project:

$$\beta_{PROJECT} = \beta_{ASSET} \left\{ 1 + \left[(1-t)\dfrac{D}{E} \right] \right\}$$

4. Use the CAPM to estimate the required return on equity to use when evaluating the project.

5. Calculate the WACC for the firm using the project's required return on equity.

LOS 37.j

A country risk premium should be added to the market risk premium in the CAPM to reflect the added risk associated with investing in a developing market.

The country risk premium for a developing country can be estimated as the spread between the developing country's sovereign debt (denominated in a developed country's currency) and the developed country's sovereign debt (e.g., U.S. T-bills), multiplied by the ratio of the volatility of the developing country's equity market to the volatility of the market for its developed-country-denominated sovereign debt.

LOS 37.k

The marginal cost of capital schedule shows the WACC for successively greater amounts of new capital investment for a period, such as the coming year.

The MCC schedule is typically upward-sloping because raising greater amounts of capital increases the cost of equity and debt financing. Break points (increases) in the marginal cost of capital schedule occur at amounts of total capital raised equal to the amount of each source of capital at which the component cost of capital increases, divided by the target weight for that source of capital.

LOS 37.l

The correct method to account for flotation costs of raising new equity capital is to increase a project's initial cash outflow by the flotation cost attributable to the project when calculating the project's NPV.

CONCEPT CHECKERS

1. A company has $5 million in debt outstanding with a coupon rate of 12%. Currently, the yield to maturity (YTM) on these bonds is 14%. If the firm's tax rate is 40%, what is the company's after-tax cost of debt?
   A. 5.6%.
   B. 8.4%.
   C. 14.0%.

2. The cost of preferred stock is equal to:
   A. the preferred stock dividend divided by its par value.
   B. [(1 – tax rate) times the preferred stock dividend] divided by price.
   C. the preferred stock dividend divided by its market price.

3. A company's $100, 8% preferred is currently selling for $85. What is the company's cost of preferred equity?
   A. 8.0%.
   B. 9.4%.
   C. 10.8%.

4. The expected dividend is $2.50 for a share of stock priced at $25. What is the cost of equity if the long-term growth in dividends is projected to be 8%?
   A. 15%.
   B. 16%.
   C. 18%.

5. An analyst gathered the following data about a company:

Capital structure	Required rate of return
30% debt	10% for debt
20% preferred stock	11% for preferred stock
50% common stock	18% for common stock

   Assuming a 40% tax rate, what after-tax rate of return must the company earn on its investments?
   A. 13.0%.
   B. 14.2%.
   C. 18.0%.

6. A company is planning a $50 million expansion. The expansion is to be financed by selling $20 million in new debt and $30 million in new common stock. The before-tax required return on debt is 9% and 14% for equity. If the company is in the 40% tax bracket, the company's marginal cost of capital is *closest* to:
   A. 7.2%.
   B. 10.6%.
   C. 12.0%.

Use the following data to answer Questions 7 through 10.

- The company has a target capital structure of 40% debt and 60% equity.
- Bonds with face value of $1,000 pay a 10% coupon (semiannual), mature in 20 years, and sell for $849.54 with a yield to maturity of 12%.
- The company stock beta is 1.2.
- Risk-free rate is 10%, and market risk premium is 5%.
- The company is a constant-growth firm that just paid a dividend of $2, sells for $27 per share, and has a growth rate of 8%.
- The company's marginal tax rate is 40%.

7.   The company's after-tax cost of debt is:
      A. 7.2%.
      B. 8.0%.
      C. 9.1%.

8.   The company's cost of equity using the capital asset pricing model (CAPM) approach is:
      A. 16.0%.
      B. 16.6%.
      C. 16.9%.

9.   The company's cost of equity using the dividend discount model is:
      A. 15.4%.
      B. 16.0%.
      C. 16.6%.

10.   The company's weighted average cost of capital (using the cost of equity from CAPM) is *closest* to:
      A. 12.5%.
      B. 13.0%.
      C. 13.5%.

11.   What happens to a company's weighted average cost of capital (WACC) if the firm's corporate tax rate increases and if the Federal Reserve causes an increase in the risk-free rate, respectively? (Consider the events independently and assume a beta of less than one.)

Tax rate increase	Increase in risk-free rate
A. Decrease WACC	Increase WACC
B. Decrease WACC	Decrease WACC
C. Increase WACC	Increase WACC

12. Given the following information on a company's capital structure, what is the company's weighted average cost of capital? The marginal tax rate is 40%.

Type of capital	Percent of capital structure	Before-tax component cost
Bonds	40%	7.5%
Preferred stock	5%	11%
Common stock	55%	15%

A. 10.0%.
B. 10.6%.
C. 11.8%.

13. Derek Ramsey is an analyst with Bullseye Corporation, a major U.S.-based discount retailer. Bullseye is considering opening new stores in Brazil and wants to estimate its cost of equity capital for this investment. Ramsey has found that:
- The yield on a Brazilian government 10-year U.S. dollar-denominated bond is 7.2%.
- A 10-year U.S. Treasury bond has a yield of 4.9%.
- The annualized standard deviation of the Sao Paulo Bovespa stock index in the most recent year is 24%.
- The annualized standard deviation of Brazil's U.S. dollar-denominated 10-year government bond over the last year was 18%.
- The appropriate beta to use for the project is 1.3.
- The market risk premium is 6%.
- The risk-free interest rate is 4.5%.

Which of the following choices is *closest* to the appropriate country risk premium for Brazil and the cost of equity that Ramsey should use in his analysis?

Country risk premium for Brazil	Cost of equity for project
A. 2.5%	15.6%
B. 2.5%	16.3%
C. 3.1%	16.3%

14. Manigault Industries currently has assets on its balance sheet of $200 million that are financed with 70% equity and 30% debt. The executive management team at Manigault is considering a major expansion that would require raising additional capital. Rosannna Stallworth, the CFO of Manigault, has put together the following schedule for the costs of debt and equity:

Amount of New Debt (in millions)	After-Tax Cost of Debt	Amount of New Equity (in millions)	Cost of Equity
$0 to $49	4.0%	$0 to $99	7.0%
$50 to $99	4.2%	$100 to $199	8.0%
$100 to $149	4.5%	$200 to $299	9.0%

In a presentation to Manigault's Board of Directors, Stallworth makes the following statements:

Statement 1: If we maintain our target capital structure of 70% equity and 30% debt, the break point at which our cost of equity will increase to 8.0% is $185 million in new capital.

Statement 2: If we want to finance total assets of $450 million, our marginal cost of capital will increase to 7.56%.

Are Stallworth's Statements 1 and 2 *most likely* correct or incorrect?

	Statement 1	Statement 2
A.	Correct	Correct
B.	Incorrect	Correct
C.	Incorrect	Incorrect

15. Black Pearl Yachts is considering a project that requires a $180,000 cash outlay and is expected to produce cash flows of $50,000 per year for the next five years. Black Pearl's tax rate is 25%, and the before-tax cost of debt is 8%. The current share price for Black Pearl's stock is $56 and the expected dividend next year is $2.80 per share. Black Pearl's expected growth rate is 5%. Assume that Black Pearl finances the project with 60% equity and 40% debt, and the flotation cost for equity is 4.0%. The appropriate discount rate is the weighted average cost of capital (WACC). Which of the following choices is *closest* to the dollar amount of the flotation costs and the NPV for the project, assuming that flotation costs are accounted for properly?

	Dollar amount of flotation costs	NPV of project
A.	$4,320	$17,548
B.	$4,320	$13,228
C.	$7,200	$17,548

16. Jay Company has a debt-to-equity ratio of 2.0. Jay is evaluating the cost of equity for a project in the same line of business as Cass Company and will use the pure-play method with Cass as the comparable firm. Cass has a beta of 1.2 and a debt-to-equity ratio of 1.6. The project beta *most likely*:
   A. will be less than Jay Company's beta.
   B. will be greater than Jay Company's beta.
   C. could be greater than or less than Jay Company's beta.

ANSWERS – CONCEPT CHECKERS

1. **B** $k_d(1 - t) = (0.14)(1 - 0.4) = 8.4\%$

2. **C**   Cost of preferred stock $= k_{ps} = D_{ps} / P$

3. **B** $k_{ps} = D_{ps} / P_{ps}$, $D_{ps} = \$100 \times 8\% = \$8$, $k_{ps} = 8 / 85 = 9.4\%$

4. **C**   Using the dividend yield plus growth rate approach: $k_{ce} = (D_1 / P_0) + g = (2.50 / 25.00) + 8\% = 18\%$.

5. **A**   WACC $= (w_d)(k_d)(1 - t) + (w_{ps})(k_{ps}) + (w_{ce})(k_{ce}) = (0.3)(0.1)(1 - 0.4) + (0.2)(0.11) + (0.5)(0.18) = 13\%$

6. **B** $w_d = 20 / (20 + 30) = 0.4$, $w_{ce} = 30 / (20 + 30) = 0.6$

    WACC $= (w_d)(k_d)(1 - t) + (w_{ce})(k_{ce}) = (0.4)(9)(1 - 0.4) + (0.6)(14) = 10.56\% = $ MCC

7. **A** $k_d(1 - t) = 12(1 - 0.4) = 7.2\%$

8. **A**   Using the CAPM formula, $k_{ce} = $ RFR $+ \beta[E(R_{mkt}) - $ RFR$] = 10 + 1.2(5) = 16\%$.

9. **B** $D_1 = D_0 (1 + g) = 2(1.08) = 2.16$; $k_{ce} = (D_1 / P_0) + g = (2.16 / 27) + 0.08 = 16\%$

10. **A**   WACC $= (w_d)(k_d)(1 - t) + (w_{ce})(k_{ce}) = (0.4)(7.2) + (0.6)(16) = 12.48\%$

11. **A**   An increase in the corporate tax rate will reduce the after-tax cost of debt, causing the WACC to fall. More specifically, because the after-tax cost of debt $= (k_d)(1 - t)$, the term $(1 - t)$ decreases, decreasing the after-tax cost of debt. If the risk-free rate were to increase, the costs of debt and equity would both increase, thus causing the firm's cost of capital to increase.

12. **B**   WACC $= (w_d)(k_d)(1 - t) + (w_{ps})(k_{ps}) + (w_{ce})(k_{ce}) = (0.4)(7.5)(1 - 0.4) + (0.05)(11) + (0.55)(15) = 10.6\%$

13. **C** $$\text{CRP} = \text{sovereign yield spread} \left(\frac{\text{annualized standard deviation of equity index of developing country}}{\text{annualized standard deviation of sovereign bond market in terms of the developed market currency}} \right)$$

    $$= (0.072 - 0.049)\left(\frac{0.24}{0.18}\right) = 0.031, \text{ or } 3.1\%$$

    $$\begin{aligned} k &= R_F + \beta\left[E(R_{MKT}) - R_F + \text{CRP}\right] \\ &= 0.045 + 1.3[0.06 + 0.031] \\ &= 0.163, \text{ or } 16.3\% \end{aligned}$$

14. **C**   Statement 1 is incorrect. The break point at which the cost of equity changes to 8.0% is:

$$\text{break point} = \frac{\text{amount of capital at which the component's cost of capital changes}}{\text{weight of the component in the WACC}}$$

$$= \frac{\$100 \text{ million}}{0.70} = \$142.86 \text{ million}$$

Statement 2 is also incorrect. If Manigault wants to finance $450 million of total assets, that means that the firm will need to raise $450 − $200 = $250 million in additional capital. Using the target capital structure of 70% equity, 30% debt, the firm will need to raise 0.70 × $250 = $175 million in new equity and 0.30 × $250 = $75 in new debt. Looking at the capital schedule, the cost associated with $75 million in new debt is 4.2%, and the cost associated with $175 million in new equity is 8.0%. The marginal cost of capital at that point will be (0.3 × 4.2%) + (0.7 × 8.0%) = 6.86%.

15. **B**   Because the project is financed with 60% equity, the amount of equity capital raised is 0.60 × $180,000 = $108,000.

Flotation costs are 4.0%, which equates to a dollar cost of $108,000 × 0.04 = $4,320.

After-tax cost of debt = 8.0% (1 − 0.25) = 6.0%

$$\text{Cost of equity} = \left(\frac{\$2.80}{\$56.00} \right) + 0.05 = 0.10, \text{ or } 10.0\%$$

WACC = 0.60(0.10) + 0.40(0.06) = 8.4%

NPV =

$$-\$180,000 - \$4,320 + \frac{\$50,000}{1.084} + \frac{\$50,000}{(1.084)^2} + \frac{\$50,000}{(1.084)^3} + \frac{\$50,000}{(1.084)^4} + \frac{\$50,000}{(1.084)^5} = \$13,228$$

16. **C**   The project beta calculated using the pure-play method is not necessarily related in a predictable way to the beta of the firm that is performing the project.

The following is a review of the Corporate Finance principles designed to address the learning outcome statements set forth by CFA Institute. This topic is also covered in:

MEASURES OF LEVERAGE

Study Session 11

EXAM FOCUS

Here we define and calculate various measures of leverage and the firm characteristics that affect the levels of operating and financial leverage. Operating leverage magnifies the effect of changes in sales on operating earnings. Financial leverage magnifies the effect of changes in operating earnings on net income (earnings per share). The breakeven quantity of sales is that quantity of sales for which total revenue just covers total costs. The operating breakeven quantity of sales is the quantity of sales for which total revenue just covers total operating costs. Be sure you understand how a firm's decisions regarding its operating structure and scale and its decisions regarding the use of debt and equity financing (its capital structure) affect its breakeven levels of sales and the uncertainty regarding its operating earnings and net income.

LOS 38.a: Define and explain leverage, business risk, sales risk, operating risk, and financial risk, and classify a risk, given a description.

CFA® Program Curriculum, Volume 4, page 80

Leverage, in the sense we use it here, refers to the amount of fixed costs a firm has. These fixed costs may be fixed operating expenses, such as building or equipment leases, or fixed financing costs, such as interest payments on debt. Greater leverage leads to greater variability of the firm's after-tax operating earnings and net income. A given change in sales will lead to a greater change in operating earnings when the firm employs operating leverage; a given change in operating earnings will lead to a greater change in net income when the firm employs financial leverage.

 Professor's Note: The British refer to leverage as "gearing."

Business risk refers to the risk associated with a firm's operating income and is the result of uncertainty about a firm's revenues and the expenditures necessary to produce those revenues. Business risk is the combination of sales risk and operating risk.

- **Sales risk** is the uncertainty about the firm's sales.
- **Operating risk** refers to the additional uncertainty about operating earnings caused by fixed operating costs. The greater the proportion of fixed costs to variable costs, the greater a firm's operating risk.

Financial risk refers to the additional risk that the firm's common stockholders must bear when a firm uses fixed cost (debt) financing. When a company finances its operations with debt, it takes on fixed expenses in the form of interest payments. The greater the proportion of debt in a firm's capital structure, the greater the firm's financial risk.

LOS 38.b: Calculate and interpret the degree of operating leverage, the degree of financial leverage, and the degree of total leverage.

CFA® Program Curriculum, Volume 4, page 83

The **degree of operating leverage** (DOL) is defined as the percentage change in operating income (EBIT) that results from a given percentage change in sales:

$$DOL = \frac{\text{percentage change in EBIT}}{\text{percentage change in sales}} = \frac{\dfrac{\Delta EBIT}{EBIT}}{\dfrac{\Delta Q}{Q}}$$

To calculate a firm's DOL for a particular level of unit sales, Q, DOL is:

$$DOL = \frac{Q(P-V)}{Q(P-V)-F}$$

where:
Q = quantity of units sold
P = price per unit
V = variable cost per unit
F = fixed costs

Multiplying, we have:

$$DOL = \frac{S-TVC}{S-TVC-F}$$

where:
S = sales
TVC = total variable costs
F = fixed costs

Note that in this form, the denominator is operating earnings (EBIT).

Example: Degree of operating leverage

Consider the costs for the projects presented in the following table. Assuming that 100,000 units are produced for each firm, calculate the DOL for Atom Company and Beta Company.

Operating Costs for Atom Company and Beta Company

	Atom Company	Beta Company
Price	$4.00	$4.00
Variable costs	$3.00	$2.00
Fixed costs	$40,000	$120,000
Revenue	$400,000	$400,000

Answer:

For Atom Company:

$$DOL(Atom) = \frac{Q(P-V)}{[Q(P-V)-F]} = \frac{100,000(4-3)}{[100,000(4-3)-40,000]}$$

$$DOL(Atom) = \frac{100,000}{60,000} = 1.67$$

For Beta Company:

$$DOL(Beta) = \frac{Q(P-V)}{[Q(P-V)-F]} = \frac{100,000(4-2)}{[100,000(4-2)-120,000]}$$

$$DOL(Beta) = \frac{200,000}{80,000} = 2.50$$

The results indicate that if Beta Company has a 10% increase in sales, its EBIT will increase by 2.50 × 10% = 25%, while for Atom Company, the increase in EBIT will be 1.67 × 10% = 16.7%.

It is important to note that the degree of operating leverage for a company depends on the level of sales. For example, if Atom Company sells 300,000 units, the DOL is decreased:

$$DOL(Atom) = \frac{Q(P-V)}{[Q(P-V)-F]} = \frac{300,000(4-3)}{[300,000(4-3)-40,000]} = \frac{300,000}{260,000} = 1.15$$

DOL is highest at low levels of sales and declines at higher levels of sales.

The **degree of financial leverage** (DFL) is interpreted as the ratio of the percentage change in net income (or EPS) to the percentage change in EBIT:

$$DFL = \frac{\text{percentage change in EPS}}{\text{percentage change in EBIT}}$$

For a particular level of operating earnings, DFL is calculated as:

$$DFL = \frac{EBIT}{EBIT - \text{interest}}$$

 Professor's Note: The terms "earnings per share" (EPS) and "net income" are used interchangeably in this topic review.

Example: Degree of financial leverage

From the previous example, Atom Company's operating income for selling 100,000 units is $60,000. Assume that Atom Company has annual interest expense of $18,000. If Atom's EBIT increases by 10%, by how much will its earnings per share increase?

Answer:

$$DFL = \frac{EBIT}{EBIT - I} = \frac{\$60,000}{\$60,000 - \$18,000} = 1.43$$

$$\%\Delta EPS = DFL \times \%\Delta EBIT = 1.43 \times 10\% = 14.3\%$$

Hence, earnings per share will increase by 14.3%.

 Professor's Note: Look back at the formulas for DOL and DFL and convince yourself that if there are no fixed costs, DOL is equal to one, and that if there are no interest costs, DFL is equal to one. Values of one mean no leverage. No fixed costs, no operating leverage. No interest costs, no financial leverage. This should help tie these formulas to the concepts and help you know when you have the formulas right (or wrong). If you plug in zero for fixed costs, DOL should be one, and if you plug in zero for interest, DFL should be one.

The **degree of total leverage** (DTL) combines the degree of operating leverage and financial leverage. DTL measures the sensitivity of EPS to change in sales. DTL is computed as:

$$DTL = DOL \times DFL$$

$$DTL = \frac{\%\Delta EBIT}{\%\Delta sales} \times \frac{\%\Delta EPS}{\%\Delta EBIT} = \frac{\%\Delta EPS}{\%\Delta sales}$$

$$DTL = \frac{Q(P-V)}{Q(P-V)-F-I}$$

$$DTL = \frac{S-TVC}{S-TVC-F-I}$$

Example: Degree of total leverage

Continuing with our previous example, how much will Atom's EPS increase if Atom increases its sales by 10%?

Answer:

From the previous examples:

$$DOL_{Atom} = 1.67$$

$$DFL_{Atom} = 1.43$$

$$DTL = DOL \times DFL = 1.67 \times 1.43 = 2.39$$

 Professor's Note: There is some rounding here. If we use 1.6666 for DOL and 1.42857 for DFL, we obtain the DTL of 2.38.

Note that we also could have calculated the DTL the long way. From the previous example, the current value of Atom's dollar sales is $4 × 100,000 = $400,000.

$$DTL = \frac{S-TVC}{S-TVC-F-I} = \frac{\$400,000-\$300,000}{\$400,000-\$300,000-\$40,000-\$18,000} = 2.38$$

$$\%\Delta EPS = DTL \times \%\Delta sales = 2.38 \times 10\% = 23.8\%$$

EPS will increase by 23.8%.

LOS 38.c: Describe the effect of financial leverage on a company's net income and return on equity.

CFA® Program Curriculum, Volume 4, page 89

The use of financial leverage significantly increases the risk and potential reward to common stockholders. The following examples involving Beta Company illustrate how financial leverage affects net income and shareholders' return on equity (ROE).

Example 1: Beta Company financed with 100% equity

Assume that the Beta Company has $500,000 in assets that are financed with 100% equity. Fixed costs are $120,000. Beta is expected to sell 100,000 units, resulting in operating income of [100,000 ($4 − $2)] − $120,000 = $80,000. Beta's tax rate is 40%. Calculate Beta's net income and return on equity if its EBIT increases or decreases by 10%.

Answer:

Beta's Return on Equity With 100% Equity Financing

	EBIT Less 10%	*Expected EBIT*	*EBIT Plus 10%*
EBIT	$72,000	$80,000	$88,000
Interest expense	0	0	0
Income before taxes	$72,000	$80,000	$88,000
Taxes at 40%	28,800	32,000	35,200
Net income	$43,200	$48,000	$52,800
Shareholders' equity	$500,000	$500,000	$500,000
Return on equity (ROE)	**8.64%**	**9.60%**	**10.56%**

Example 2: Beta Company financed with 50% equity and 50% debt

Continuing the previous example, assume that Beta Company is financed with 50% equity and 50% debt. The interest rate on the debt is 6%. Calculate Beta's net income and return on equity if its EBIT increases or decreases by 10%. Beta's tax rate is 40%.

Answer:

Beta's Return on Equity with 50% Equity Financing

	EBIT Less 10%	*Expected EBIT*	*EBIT Plus 10%*
EBIT	$72,000	$80,000	$88,000
Interest expense at 6%	15,000	15,000	15,000
Income before taxes	$57,000	$65,000	$73,000
Taxes at 40%	22,800	26,000	29,200
Net income	$34,200	$39,000	$43,800
Shareholders' equity	$250,000	$250,000	$250,000
Return on equity (ROE)	**13.68%**	**15.60%**	**17.52%**

The interest expense associated with using debt represents a fixed cost that reduces net income. However, the lower net income value is spread over a smaller base of shareholders' equity, serving to magnify the ROE. In all three of the scenarios shown in the two examples, ROE is higher using leverage than it is without leverage.

Further analyzing the differences between the examples, we can see that the use of financial leverage not only increases the *level* of ROE, it also increases the *rate of change* for ROE. In the unleveraged scenario, ROE varies directly with the change in EBIT. For an increase in EBIT of 10%, the ROE increases from 9.60% to 10.56%, for a rate of change of 10%. In the leveraged scenario, ROE is more volatile. For an increase in EBIT of 10%, the ROE increases from 15.60% to 17.52%, for a rate of change of 12.3%.

The use of financial leverage increases the risk of default but also increases the potential return for equity holders.

Professor's Note: Recall how this relationship is reflected in the DuPont formula used to analyze ROE. One of the components of the DuPont formula is the equity multiplier (assets/equity), which captures the effect of financial leverage on ROE.

LOS 38.d: Calculate the breakeven quantity of sales and determine the company's net income at various sales levels.

LOS 38.e: Calculate and interpret the operating breakeven quantity of sales.

CFA® Program Curriculum, Volume 4, page 95

The level of sales that a firm must generate to cover all of its fixed and variable costs is called the breakeven quantity. The **breakeven quantity of sales** is the quantity of sales for which revenues equal total costs, so that net income is zero. We can calculate the breakeven quantity by simply determining how many units must be sold to just cover total fixed costs.

For each unit sold, the **contribution margin**, which is the difference between price and variable cost per unit, is available to help cover fixed costs. We can thus describe the breakeven quantity of sales, Q_{BE}, as:

$$Q_{BE} = \frac{\text{fixed operating costs} + \text{fixed financing costs}}{\text{price} - \text{variable cost per unit}}$$

Example: Breakeven quantity of sales

Consider the prices and costs for Atom Company and Beta Company shown in the following table. Compute and illustrate the breakeven quantity of sales for each company.

Operating Costs for Atom Company and Beta Company

	Atom Company	*Beta Company*
Price	$4.00	$4.00
Variable costs	$3.00	$2.00
Fixed operating costs	$10,000	$80,000
Fixed financing costs	$30,000	$40,000

Answer:

For Atom Company, the breakeven quantity is:

$$Q_{BE}(Atom) = \frac{\$10,000 + \$30,000}{\$4.00 - \$3.00} = 40,000 \text{ units}$$

Similarly, for Beta Company, the breakeven quantity is:

$$Q_{BE}(Beta) = \frac{\$80,000 + \$40,000}{\$4.00 - \$2.00} = 60,000 \text{ units}$$

The breakeven quantity and the relationship between sales revenue, total costs, net income, and net loss are illustrated in Figures 1 and 2.

Figure 1: Breakeven Analysis for Atom Company

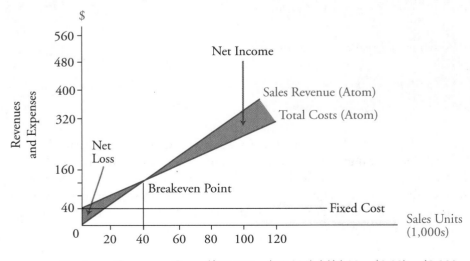

For Atom Company: Q_{BE} = ($30,000 + $10,000) / ($4.00 – $3.00) = 40,000 units

Figure 2: Breakeven Analysis for Beta Company

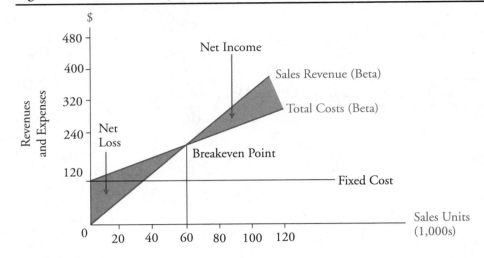

For Beta Company: $Q_{BE} = (\$80{,}000 + \$40{,}000) / (\$4.00 - \$2.00) = 60{,}000$ units

We can also calculate an **operating breakeven quantity of sales**. In this case, we consider only fixed operating costs and ignore fixed financing costs. The calculation is simply:

$$Q_{OBE} = \frac{\text{fixed operating costs}}{\text{price} - \text{variable cost per unit}}$$

Example: Operating breakeven quantity of sales

Calculate the operating breakeven quantity of sales for Atom and Beta, using the same data from the previous example.

Answer:

For Atom, the operating breakeven quantity of sales is:

$$\$10{,}000 / (\$4.00 - \$3.00) = 10{,}000 \text{ units}$$

For Beta, the operating breakeven quantity of sales is:

$$\$80{,}000 / (\$4.00 - \$2.00) = 40{,}000 \text{ units}$$

We can summarize the effects of leverage on net income through an examination of Figures 1 and 2. Other things equal, a firm that chooses operating and financial structures that result in greater total fixed costs will have a higher breakeven quantity of sales. Leverage of either type magnifies the effects of changes in sales on net income. The further a firm's sales are from its breakeven level of sales, the greater the magnifying effects of leverage on net income.

These same conclusions apply to operating leverage and the operating breakeven quantity of sales. One company may choose a larger scale of operations (larger factory), resulting in a greater operating breakeven quantity of sales and greater leverage, other things equal.

Note that the degree of total leverage is calculated for a particular level of sales. The slope of the net income line in Figures 1 and 2 is related to total leverage but is not the same thing. The degree of total leverage is different for every level of sales.

KEY CONCEPTS

LOS 38.a

Leverage increases the risk and potential return of a firm's earnings and cash flows.

Operating leverage increases with fixed operating costs.

Financial leverage increases with fixed financing costs.

Sales risk is uncertainty about the firm's sales.

Business risk refers to the uncertainty about operating earnings (EBIT) and results from variability in sales and expenses. Business risk is magnified by operating leverage.

Financial risk refers to the additional variability of EPS compared to EBIT. Financial risk increases with greater use of fixed cost financing (debt) in a company's capital structure.

LOS 38.b

The degree of operating leverage (DOL) is calculated as $\dfrac{Q(P-V)}{Q(P-V)-F}$ and is interpreted as $\dfrac{\%\Delta EBIT}{\%\Delta sales}$.

The degree of financial leverage (DFL) is calculated as $\dfrac{EBIT}{EBIT-I}$ and is interpreted as $\dfrac{\%\Delta EPS}{\%\Delta EBIT}$.

The degree of total leverage (DTL) is the combination of operating and financial leverage and is calculated as DOL × DFL and interpreted as $\dfrac{\%\Delta EPS}{\%\Delta sales}$.

LOS 38.c

Using more debt and less equity in a firm's capital structure reduces net income through added interest expense but also reduces net equity. The net effect can be to either increase or decrease ROE.

LOS 38.d

The breakeven quantity of sales is the amount of sales necessary to produce a net income of zero (total revenue just covers total costs) and can be calculated as:

$$\frac{\text{fixed operating costs} + \text{fixed financing costs}}{\text{price} - \text{variable cost per unit}}$$

Net income at various sales levels can be calculated as total revenue (i.e., price × quantity sold) minus total costs (i.e., total fixed costs plus total variable costs).

LOS 38.e

The operating breakeven quantity of sales is the amount of sales necessary to produce an operating income of zero (total revenue just covers total operating costs) and can be calculated as:

$$\frac{\text{fixed operating costs}}{\text{price} - \text{variable cost per unit}}$$

CONCEPT CHECKERS

1. Business risk is the combination of:
    A. operating risk and financial risk.
    B. sales risk and financial risk.
    C. operating risk and sales risk.

2. Which of the following is a key determinant of operating leverage?
    A. Level and cost of debt.
    B. The competitive nature of the business.
    C. The trade-off between fixed and variable costs.

3. Which of the following statements about capital structure and leverage is *most accurate*?
    A. Financial leverage is directly related to operating leverage.
    B. Increasing the corporate tax rate will not affect capital structure decisions.
    C. A firm with low operating leverage has a small proportion of its total costs in fixed costs.

4. Jayco, Inc., sells blue ink for $4 a bottle. The ink's variable cost per bottle is $2. Ink has fixed operating costs of $4,000 and fixed financing costs of $6,000. What is Jayco's breakeven quantity of sales, in units?
    A. 2,000.
    B. 3,000.
    C. 5,000.

5. Jayco, Inc., sells blue ink for $4 a bottle. The ink's variable cost per bottle is $2. Ink has fixed operating costs of $4,000 and fixed financing costs of $6,000. What is Jayco's operating breakeven quantity of sales, in units?
    A. 2,000.
    B. 3,000.
    C. 5,000.

6. If Jayco's sales increase by 10%, Jayco's EBIT increases by 15%. If Jayco's EBIT increases by 10%, Jayco's EPS increases by 12%. Jayco's degree of operating leverage (DOL) and degree of total leverage (DTL) are *closest* to:
    A. 1.2 DOL and 1.5 DTL.
    B. 1.2 DOL and 2.7 DTL.
    C. 1.5 DOL and 1.8 DTL.

Use the following data to answer Questions 7 and 8.

Jayco, Inc., sells 10,000 units at a price of $5 per unit. Jayco's fixed costs are $8,000, interest expense is $2,000, variable costs are $3 per unit, and EBIT is $12,000.

7. Jayco's degree of operating leverage (DOL) and degree of financial leverage (DFL) are *closest* to:
    A. 2.50 DOL and 1.00 DFL.
    B. 1.67 DOL and 2.00 DFL.
    C. 1.67 DOL and 1.20 DFL.

8. Jayco's degree of total leverage (DTL) is *closest* to:
   A. 2.00.
   B. 1.75.
   C. 1.50.

9. Vischer Concrete has $1.2 million in assets that are currently financed with 100% equity. Vischer's EBIT is $300,000, and its tax rate is 30%. If Vischer changes its capital structure (recapitalizes) to include 40% debt, what is Vischer's ROE before and after the change? Assume that the interest rate on debt is 5%.

	ROE at 100% equity	ROE at 60% equity
A.	17.5%	26.8%
B.	25.0%	26.8%
C.	25.0%	37.5%

ANSWERS – CONCEPT CHECKERS

1. **C**   Business risk refers to the risk associated with a firm's operating income and is the result of uncertainty about a firm's revenues and the expenditures necessary to produce those revenues. Business risk is the combination of sales risk (the uncertainty associated with the price and quantity of goods and services sold) and operating risk (the leverage created by the use of fixed costs in the firm's operations).

2. **C**   The extent to which costs are fixed determines operating leverage.

3. **C**   If fixed costs are a small percentage of total costs, operating leverage is low. Operating leverage is separate from financial leverage, which depends on the amount of debt in the capital structure. Increasing the tax rate would make the after-tax cost of debt cheaper.

4. **C** $Q_{BE} = \dfrac{\$4,000 + \$6,000}{\$4.00 - \$2.00} = 5,000$ units

5. **A** $Q_{OBE} = \dfrac{\$4,000}{\$4.00 - \$2.00} = 2,000$ units

6. **C** $DOL = \dfrac{15\%}{10\%} = 1.5$

   $DFL = \dfrac{12\%}{10\%} = 1.2$

   $DTL = DOL \times DFL = 1.5 \times 1.2 = 1.8$

7. **C** $DOL = \dfrac{Q(P-V)}{[Q(P-V)-F]} = \dfrac{10,000(5-3)}{[10,000(5-3)-8,000]} = 1.67$

   $DFL = \dfrac{EBIT}{EBIT-I} = \dfrac{12,000}{12,000-2,000} = 1.2$

8. **A** $DTL = \dfrac{Q(P-V)}{[Q(P-V)-F-I]} = \dfrac{10,000(5-3)}{[10,000(5-3)-8,000-2,000]} = 2$, or because we

   calculated the components in Question 7, DTL = DOL × DFL = 1.67 × 1.2 = 2.0

9. **A** With 100% equity:

EBIT	$300,000
Interest expense	0
Income before taxes	$300,000
Taxes at 30%	90,000
Net income	$210,000
Shareholder's equity	$1,200,000
ROE = NI/equity	17.5%

With 60% equity:

EBIT	$300,000
Interest expense ($480,000 at 5%)	24,000
Income before taxes	$276,000
Taxes at 30%	82,800
Net income	$193,200
Shareholders' equity	$720,000
ROE = NI/equity	26.8%

DIVIDENDS AND SHARE REPURCHASES: BASICS

EXAM FOCUS

Dividends have been a large component of the total returns that stocks have provided over time. Cash dividends and share repurchases are two ways that firms can pay out earnings to current shareholders. In this topic review, you will learn the terminology and mechanics of dividend payments. You should also get comfortable with calculating the EPS and book value of a firm after a share repurchase, given the relevant information about the firm and the source of the funds.

LOS 39.a: Describe regular cash dividends, extra dividends, stock dividends, stock splits, and reverse stock splits, including their expected effect on a shareholder's wealth and a company's financial ratios.

CFA® Program Curriculum, Volume 4, page 108

Cash dividends, as the name implies, are payments made to shareholders in cash. They come in three forms:

1. **Regular dividends** occur when a company pays out a portion of profits on a consistent schedule (e.g., quarterly). A long-term record of stable or increasing dividends is widely viewed by investors as a sign of a company's financial stability.

2. **Special dividends** are used when favorable circumstances allow the firm to make a one-time cash payment to shareholders, in addition to any regular dividends the firm pays. Many cyclical firms (e.g., automakers) will use a special dividend to share profits with shareholders when times are good but maintain the flexibility to conserve cash when profits are down. Other names for special dividends include *extra dividends* and *irregular dividends*.

3. **Liquidating dividends** occur when a company goes out of business and distributes the proceeds to shareholders. For tax purposes, a liquidating dividend is treated as a return of capital and amounts over the investor's tax basis are taxed as capital gains.

No matter which form cash dividends take, their net effect is to transfer cash from the company to its shareholders. The payment of a cash dividend reduces a company's assets and the market value of its equity. This means that immediately after a dividend is paid, the price of the stock should drop by the amount of the dividend. For example, if a company's stock price is $25 per share and the company pays $1 per share as a dividend, the price of the stock should immediately drop to $24 per share to account for the lower asset and equity values of the firm.

Stock dividends are dividends paid out in new shares of stock rather than cash. In this case, there will be more shares outstanding, but each one will be worth less. Stock dividends are commonly expressed as a percentage. A 20% stock dividend means every shareholder gets 20% more stock.

Example: Stock dividend

Dwight Craver owns 100 shares of Carson Construction Company at a current price of $30 per share. Carson has 1,000,000 shares of stock outstanding, and its earnings per share (EPS) for the last year were $1.50. Carson declares a 20% stock dividend to all shareholders of record as of June 30.

What is the effect of the stock dividend on the market price of the stock, and what is the impact of the dividend on Craver's ownership position in the company?

Answer:

Impact of 20% Stock Dividend on Shareholders

	Before Stock Dividend	After Stock Dividend
Shares outstanding	1,000,000	1,000,000 × 1.20 = 1,200,000
Earnings per share	$1.50	$1.50 / 1.20 = $1.25
Stock price	$30.00	$30.00 / 1.20 = $25.00
Total market value	1,000,000 × $30 = $30,000,000	1,200,000 × $25 = $30,000,000
Shares owned	100	100 × 1.20 = 120
Ownership value	100 × $30 = $3,000	120 × $25 = $3,000
Ownership stake	100 / 1,000,000 = 0.01%	120 / 1,200,000 = 0.01%

The effect of the stock dividend is to increase the number of shares outstanding by 20%. However, because company earnings stay the same, EPS decline and the price of the firm's stock drops from $30 to $25. Craver's receipt of more shares is exactly offset by the drop in stock price, and his wealth and ownership position in the company are unchanged.

Stock splits divide each existing share into multiple shares, thus creating more shares. There are now more shares, but the price of each share will drop correspondingly to the number of shares created, so there is no change in the owner's wealth. Splits are expressed as a ratio. In a 3-for-1 stock split, each old share is split into three new shares. Stock splits are more common today than stock dividends.

Example: Stock split

Carson Construction Company declares a 3-for-2 stock split. The current stock price is $30, earnings for last year were $1.50, dividends were $0.60 per share, and there are 1 million shares outstanding. What is the impact on Carson's shares outstanding, stock price, EPS, dividends per share, dividend yield, P/E, and market value?

Answer:

Impact of a 3-for-2 Stock Split on Shareholders

	Before Stock Split	*After Stock Split*
Shares outstanding	1,000,000	1,000,000 × (3/2) = 1,500,000
Stock price	$30.00	$30.00 / (3/2) = $20.00
Earnings per share	$1.50	$1.50 / (3/2) = $1.00
Dividends per share	$0.60	$0.60 / (3/2) = $0.40
Dividend yield	$0.60 / $30.00 = 2.0%	$0.40 / $20.00 = 2.0%
P/E ratio	$30.00 / $1.50 = 20	$20.00 / $1.00 = 20
Total market value	1,000,000 × $30 = $30,000,000	1,500,000 × $20 = $30,000,000

The number of shares outstanding increases, but the stock price, EPS, and dividends per share decrease by a proportional amount. The dividend yield, P/E ratio, and total market value of the firm remain the same. As in our prior example, the effect on the firm's shareholders also remains the same. The number of shares would increase (100 × 3 / 2 = 150), but the ownership value and stake are unchanged.

The bottom line for stock splits and stock dividends is that they increase the total number of shares outstanding, but because the stock price and earnings per share are adjusted proportionally, the value of a shareholder's total shares is unchanged.

Some firms use stock splits and stock dividends to keep stock prices within a perceived optimal trading range of $20 to $80 per share. What does academic research have to say about this?

- Stock prices tend to rise after a split or stock dividend.
- Price increases appear to occur because stock splits are taken as a positive signal from management about future earnings.
- If a report of good earnings does not follow a stock split, prices tend to revert to their original (split-adjusted) levels.
- Stock splits and dividends tend to reduce liquidity due to higher percentage brokerage fees on lower-priced stocks.

The conclusion is that stock splits and stock dividends create more shares but don't increase shareholder value.

Reverse stock splits are the opposite of stock splits. After a reverse split, there are fewer shares outstanding but a higher stock price. Because these factors offset one another, shareholder wealth is unchanged. The logic behind a reverse stock split is that the perceived optimal stock price range is $20 to $80 per share, and most investors consider a stock with a price less than $5 per share less than investment grade. Exchanges may impose a minimum stock price and delist those that fall below that price. A company in financial distress whose stock has fallen dramatically may declare a reverse stock split to increase the stock price.

Effects on Financial Ratios

Paying a cash dividend decreases assets (cash) and shareholders' equity (retained earnings). Other things equal, the decrease in cash will decrease a company's liquidity ratios and increase its debt-to-assets ratio, while the decrease in shareholders' equity will increase its debt-to-equity ratio.

Stock dividends, stock splits, and reverse stock splits have no effect on a company's leverage ratios or liquidity ratios. These transactions do not change the value of a company's assets or shareholders' equity; they merely change the number of equity shares.

LOS 39.b: Describe dividend payment chronology, including the significance of declaration, holder-of-record, ex-dividend, and payment dates.

CFA® Program Curriculum, Volume 4, page 115

An example of a typical dividend payment schedule is shown in Figure 1.

Figure 1: Dividend Payment Chronology

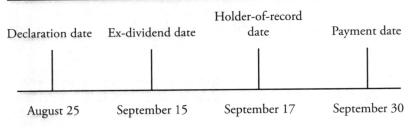

- **Declaration date.** The date the board of directors approves payment of the dividend.
- **Ex-dividend date.** The first day a share of stock trades without the dividend. The ex-dividend date is also the cutoff date for receiving the dividend and occurs two business days before the holder-of-record date. If you buy the share on or after the ex-dividend date, you will not receive the dividend.
- **Holder-of-record date.** The date on which the shareholders of record are designated to receive the dividend.
- **Payment date.** The date the dividend checks are mailed out or when the payment is electronically transferred to shareholder accounts.

Stocks are traded ex-dividend on and after the ex-dividend date, so stock prices should fall by the amount of the dividend on the ex-dividend date. Because of taxes, however, the drop in price may be closer to the after-tax value of dividends.

 Professor's Note: The reason that the holder-of-record date is two business days after the ex-dividend date has to do with the fact that the settlement date for stocks is three business days after the trade date (t + 3). If an investor buys a stock the day before the ex-dividend date, the trade will settle three business days later on the holder-of-record date, and the investor will receive the dividend.

LOS 39.c: Compare share repurchase methods.

CFA® Program Curriculum, Volume 4, page 120

A **share repurchase** is a transaction in which a company buys back shares of its own common stock. Companies use three methods to repurchase shares:

1. **Buy in the open market.** Companies may repurchase stock in the open market at the prevailing market price. A share repurchase is authorized by the board of directors for a certain number of shares. Buying in the open market gives the company the flexibility to choose the timing of the transaction.

2. **Buy a fixed number of shares at a fixed price.** A company may repurchase stock by making a **tender offer** to repurchase a specific number of shares at a price that is usually at a premium to the current market price. Shareholders may tender their shares according to the terms of the offer. If shareholders try to tender more shares than the total repurchase, the company will typically buy back a pro rata amount from each shareholder. The company may select a tender offer price or use a **Dutch auction** (described in the Economics topic review for Demand and Supply Analysis: Introduction) to determine the lowest price at which it can repurchase the number of shares desired.

3. **Repurchase by direct negotiation.** Companies may negotiate directly with a large shareholder to buy back a block of shares, usually at a premium to the market price. A company may engage in direct negotiation in order to keep a large block of shares from coming into the market and reducing the stock price or to repurchase shares from a potential acquirer after an unsuccessful takeover attempt. If the firm pays more than market value for the shares, the result is an increase in wealth for the seller and an equal decrease in wealth for remaining firm shareholders.

LOS 39.d: Calculate and compare the effects of a share repurchase on earnings per share when 1) the repurchase is financed with the company's excess cash and 2) the company uses funded debt to finance the repurchase.

CFA® Program Curriculum, Volume 4, page 122

A share repurchase will reduce the number of shares outstanding, which will tend to increase earnings per share. On the other hand, purchasing shares with company funds will reduce interest income and earnings, and purchasing shares with borrowed funds incurs interest costs, which will reduce earnings directly by the after-tax cost of the borrowed funds. The relation of the percentage decrease in earnings and the percentage decrease in the number of shares used to calculate EPS will determine whether the effect of a stock repurchase on EPS will be positive or negative.

Before we look at the calculations involved in determining the effect of a share repurchase on EPS, consider the following intuitive approach. The earnings yield for a share of stock is simply EPS divided by the share price. A $20 stock with EPS of $1 has an earnings yield of 5%. If the after-tax yield on company funds used to repurchase shares, or the after-tax cost of borrowed funds used to repurchase shares, is greater than 5%, EPS will fall as a result of the repurchase. If the after-tax yield on company funds used to repurchase shares, or the after-tax cost of borrowed funds used to repurchase shares, is less than 5%, EPS will rise as a result of the repurchase.

Example: Share repurchase when after-tax cost of debt is less than earnings yield

Spencer Pharmaceuticals, Inc., (SPI) plans to borrow $30 million that it will use to repurchase shares. SPI's chief financial officer has compiled the following information:

- Share price at the time of buyback = $50.
- Shares outstanding before buyback = 20,000,000.
- EPS before buyback = $5.00.
- Earnings yield = $5.00 / $50 = 10%.
- After-tax cost of borrowing = 8%.
- Planned buyback = 600,000 shares.

Calculate the EPS after the buyback.

Answer:

total earnings = $5.00 × 20,000,000 = $100,000,000

$$\text{EPS after buyback} = \frac{\text{total earnings} - \text{after-tax cost of funds}}{\text{shares outstanding after buyback}}$$

$$= \frac{\$100,000,000 - (600,000 \text{ shares} \times \$50 \times 0.08)}{(20,000,000 - 600,000) \text{ shares}}$$

$$= \frac{\$100,000,000 - \$2,400,000}{19,400,000 \text{ shares}}$$

$$= \frac{\$97,600,000}{19,400,000 \text{ shares}}$$

$$= \$5.03$$

Because the 8% after-tax cost of borrowing is less than the 10% earnings yield (E/P) of the shares, the share repurchase will increase the company's EPS.

Example: Share repurchase when after-tax cost of debt is greater than earnings yield

Spencer Pharmaceuticals, Inc., (SPI) plans to borrow $30 million that it will use to repurchase shares. Creditors perceive the company to be a significant credit risk, and the after-tax cost of borrowing is 15%. Using the other information from the previous example, calculate the EPS after the buyback.

Answer:

$$\text{EPS after buyback} = \frac{\text{total earnings} - \text{after-tax cost of funds}}{\text{shares outstanding after buyback}}$$

$$= \frac{\$100,000,000 - (600,000 \text{ shares} \times \$50 \times 0.15)}{(20,000,000 - 600,000) \text{ shares}}$$

$$= \frac{\$100,000,000 - \$4,500,000}{19,400,000 \text{ shares}}$$

$$= \frac{\$95,500,000}{19,400,000 \text{ shares}}$$

$$= \$4.92$$

Because the after-tax cost of borrowing of 15% exceeds the earnings yield of 10%, the added interest paid reduces EPS after the buyback.

The conclusion is that a share repurchase using borrowed funds will increase EPS if the after-tax cost of debt used to buy back shares is less than the earnings yield of the shares before the repurchase. It will decrease EPS if the cost of debt is greater than the earnings yield, and it will not change EPS if the two are equal.

LOS 39.e: Calculate the effect of a share repurchase on book value per share.

CFA® Program Curriculum, Volume 4, page 124

Share repurchases may also have an impact on the book value of a share of stock.

Example: Effect of a share repurchase on book value per share

The share prices of Blue, Inc., and Red Company are both $25 per share, and each company has 20 million shares outstanding. Both companies have announced a $10 million stock buyback. Blue, Inc., has a book value of $300 million, while Red Company has a book value of $700 million.

Calculate the book value per share (BVPS) of each company after the share repurchase.

Answer:

Share buyback for both companies = $10 million / $25 per share = 400,000 shares.

Remaining shares for both companies = 20 million − 400,000 = 19.6 million.

Blue, Inc.'s current BVPS = $300 million / 20 million = $15.
The market price per share of $25 is greater than the BVPS of $15.

   Book value after repurchase: $300 million − $10 million = $290 million
   BVPS = $290 million / 19.6 million = $14.80
   BVPS decreased by $0.20

Red Company's current BVPS = $700 million / 20 million = $35.
The market price per share of $25 is less than the BVPS of $35.

   Book value after repurchase: $700 million − $10 million = $690 million
   BVPS = $690 million / 19.6 million = $35.20
   BVPS increased by $0.20

The conclusion is that BVPS will decrease if the repurchase price is greater than the original BVPS and increase if the repurchase price is less than the original BVPS.

LOS 39.f: Explain why a cash dividend and a share repurchase of the same amount are equivalent in terms of the effect on shareholders' wealth, all else being equal.

CFA® Program Curriculum, Volume 4, page 125

Because shares are repurchased using a company's own cash, a share repurchase can be considered an alternative to a cash dividend as a way of distributing earnings to shareholders.

Assuming the tax treatment of the two alternatives is the same, a share repurchase has the same impact on shareholder wealth as a cash dividend payment of an equal amount.

Example: Impact of share repurchase and cash dividend of equal amounts

Spencer Pharmaceuticals, Inc., (SPI) has 20,000,000 shares outstanding with a current market value of $50 per share. SPI made $100 million in profits for the recent quarter, and because only 70% of these profits will be reinvested back into the company, SPI's Board of Directors is considering two alternatives for distributing the remaining 30% to shareholders:

- Pay a cash dividend of $30,000,000 / 20,000,000 shares = $1.50 per share.
- Repurchase $30,000,000 worth of common stock.

Assume that dividends are received when the shares go ex-dividend, the stock can be repurchased at the market price of $50 per share, and there are no differences in tax treatment between the two alternatives. How would the wealth of an SPI shareholder be affected by the board's decision on the method of distribution?

Answer:

(1) Cash dividend

After the shares go ex-dividend, a shareholder of a single share would have $1.50 in cash and a share worth $50 − $1.50 = $48.50.

The ex-dividend value of $48.50 can also be calculated as the market value of equity after the distribution of the $30 million, divided by the number of shares outstanding after the dividend payment:

$$\frac{(20,000,000)(\$50) - \$30,000,000}{20,000,000} = \$48.50$$

total wealth from the ownership of one share = $48.50 + $1.50 = $50

(2) Share repurchase

With $30,000,000, SPI could repurchase $30,000,000 / $50 = 600,000 shares of common stock. The share price after the repurchase is calculated as the market value of equity after the $30,000,000 repurchase divided by the shares outstanding after the repurchase:

$$\frac{(20,000,000)(\$50) - \$30,000,000}{20,000,000 - 600,000} = \frac{\$970,000,000}{19,400,000} = \$50$$

total wealth from the ownership of one share = $50

KEY CONCEPTS

LOS 39.a

Cash dividends are a payment from a company to a shareholder that reduces both the value of the company's assets and the market value of equity. They can come in the forms of regular, special, or liquidating dividends.

Stock dividends are distributions of new shares rather than cash. Stock splits divide each existing share into multiple shares. Both create more shares, but there is a proportionate drop in the price per share, so there is no effect on the total value of each shareholder's shares.

Other things equal, paying a cash dividend decreases liquidity ratios and increases leverage ratios. Stock dividends and stock splits do not affect liquidity or leverage ratios.

LOS 39.b

The chronology of a dividend payout is:
* Declaration date.
* Ex-dividend date.
* Holder-of-record date.
* Payment date.

Stocks purchased on or after the ex-dividend date will not receive the dividend. The ex-dividend date is two business days prior to the holder-of-record date.

LOS 39.c

Companies can repurchase shares of their own stock by buying shares in the open market, buying back a fixed number of shares at a fixed price through a tender offer, or directly negotiating to buy a large block of shares from a large shareholder.

LOS 39.d

The effect of share repurchases using borrowed funds on EPS is:
* If the company's E/P is equal to the after-tax cost of borrowing, there will be no effect on EPS.
* If the company's E/P is greater than the after-tax cost of borrowing, EPS will increase.
* If the company's E/P is less than the after-tax cost of borrowing, EPS will decrease.

LOS 39.e

The effect of a share repurchase on book value per share is:
* An increase if the share price is less than the original BVPS.
* A decrease if the share price is greater than the original BVPS.

LOS 39.f

A share repurchase is economically equivalent to a cash dividend of an equal amount, assuming the tax treatment of the two alternatives is the same.

CONCEPT CHECKERS

1. Which of the following is *most likely* to increase shareholders' wealth?
   A. A stock dividend.
   B. A stock split.
   C. A special dividend.

2. Which of the following is *most accurate*? The purchaser of a stock will not receive the dividend if the stock was purchased on or after the:
   A. declaration date.
   B. ex-dividend date.
   C. holder-of-record date.

3. A share repurchase that begins with a company communicating to shareholders a specific number of shares and a range of acceptable prices is *most likely* to be a(n):
   A. open market repurchase.
   B. fixed price tender offer.
   C. Dutch auction.

4. If a company's after-tax borrowing rate is greater than the company's earning yield when the company repurchases stock with borrowed money, going forward, the earnings per share is *most likely* to:
   A. increase.
   B. decrease.
   C. remain unchanged.

5. After a share repurchase, book value per share is *most likely* to increase if, pre-purchase, BVPS was:
   A. greater than the market price per share.
   B. less than the market price per share.
   C. negative.

6. A company is considering either an open market share repurchase or a cash dividend of an equal amount. Compared to the open market share repurchase, the cash dividend is *most likely* to:
   A. increase a shareholder's wealth by a greater amount.
   B. increase a shareholder's wealth by a lesser amount.
   C. have a relative impact that depends on the tax treatment of the two alternatives.

7. Studdard Controls recently declared a quarterly dividend of $1.25 payable on Thursday, April 25, to holders of record on Friday, April 12. What is the last day an investor could purchase Studdard stock and still receive the quarterly dividend?
   A. April 9.
   B. April 10.
   C. April 12.

8.   Arizona Seafood, Inc., plans $45 million in new borrowing to repurchase 3,600,000 shares at their market price of $12.50. The yield on the new debt will be 12%. The company has 36 million shares outstanding and EPS of $0.60 before the repurchase. The company's tax rate is 40%. The company's EPS after the share repurchase will be *closest* to:
      A. $0.50.
      B. $0.57.
      C. $0.67.

9.   Northern Financial Co. has a BVPS of $5. The company has announced a $15 million share buyback. The share price is $60 and the company has 40 million shares outstanding. After the share repurchase, the company's BVPS will be *closest* to:
      A. $4.65.
      B. $4.90.
      C. $5.03.

ANSWERS – CONCEPT CHECKERS

1. **C** "Special" dividends (also known as "extra" or "irregular" dividends) are likely to be associated with increased shareholder wealth because they are usually used to distribute excess profits to shareholders after a period of unusually high earnings. Stock dividends and stock splits create more shares; however, there is a proportionate drop in the price per share, so there is no effect on shareholder wealth.

2. **B** The chronology of a dividend payout is declaration date, ex-dividend date, holder-of-record date, and payment date. The ex-dividend date is the cutoff date for receiving the dividend: stocks purchased on or after the ex-dividend date will not receive the dividend.

3. **C** Dutch auctions begin with the company communicating to shareholders a specific number of shares and a range of acceptable prices. When companies repurchase shares in the open market, they buy at market prices and in quantities as conditions warrant. In a fixed price tender offer, the company announces a fixed number of shares to be repurchased and a fixed price.

4. **B** Earnings per share is expected to decrease after a share repurchase if the company's after-tax borrowing rate is greater than the company's earning yield.

5. **A** Book value per share will increase after a share repurchase if book value per share was greater than market price per share. BVPS will decrease after a share repurchase if BVPS was less than market price.

6. **C** A share repurchase is economically equivalent to a cash dividend of an equal amount, assuming the tax treatment of the two alternatives is the same.

7. **A** If an investor purchases shares of stock on or after the ex-dividend date, she will NOT receive the dividend. Therefore, to receive the dividend, the investor must purchase stock the day before the ex-dividend date. The ex-dividend day is always two business days before the holder-of-record date. Two days before April 12 is April 10; therefore, the last day the investor can purchase shares and still receive the dividend is April 9.

8. **B** Total earnings are $0.60 \times 36,000,000 = \$21,600,000$.

   After-tax cost of debt is $12\% \times (1 - 0.40) = 7.2\%$.

   $$\text{EPS after buyback} = \frac{\text{total earnings} - \text{after-tax cost of funds}}{\text{shares outstanding after buyback}}$$

   $$= \frac{\$21,600,000 - (3,600,000 \text{ shares} \times \$12.50 \times 0.072)}{36,000,000 \text{ shares} - 3,600,000 \text{ shares}}$$

   $$= \frac{\$21,600,000 - \$3,240,000}{32,400,000 \text{ shares}} = \frac{\$18,360,000}{32,400,000 \text{ shares}}$$

   EPS = $0.57

9. **A**   Shares to be repurchased are $15 million / $60 = 250,000 shares.

Remaining shares after the repurchase will be 40,000,000 − 250,000 = 39,750,000 shares.

Book value before the repurchase is 40,000,000 × $5.00 = $200,000,000.

Book value after the repurchase will be $200,000,000 − $15,000,000 = $185,000,000.

BVPS = $185,000,000 / 39,750,000 = $4.654 per share.

Working Capital Management

Exam Focus

Firm liquidity is an important concern for an analyst. How a firm manages its working capital, its short-term financing policy, and its sources of short-term financing for liquidity needs are therefore important concerns for the analyst. A good portion of this topic review repeats material on ratios and yield calculations from previous readings and introduces types of debt securities that will also be covered in the topic reviews for fixed income investments.

New concepts introduced here are the management of current assets and liabilities, types of short-term bank financing, and the receivables aging schedule. Understand well why the management of inventory, receivables, and payables is important to a firm's overall profitability and value. The general guidelines for establishing and evaluating a firm's short-term investment policies and for evaluating short-term funding strategy and policy should be sufficient here. Focus on the overall objectives and how they can be met.

LOS 40.a: Describe primary and secondary sources of liquidity and factors that influence a company's liquidity position.

CFA® Program Curriculum, Volume 4, page 137

A company's **primary sources of liquidity** are the sources of cash it uses in its normal day-to-day operations. The company's *cash balances* result from selling goods and services, collecting receivables, and generating cash from other sources such as short-term investments. Typical sources of *short-term funding* include trade credit from vendors and lines of credit from banks. Effective *cash flow management* of a firm's collections and payments can also be a source of liquidity for a company.

Secondary sources of liquidity include liquidating short-term or long-lived assets, negotiating debt agreements (i.e., renegotiating), or filing for bankruptcy and reorganizing the company. While using its primary sources of liquidity is unlikely to change the company's normal operations, resorting to secondary sources of liquidity such as these can change the company's financial structure and operations significantly and may indicate that its financial position is deteriorating.

Factors That Influence a Company's Liquidity Position

In general, a company's liquidity position improves if it can get cash to flow in more quickly and flow out more slowly. Factors that weaken a company's liquidity position are called *drags and pulls* on liquidity.

Drags on liquidity delay or reduce cash inflows, or increase borrowing costs. Examples include uncollected receivables and bad debts, obsolete inventory (takes longer to sell and can require sharp price discounts), and tight short-term credit due to economic conditions.

Pulls on liquidity accelerate cash outflows. Examples include paying vendors sooner than is optimal and changes in credit terms that require repayment of outstanding balances.

LOS 40.b: Compare a company's liquidity measures with those of peer companies.

CFA® Program Curriculum, Volume 4, page 139

Some companies tend to have chronically weak liquidity positions, often due to specific factors that affect the company or its industry. These companies typically need to borrow against their long-lived assets to acquire working capital.

Liquidity ratios are employed by analysts to determine the firm's ability to pay its short-term liabilities.

- The *current ratio* is the best-known measure of liquidity:

$$\text{current ratio} = \frac{\text{current assets}}{\text{current liabilities}}$$

The higher the current ratio, the more likely it is that the company will be able to pay its short-term bills. A current ratio of less than one means that the company has negative working capital and is probably facing a liquidity crisis. Working capital equals current assets minus current liabilities.

- The *quick ratio* or *acid-test ratio* is a more stringent measure of liquidity because it does not include inventories and other assets that might not be very liquid:

$$\text{quick ratio} = \frac{\text{cash + short-term marketable securities + receivables}}{\text{current liabilities}}$$

The higher the quick ratio, the more likely it is that the company will be able to pay its short-term bills.

The current and quick ratios differ only in the assumed liquidity of the current assets that the analyst projects will be used to pay off current liabilities.

- A measure of accounts receivable liquidity is the *receivables turnover*:

$$\text{receivables turnover} = \frac{\text{credit sales}}{\text{average receivables}}$$

It is considered desirable to have a receivables turnover figure close to the industry norm.

Professor's Note: This formula for the receivables turnover ratio uses credit sales in the numerator, rather than total sales as shown in the earlier topic review on ratio analysis. While an analyst within a company will know what proportion of sales are credit or cash sales, an external analyst will likely not have this information but may be able to estimate it based on standard industry practice.

In most cases when a ratio compares a balance sheet account (such as receivables) with an income or cash flow item (such as sales), the balance sheet item will be the average of the account instead of simply the end-of-year balance. Averages are calculated by adding the beginning-of-year account value and the end-of-year account value, then dividing the sum by two.

- The inverse of the receivables turnover multiplied by 365 is the *number of days of receivables* (also called *average days' sales outstanding*), which is the average number of days it takes for the company's customers to pay their bills:

$$\text{number of days of receivables} = \frac{365}{\text{receivables turnover}} = \frac{\text{average receivables}}{\text{average day's credit sales}}$$

It is considered desirable to have a collection period (and receivables turnover) close to the industry norm. The firm's credit terms are another important benchmark used to interpret this ratio. A collection period that is too high might mean that customers are too slow in paying their bills, which means too much capital is tied up in assets. A collection period that is too low might indicate that the firm's credit policy is too rigorous, which might be hampering sales.

- A measure of a firm's efficiency with respect to its processing and inventory management is the *inventory turnover*:

$$\text{inventory turnover} = \frac{\text{cost of goods sold}}{\text{average inventory}}$$

Professor's Note: Pay careful attention to the numerator in the turnover ratios. For inventory turnover, be sure to use cost of goods sold, not sales.

- The inverse of the inventory turnover multiplied by 365 is the *average inventory processing period* or *number of days of inventory*:

$$\text{number of days of inventory} = \frac{365}{\text{inventory turnover}} = \frac{\text{average inventory}}{\text{average day's COGS}}$$

As is the case with accounts receivable, it is considered desirable to have an inventory processing period (and inventory turnover) close to the industry norm. A processing period that is too high might mean that too much capital is tied up in inventory and could mean that the inventory is obsolete. A processing period that is too low might indicate that the firm has inadequate stock on hand, which could hurt sales.

- A measure of the use of trade credit by the firm is the *payables turnover ratio*:

$$\text{payables turnover ratio} = \frac{\text{purchases}}{\text{average trade payables}}$$

- The inverse of the payables turnover ratio multiplied by 365 is the *payables payment period* or *number of days of payables*, which is the average amount of time it takes the company to pay its bills:

$$\text{number of days of payables} = \frac{365}{\text{payables turnover ratio}} = \frac{\text{average payables}}{\text{average day's purchases}}$$

LOS 40.c: Evaluate working capital effectiveness of a company based on its operating and cash conversion cycles, and compare the company's effectiveness with that of peer companies.

CFA® Program Curriculum, Volume 4, page 139

- The **operating cycle**, the average number of days that it takes to turn raw materials into cash proceeds from sales, is:

    operating cycle = days of inventory + days of receivables

- The *cash conversion cycle* or *net operating cycle* is the length of time it takes to turn the firm's cash investment in inventory back into cash, in the form of collections from the sales of that inventory. The cash conversion cycle is computed from the average receivables collection period, average inventory processing period, and the payables payment period:

$$\text{cash conversion cycle} = \left(\begin{array}{c} \text{average days} \\ \text{of receivables} \end{array} \right) + \left(\begin{array}{c} \text{average days} \\ \text{of inventory} \end{array} \right) - \left(\begin{array}{c} \text{average days} \\ \text{of payables} \end{array} \right)$$

High cash conversion cycles are considered undesirable. A conversion cycle that is too high implies that the company has an excessive amount of investment in working capital.

LOS 40.d: Explain the effect of different types of cash flows on a company's net daily cash position.

CFA® Program Curriculum, Volume 4, page 143

Daily cash position refers to uninvested cash balances a firm has available to make routine purchases and pay expenses as they come due. The purpose of managing a firm's daily cash position is to have sufficient cash on hand (that is, make sure the firm's net daily cash position never becomes negative) but to avoid keeping excess cash because of the interest income foregone by not investing the cash.

Typical cash inflows for a firm include its cash from sales and collections of receivables; cash received from subsidiaries; dividends, interest, and principal received from investments in securities; tax refunds; and borrowing. Typical cash outflows include payments to employees and vendors; cash transferred to subsidiaries; payments of interest and principal on debt; investments in securities; taxes paid; and dividends paid.

To manage its cash position effectively, a firm should analyze its typical cash inflows and outflows by category and prepare forecasts over short-term (daily or weekly balances for the next several weeks), medium-term (monthly balances for the next year), and long-term time horizons. A firm can use these forecasts to identify periods when its cash balance may become low enough to require short-term borrowing, or high enough to invest excess cash in short-term securities.

LOS 40.e: Calculate and interpret comparable yields on various securities, compare portfolio returns against a standard benchmark, and evaluate a company's short-term investment policy guidelines.

CFA® Program Curriculum, Volume 4, page 149

Short-term securities in which a firm can invest cash include:

- U.S. Treasury bills.
- Short-term federal agency securities.
- Bank certificates of deposit.
- Banker's acceptances.
- Time deposits.
- Repurchase agreements.
- Commercial paper.
- Money market mutual funds.
- Adjustable-rate preferred stock.

Adjustable-rate preferred stock has a dividend rate that is reset quarterly to current market yields and offers corporate holders a tax advantage because a percentage of the dividends received are exempt from federal tax. The other securities listed are all described in more detail in the topic reviews on fixed income securities.

We covered the yield calculations for short-term discount securities in the "Discounted Cash Flow Applications" topic review in Quantitative Methods.

The percentage discount from face value is:

$$\% \text{ discount} = \left(\frac{\text{face value} - \text{price}}{\text{face value}} \right)$$

The discount-basis yield (bank discount yield or BDY) is:

$$\text{discount-basis yield} = \left(\frac{\text{face value} - \text{price}}{\text{face value}}\right)\left(\frac{360}{\text{days}}\right) = \% \text{ discount} \times \left(\frac{360}{\text{days}}\right)$$

The money market yield is:

$$\text{money market yield} = \left(\frac{\text{face value} - \text{price}}{\text{price}}\right)\left(\frac{360}{\text{days}}\right) = \text{holding period yield} \times \left(\frac{360}{\text{days}}\right)$$

where:
"days" = days to maturity
"price" = purchase price of the security

The bond equivalent yield measure for short-term discount securities is calculated as:

$$\text{bond equivalent yield} = \left(\frac{\text{face value} - \text{price}}{\text{price}}\right)\left(\frac{365}{\text{days to maturity}}\right)$$

$$= \text{holding period yield} \times \left(\frac{365}{\text{days}}\right)$$

 Professor's Note: In Quantitative Methods, the bond equivalent yield was defined differently as two times the effective semiannual yield.

Returns on the firm's short-term securities investments should be stated as bond equivalent yields. The return on the portfolio should be expressed as a weighted average of these yields.

Cash Management Investment Policy

Typically, the objective of cash management is to earn a market return without taking on much risk, either liquidity risk or default risk. Firms invest cash that may be needed in the short term in securities of relatively high credit quality and relatively short maturities to minimize these risks.

It is advisable to have a written investment policy statement. An investment policy statement typically begins with a statement of the purpose and objective of the investment portfolio, some general guidelines about the strategy to be employed to achieve those objectives, and the types of securities that will be used. The investment policy statement will also include specific information on who is allowed to purchase securities, who is responsible for complying with company guidelines, and what steps will be taken if the investment guidelines are not followed. Finally, the investment policy statement will include limitations on the specific types of securities permitted for investment of short-term funds, limitations on the credit ratings of portfolio securities, and limitations on the proportions of the total short-term securities portfolio that can be invested in the various types of permitted securities.

An investment policy statement should be evaluated on how well the policy can be expected to satisfy the goals and purpose of short-term investments, generating yield without taking on excessive credit or liquidity risk. The policy should not be overly restrictive in the context of meeting the goals of safety and liquidity.

LOS 40.f: Evaluate a company's management of accounts receivable, inventory, and accounts payable over time and compared to peer companies.

CFA® Program Curriculum, Volume 4, page 153

The management of accounts receivable begins with calculating the average days of receivables and comparing this ratio to the firm's historical performance or to the average ratios for a group of comparable companies. More detail about the accounts receivable performance can be gained by using an **aging schedule** such as that presented in Figure 1.

Figure 1: Receivables Aging (thousands of dollars)

Days Outstanding	March	April	May
< 31 days	200	212	195
31–60 days	150	165	140
61–90 days	100	90	92
> 90 days	50	70	66

In March, $200,000 of accounts receivable were current—that is, had been outstanding less than 31 days; $50,000 of the receivables at the end of March had been outstanding for more than 90 days.

Presenting this data as percentages of total outstanding receivables can facilitate analysis of how the aging schedule for receivables is changing over time. An example is presented in Figure 2.

Figure 2: Receivables Aging (% of totals)

Days Outstanding	March	April	May
< 31 days	40%	39%	40%
31–60 days	30%	31%	28%
61–90 days	20%	17%	19%
> 90 days	10%	13%	13%

Another useful metric for monitoring the accounts receivable performance is the *weighted average collection period*, which indicates the average days outstanding per dollar of receivables. As illustrated in Figure 3, the weights are the percentage of total receivables in each category, and these are multiplied by the average days to collect accounts within each aging category.

Figure 3: Weighted Average Collection Period—March

Days Outstanding	Average Collection Days	% Weight	Days × Weight
< 31 days	22	40%	8.8
31–60 days	44	30%	13.2
61–90 days	74	20%	14.8
> 90 days	135	10%	13.5
Weighted Average Collection Period			50.3 days

The information necessary to compare a firm's aging schedule and weighted average collection period to other firms is not available. However, analysis of the historical trends and significant changes in a firm's aging schedule and weighted average collection days can give a clearer picture of what is driving changes in the simpler metric of average days of receivables. The company must always evaluate the trade-off between stricter credit terms (and borrower creditworthiness) and the ability to make sales. Terms that are too strict will lead to less-than-optimal sales. Terms that are too lenient will increase sales at the cost of longer average days of receivables, which must be funded at some cost, and will increase bad accounts, directly affecting profitability.

Inventory Management

Inventory management involves a trade-off as well. Inventory levels that are too low will result in lost sales due to stock-outs, while inventory that is too large will have carrying costs because the firm's capital is tied up in inventory. Reducing inventory will free up cash that can be invested in interest-bearing securities or used to reduce debt or equity funding. Increasing average days' inventory or a decreasing inventory turnover ratio can both indicate that inventory is too large. A large inventory can lead to greater losses from obsolete items and can also indicate that obsolete items that no longer sell well are included in inventory.

Comparing average days of inventory and inventory turnover ratios between industries, or even between two firms that have different business strategies, can be misleading. The grocery business typically has high inventory turnover, while an art gallery's inventory turnover will typically be low. An auto parts firm that stocks hard-to-find parts for antique cars will likely have a low inventory turnover (and charge premium prices) compared to a chain auto parts store that does most of its business in standard items like oil filters, brake parts, and antifreeze. In any business, inventory management is an important component of effective overall financial management.

Accounts Payable Management

Just as a company must manage its receivables because they require working capital (and therefore have a funding cost), payables must be managed well because they represent a source of working capital to the firm. If the firm pays its payables prior to their due dates, cash is used unnecessarily and interest on it is sacrificed. If a firm pays its payables late, it can damage relationships with suppliers and lead to more restrictive credit terms or even the requirement that purchases be made for cash. Late payment can also result in interest charges that are high compared to other sources of short-term financing.

Typical terms on payables (trade credit) contain a discount available to those who pay quickly as well as a due date. Terms of "2/10 net 60" mean that if the invoice is paid within ten days, the company gets a 2% discount on the invoiced amount and that if the company does not take advantage of the discount, the net amount is due 60 days from the date of the invoice.

The cost to the company of not taking the discount for early payment can be evaluated as an annualized rate:

$$\text{cost of trade credit} = \left(1 + \frac{\% \text{ discount}}{1 - \% \text{ discount}}\right)^{\frac{365}{\text{days past discount}}} - 1$$

where:
days past discount = number of days after the end of the discount period

 Professor's Note: You should recognize this from Quantitative Methods as the formula for converting a short-term rate to an effective annual rate. The term [% discount / (1 – % discount)] is the holding period return to the firm of taking advantage of a discount, in the same way that the holding period return on a pure discount security is [discount / (face – discount)].

Trade credit can be a source of liquidity for a company. However, when the cost of trade credit is greater than the company's cost of short-term liquidity from other sources, the company is better off paying the invoice within (ideally at the end of) the discount period.

Example: Cost of trade credit

Calculate and interpret the annualized cost of trade credit for invoice terms of 2/10 net 60, when the invoice is paid on the 40th, 50th, or 60th day.

Answer:

The discount is 2%. The annualized cost of not taking the discount can be calculated when the invoice is paid on:

$$\text{Day 40:} \quad \left(1 + \frac{0.02}{1 - 0.02}\right)^{\frac{365}{40-10}} - 1 = 27.9\%$$

$$\text{Day 50:} \quad \left(1 + \frac{0.02}{1 - 0.02}\right)^{\frac{365}{50-10}} - 1 = 20.2\%$$

$$\text{Day 60:} \quad \left(1 + \frac{0.02}{1 - 0.02}\right)^{\frac{365}{60-10}} - 1 = 15.9\%$$

The annualized cost of trade credit decreases as the payment period increases. If the company does not take the 2% discount within the first ten days, it should wait until the due date (day 60) to pay the invoice.

Our primary quantitative measure of payables management is average days of payables outstanding, which can also be calculated as:

$$\text{number of days of payables} = \frac{\text{accounts payable}}{\text{average day's purchases}}$$

where:

$$\text{average day's purchases} = \frac{\text{annual purchases}}{365}$$

A company with a short payables period (high payables turnover) may simply be taking advantage of discounts for paying early because it has good low-cost funds available to finance its working capital needs. A company with a long payables period may be such an important buyer that it can effectively utilize accounts payable as a source of short-term funding with relatively little cost (because suppliers will put up with it). Monitoring the changes in days' payables outstanding over time for a single firm will, however, aid the analyst. An extension of days' payables may serve as an early warning of deteriorating short-term liquidity.

LOS 40.g: Evaluate the choices of short-term funding available to a company and recommend a financing method.

CFA® Program Curriculum, Volume 4, page 167

There are several sources of short-term funding available to a company, from both bank and non-bank sources. We list the most important of these here.

Sources of Short-Term Funding From Banks

Lines of credit are used primarily by large, financially sound companies.

- *Uncommitted line of credit.* A bank extends an offer of credit for a certain amount but may refuse to lend if circumstances change.
- *Committed (regular) line of credit.* A bank extends an offer of credit that it "commits to" for some period of time. The fact that the bank has committed to extend credit in amounts up to the credit line makes this a more reliable source of short-term funding than an uncommitted line of credit. Banks charge a fee for making such a commitment. Loans under the agreement are typically for periods of less than a year, and interest charges are stated in terms of a short-term reference rate, such as LIBOR or the U.S. prime rate, plus a margin to compensate for the credit risk of the loan. Outside the United States, similar arrangements are referred to as *overdraft lines of credit.*
- *Revolving line of credit.* An even more reliable source of short-term financing than a committed line of credit, revolving lines of credit are typically for longer terms, sometimes as long as years. Along with committed lines of credit, revolving credit lines can be verified and can be listed on a firm's financial statements in the footnotes as a source of liquidity.

Companies with weaker credit may have to pledge assets as collateral for bank borrowings. Fixed assets, inventory, and accounts receivable may all serve as collateral for loans. Short-term financing is typically collateralized by receivables or inventory and longer-term loans are secured with a claim to fixed (longer-term) assets. The bank may also have a *blanket lien* which gives it a claim to all current and future firm assets as collateral in case the primary collateral is insufficient and the borrowing firm defaults. When a firm assigns its receivables to the bank making a loan, the company still services the receivables and remains responsible for any receivables that are not paid.

Banker's acceptances are used by firms that export goods. A banker's acceptance is a guarantee from the bank of the firm that has ordered the goods stating that a payment will be made upon receipt of the goods. The exporting company can then sell this acceptance at a discount in order to generate immediate funds.

Factoring refers to the actual sale of receivables at a discount from their face values. The size of the discount will depend on how long it is until the receivables are due, the creditworthiness of the firm's credit customers, and the firm's collection history on its receivables. The "factor" (the buyer of the receivables) takes on the responsibility for collecting receivables and the credit risk of the receivables portfolio.

Non-Bank Sources of Short-Term Funding

Smaller firms and firms with poor credit may use nonbank *finance companies* for short-term funding. The cost of such funding is higher than other sources and is used by firms for which normal bank sources of short-term funding are not available.

Large, creditworthy companies can issue short-term debt securities called **commercial paper**. Whether the firm sells the paper directly to investors (direct placement) or sells it through dealers (dealer-placed paper), the interest costs are typically slightly less than the rate they could get from a bank.

In managing its short-term financing, a firm should focus on the objectives of having sufficient sources of funding for current, as well as future foreseeable, cash needs and should seek the most cost-effective rates available given its needs, assets, and creditworthiness. The firm should have the ability to prepay short-term borrowings when cash flow permits and have the flexibility to structure its short-term financing so that the debt matures without peaks and can be matched to expected cash flows. For large borrowers, it is important that the firm has alternative sources of short-term funding and even alternative lenders for a particular type of financing. It is often worth having slightly higher overall short-term funding costs in order to have flexibility and redundant sources of financing.

KEY CONCEPTS

LOS 40.a
Primary sources of liquidity are the sources of cash a company uses in its normal operations. If its primary sources are inadequate, a company can use secondary sources of liquidity such as asset sales, debt negotiation, and bankruptcy reorganization.

A company's liquidity position depends on the effectiveness of its cash flow management and is influenced by drags on its cash inflows (e.g., uncollected receivables, obsolete inventory) and pulls on its cash outflows (e.g., early payments to vendors, reductions in credit limits).

LOS 40.b
Measures of a company's short-term liquidity include:
- Current ratio = current assets / current liabilities.
- Quick ratio = (cash + marketable securities + receivables) / current liabilities.

Measures of how well a company is managing its working capital include:
- Receivables turnover = credit sales / average receivables.
- Number of days of receivables = 365 / receivables turnover.
- Inventory turnover = cost of goods sold / average inventory.
- Number of days of inventory = 365 / inventory turnover.
- Payables turnover = purchases / average trade payables.
- Number of days of payables = 365 / payables turnover.

LOS 40.c
The operating cycle and the cash conversion cycle are summary measures of the effectiveness of a company's working capital management.
- Operating cycle = days of inventory + days of receivables.
- Cash conversion cycle = days of inventory + days of receivables – days of payables.

Operating and cash conversion cycles that are high relative to a company's peers suggest the company has too much cash tied up in working capital.

LOS 40.d
To manage its net daily cash position, a firm needs to forecast its cash inflows and outflows and identify periods when its cash balance may be lower than needed or higher than desired. Cash inflows include operating receipts, cash from subsidiaries, cash received from securities investments, tax refunds, and borrowing. Cash outflows include purchases, payroll, cash transfers to subsidiaries, interest and principal paid on debt, investments in securities, taxes paid, and dividends paid.

LOS 40.e

Commonly used annualized yields for short-term pure discount securities are based on the days to maturity (days) of the securities and include:

- Discount-basis yields = % discount from face value × (360/days).
- Money market yields = HPY × (360/days).
- Bond-equivalent yields = HPY × (365/days).

The overall objective of short-term cash management is to earn a reasonable return while taking on only very limited credit and liquidity risk. Returns on the firm's short-term securities investments should be stated as bond equivalent yields. The return on the portfolio should be expressed as a weighted average of these yields.

An investment policy statement should include the objectives of the cash management program, details of who is authorized to purchase securities, authorization for the purchase of specific types of securities, limitations on portfolio proportions of each type, and procedures in the event that guidelines are violated.

LOS 40.f

A firm's inventory, receivables, and payables management can be evaluated by comparing days of inventory, days of receivables, and days of payables for the firm over time and by comparing them to industry averages or averages for a group of peer companies.

A receivables aging schedule and a schedule of weighted average days of receivables can each provide additional detail for evaluating receivables management.

LOS 40.g

There are many choices for short-term borrowing. The firm should keep costs down while also allowing for future flexibility and alternative sources.

The choice of short-term funding sources depends on a firm's size and creditworthiness. Sources available, in order of decreasing firm creditworthiness and increasing cost, include:

- Commercial paper.
- Bank lines of credit.
- Collateralized borrowing.
- Nonbank financing.
- Factoring.

CONCEPT CHECKERS

1. Firm A and Firm B have the same quick ratio, but Firm A has a greater current ratio than Firm B. Compared to Firm B, it is *most likely* that Firm A has:
    A. greater inventory.
    B. greater payables.
    C. a higher receivables turnover ratio.

2. An increase in Rowley Corp's cash conversion cycle and a decrease in Rowley's operating cycle could result from:

Cash conversion cycle ↑	Operating cycle ↓
A. Decreased receivables turnover	Increased payables turnover
B. Decreased receivables turnover	Decrease in days of inventory
C. Increased inventory turnover	Increased payables turnover

3. An example of a primary source of liquidity is:
    A. liquidating assets.
    B. negotiating debt contracts.
    C. short-term investment portfolios.

4. Which of the following statements *most accurately* describes a key aspect of managing a firm's net daily cash position?
    A. Analyze cash inflows and outflows to forecast future needs for cash.
    B. Maximize the firm's cash inflows and minimize its cash outflows.
    C. Minimize uninvested cash balances because they earn a return of zero.

5. Boyle, Inc., just purchased a banker's acceptance for $25,400. It will mature in 80 days for $26,500. The discount-basis yield and the bond equivalent yield for this security are *closest* to:

Discount-basis	Bond equivalent
A. 18.7%	18.7%
B. 18.7%	19.8%
C. 4.2%	19.8%

6. Blodnick Corp. has found that its weighted average collection period has increased from 50 days last year to 55 days this year, and its average days of receivables this year is 48 compared to 52 last year. It is *most likely* that:
    A. Blodnick has relaxed its credit standards this year.
    B. Blodnick's credit customers are paying more slowly this year.
    C. credit sales are a greater part of Blodnick's business this year.

7. Chapmin Corp. is a large domestic services firm with a good credit rating. The source of short-term financing it would *most likely* use is:
    A. factoring of receivables.
    B. issuing commercial paper.
    C. issuing bankers' acceptances.

ANSWERS – CONCEPT CHECKERS

1. **A**   Inventory is in the numerator of the current ratio but not in the quick ratio. Greater inventory for Firm A is consistent with a greater current ratio for Firm A.

2. **B**   A decrease in receivables turnover would increase days of receivables and increase the cash conversion cycle. A decrease in days of inventory would decrease the operating cycle.

3. **C**   Primary sources of liquidity include ready cash balances, short-term funds (e.g., short-term investment portfolios), and cash flow management. Secondary sources of liquidity include negotiating debt contracts, liquidating assets, and filing for bankruptcy protection and reorganization.

4. **A**   The goal of managing the net daily cash position is to ensure that adequate cash is available to prevent the firm from having to arrange financing on short notice (and thus at high cost), while earning a return on cash balances when they are temporarily high by investing in short-term securities. A firm can meet this goal by forecasting its cash inflows and outflows to identify periods when its cash balance is expected to be lower or higher than needed. "Minimizing uninvested cash balances" is inaccurate because a firm should maintain some target amount of available cash.

5. **B**   The actual discount on the acceptance is $(26,500 - 25,400) / 26,500 = 4.151\%$. The annualized discount, or discount-basis yield, is $4.151(360/80) = 18.68\%$.

    The holding period yield is $(26,500 - 25,400) / 25,400 = 4.331\%$. The bond equivalent yield is $4.331(365/80) = 19.76\%$.

6. **B**   Outstanding accounts are paying more slowly because the average collection period is up. Relaxed credit standards or a greater reliance on credit sales would tend to increase average days of receivables. The decrease in days of receivables suggests neither of these is likely.

7. **B**   Large firms with good credit have access to the commercial paper market and can get lower financing costs with commercial paper than they can with bank borrowing. Bankers' acceptances are used by companies involved in international trade. Factoring of receivables is a higher-cost source of funds and is used more by smaller firms that do not have particularly strong credit.

THE CORPORATE GOVERNANCE OF LISTED COMPANIES: A MANUAL FOR INVESTORS

Study Session 11

EXAM FOCUS

Due to the collapses of some major corporations and associated investor losses, corporate governance has become a hot topic in the investment community. The prominence of the issue has likely been a factor in the decision to include this topic in the curriculum. Corporate governance encompasses the internal controls that outline how a firm is managed. The material here is not particularly challenging, but given all the lists of "things to consider" in the CFA curriculum concerning corporate governance, we have not covered them all here. You need to understand the specific issues that are covered under the heading of "corporate governance" and which practices are considered good. You should know the characteristics of an independent and effective board of directors. Much of the rest of the material has to do with shareholder interests and whether a firm's actions and procedures promote the interests of shareholders.

LOS 41.a: Define corporate governance.

CFA® Program Curriculum, Volume 4, page 182

Corporate governance is the set of internal controls, processes, and procedures by which firms are managed. It defines the appropriate rights, roles, and responsibilities of management, the board of directors, and shareholders within an organization. It is the firm's checks and balances. Good corporate governance practices seek to ensure that:

- The board of directors protects shareholder interests.
- The firm acts lawfully and ethically in dealings with shareholders.
- The rights of shareholders are protected and shareholders have a voice in governance.
- The board acts independently from management.
- Proper procedures and controls cover management's day-to-day operations.
- The firm's financial, operating, and governance activities are reported to shareholders in a fair, accurate, and timely manner.

LOS 41.b: Describe practices related to board and committee independence, experience, compensation, external consultants, and frequency of elections, and determine whether they are supportive of shareowner protection.

CFA® Program Curriculum, Volume 4, page 183

The duty of the board is to act in the shareholders' long-term interests. An effective board needs to have the independence, experience, and resources necessary to perform this duty. To properly protect their long-term interests as shareholders, investors should consider whether the following statements hold true:

- A majority of the board of directors is comprised of independent members (not management).
- The board meets regularly outside the presence of management.
- The chairman of the board is also the CEO or a former CEO of the firm. This may impair the ability and willingness of independent board members to express opinions contrary to those of management.
- Independent board members have a primary or leading board member in cases where the chairman is not independent.
- Board members are closely aligned with a firm supplier, customer, share-option plan, or pension adviser. Can board members recuse themselves on any potential areas of conflict?

An independent board is less likely to make decisions that unfairly or improperly benefit management and those who have influence over management.

There is often a need for specific, specialized, independent advice on various firm issues and risks, including compensation; mergers and acquisitions; legal, regulatory, and financial matters; and issues relating to the firm's reputation. A truly independent board will have the ability to hire external consultants without management approval. This enables the board to receive specialized advice on technical issues and provides the board with independent advice that is not influenced by management interests.

Frequency of Board Elections

Anything that prevents shareholders from being able to approve or reject board members annually limits shareowners' abilities to change the board's composition if board members fail to represent shareowners' interests fairly.

While reviewing firm policy regarding election of the board, investors should consider:

- Whether there are annual elections or staggered multiple-year terms (a **classified board**). A classified board may serve another purpose—to act as a takeover defense.
- Whether the board filled a vacant position for a remaining term without shareholder approval.
- Whether shareholders can remove a board member.
- Whether the board is the proper size for the specific facts and circumstances of the firm.

LOS 41.c: Describe board independence and explain the importance of independent board members in corporate governance.

CFA® Program Curriculum, Volume 4, page 188

A board can be considered independent if its decisions are not controlled or biased by the management of the firm. Although the definition of independence may vary across firms, typically to be considered independent, a board member must not have any material business or other relationship with:

- The firm and its subsidiaries, including former employees, executives, and their families.
- Individuals or groups, such as a shareholder(s) with a controlling interest, which can influence the firm's management.
- Executive management and their families.
- The firm's advisers, auditors, and their families.
- Any entity which has a cross directorship with the firm.

An independent board member must work to protect shareholders' long-term interests. Board members need to have not only independence, but experience and resources. The board of directors must have autonomy to operate independently from management.

If board members are not independent, they may be more likely to make decisions that benefit either management or those who have influence over management, thus harming shareholders' long-term interests.

To make sure board members act independently, the firm should have policies in place to discourage board members from receiving consulting fees for work done on the firm's behalf or receiving finders' fees for bringing mergers, acquisitions, and sales to management's attention. Further, procedures should limit board members' and associates' ability to receive compensation beyond the scope of their board responsibilities.

The firm should disclose all material related-party transactions or commercial relationships it has with board members or nominees. The same goes for any property that is leased, loaned, or otherwise provided to the firm by board members or executive officers. Receiving personal benefits from the firm can create conflicts of interest.

LOS 41.d: Identify factors that an analyst should consider when evaluating the qualifications of board members.

CFA® Program Curriculum, Volume 4, page 189

Board members without the requisite skills and experience are more likely to defer to management when making decisions. This can be a threat to shareholder interests.

When evaluating the qualifications of board members, consider whether board members:

- Can make informed decisions about the firm's future.
- Can act with care and competence as a result of their experience with:
  - Technologies, products, and services which the firm offers.

- ◆ Financial operations and accounting and auditing topics.
- ◆ Legal issues.
- ◆ Strategies and planning.
- ◆ Business risks the firm faces.
- Have made any public statements indicating their ethical stances.
- Have had any legal or regulatory problems as a result of working for or serving on the firm's board or the board of another firm.
- Have other board experience.
- Regularly attend meetings.
- Are committed to shareholders. Do they have significant stock positions? Have they eliminated any conflicts of interest?
- Have necessary experience and qualifications.
- Have served on the board for more than ten years. While this adds experience, these board members may be too closely allied with management.

Investors should also consider how many board and committee meetings are held, and the attendance record of the meetings; whether the board and its committees conduct self-assessments; and whether the board provides adequate training for its members.

LOS 41.e: Describe the responsibilities of the audit, compensation, and nominations committees and identify factors an investor should consider when evaluating the quality of each committee.

CFA® Program Curriculum, Volume 4, page 194

Board committees are responsible for examining specific issues and reporting to the board, which is responsible for making final decisions.

Audit Committee

This committee ensures that the financial information provided to shareholders is complete, accurate, reliable, relevant, and timely. Investors must determine whether:

- Proper accounting and auditing procedures have been followed.
- The external auditor is free from management influence.
- Any conflicts between the external auditor and the firm are resolved in a manner that favors the shareholder.
- Independent auditors have authority over the audit of all the company's affiliates and divisions.
- All board members serving on the audit committee are independent.
- Committee members are financial experts.
- The shareholders vote on the approval of the board's selection of the external auditor.
- The audit committee has authority to approve or reject any proposed non-audit engagements with the external audit firm.
- The firm has provisions and procedures that specify to whom the internal auditor reports. Internal auditors must have no restrictions on their contact with the audit committee.

- There have been any discussions between the audit committee and the external auditor resulting in a change in financial reports due to questionable interpretation of accounting rules, fraud, and the like.
- The audit committee controls the audit budget.

Remuneration/Compensation Committee

Investors should be sure a committee of independent board members sets executive compensation, commensurate with responsibilities and performance. The committee can further these goals by making sure all committee members are independent and by linking compensation to long-term firm performance and profitability.

Investors, when analyzing this committee, should determine whether:

- Executive compensation is appropriate.
- The firm has provided loans or the use of company property to board members.
- Committee members attend regularly.
- Policies and procedures for this committee are in place.
- The firm has provided details to shareholders regarding compensation in public documents.
- Terms and conditions of options granted are reasonable.
- Any obligations regarding share-based compensation are met through issuance of new shares.
- The firm and the board are required to receive shareholder approval for any share-based remuneration plans, because these plans can create potential dilution issues.
- Senior executives from other firms have cross-directorship links with the firm or committee members. Watch for situations where individuals may benefit directly from reciprocal decisions on board compensation.

Nominations Committee

The nominations committee handles recruiting of new (independent) board members. It is responsible for:

- Recruiting qualified board members.
- Regularly reviewing performance, independence, skills, and experience of existing board members.
- Creating nomination procedures and policies.
- Preparing an executive management succession plan.

Candidates proposed by this committee will affect whether or not the board works for the benefit of shareholders. Performance assessment of board members should be fair and appropriate. Investors should review company reports over several years to see if this committee has properly recruited board members who have fairly protected shareholder interests. Investors should also review:

- Criteria for selecting new board members.
- Composition, background, and expertise of present board members. How do proposed new members complement the existing board?
- The process for finding new members (i.e., input from outside the firm versus management suggestions).
- Attendance records.

- Succession plans for executive management (if such plans exist).
- The committee's report, including any actions, decisions, and discussion.

Other Board Committees

Additional committees can provide more insight into goals and strategies of the firm. These committees are more likely to fall outside typical corporate governance codes, so they are more likely to be comprised of members of executive management. Be wary of this—independence is once again critical to maintain shareowners' best interests.

LOS 41.f: Explain the provisions that should be included in a strong corporate code of ethics.

CFA® Program Curriculum, Volume 4, page 201

A code of ethics for a firm sets the standard for basic principles of integrity, trust, and honesty. It gives the staff behavioral standards and addresses conflicts of interest. Ethical breaches can lead to big problems for firms, resulting in sanctions, fines, management turnover, and unwanted negative publicity. Having an ethical code can be a mitigating factor with regulators if a breach occurs.

With respect to board members and persons related to board members, it is important to discourage consultancy contracts, finder's fees for identifying merger or acquisition targets, and other compensation from the company as this can compromise the independence of board members from management. With respect to other corporate personnel and their friends and relations, it is important to discourage related-party transactions as well so that shareholders can be confident that company transactions are to their benefit rather than to the benefit of company insiders. The same holds true for personal use of company assets by board members as well as company management and their families. Personal use of company assets should be discouraged to preserve and promote board member independence and to ensure that company assets are used exclusively to generate value for the company and its shareholders.

In the United States and many other countries, investors can get information about either of these practices in the annual report (under related-party transactions), the annual corporate governance report, or in proxy statements. In the case of newly public companies, the prospectus will disclose any stock sales to insiders and related persons that have been recently made at prices less than the offering price, because such transactions will tend to dilute shareholder interests.

When analyzing ethics codes, these are items to consider:

- Make sure the board of directors receives relevant corporate information in a timely manner.
- Ethics codes should be in compliance with the corporate governance laws of the location country and with the governance requirements set forth by the local stock exchange. Firms should disclose whether they adhered to their own ethical code, including any reasons for failure.
- The ethical code should prohibit advantages to the firm's insiders that are not offered to shareowners.

©2012 Kaplan, Inc.

Study Session 11

Cross-Reference to CFA Institute Assigned Reading #41 – The Corporate Governance of Listed Companies: A Manual for Investors

- A person should be designated to be responsible for corporate governance.
- If selected management personnel receive waivers from the ethics code, reasons should be given.
- If any provisions of the ethics code were waived recently, the firm should explain why.
- The firm's ethics code should be audited and improved periodically.

In evaluating management, investors should:

- Verify that the firm has committed to an ethical framework and adopted a code of ethics.
- See if the firm permits board members or management to use firm assets for personal reasons.
- Analyze executive compensation to assess whether it is commensurate with responsibilities and performance.
- Look into the size, purpose, means of financing, and duration of any share-repurchase programs.

LOS 41.g: Evaluate, from a shareowner's perspective, company policies related to voting rules, shareowner sponsored proposals, common stock classes, and takeover defenses.

CFA® Program Curriculum, Volume 4, page 208

The ability to vote proxies is a fundamental shareholder right. If the firm makes it difficult to vote proxies, it limits the ability of shareholders to express their views and affect the firm's future direction.

Investors should consider whether the firm:

- Limits the ability to vote shares by requiring attendance at the annual meeting.
- Groups its meetings to be held the same day as other companies in the same region and also requires attendance to cast votes.
- Allows proxy voting by some remote mechanism.
- Is allowed under its governance code to use **share blocking**, a mechanism that prevents investors who wish to vote their shares from trading their shares during a period prior to the annual meeting.

Confidential Voting

Investors should determine if shareholders are able to cast confidential votes. This can encourage unbiased voting. In looking at this issue, investors should consider whether:

- The firm uses a third party to tabulate votes.
- The third party or the firm retains voting records.
- The tabulation is subject to audit.
- Shareholders are entitled to vote only if present.

Cumulative Voting

Shareholders may be able to cast the cumulative number of votes allotted to their shares for one or a limited number of board nominees. Cumulative voting is generally viewed as favorable for shareholders. However, investors should be cautious in the event the firm has a considerable minority shareholder group, such as a founding family, that can serve its own interests through cumulative voting.

Information on possible cumulative voting rights will be contained in the articles of organization and bylaws, the prospectus, or Form 8-A, which must be filed with the Securities and Exchange Commission in the United States.

Voting for Other Corporate Changes

Changes to corporate structure or policies can change the relationship between shareholders and the firm. Watch for changes to:

- Articles of organization.
- Bylaws.
- Governance structures.
- Voting rights and procedures.
- Poison pill provisions (these are impediments to an acquisition of the firm).
- Provisions for change-in-control.

Regarding issues requiring shareholder approval, consider whether shareholders:

- Must approve corporate change proposals with supermajority votes.
- Will be able to vote on the sale of the firm, or part of it, to a third-party buyer.
- Will be able to vote on major executive compensation issues.
- Will be able to approve any anti-takeover measures.
- Will be able to periodically reconsider and re-vote on rules that require supermajority voting to revise any governance documents.
- Have the ability to vote for changes in articles of organization, bylaws, governance structures, and voting rights and procedures.
- Have the ability to use their relatively small ownership interest to force a vote on a special interest issue.

Investors should also be able to review issues such as:

- Share buy-back programs that may be used to fund share-based compensation grants.
- Amendments or other changes to a firm's charter and bylaws.
- Issuance of new capital stock.

Shareowner-Sponsored Board Nominations

Investors need to determine whether the firm's shareholders have the power to put forth an independent board nominee. Having such flexibility is positive for investors as it allows them to address their concerns and protect their interests through direct board representation. Additional items to consider:

- Under what circumstances can a shareholder nominate a board member?

Study Session 11

Cross-Reference to CFA Institute Assigned Reading #41 – The Corporate Governance of Listed Companies: A Manual for Investors

- Can shareowners vote to remove a board member?
- How does the firm handle contested board elections?

The proxy statement is a good source document for information about these issues in the United States. In many jurisdictions, articles of organization and corporate bylaws are other good sources of information on shareholder rights.

Shareowner-Sponsored Resolutions

The right to propose initiatives for consideration at the annual meeting is an important shareholder method to send a message to management.

Investors should look at whether:

- The firm requires a simple majority or a supermajority vote to pass a resolution.
- Shareholders can hold a special meeting to vote on a special initiative.
- Shareholder-proposed initiatives will benefit all shareholders rather than just a small group.

Advisory or Binding Shareowner Proposals

Investors should find out if the board and management are required to actually implement any shareholder-approved proposals. Investors should determine whether:

- The firm has implemented or ignored such proposals in the past.
- The firm requires a supermajority of votes to approve changes to its bylaws and articles of organization.
- Any regulatory agencies have pressured firms to act on the terms of any approved shareholder initiatives.

Different Classes of Common Equity

Different classes of common equity within a firm may separate the voting rights of those shares from their economic value.

Firms with dual classes of common equity could encourage prospective acquirers to only deal directly with shareholders holding the supermajority rights. Firms that separate voting rights from economic rights have historically had more trouble raising equity capital for fixed investment and product development than firms that combine those rights.

When looking at a firm's ownership structure, examine whether:

- Safeguards in the bylaws and articles of organization protect shareholders who have inferior voting rights.
- The firm was recently privatized by a government entity and the selling entity retained voting rights. This may prevent shareholders from receiving full value for their shares.
- Any super-voting rights kept by certain classes of shareholders impair the firm's ability to raise equity capital. If a firm has to turn to debt financing, the increase in leverage can harm the firm.

Information on these issues can be found in the proxy, Web site, prospectus, or notes to the financial statements.

Shareowner Legal Rights

Examine whether the investor has the legal right under the corporate governance code and other legal statutes of the jurisdiction in which the firm is headquartered to seek legal redress or regulatory action to enforce and protect shareholder rights.

Investors should determine whether:

- Legal statutes allow shareholders to take legal actions to enforce ownership rights.
- The local market regulator, in similar situations, has taken action to enforce shareholder rights.
- Shareholders are allowed to take legal or regulatory action against the firm's management or board in the case of fraud.
- Shareholders have "dissenters' rights," which require the firm to repurchase their shares at fair market value in the event of a problem.

Takeover Defenses

Takeover defenses are provisions that are designed to make a company less attractive to a hostile bidder. Examples of takeover defenses include golden parachutes (rich severance packages for top managers who lose their jobs as a result of a takeover), poison pills (provisions that grant rights to existing shareholders in the event a certain percentage of a company's shares are acquired), and greenmail (use of corporate funds to buy back the shares of a hostile acquirer at a premium to their market value). All of these defenses may be used to counter a hostile bid, and their probable effect is to decrease share value.

When reviewing the firm's takeover defenses, investors should:

- Ask whether the firm requires shareholder approval to implement such takeover measures.
- Ask whether the firm has received any acquisition interest in the past.
- Consider that the firm may use its cash to "pay off" a hostile bidder. Shareholders should take steps to discourage this activity.
- Consider whether any change of control issues would invoke the interest of a national or local government and, as a result, pressure the seller to change the terms of the acquisition or merger.

Study Session 11

Cross-Reference to CFA Institute Assigned Reading #41 – The Corporate Governance of Listed Companies: A Manual for Investors

KEY CONCEPTS

LOS 41.a

Corporate governance is the set of internal controls, processes, and procedures by which firms are managed. Good corporate governance practices ensure that the board of directors is independent of management and that the firm and its managers act lawfully, ethically, and in the interests of shareholders.

LOS 41.b

A majority of board and committee members should be independent (not management), and the board should meet regularly without management present.

Board members should have the experience and knowledge necessary to advise management and review its activities.

The board should have the resources it needs to act independently, including the ability to hire outside consultants without approval from management.

LOS 41.c

A board can be considered independent if its decisions are not controlled or biased by the management of the firm.

An independent board member must work to protect the long-term interests of shareholders.

LOS 41.d

Board members should have the skills and experience required to make informed decisions about the firm's future.

A qualified board member should have experience with:
- The products or services the firm produces.
- Financial operations, accounting, and auditing.
- Legal issues.
- Strategies and planning.
- The firm's business and financial risks.

Members who serve on the board for a long time (more than ten years) may become too closely aligned with management to be considered independent.

LOS 41.e

The audit committee is responsible for providing financial information to shareholders. The audit committee should:

- Follow proper accounting and auditing procedures.
- Appoint an external auditor that is free from management influence.
- Resolve conflicts between the auditor and management in a way that favors shareholders.
- Approve or reject any non-audit engagements with the external auditor.
- Have no restrictions on its communications with the firm's internal auditors.
- Control the audit budget.

The compensation (remuneration) committee sets the compensation for the firm's executives. The compensation committee should:

- Determine whether executives' compensation is appropriate and linked to the firm's long-term profitability.
- Provide shareholders with details about executive compensation in public documents.
- Require the firm and the board to seek shareholder approval for any share-based compensation plans.

The nominations committee is responsible for recruiting new, qualified, independent board members. The nominations committee should:

- Review the performance, independence, and skills of existing board members.
- Create nomination procedures and policies.
- Prepare a succession plan for senior management.

LOS 41.f

A firm's code of ethics sets the standard for basic principles of integrity, trust, and honesty. Having a code of ethics can be a mitigating factor with regulators if a breach occurs.

A strong code of ethics should:

- Comply with corporate governance standards of the company's home country and stock exchange.
- Prohibit the company from giving advantages to company insiders that are not available to shareholders.
- Discourage payments to board members of consultancy fees or finder's fees for acquisition targets.
- Designate a person responsible for corporate governance.

A company with a weak code of ethics may allow practices such as transactions with parties related to management or personal use of company assets by management or board members. Such practices benefit company insiders rather than shareholders.

©2012 Kaplan, Inc.

Study Session 11

Cross-Reference to CFA Institute Assigned Reading #41 – The Corporate Governance of Listed Companies: A Manual for Investors

LOS 41.g
Consider whether company policies make it difficult to vote proxies and whether a significant minority shareholder group can serve their own interests through cumulative voting. Confidential voting and remote proxy voting promote the interests of shareholders.

Investors should determine whether a firm permits shareholders to nominate board members and propose initiatives to be discussed at the annual meeting and whether the firm regards shareholder proposals as binding or advisory.

Corporate structure changes can alter the relationship between shareholders and the firm. Different classes of equity may separate the voting rights of shares from their economic value.

Takeover defenses are provisions that make a company less attractive to a hostile bidder or more difficult to acquire. They are generally not in shareholders' interests.

CONCEPT CHECKERS

1. Which of the following board characteristics would *least likely* be an indication of high-quality corporate governance?
    A. Board members have staggered terms.
    B. The board can hire independent consultants.
    C. The board has a separate committee to set executive pay.

2. Which of the following board members would *most likely* be considered well chosen based on the principles of good corporate governance?
    A. A board member of Company B who is also the CEO of Company B.
    B. A board member of Company B who is a partner in an accounting firm that competes with the firm's auditor.
    C. A board member of Company A who is president of Company B, when the CFO of Company A sits on Company B's board.

3. Which of the following is *least likely* to enable a corporate board to exercise its duty by acting in the long-term interest of shareholders?
    A. The board meets regularly outside the presence of management.
    B. A majority of the board members are independent of firm management.
    C. The board has representatives from key suppliers and important customers.

4. Which of the following would *most likely* be considered a negative factor in assessing the suitability of a board member? The board member:
    A. has served for ten years.
    B. has served on other boards.
    C. is a former CEO of another firm.

5. Which of the following would *least likely* be an indication of poor corporate governance?
    A. A board member leases office space to the company in a building he owns.
    B. There are board members who do not have previous experience in the industry in which the firm operates.
    C. A board member has a consulting contract with the firm to provide strategic vision for the technology research and development effort.

6. Which of the following would *most likely* be considered a poor corporate practice in terms of promoting shareholder interests?
    A. The firm can use "share blocking."
    B. The firm uses a third party to tabulate shareholder votes.
    C. Voting for board members does not allow cumulative voting by shareholders of all votes allotted to their shares.

Study Session 11

Cross-Reference to CFA Institute Assigned Reading #41 – The Corporate Governance of Listed Companies: A Manual for Investors

7. Two analysts are discussing shareholder defenses against hostile takeovers. Alice states, "It is positive for shareholders that the board has shown a willingness to buy back shares from holders who may be in a position to effect a hostile takeover of the firm at less than its long-term value to shareholders." Bradley states, "Firms that are likely takeover targets should offer valuable exit packages in the event of a hostile takeover because they are necessary to recruit highly talented top executives, such as the CEO." From the perspective of good corporate governance, are these statements correct?
    A. Both statements are correct.
    B. Neither statement is correct.
    C. Only one of the statements is correct.

Study Session 11
Cross-Reference to CFA Institute Assigned Reading #41 – The Corporate Governance of Listed Companies: A Manual for Investors

Study Session 11

ANSWERS – CONCEPT CHECKERS

1. **A**   Staggered terms make it more difficult for shareholders to change the board of directors. Annual elections of all members make the board more responsive to shareholder wishes.

2. **B**   A board member who is a partner in an unrelated accounting firm would be considered independent, has no particular relation to firm management, and could be a valuable addition to the board.

3. **C**   Board members should not be closely aligned with a firm's suppliers or customers because they may act in the interest of suppliers and customers rather than in the interest of shareholders.

4. **A**   While experience may be a good thing, a board member with long tenure may be too closely aligned with management to be considered an independent member.

5. **B**   Lack of previous experience in the firm's industry is not necessarily a negative and can be consistent with an independent board member who acts in shareholders' long-term interests. Examples might be board members with specialized knowledge of finance, marketing, management, accounting, or auditing. The other answers indicate possible conflicts of interest.

6. **A**   Share blocking prevents shareholders from trading their shares over a period prior to the annual meeting and is considered a restriction on the ability of shareholders to express their opinions and act in their own interests. Cumulative voting can allow a minority group, such as a founding family, to serve its own interests. Third party tabulation of shareowner votes is considered a good corporate governance practice.

7. **B**   Defenses against hostile takeovers such as greenmail (Alice) or golden parachutes (Bradley) tend to protect entrenched or poorly performing managements and typically decrease share values. Shareholders as a group always have the choice not to sell when a takeover offer is not in their long-term interests.

10 questions: 15 minutes

1. An analyst calculates the following leverage ratios for Burkhardt Company and Dutchin Company:

	Degree of Operating Leverage	*Degree of Financial Leverage*
Burkhardt	1.6	3.0
Dutchin	1.2	4.0

    If both companies' sales increase by 5%, what are the *most likely* effects on the companies' earnings before interest and taxes (EBIT) and earnings per share (EPS)?
    A. Both companies' EBIT will increase by the same percentage.
    B. Dutchin's EPS will increase by a larger percentage than Burkhardt's EPS.
    C. Burkhardt's EBIT will increase by a larger percentage than Dutchin's EBIT.

2. Which of the following would *most likely* lead to an increase in a typical firm's capital investment for the current period?
    A. A need to increase inventory.
    B. An increase in the firm's expected marginal tax rate.
    C. A decrease in the market value of the firm's debt.

3. Which of the following changes in a firm's working capital management is *most likely* to result in a shorter operating cycle?
    A. Reducing stock-outs by carrying greater quantities of inventory.
    B. Stretching its payables by paying on the last permitted date.
    C. Changing its credit terms for customers from 2/10, net 60 to 2/10, net 30.

4. A company's operations analyst is evaluating a plant expansion project that is likely to be financed in part by issuing new common equity. Flotation costs are expected to be 4% of the amount of new equity capital raised. The *most appropriate* way for the analyst to treat the flotation costs is to:
    A. ignore them, because flotation costs for common equity are likely to be nonmaterial.
    B. estimate the cost of equity capital based on a share price 4% less than the current price.
    C. determine the flotation cost attributable to this project and treat it as part of the project's initial cash outflow.

5. A board of directors is *most likely* to act in the long-term interest of shareholders if:
    A. all board members are elected annually.
    B. most board members are selected from outside the company's industry.
    C. there are board members who represent the company's key supplier and largest customer.

6. The manufacturer of Pow Detergent has developed New Improved Pow with Dirteaters and is considering adding it to its product line. New Improved Pow would sell at a premium price compared to Pow. In order to manufacture New Improved Pow, the firm will need to build a new facility and purchase new equipment. Which of the following is *least likely* included when calculating the appropriate cash flows for analysis of whether to add New Improved Pow to its product line?
    A. Expected depreciation on the new facility and equipment for tax purposes.
    B. Costs of a marketing survey performed last month to decide whether to introduce New Improved Pow.
    C. Reduced sales of Pow that result from the introduction of New Improved Pow.

7. Acme Corp. has reported the following financial ratios for the past two years:

Year	Net Profit Margin	Financial Leverage	Total Asset Turnover
20X0	14%	1.3	1.1
20X1	13%	1.8	0.9

    Based only on these results, an analyst would *most correctly* conclude that the results in year 20X1 compared to those in year 20X0 indicate that Acme's ROE has:
    A. declined, in part due to lower profitability.
    B. increased because the company has used more debt financing.
    C. increased because of the improvement in asset utilization.

8. The use of secondary sources of liquidity would *most likely* be considered:
    A. a normal part of daily business for a company.
    B. a signal that a company's financial position is deteriorating.
    C. a lower-cost source of short-term financing compared to primary sources of liquidity.

9. A firm's debt-to-equity ratio is *most likely* to increase as a result of a(n):
    A. extra dividend.
    B. stock dividend.
    C. purchase of a machine for cash.

10. A firm is evaluating two mutually exclusive projects of the same risk class, Project X and Project Y. Both have the same initial cash outlay and both have positive NPVs. Which of the following is a sufficient reason to choose Project X over Project Y?
    A. Project Y has a lower profitability index than Project X.
    B. Project X has both a shorter payback period and a shorter discounted payback period compared to Project Y.
    C. Project Y has a lower internal rate of return than Project X.

SELF-TEST ANSWERS: CORPORATE FINANCE

1. **C** The DOL is the percent change in operating income (EBIT) that will result from a 1% change in sales. Because Burkhardt has a higher DOL than Dutchin, Burkhardt's EBIT will increase by a larger percentage if both companies' sales increase by the same percentage. The percentage change in EPS resulting from a change in sales of 1% is measured by the degree of total leverage. The DTL for Burkhardt is 1.6 × 3.0 = 4.8, and the DTL for Dutchin is 1.2 × 4.0 = 4.8. If both companies' sales increase by the same percentage, their EPS will also increase by the same percentage.

2. **B** Because a typical firm has both equity and debt financing, an increase in the firm's tax rate will decrease the after-tax cost of debt and consequently decrease the firm's WACC, which can change a project's NPV from negative to positive. A decrease in the market value of the firm's debt will increase the market yield on the debt, which will increase the after-tax cost of debt and the firm's WACC. Increases in inventory increase current assets and working capital needs, not capital investment.

3. **C** The operating cycle is average days of receivables plus average days of inventory. Changing its credit terms for customers from "net 60" to "net 30" would likely decrease the firm's average days of receivables and shorten its operating cycle. Increasing inventory quantities would increase average days of inventory and lengthen the operating cycle. Stretching payables by waiting until their due date to pay would increase the firm's average days of payables. This would shorten the firm's cash conversion cycle (days of receivables + days of inventory − days of payables) but would not affect its operating cycle.

4. **C** The correct treatment of flotation costs is to treat them as a cash outflow at the project's initiation. Methods that adjust the cost of equity capital (and therefore the WACC) for flotation costs are incorrect because the cost of capital is an ongoing expense, whereas flotation costs are actually a one-time expense. Flotation costs for common equity are typically large enough that they must be considered in computing a project's NPV.

5. **A** Annual elections of all board members (as compared to longer terms) make a board more likely to represent shareholders' long-term interests because it is easier for shareholders to nominate and elect new members. Board members who do not have direct experience in the company's industry might lack the specific knowledge they need to give proper oversight to management's decisions and, therefore, tend to defer to management. Board members who are aligned with the company's customers and suppliers might have interests that conflict with shareholders' interests.

6. **B** Costs that are incurred prior to the decision of whether or not to pursue a project are sunk costs and should not be used in the NPV calculation. Only cash flows that result from the decision to actually do the project should be considered in the analysis. Taxes must be deducted so the project's cash flows can be analyzed on an after-tax basis. Because depreciation is tax deductible, expected depreciation will affect annual taxes and after-tax cash flows. Cannibalization of sales of an existing product is an externality that should be included in the estimation of incremental project cash flows.

7. **B** ROE was (14%)(1.3)(1.1) = 20% in 20X0 and (13%)(1.8)(0.9) = 21% in 20X1. Both the decrease in profitability and the decrease in total asset turnover in 20X1 will tend to decrease ROE. The only reason ROE increased in 20X1 is that more debt was used in the capital structure, increasing the financial leverage ratio.

8. **B**   Secondary sources of liquidity include negotiating debt contracts, liquidating assets, and filing for bankruptcy protection and reorganization. The use of these sources of funds is typically a signal that a company's financial position is deteriorating. The liquidity provided by these sources usually comes at a substantially higher cost than liquidity provided by primary sources.

9. **A**   An extra dividend is a cash payment to shareholders. This decreases assets (cash) and shareholders' equity (retained earnings) but does not affect liabilities. Unchanged debt and lower equity results in a higher debt-to-equity ratio. Stock splits, reverse stock splits, and stock dividends change the number of shares outstanding but do not change the value of shareholders' equity or require any use of the firm's assets. Purchasing a machine for cash exchanges one asset for another asset and does not affect debt or equity.

10. **A**   The correct method of choosing between two mutually exclusive projects is to choose the one with the higher NPV. The profitability index is calculated as the present value of the future cash flows divided by the initial outlay for the project. Because both projects have the same initial cash outlay, the one with the higher profitability index has both higher present value of future cash flows and the higher NPV. Ranking projects on their payback periods or their internal rates of return can lead to incorrect ranking.

PORTFOLIO MANAGEMENT: AN OVERVIEW

EXAM FOCUS

Here, we introduce the portfolio management process and the investment policy statement. In this topic review, you will learn the investment needs of different types of investors, as well as the different kinds of pooled investments. Later, our topic review of "Basics of Portfolio Planning and Construction" will provide more detail on investment policy statements and investor objectives and constraints.

LOS 42.a: Describe the portfolio approach to investing.

CFA® Program Curriculum, Volume 4, page 225

The **portfolio perspective** refers to evaluating individual investments by their contribution to the risk and return of an investor's portfolio. The alternative to taking a portfolio perspective is to examine the risk and return of individual investments in isolation. An investor who holds all his wealth in a single stock because he believes it to be the best stock available is not taking the portfolio perspective—his portfolio is very risky compared to holding a diversified portfolio of stocks. Modern portfolio theory concludes that the extra risk from holding only a single security is not rewarded with higher expected investment returns. Conversely, diversification allows an investor to reduce portfolio risk without necessarily reducing the portfolio's expected return.

In the early 1950s, the research of Professor Harry Markowitz provided a framework for measuring the risk-reduction benefits of diversification. Using the standard deviation of returns as the measure of investment risk, he investigated how combining risky securities into a portfolio affected the portfolio's risk and expected return. One important conclusion of his model is that unless the returns of the risky assets are perfectly positively correlated, risk is reduced by diversifying across assets.

In the 1960s, professors Treynor, Sharpe, Mossin, and Lintner independently extended this work into what has become known as modern portfolio theory (MPT). MPT results in equilibrium expected returns for securities and portfolios that are a linear function of each security's or portfolio's market risk (the risk that cannot be reduced by diversification).

One measure of the benefits of diversification is the **diversification ratio**. It is calculated as the ratio of the risk of an equally weighted portfolio of *n* securities (measured by its standard deviation of returns) to the risk of a single security selected at random from the *n* securities. Note that the expected return of an equal-weighted portfolio is also the expected return from selecting one of the *n* portfolio securities at random (the simple average of expected security returns in both instances). If the average standard deviation of returns for the *n* stocks is 25%, and the standard deviation of returns for an equally weighted portfolio of the *n* stocks is 18%, the diversification ratio is 18 / 25 = 0.72.

While the diversification ratio provides a quick measure of the potential benefits of diversification, an equal-weighted portfolio is not necessarily the portfolio that provides the greatest reduction in risk. Computer optimization can calculate the portfolio weights that will produce the lowest portfolio risk (standard deviation of returns) for a given group of securities.

Portfolio diversification works best when financial markets are operating normally; diversification provides less reduction of risk during market turmoil, such as the credit contagion of 2008. During periods of financial crisis, correlations tend to increase, which reduces the benefits of diversification.

LOS 42.b: Describe types of investors and distinctive characteristics and needs of each.

CFA® Program Curriculum, Volume 4, page 233

Individual investors save and invest for a variety of reasons, including purchasing a house or educating their children. In many countries, special accounts allow citizens to invest for retirement and to defer any taxes on investment income and gains until the funds are withdrawn. **Defined contribution (DC) pension plans** are popular vehicles for these investments. In a DC plan, the individual makes the investment decisions and takes on the investment risk. There is no guarantee of specific future pension payments.

Many types of **institutions** have large investment portfolios. **Defined benefit (DB) pension plans** are funded by company contributions and have an obligation to provide specific benefits to retirees, such as a lifetime income based on employee earnings. DB plans typically have a very long time horizon. They typically select investments that will most reliably meet the goal of providing the benefits owed to retirees.

An **endowment** is a fund that is dedicated to providing financial support on an ongoing basis for a specific purpose. For example, in the United States, many universities have large endowment funds to support their programs. A **foundation** is a fund established for charitable purposes to support specific types of activities or to fund research related to a particular disease. A typical foundation's investment objective is to fund the activity or research on a continuing basis without decreasing the real (inflation adjusted) value of the portfolio assets. Foundations and endowments typically have long investment horizons, high risk tolerance, and, aside from their planned spending needs, little need for additional liquidity.

The investment objective of a **bank**, simply put, is to earn more on the bank's loans and investments than the bank pays for deposits of various types. Banks seek to keep risk low and need adequate liquidity to meet investor withdrawals as they occur.

Insurance companies invest customer premiums with the objective of funding customer claims as they occur. Life insurance companies have a relatively long-term investment horizon, while property and casualty (P&C) insurers have a shorter investment horizon because claims are expected to arise sooner than for life insurers.

Investment companies manage the pooled funds of many investors. **Mutual funds** manage these pooled funds in particular styles (e.g., index investing, growth investing, bond investing) and restrict their investments to particular subcategories of investments (e.g., large-firm stocks, energy stocks, speculative bonds) or particular regions (emerging market stocks, international bonds, Asian-firm stocks).

Sovereign wealth funds refer to pools of assets owned by a government. For example, the Abu Dhabi Investment Authority, a sovereign wealth fund in the United Arab Emirates funded by Abu Dhabi government surpluses, has an estimated US$627 billion in assets.[1]

Figure 1 provides a summary of the risk tolerance, investment horizon, liquidity needs, and income objectives for different types of investors.

Figure 1: Characteristics of Different Types of Investors

Investor	Risk Tolerance	Investment Horizon	Liquidity Needs	Income Needs
Individuals	Depends on individual	Depends on individual	Depends on individual	Depends on individual
DB pensions	High	Long	Low	Depends on age
Banks	Low	Short	High	Pay interest
Endowments	High	Long	Low	Spending level
Insurance	Low	Long—life Short—P&C	High	Low
Mutual funds	Depends on fund	Depends on fund	High	Depends on fund

LOS 42.c: Describe the steps in the portfolio management process.

CFA® Program Curriculum, Volume 4, page 239

There are three major steps in the portfolio management process:

Step 1: The **planning step** begins with an analysis of the investor's risk tolerance, return objectives, time horizon, tax exposure, liquidity needs, income needs, and any unique circumstances or investor preferences.

This analysis results in an **investment policy statement** (IPS) that details the investor's investment objectives and constraints. It should also specify an objective benchmark (such as an index return) against which the success of the portfolio management process will be measured. The IPS should be updated at least every few years and any time the investor's objectives or constraints change significantly.

---

1. Source: SWF Institute (*www.swfinstitute.org/fund-rankings*).

Step 2: The **execution step** involves an analysis of the risk and return characteristics of various asset classes to determine how funds will be allocated to the various asset types. Often, in what is referred to as a *top-down* analysis, a portfolio manager will examine current economic conditions and forecasts of such macroeconomic variables as GDP growth, inflation, and interest rates, in order to identify the asset classes that are most attractive. The resulting portfolio is typically diversified across such asset classes as cash, fixed-income securities, publicly traded equities, hedge funds, private equity, and real estate, as well as commodities and other real assets.

Once the asset class allocations are determined, portfolio managers may attempt to identify the most attractive securities within the asset class. Security analysts use model valuations for securities to identify those that appear undervalued in what is termed *bottom-up* security analysis.

Step 3: The **feedback step** is the final step. Over time, investor circumstances will change, risk and return characteristics of asset classes will change, and the actual weights of the assets in the portfolio will change with asset prices. The portfolio manager must monitor these changes and **rebalance** the portfolio periodically in response, adjusting the allocations to the various asset classes back to their desired percentages. The manager must also measure portfolio performance and evaluate it relative to the return on the benchmark portfolio identified in the IPS.

LOS 42.d: Describe mutual funds and compare them with other pooled investment products.

CFA® Program Curriculum, Volume 4, page 243

Mutual funds are one form of **pooled investments** (i.e., a single portfolio that contains investment funds from multiple investors). Each investor owns shares representing ownership of a portion of the overall portfolio. The total net value of the assets in the fund (pool) divided by the number of such shares issued is referred to as the **net asset value** (NAV) of each share.

With an **open-end fund**, investors can buy newly issued shares at the NAV. Newly invested cash is invested by the mutual fund managers in additional portfolio securities. Investors can **redeem** their shares (sell them back to the fund) at NAV as well. All mutual funds charge a fee for the ongoing management of the portfolio assets, which is expressed as a percentage of the net asset value of the fund. **No-load funds** do not charge additional fees for purchasing shares (up-front fees) or for redeeming shares (redemption fees). **Load funds** charge either up-front fees, redemption fees, or both.

Closed-end funds are professionally managed pools of investor money that do not take new investments into the fund or redeem investor shares. The shares of a closed-end fund trade like equity shares (on exchanges or over-the-counter). As with open-end funds, the portfolio management firm charges ongoing management fees.

Types of Mutual Funds

Money market funds invest in short-term debt securities and provide interest income with very low risk of changes in share value. Fund NAVs are typically set to one currency unit, but there have been instances over recent years in which the NAV of some funds declined when the securities they held dropped dramatically in value. Funds are differentiated by the types of money market securities they purchase and their average maturities.

Bond mutual funds invest in fixed-income securities. They are differentiated by bond maturities, credit ratings, issuers, and types. Examples include government bond funds, tax-exempt bond funds, high-yield (lower rated corporate) bond funds, and global bond funds.

A great variety of **stock mutual funds** are available to investors. **Index funds** are **passively managed**; that is, the portfolio is constructed to match the performance of a particular index, such as the Standard & Poor's 500 Index. **Actively managed** funds refer to funds where the management selects individual securities with the goal of producing returns greater than those of their benchmark indexes. Annual management fees are higher for actively managed funds, and actively managed funds have higher turnover of portfolio securities (the percentage of investments that are changed during the year). This leads to greater tax liabilities compared to passively managed index funds.

Other Forms of Pooled Investments

Exchange-traded funds (ETFs) are similar to closed-end funds in that purchases and sales are made in the market rather than with the fund itself. There are important differences, however. While closed-end funds are often actively managed, ETFs are most often invested to match a particular index (passively managed). With closed-end funds, the market price of shares can differ significantly from their NAV due to imbalances between investor supply and demand for shares at any point in time. Special redemption provisions for ETFs are designed to keep their market prices very close to their NAVs.

ETFs can be sold short, purchased on margin, and traded at intraday prices, whereas open-end funds are typically sold and redeemed only daily, based on the share NAV calculated with closing asset prices. Investors in ETFs must pay brokerage commissions when they trade, and there is a spread between the bid price at which market makers will buy shares and the ask price at which market makers will sell shares. With most ETFs, investors receive any dividend income on portfolio stocks in cash, while open-end funds offer the alternative of reinvesting dividends in additional fund shares. One final difference is that ETFs may produce less capital gains liability compared to open-end index funds. This is because investor sales of ETF shares do not require the fund to sell any securities. If an open-end fund has significant redemptions that cause it to sell appreciated portfolio shares, shareholders incur a capital gains tax liability.

A **separately managed account** is a portfolio that is owned by a single investor and managed according to that investor's needs and preferences. No shares are issued, as the single investor owns the entire account.

Hedge funds are pools of investor funds that are not regulated to the extent that mutual funds are. Hedge funds are limited in the number of investors who can invest in the fund and are often sold only to qualified investors who have a minimum amount of overall portfolio wealth. Minimum investments can be quite high, often between $250,000 and $1 million.

There is a great variety of hedge fund strategies, and major hedge fund categories are based on the investment strategy that the funds pursue:

- **Long/short funds** buy securities that are expected to outperform the overall market and sell securities short that are expected to underperform the overall market.
- **Equity market-neutral funds** are long/short funds with long stock positions that are just offset in value by stocks sold short. These funds are designed to be neutral with respect to overall market movements so that they can be profitable in both up and down markets as long as their longs outperform their shorts.
- An equity hedge fund with a **bias** is a long/short fund dedicated to a larger long position relative to short sales (a **long bias**) or to a greater short position relative to long positions (a **short bias**).
- **Event-driven funds** invest in response to one-time corporate events, such as mergers and acquisitions.
- **Fixed-income arbitrage funds** take long and short positions in debt securities, attempting to profit from minor mispricings while minimizing the effects of interest rate changes on portfolio values.
- **Convertible bond arbitrage funds** take long and short positions in convertible bonds and the equity shares they can be converted into in order to profit from a relative mispricing between the two.
- **Global macro funds** speculate on changes in international interest rates and currency exchange rates, often using derivative securities and a great amount of leverage.

Buyout funds (private equity funds) typically buy entire public companies and take them private (their shares no longer trade). The purchase of the companies is often funded with a significant increase in the firm's debt (a leveraged buyout). The fund attempts to reorganize the firm to increase its cash flow, pay down its debt, increase the value of its equity, and then sell the restructured firm or its parts in a public offering or to another company over a fairly short time horizon of three to five years.

Venture capital funds typically invest in companies in their start-up phase, with the intent to grow them into valuable companies that can be sold publicly via an IPO or sold to an established firm. Both buyout funds and venture capital funds are very involved in the management of their portfolio companies and often have expertise in the industries on which they focus.

KEY CONCEPTS

LOS 42.a

A diversified portfolio produces reduced risk for a given level of expected return, compared to investing in an individual security. Modern portfolio theory concludes that investors that do not take a portfolio perspective bear risk that is not rewarded with greater expected return.

LOS 42.b

Types of investment management clients and their characteristics:

Investor Type	Risk Tolerance	Investment Horizon	Liquidity Needs	Income Needs
Individuals	Depends on individual	Depends on individual	Depends on individual	Depends on individual
DB pension	High	Long	Low	Depends on age
Banks	Low	Short	High	Pay interest
Endowments	High	Long	Low	Spending level
Insurance	Low	Long—life Short—P&C	High	Low
Mutual funds	Depends on fund	Depends on fund	High	Depends on fund

LOS 42.c

The three steps in the portfolio management process are:

1. **Planning**: Determine client needs and circumstances, including the client's return objectives, risk tolerance, constraints, and preferences. Create, and then periodically review and update, an investment policy statement (IPS) that spells out these needs and circumstances.

2. **Execution**: Construct the client portfolio by determining suitable allocations to various asset classes based on the IPS and on expectations about macroeconomic variables such as inflation, interest rates, and GDP growth (top-down analysis). Identify attractively priced securities within an asset class for client portfolios based on valuation estimates from security analysts (bottom-up analysis).

3. **Feedback**: Monitor and rebalance the portfolio to adjust asset class allocations and securities holdings in response to market performance. Measure and report performance relative to the performance benchmark specified in the IPS.

LOS 42.d

Mutual funds combine funds from many investors into a single portfolio that is invested in a specified class of securities or to match a specific index. Many varieties exist, including money market funds, bond funds, stock funds, and balanced (hybrid) funds. Open-ended shares can be bought or sold at the net asset value. Closed-ended funds have a fixed number of shares that trade at a price determined by the market.

Exchange-traded funds are similar to mutual funds, but investors can buy and sell ETF shares in the same way as shares of stock. Management fees are generally low, though trading ETFs results in brokerage costs.

Separately managed accounts are portfolios managed for individual investors who have substantial assets. In return for an annual fee based on assets, the investor receives personalized investment advice.

Hedge funds are available only to accredited investors and are exempt from most reporting requirements. Many different hedge fund strategies exist. A typical annual fee structure is 20% of excess performance plus 2% of assets under management.

Buyout funds involve taking a company private by buying all available shares, usually funded by issuing debt. The company is then restructured to increase cash flow. Investors typically exit the investment within three to five years.

Venture capital funds are similar to buyout funds, except that the companies purchased are in the start-up phase. Venture capital funds, like buyout funds, also provide advice and expertise to the start-ups.

CONCEPT CHECKERS

1. Compared to investing in a single security, diversification provides investors a way to:
    A. increase the expected rate of return.
    B. decrease the volatility of returns.
    C. increase the probability of high returns.

2. Portfolio diversification is *least likely* to protect against losses:
    A. during severe market turmoil.
    B. when markets are operating normally.
    C. when the portfolio securities have low return correlation.

3. In a defined contribution pension plan:
    A. the employee accepts the investment risk.
    B. the plan sponsor promises a predetermined retirement income to participants.
    C. the plan manager attempts to match the fund's assets to its liabilities.

4. Low risk tolerance and high liquidity requirements *best* describe the typical investment needs of a(n):
    A. defined-benefit pension plan.
    B. foundation.
    C. insurance company.

5. A long time horizon and low liquidity requirements *best* describe the investment needs of a(n):
    A. endowment.
    B. insurance company.
    C. bank.

6. Which of the following is *least likely* to be considered an appropriate schedule for reviewing and updating an investment policy statement?
    A. At regular intervals (e.g., every year).
    B. When there is a major change in the client's constraints.
    C. Frequently, based on the recent performance of the portfolio.

7. A top-down security analysis begins by:
    A. analyzing a firm's business prospects and quality of management.
    B. identifying the most attractive companies within each industry.
    C. examining economic conditions.

8. Compared to exchange-traded funds (ETFs), open-end mutual funds are typically associated with lower:
    A. brokerage costs.
    B. minimum investment amounts.
    C. management fees.

9. Both buyout funds and venture capital funds:
   A. expect that only a small percentage of investments will pay off.
   B. play an active role in the management of companies.
   C. restructure companies to increase cash flow.

10. Hedge funds *most likely*:
   A. have stricter reporting requirements than a typical investment firm because of their use of leverage and derivatives.
   B. hold equal values of long and short securities.
   C. are not offered for sale to the general public.

ANSWERS – CONCEPT CHECKERS

1. **B**   Diversification provides an investor reduced risk. However, the expected return is generally similar or less than that expected from investing in a single risky security. Very high or very low returns become less likely.

2. **A**   Portfolio diversification has been shown to be relatively ineffective during severe market turmoil. Portfolio diversification is most effective when the securities have low correlation and the markets are operating normally.

3. **A**   In a defined contribution pension plan, the employee accepts the investment risk. The plan sponsor and manager neither promise a specific level of retirement income to participants nor make investment decisions. These are features of a defined benefit plan.

4. **C**   Insurance companies need to be able to pay claims as they arise, which leads to insurance firms having low risk tolerance and high liquidity needs. Defined benefit pension plans and foundations both have high risk tolerance and low liquidity needs.

5. **A**   An endowment has a long time horizon and low liquidity needs, as an endowment generally intends to fund its causes perpetually. Both insurance companies and banks require high liquidity.

6. **C**   An IPS should be updated at regular intervals and whenever there is a major change in the client's objectives or constraints. Updating an IPS based on portfolio performance is not recommended.

7. **C**   A top-down analysis begins with an analysis of broad economic trends. After an industry that is expected to perform well is chosen, the most attractive companies within that industry are identified. A bottom-up analysis begins with criteria such as firms' business prospects and quality of management.

8. **A**   Open-end mutual funds do not have brokerage costs, as the shares are purchased from and redeemed with the fund company. Minimum investment amounts and management fees are typically higher for mutual funds.

9. **B**   Both buyout funds and venture capital funds play an active role in the management of companies. Unlike venture capital funds, buyout funds expect that the majority of investments will pay off. Venture capital funds do not typically restructure companies.

10. **C**   Hedge funds may not be offered for sale to the general public; they can be sold only to qualified investors who meet certain criteria. Hedge funds that hold equal values of long and short securities today make up only a small percentage of funds; many other kinds of hedge funds exist that make no attempt to be market neutral. Hedge funds have reporting requirements that are less strict than those of a typical investment firm.

The following is a review of the Portfolio Management principles designed to address the learning outcome statements set forth by CFA Institute. This topic is also covered in:

PORTFOLIO RISK AND RETURN: PART I

Study Session 12

EXAM FOCUS

This topic review makes use of many of the statistical and returns measures we covered in Quantitative Methods. You should understand the historical return and risk rankings of the major asset classes and how the correlation (covariance) of returns between assets and between various asset classes affects the risk of portfolios. Risk aversion describes an investor's preferences related to the tradeoff between risk and return. These preferences, along with the risk and return characteristics of available portfolios, can be used to illustrate the selection of an optimal portfolio for a given investor, that is, the portfolio that maximizes the investor's expected utility.

LOS 43.a: Calculate and interpret major return measures and describe their appropriate uses.

CFA® Program Curriculum, Volume 4, page 260

Holding period return (HPR) is simply the percentage increase in the value of an investment over a given time period:

$$\text{holding period return} = \frac{\text{end-of-period value}}{\text{beginning-of-period value}} - 1 = \frac{P_t + \text{Div}_t}{P_0} - 1 = \frac{P_t - P_0 + \text{Div}_t}{P_0}$$

If a stock is valued at €20 at the beginning of the period, pays €1 in dividends over the period, and at the end of the period is valued at €22, the HPR is:

$$\text{HPR} = (22 + 1) / 20 - 1 = 0.15 = 15\%$$

Average Returns

The **arithmetic mean return** is the simple average of a series of periodic returns. It has the statistical property of being an unbiased estimator of the true mean of the underlying distribution of returns:

$$\text{arithmetic mean return} = \frac{(R_1 + R_2 + R_3 + ... + R_n)}{n}$$

The **geometric mean return** is a compound annual rate. When periodic rates of return vary from period to period, the geometric mean return will have a value less than the arithmetic mean return:

$$\text{geometric mean return} = \sqrt[n]{(1+R_1) \times (1+R_2) \times (1+R_3) \times \ldots \times (1+R_n)} - 1$$

For example, for returns R_t over three annual periods, the geometric mean return is calculated as follows:

$$\text{geometric mean return} = \sqrt[3]{(1+R_1)(1+R_2)(1+R_3)} - 1$$

Example: Return measures

An investor purchased $1,000 of a mutual fund's shares. The fund had the following total returns over a 3-year period: +5%, –8%, +12%. Calculate the value at the end of the 3-year period, the holding period return, the mean annual return, and the geometric mean annual return.

Answer:

Ending value = (1,000)(1.05)(0.92)(1.12) = $1,081.92.

Holding period return = (1.05)(0.92)(1.12) − 1 = 0.08192 = 8.192%, which can also be calculated as 1,081.92 / 1,000 − 1 = 8.192%.

Arithmetic mean return = (5% − 8% + 12%) / 3 = 3%.

Geometric mean return = $\sqrt[3]{(1.05)(0.92)(1.12)} - 1 = 0.02659 = 2.66\%$, which can also be calculated as geometric mean return = $\sqrt[3]{1 + \text{HPR}} - 1 = \sqrt[3]{1.08192} - 1 = 2.66\%$.

The **money-weighted rate of return** is the internal rate of return on a portfolio based on all of its cash inflows and outflows. To calculate a money-weighted rate of return, consider the beginning value and additional deposits of cash by the investor to be inflows and consider withdrawals of cash, interest, and dividends (which are additional cash available to be withdrawn) and the ending value to be outflows.

Example: Money-weighted rate of return

Assume an investor buys a share of stock for $80 at t = 0 and at the end of the next year (t = 1), she buys an additional share for $70. At the end of Year 2, the investor sells both shares for $85 each. At the end of each year in the holding period, the stock paid a $1.50 per share dividend. What is the money-weighted rate of return?

Answer:

Step 1: Determine the timing of each cash flow and whether the cash flow is an inflow (+), into the account, or an outflow (–), available from the account.

t = 0:	purchase of first share	= +$80.00 inflow to account
t = 1:	purchase of second share	= +$70.00
	dividend from first share	= –$1.50
	Subtotal, t = 1	+$68.50 inflow to account
t = 2:	dividend from two shares	= –$3.00
	proceeds from selling shares	= –$170.00
	Subtotal, t = 2	–$173.00 outflow from account

Step 2: Net the cash flows for each time period and set the PV of cash inflows equal to the present value of cash outflows.

$$PV_{inflows} = PV_{outflows}$$

$$\$80 + \frac{\$68.50}{(1+r)} = \frac{\$173.00}{(1+r)^2}$$

Step 3: Solve for r to find the money-weighted rate of return.

Net cash flows: $CF_0 = +80$; $CF_1 = +68.5$; $CF_2 = -173$

The money-weighted rate of return is 10.35%.

In the previous example, the cash flows in and out of the account occur at 1-year intervals so that we solved for an annual money-weighted rate of return. More generally, we must use the shortest period between significant cash flows into or out of the account when setting up the internal rate of return calculation. For example, if we use one month as our period (zero cash flow for months with no cash flows), the internal rate of return calculation will yield a monthly rate of return. In that case, we would need to compound the monthly money-weighted return for 12 months to translate it into an effective annual rate.

Other Return Measures

Gross return refers to the total return on a security portfolio before deducting fees for the management and administration of the investment account. **Net return** refers to the return after these fees have been deducted. Note that commissions on trades and other costs that are necessary to generate the investment returns are deducted in both gross and net return measures.

Pretax nominal return refers to the return prior to paying taxes. Dividend income, interest income, short-term capital gains, and long-term capital gains may all be taxed at different rates.

After-tax nominal return refers to the return after the tax liability is deducted.

Real return is nominal return adjusted for inflation. Consider an investor who earns a nominal return of 7% over a year when inflation is 2%. The investor's approximate real return is simply 7 – 2 = 5%. The investor's exact real return is slightly lower, 1.07 / 1.02 – 1 = 0.049 = 4.9%.

Real return measures the increase in an investor's purchasing power: how much more goods she can purchase at the end of one year due to the increase in the value of her investments. If she invests $1,000 and earns a nominal return of 7%, she will have $1,070 at the end of the year. If the price of the goods she consumes has gone up 2%, from $1.00 to $1.02, she will be able to consume 1,070 / 1.02 = 1,049 units. She has given up consuming 1,000 units today but instead is able to purchase 1,049 units at the end of one year. Her purchasing power has gone up 4.9%; this is her real return.

A **leveraged return** refers to a return to an investor that is a multiple of the return on the underlying asset. The leveraged return is calculated as the gain or loss on the investment as a percentage of an investor's cash investment. An investment in a derivative security, such as a futures contract, produces a leveraged return because the cash deposited is only a fraction of the value of the assets underlying the futures contract. Leveraged investments in real estate are very common: investors pay for only part of the cost of the property with their own cash, and the rest of the amount is paid for with borrowed money.

LOS 43.b: Calculate and interpret the mean, variance, and covariance (or correlation) of asset returns based on historical data.

CFA® Program Curriculum, Volume 4, page 261

Variance (Standard Deviation) of Returns for an Individual Security

In finance, the variance and standard deviation of returns are common measures of investment risk. Both of these are measures of the variability of a distribution of returns about its mean or expected value.

We can calculate the population variance, σ^2, when we know the return R_t for each period, the total number periods (T), and the mean or expected value of the population's distribution (μ), as follows:

$$\sigma^2 = \frac{\sum_{t=1}^{T}(R_t - \mu)^2}{T}$$

In the world of finance, we are typically analyzing only a sample of returns data, rather than the entire population. To calculate sample variance, s^2, using a sample of T historical returns and the mean, $\overline{R}$, of the observations, we use the following formula:

$$s^2 = \frac{\sum_{t=1}^{T}\left(R_t - \overline{R}\right)^2}{T-1}$$

Covariance and Correlation of Returns for Two Securities

Covariance measures the extent to which two variables move together over time. A positive covariance means that the variables (e.g., rates of return on two stocks) tend to move together. Negative covariance means that the two variables tend to move in opposite directions. A covariance of zero means there is no linear relationship between the two variables. To put it another way, if the covariance of returns between two assets is zero, knowing the return for the next period on one of the assets tells you nothing about the return of the other asset for the period.

Here we will focus on the calculation of the covariance between two assets' returns using **historical data**. The calculation of the sample covariance is based on the following formula:

$$Cov_{1,2} = \frac{\sum_{t=1}^{n}\left\{\left[R_{t,1} - \overline{R}_1\right]\left[R_{t,2} - \overline{R}_2\right]\right\}}{n-1}$$

where:

$R_{t,1}$ = return on Asset 1 in period t

$R_{t,2}$ = return on Asset 2 in period t

$\overline{R}_1$ = mean return on Asset 1

$\overline{R}_2$ = mean return on Asset 2

n = number of periods

The magnitude of the covariance depends on the magnitude of the individual stocks' standard deviations and the relationship between their co-movements. Covariance is an absolute measure and is measured in return units squared.

The covariance of the returns of two securities can be standardized by dividing by the product of the standard deviations of the two securities. This standardized measure of co-movement is called **correlation** and is computed as:

$$\rho_{1,2} = \frac{Cov_{1,2}}{\sigma_1 \sigma_2}$$

The relation can also be written as:

$$Cov_{1,2} = \rho_{1,2}\sigma_1\sigma_2$$

The term $\rho_{1,2}$ is called the *correlation coefficient* between the returns of securities 1 and 2. The correlation coefficient has no units. It is a pure measure of the co-movement of the two stocks' returns and is bounded by −1 and +1.

How should you interpret the correlation coefficient?

- A correlation coefficient of +1 means that deviations from the mean or expected return are always proportional in the same direction. That is, they are perfectly positively correlated.
- A correlation coefficient of −1 means that deviations from the mean or expected return are always proportional in opposite directions. That is, they are perfectly negatively correlated.
- A correlation coefficient of zero means that there is no linear relationship between the two stocks' returns. They are uncorrelated. One way to interpret a correlation (or covariance) of zero is that, in any period, knowing the actual value of one variable tells you nothing about the value of the other.

Example: Calculating mean return, returns variance, returns covariance, and correlation

Given the six years of percentage returns for Stocks 1 and 2 in the following table, calculate the mean return, sample variance, sample covariance, and correlation for the two returns series.

Year	Stock 1 Return	Stock 2 Return	$(R_t - \bar{R}_1)$	$(R_t - \bar{R}_2)$	$(R_t - \bar{R}_1)(R_t - \bar{R}_2)$
20X4	+0.10	+0.20	+0.05	+0.10	+0.005
20X5	−0.15	−0.20	−0.20	−0.30	+0.060
20X6	+0.20	−0.10	+0.15	−0.20	−0.030
20X7	+0.25	+0.30	+0.20	+0.20	+0.040
20X8	−0.30	−0.20	−0.35	−0.30	+0.105
20X9	+0.20	+0.60	+0.15	+0.50	+0.075
	$\sum R_1 = 0.30$ $\bar{R}_1 = 0.05$	$\sum R_2 = 0.60$ $\bar{R}_2 = 0.10$			$\Sigma = 0.255$

Answer:

To calculate the mean returns for the samples, we sum the returns for each stock and divide by the number of years. The mean returns are $\overline{R}_1 = 30 / 6 = 5\%$ for Stock 1 and $\overline{R}_2 = 60 / 6 = 10\%$ for Stock 2.

Using the deviations of each year's returns from the mean return for Stock 1, we can calculate the sample variance as follows:

$$s_1^2 = \frac{(0.05)^2 + (-0.20)^2 + (0.15)^2 + (0.20)^2 + (-0.35)^2 + (0.15)^2}{6-1} = 0.05$$

Using the deviations of each year's returns from the mean return for Stock 2, we can calculate the sample variance as follows:

$$s_2^2 = \frac{(0.10)^2 + (-0.30)^2 + (-0.20)^2 + (0.20)^2 + (-0.30)^2 + (0.50)^2}{6-1} = 0.104$$

In the right-hand column of the table, we have summed the products of the deviations of Stocks 1 and 2 from their means to get 0.255.

The sample covariance is calculated as 0.255 / (6 − 1) = 0.051.

To convert the covariance into correlation, we use the sample standard deviations of returns for the two stocks:

$$s_1 = \sqrt{0.05} = 0.2236 = 22.36\%$$

$$s_2 = \sqrt{0.104} = 0.3225 = 32.25\%$$

Finally, we can calculate the correlation coefficient for the two stocks' returns as follows:

$$\rho_{1,2} = \text{sample correlation } (r_{1,2}) = \frac{Cov_{1,2}}{s_1 s_2} = \frac{0.0510}{0.2236 \times 0.3225} = 0.7072$$

LOS 43.c: Describe the characteristics of the major asset classes that investors consider in forming portfolios.

CFA® Program Curriculum, Volume 4, page 260

An examination of the returns and standard deviation of returns for the major investable asset classes supports the idea of a tradeoff between risk and return. Using U.S. data over the period 1926–2008 as an example, shown in Figure 1, small-capitalization stocks have had the greatest average returns and greatest risk over the period. T-bills had the lowest average returns and the lowest standard deviation of returns.

Figure 1: Risk and Return of Major Asset Classes in the United States (1926–2008)[1]

Assets Class	Average Annual Return (Geometric Mean)	Standard Deviation (Annualized Monthly)
Small-cap stocks	11.7%	33.0%
Large-cap stocks	9.6%	20.9%
Long-term corporate bonds	5.9%	8.4%
Long-term Treasury bonds	5.7%	9.4%
Treasury bills	3.7%	3.1%
Inflation	3.0%	4.2%

Results for other markets around the world are similar: asset classes with the greatest average returns also have the highest standard deviations of returns.

The annual nominal return on U.S. equities has varied greatly from year to year, ranging from losses greater than 40% to gains of more than 50%. We can approximate the real returns over the period by subtracting inflation. The asset class with the least risk, T-bills, had a real return of only approximately 0.7% over the period, while the approximate real return on U.S. large-cap stocks was 6.6%. Because annual inflation fluctuated greatly over the period, real returns have been much more stable than nominal returns.

Evaluating investments using expected return and variance of returns is a simplification because returns do not follow a normal distribution; distributions are negatively skewed, with greater kurtosis (fatter tails) than a normal distribution. The negative skew reflects a tendency towards large downside deviations, while the positive excess kurtosis reflects frequent extreme deviations on both the upside and downside. These non-normal characteristics of skewness ($\neq 0$) and kurtosis ($\neq 3$) should be taken into account when analyzing investments.

Liquidity is an additional characteristic to consider when choosing investments because liquidity can affect the price and, therefore, the expected return of a security. Liquidity can be a major concern in emerging markets and for securities that trade infrequently, such as low-quality corporate bonds.

LOS 43.d: Explain risk aversion and its implications for portfolio selection.

CFA® Program Curriculum, Volume 4, page 282

A **risk-averse** investor is simply one that dislikes risk (i.e., prefers less risk to more risk). Given two investments that have equal expected returns, a risk-averse investor will choose the one with less risk (standard deviation, σ).

---

1.   2009 Ibbotson SBBI Classic Yearbook.

A **risk-seeking** (risk-loving) investor actually prefers more risk to less and, given equal expected returns, will choose the more risky investment. A **risk-neutral** investor has no preference regarding risk and would be indifferent between two such investments.

Consider this gamble: A coin will be flipped; if it comes up heads, you receive $100; if it comes up tails, you receive nothing. The expected payoff is 0.5($100) + 0.5($0) = $50. A risk-averse investor would choose a payment of $50 (a certain outcome) over the gamble. A risk-seeking investor would prefer the gamble to a certain payment of $50. A risk-neutral investor would be indifferent between the gamble and a certain payment of $50.

If expected returns are identical, a risk-averse investor will always choose the investment with the least risk. However, an investor may select a very risky portfolio despite being risk averse; a risk-averse investor will hold very risky assets if he feels that the extra return he expects to earn is adequate compensation for the additional risk.

LOS 43.e: Calculate and interpret portfolio standard deviation.

CFA® Program Curriculum, Volume 4, page 290

The variance of returns for a portfolio of two risky assets is calculated as follows:

$$\text{Var}_{\text{portfolio}} = w_1^2 \sigma_1^2 + w_2^2 \sigma_2^2 + 2 w_1 w_2 \text{Cov}_{12}$$

where w_1 is the proportion of the portfolio invested in Asset 1, and w_2 is the proportion of the portfolio invested in Asset 2. w_2 must equal $(1 - w_1)$.

Previously, we established that the correlation of returns for two assets is calculated as:

$$\rho_{12} = \frac{\text{Cov}_{12}}{\sigma_1 \sigma_2}, \text{ so that we can also write } \text{Cov}_{12} = \rho_{12} \sigma_1 \sigma_2.$$

Substituting this term for Cov_{12} in the formula for the variance of returns for a portfolio of two risky assets, we have the following:

$$\text{Var}_{\text{portfolio}} = w_1^2 \sigma_1^2 + w_2^2 \sigma_2^2 + 2 w_1 w_2 \rho_{12} \sigma_1 \sigma_2$$

Because $\text{Var}_{\text{portfolio}} = \sigma_{\text{portfolio}}^2$:

$$\sigma_{\text{portfolio}} = \sqrt{w_1^2 \sigma_1^2 + w_2^2 \sigma_2^2 + 2 w_1 w_2 \rho_{12} \sigma_1 \sigma_2}$$

Writing the formula in this form allows us to easily see the effect of the correlation of returns between the two assets on portfolio risk.

LOS 43.f: Describe the effect on a portfolio's risk of investing in assets that are less than perfectly correlated.

CFA® Program Curriculum, Volume 4, page 292

If two risky asset returns are perfectly positively correlated, ρ_{12} = +1, then the square root of portfolio variance (the portfolio standard deviation of returns) is equal to:

$$\sigma_{portfolio} = \sqrt{Var_{portfolio}} = \sqrt{w_1^2\sigma_1^2 + w_2^2\sigma_2^2 + 2w_1w_2\sigma_1\sigma_2(1)} = w_1\sigma_1 + w_2\sigma_2$$

Professor's Note: This might be easier to see if we do the algebra in reverse. If $w_1\sigma_1 + w_2\sigma_2$ equals the square root of the term under the radical in this special case, then $(w_1\sigma_1 + w_2\sigma_2)^2$ should equal the term under the radical. If we expand $(w_1\sigma_1 + w_2\sigma_2)^2$, we get:

$$(w_1\sigma_1 + w_2\sigma_2)^2 = (w_1\sigma_1)^2 + (w_1\sigma_1)(w_2\sigma_2) + (w_2\sigma_2)(w_1\sigma_1) + (w_2\sigma_2)^2$$

$$= (w_1\sigma_1)^2 + (w_2\sigma_2)^2 + 2(w_1\sigma_1)(w_2\sigma_2)$$

$$= w_1^2\sigma_1^2 + w_2^2\sigma_2^2 + 2w_1\sigma_1w_2\sigma_2$$

In this unique case, with ρ_{12} = 1, the portfolio standard deviation is simply a weighted average of the standard deviations of the individual asset returns. A portfolio 25% invested in Asset 1 and 75% invested in Asset 2 will have a standard deviation of returns equal to 25% of the risk (σ_1) of Asset 1's return, plus 75% of the risk of Asset 2's return.

Focusing on returns correlation, we can see that the greatest portfolio risk results when the correlation between asset returns is +1. For any value of correlation less than +1, portfolio variance is reduced. Note that for a correlation of zero, the entire third term in the portfolio variance equation is zero. For negative values of correlation ρ_{12}, the third term becomes negative and further reduces portfolio variance and standard deviation.

We will illustrate this property with an example.

Example: Portfolio risk as correlation varies

Consider two risky assets that have returns variances of 0.0625 and 0.0324, respectively. The assets' standard deviations of returns are then 25% and 18%, respectively. Calculate the variances and standard deviations of portfolio returns for an equal-weighted portfolio of the two assets when their correlation of returns is 1, 0.5, 0, and –0.5.

The calculations are as follows:

$$\text{variance}_{\text{portfolio}} = w_1^2\sigma_1^2 + w_2^2\sigma_2^2 + 2w_1w_2\rho_{12}\sigma_1\sigma_2$$

$$\sigma_{\text{portfolio}} = \sqrt{\text{variance}_{\text{portfolio}}}$$

$$\sigma_{\text{portfolio}} = \sqrt{w_1^2\sigma_1^2 + w_2^2\sigma_2^2 + 2w_1w_2\rho_{12}\sigma_1\sigma_2}$$

ρ = **correlation = +1:**

σ = portfolio standard deviation = 0.5(25%) + 0.5(18%) = **21.5%**

σ^2 = portfolio variance = 0.215^2 = 0.046225

ρ = **correlation = 0.5:**

$\sigma^2 = (0.5^2)0.0625 + (0.5^2)0.0324 + 2(0.5)(0.5)\textbf{(0.5)}(0.25)(0.18) = 0.034975$

σ = **18.70%**

ρ = **correlation = 0:**

$\sigma^2 = (0.5^2)0.0625 + (0.5^2)0.0324 = 0.023725$

σ = **15.40%**

ρ = **correlation = −0.5:**

$\sigma^2 = (0.5^2)0.0625 + (0.5^2)0.0324 + 2(0.5)(0.5)\textbf{(−0.5)}(0.25)(0.18) = 0.012475$

σ = **11.17%**

Note that portfolio risk falls as the correlation between the assets' returns decreases. This is an important result of the analysis of portfolio risk: The lower the correlation of asset returns, the greater the risk reduction (diversification) benefit of combining assets in a portfolio. If asset returns were perfectly negatively correlated, portfolio risk could be eliminated altogether for a specific set of asset weights.

We show these relations graphically in Figure 2 by plotting the portfolio risk and return for all portfolios of two risky assets, for assumed values of the assets' returns correlation.

Figure 2: Risk and Return for Different Values of ρ

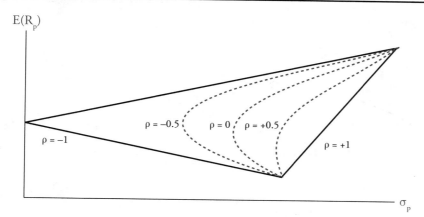

From these analyses, the risk-reduction benefits of investing in assets with low return correlations should be clear. The desire to reduce risk is what drives investors to invest in not just domestic stocks, but also bonds, foreign stocks, real estate, and other assets.

LOS 43.g: Describe and interpret the minimum-variance and efficient frontiers of risky assets and the global minimum-variance portfolio.

CFA® Program Curriculum, Volume 4, page 301

For each level of expected portfolio return, we can vary the portfolio weights on the individual assets to determine the portfolio that has the least risk. These portfolios that have the lowest standard deviation of all portfolios with a given expected return are known as **minimum-variance portfolios**. Together they make up the **minimum-variance frontier**. On a risk versus return graph, the portfolio that is farthest to the left (has the least risk) is known as the global minimum-variance portfolio.

Assuming that investors are risk averse, investors prefer the portfolio that has the greatest expected return when choosing among portfolios that have the same standard deviation of returns. Those portfolios that have the greatest expected return for each level of risk (standard deviation) make up the **efficient frontier**. The efficient frontier coincides with the top portion of the minimum-variance frontier. A risk-averse investor would only choose portfolios that are on the efficient frontier because all available portfolios that are not on the efficient frontier have lower expected returns than an efficient portfolio with the same risk. The portfolio on the efficient frontier that has the least risk is the **global minimum-variance portfolio**.

These concepts are illustrated in Figure 3.

Figure 3: Minimum-Variance and Efficient Frontiers

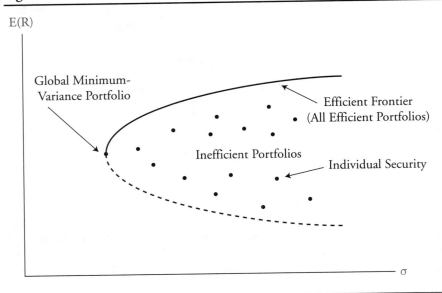

LOS 43.h: Discuss the selection of an optimal portfolio, given an investor's utility (or risk aversion) and the capital allocation line.

CFA® Program Curriculum, Volume 4, page 304

An investor's **utility function** represents the investor's preferences in terms of risk and return (i.e., his degree of risk aversion). An **indifference curve** is a tool from economics that, in this application, plots combinations of risk (standard deviation) and expected return among which an investor is indifferent. In constructing indifference curves for portfolios based on only their expected return and standard deviation of returns, we are assuming that these are the only portfolio characteristics that investors care about. In Figure 4, we show three indifference curves for an investor. The investor's expected utility is the same for all points along a single indifference curve. Indifference curve I_1 represents the most preferred portfolios in Figure 4; our investor will prefer any portfolio along I_1 to any portfolio on either I_2 or I_3.

Figure 4: Risk-Averse Investor's Indifference Curves

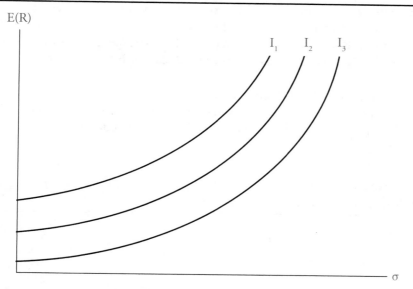

Indifference curves slope upward for risk-averse investors because they will only take on more risk (standard deviation of returns) if they are compensated with greater expected returns. An investor who is relatively more risk averse requires a relatively greater increase in expected return to compensate for a given increase in risk. In other words, a more risk-averse investor will have steeper indifference curves.

In our previous illustration of efficient portfolios available in the market, we included only risky assets. Now we will introduce a risk-free asset into our universe of available assets, and we will consider the risk and return characteristics of a portfolio that combines a portfolio of risky assets and the risk-free asset. Recall from Quantitative Methods that we can calculate the expected return and standard deviation of a portfolio with weight W_A allocated to risky Asset A and weight W_B allocated to risky Asset B using the following formulas:

$$E(R_{portfolio}) = W_A E(R_A) + W_B E(R_B)$$

$$\sigma_{portfolio} = \sqrt{W_A^2 \sigma_A^2 + W_B^2 \sigma_B^2 + 2 W_A W_B \rho_{AB} \sigma_A \sigma_B}$$

Allow Asset B to be the risk-free asset and Asset A to be the risky asset portfolio. Because a risk-free asset has zero standard deviation and zero correlation of returns with those of a risky portfolio, this results in the reduced equation:

$$\sigma_{portfolio} = \sqrt{W_A^2 \sigma_A^2} = W_A \sigma_A$$

The intuition of this result is quite simple: If we put X% of our portfolio into the risky asset portfolio, the resulting portfolio will have standard deviation of returns equal to X% of the standard deviation of the risky asset portfolio. The relationship between portfolio risk and return for various portfolio allocations is linear, as illustrated in Figure 5.

Combining a risky portfolio with a risk-free asset is the process that supports the **two-fund separation theorem**, which states that all investors' optimum portfolios will be made up of some combination of an optimal portfolio of risky assets and the risk-free asset. The line representing these possible combinations of risk-free assets and the optimal risky asset portfolio is referred to as the **capital allocation line**.

Point X on the capital allocation line in Figure 5 represents a portfolio that is 40% invested in the risky asset portfolio and 60% invested in the risk-free asset. Its expected return will be $0.40[E(R_{\text{risky asset portfolio}})] + 0.60(R_f)$, and its standard deviation will be $0.40(\sigma_{\text{risky asset portfolio}})$.

Figure 5: Capital Allocation Line and Risky Asset Weights

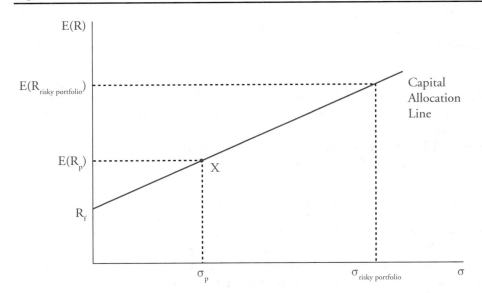

Now that we have constructed a set of the possible efficient portfolios (the capital allocation line), we can combine this with indifference curves representing an individual's preferences for risk and return to illustrate the logic of selecting an optimal portfolio (i.e., one that maximizes the investor's expected utility). In Figure 6, we can see that Investor A, with preferences represented by indifference curves I_1, I_2, and I_3, can reach the level of expected utility on I_2 by selecting portfolio X. This is the optimal portfolio for this investor, as any portfolio that lies on I_2 is preferred to all portfolios that lie on I_3 (and in fact to any portfolios that lie between I_2 and I_3). Portfolios on I_1 are preferred to those on I_2, but none of the portfolios that lie on I_1 are available in the market.

Figure 6: Risk-Averse Investor's Indifference Curves

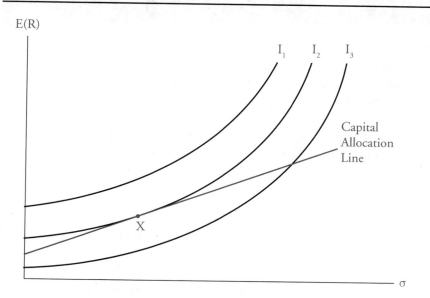

The final result of our analysis here is not surprising; investors who are less risk averse will select portfolios that are more risky. Recall that the less an investor's risk aversion, the flatter his indifference curves. As illustrated in Figure 7, the flatter indifference curve for Investor B (I_B) results in an optimal (tangency) portfolio that lies to the right of the one that results from a steeper indifference curve, such as that for Investor A (I_A). An investor who is less risk averse should optimally choose a portfolio with more invested in the risky asset portfolio and less invested in the risk-free asset.

Figure 7: Portfolio Choices Based on Investor's Indifference Curves

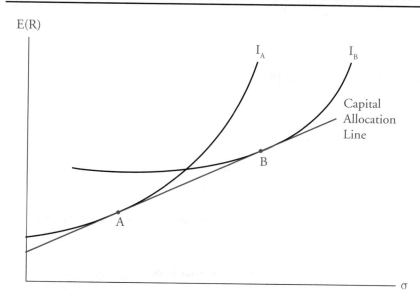

KEY CONCEPTS

LOS 43.a

Holding period return is used to measure an investment's return over a specific period. Arithmetic mean return is the simple average of a series of periodic returns. Geometric mean return is a compound annual rate.

Money-weighted rate of return is the IRR calculated using periodic cash flows into and out of an account and is the discount rate that makes the present value of cash inflows equal to the present value of cash outflows.

Gross return is total return after deducting commissions on trades and other costs necessary to generate the returns, but before deducting fees for the management and administration of the investment account. Net return is the return after management and administration fees have been deducted.

Pretax nominal return is the numerical percentage return of an investment, without considering the effects of taxes and inflation. After-tax nominal return is the numerical return after the tax liability is deducted, without adjusting for inflation. Real return is the increase in an investor's purchasing power, roughly equal to nominal return minus inflation. Leveraged return is the gain or loss on an investment as a percentage of an investor's cash investment.

LOS 43.b

We can calculate the population variance, σ^2, when we know the return R_t for period t, the total number T of periods, and the mean μ of the population's distribution:

$$\text{population variance} = \sigma^2 = \frac{\sum_{t=1}^{T}(R_t - \mu)^2}{T}$$

In finance, we typically analyze only a sample of returns, so the sample variance applies instead:

$$\text{sample variance} = S^2 = \frac{\sum_{t=1}^{T}(R_t - \overline{R})^2}{T-1}$$

Covariance measures the extent to which two variables move together over time. Positive covariance means the variables (e.g., rates of return on two stocks) tend to move together. Negative covariance means that the two variables tend to move in opposite directions. Covariance of zero means there is no linear relationship between the two variables.

Correlation is a standardized measure of co-movement that is bounded by −1 and +1:

$$\rho_{1,2} = \frac{\text{Cov}_{1,2}}{\sigma_1 \sigma_2}$$

LOS 43.c

As predicted by theory, asset classes with the greatest average returns have also had the highest risk.

Some of the major asset classes that investors consider when building a diversified portfolio include (ranked from most risk and return to least) small-capitalization stocks, large-capitalization stocks, long-term corporate bonds, long-term Treasury bonds, and Treasury bills.

In addition to risk and return, when analyzing investments, investors also take into consideration an investment's liquidity, as well as non-normal characteristics such as skewness and kurtosis.

LOS 43.d

A risk-averse investor is one that dislikes risk. Given two investments that have equal expected returns, a risk-averse investor will choose the one with less risk. However, a risk-averse investor will hold risky assets if he feels that the extra return he expects to earn is adequate compensation for the additional risk. Assets in the financial markets are priced according to the preferences of risk-averse investors.

A risk-seeking (risk-loving) investor actually prefers more risk to less and, given investments with equal expected returns, will choose the more risky investment.

A risk-neutral investor has no preference regarding risk and would be indifferent between two investments with the same expected return but different standard deviation of return.

LOS 43.e

The standard deviation of returns for a portfolio of two risky assets is calculated as follows:

$$\sigma_{portfolio} = \sqrt{w_1^2\sigma_1^2 + w_2^2\sigma_2^2 + 2w_1w_2\rho_{1,2}\sigma_1\sigma_2}$$

LOS 43.f

The greatest portfolio risk will result when the asset returns are perfectly positively correlated. As the correlation decreases from +1 to −1, portfolio risk decreases. The lower the correlation of asset returns, the greater the risk reduction (diversification) benefit of combining assets in a portfolio.

LOS 43.g

For each level of expected portfolio return, the portfolio that has the least risk is known as a minimum-variance portfolio. Taken together, these portfolios form a line called the minimum-variance frontier.

On a risk versus return graph, the one risky portfolio that is farthest to the left (has the least risk) is known as the global minimum-variance portfolio.

Those portfolios that have the greatest expected return for each level of risk make up the efficient frontier. The efficient frontier coincides with the top portion of the minimum variance frontier. Risk-averse investors would only choose a portfolio that lies on the efficient frontier.

LOS 43.h

An indifference curve plots combinations of risk and expected return that an investor finds equally acceptable. Indifference curves generally slope upward because risk-averse investors will only take on more risk if they are compensated with greater expected returns. A more risk-averse investor will have steeper indifference curves.

Flatter indifference curves (less risk aversion) result in an optimal portfolio with higher risk and higher expected return. An investor who is less risk averse will optimally choose a portfolio with more invested in the risky asset portfolio and less invested in the risk-free asset.

CONCEPT CHECKERS

1. An investor buys a share of stock for $40 at time t = 0, buys another share of the same stock for $50 at t = 1, and sells both shares for $60 each at t = 2. The stock paid a dividend of $1 per share at t = 1 and at t = 2. The periodic money-weighted rate of return on the investment is *closest* to:
   A. 22.2%.
   B. 23.0%.
   C. 23.8%.

2. Which of the following asset classes has historically had the highest returns and standard deviation?
   A. Small-cap stocks.
   B. Large-cap stocks.
   C. Long-term corporate bonds.

3. In a 5-year period, the annual returns on an investment are 5%, –3%, –4%, 2%, and 6%. The standard deviation of annual returns on this investment is *closest* to:
   A. 4.0%.
   B. 4.5%.
   C. 20.7%.

4. A measure of how the returns of two risky assets move in relation to each other is the:
   A. range.
   B. covariance.
   C. standard deviation.

5. Which of the following statements about correlation is *least accurate*?
   A. Diversification reduces risk when correlation is less than +1.
   B. If the correlation coefficient is 0, a zero variance portfolio can be constructed.
   C. The lower the correlation coefficient, the greater the potential benefits from diversification.

6. The standard deviation of returns is 0.30 for Stock A and 0.20 for Stock B. The covariance between the returns of A and B is 0.006. The correlation of returns between A and B is:
   A. 0.10.
   B. 0.20.
   C. 0.30.

7. Which of the following statements about risk-averse investors is *most accurate*? A risk-averse investor:
   A. seeks out the investment with minimum risk, while return is not a major consideration.
   B. will take additional investment risk if sufficiently compensated for this risk.
   C. avoids participating in global equity markets.

Use the following data to answer Questions 8 and 9.

A portfolio was created by investing 25% of the funds in Asset A (standard deviation = 15%) and the balance of the funds in Asset B (standard deviation = 10%).

8. If the correlation coefficient is 0.75, what is the portfolio's standard deviation?
    A. 10.6%.
    B. 12.4%.
    C. 15.0%.

9. If the correlation coefficient is –0.75, what is the portfolio's standard deviation?
    A. 2.8%.
    B. 4.2%.
    C. 5.3%.

10. Which of the following statements about covariance and correlation is *least accurate*?
    A. A zero covariance implies there is no linear relationship between the returns on two assets.
    B. If two assets have perfect negative correlation, the variance of returns for a portfolio that consists of these two assets will equal zero.
    C. The covariance of a 2-stock portfolio is equal to the correlation coefficient times the standard deviation of one stock's returns times the standard deviation of the other stock's returns.

11. Which of the following available portfolios *most likely* falls below the Markowitz efficient frontier?

Portfolio	Expected return	Expected standard deviation
A. A	7%	14%
B. B	9%	26%
C. C	12%	22%

12. The capital allocation line is a straight line from the risk-free asset through the:
    A. global maximum-return portfolio.
    B. optimal risky portfolio.
    C. global minimum-variance portfolio.

ANSWERS – CONCEPT CHECKERS

1. **C**   Using the cash flow functions on your financial calculator, enter CF0 = –40; CF1 = –50 + 1 = –49; CF2 = 60 × 2 + 2 = 122; CPT IRR = 23.82%.

2. **A**   Small-cap stocks have had the highest annual return and standard deviation of return over time. Large-cap stocks and bonds have historically had lower risk and return than small-cap stocks.

3. **B**   Mean annual return = (5% – 3% – 4% + 2% + 6%) / 5 = 1.2%

    Squared deviations from the mean:

5% – 1.2% = 3.8%	$3.8^2 = 14.44$
–3% –1.2% = –4.2%	$-4.2^2 = 17.64$
–4% –1.2% = –5.2%	$-5.2^2 = 27.04$
2% –1.2% = 0.8%	$0.8^2 = 0.64$
6% –1.2% = 4.8%	$4.8^2 = 23.04$

    Sum of squared deviations = 14.44 + 17.64 + 27.04 + 0.64 + 23.04 = 82.8

    Sample variance = 82.8 / (5 – 1) = 20.7

    Sample standard deviation = $20.7^{1/2}$ = 4.55%

4. **B**   The covariance is defined as the co-movement of the returns of two assets or how well the returns of two risky assets move together. Range and standard deviation are measures of dispersion and measure risk, not how assets move together.

5. **B**   A zero-variance portfolio can only be constructed if the correlation coefficient between assets is –1. Diversification benefits can be had when correlation is less than +1, and the lower the correlation, the greater the potential benefit.

6. **A**   Correlation = 0.006 / [(0.30)(0.20)] = 0.10

7. **B**   Risk-averse investors are generally willing to invest in risky investments, if the return of the investment is sufficient to reward the investor for taking on this risk. Participants in securities markets are generally assumed to be risk-averse investors.

8. **A** $\sqrt{(0.25)^2(0.15)^2 + (0.75)^2(0.10)^2 + 2(0.25)(0.75)(0.15)(0.10)(0.75)} =$

    $\sqrt{0.001406 + 0.005625 + 0.004219} = \sqrt{0.01125} = 0.106 = 10.6\%$

9. **C** $\sqrt{(0.25)^2(0.15)^2 + (0.75)^2(0.10)^2 + 2(0.25)(0.75)(0.15)(0.10)(-0.75)} =$

    $\sqrt{0.001406 + 0.005625 - 0.004219} = \sqrt{0.002812} = 0.053 = 5.3\%$

10. **B**   If the correlation of returns between the two assets is –1, the set of possible portfolio risk/return combinations becomes two straight lines (see Figure 2). A portfolio of these two assets will have a positive returns variance unless the portfolio weights are those that minimize the portfolio variance. Covariance is equal to the correlation coefficient multiplied by the product of the standard deviations of the returns of the two stocks in a 2-stock portfolio. If covariance is zero, then correlation is also zero, which implies that there is no linear relationship between the two stocks' returns.

11. **B** Portfolio B must be the portfolio that falls below the Markowitz efficient frontier because there is a portfolio (Portfolio C) that offers a higher return and lower risk.

12. **B** An investor's optimal portfolio will lie somewhere on the capital allocation line, which begins at the risk-free asset and runs through the optimal risky portfolio.

©2012 Kaplan, Inc.

PORTFOLIO RISK AND RETURN: PART II

EXAM FOCUS

The concepts developed here are very important to finance theory and are also used extensively in practice. You must know this material completely—not only the formulas and definitions, but the ideas that underlie their use. A model assumption that diversification is costless leads to the conclusion that only systematic risk (which cannot be reduced by further diversification) is priced in equilibrium, so that bearing nonsystematic risk does not increase expected returns.

LOS 44.a: Describe the implications of combining a risk-free asset with a portfolio of risky assets.

CFA® Program Curriculum, Volume 4, page 326

In the previous topic review, we covered the mathematics of calculating the risk and return of a portfolio with a percentage weight of W_A invested in a risky portfolio (P) and a weight of $W_B = 1 - W_A$ invested in a risk-free asset:

$$E(R_P) = W_A\, E(R_A) + W_B\, E(R_B)$$

$$\sigma_P = \sqrt{W_A^2 \sigma_A^2 + W_B^2 \sigma_B^2 + 2 W_A W_B \rho_{AB} \sigma_A \sigma_B}$$

Because a risk-free asset has zero standard deviation and zero correlation of returns with a risky portfolio, allowing Asset B to be the risk-free asset and Asset A to be the risky asset portfolio results in the following reduced equation:

$$\sigma_P = \sqrt{W_A^2 \sigma_A^2} = W_A \sigma_A$$

Our result is that the risk (standard deviation of returns) and expected return of portfolios with varying weights in the risk-free asset and a risky portfolio can be plotted as a line that begins at the risk-free rate of return and extends through the risky portfolio. This result is illustrated in Figure 1.

Figure 1: Combining a Risk-Free Asset with a Risky Asset

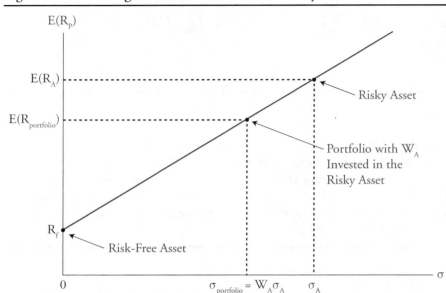

LOS 44.b: Explain the capital allocation line (CAL) and the capital market line (CML).

CFA® Program Curriculum, Volume 4, page 330

The line of possible portfolio risk and return combinations given the risk-free rate and the risk and return of a portfolio of risky assets is referred to as the **capital allocation line** (CAL). For an individual investor, the best CAL is the one that offers the most-preferred set of possible portfolios in terms of their risk and return. Figure 2 illustrates three possible investor CALs for three different risky portfolios A, B, and C. The optimal risky portfolio for this investor is Portfolio A because it results in the most preferred set of possible portfolios constructed by combining the risk-free asset with the risky portfolio. Of all the portfolios available to the investor, a combination of the risk-free asset with risky Portfolio A offers the investor the greatest expected utility.

Figure 2: Risky Portfolios and Their Associated Capital Allocation Lines

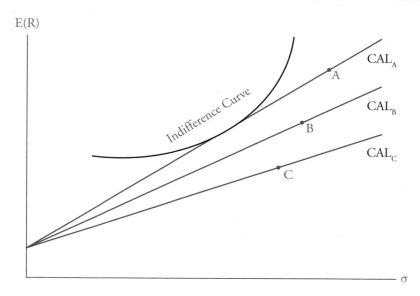

If each investor has different expectations about the expected returns of, standard deviations of, or correlations between risky asset returns, each investor will have a different optimal risky asset portfolio and a different CAL.

A simplifying assumption underlying modern portfolio theory (and the capital asset pricing model, which is introduced later in this topic review) is that investors have homogeneous expectations (i.e., they all have the same estimates of risk, return, and correlations with other risky assets for all risky assets). Under this assumption, all investors face the same efficient frontier of risky portfolios and will all have the same optimal risky portfolio and CAL.

Figure 3 illustrates the determination of the optimal risky portfolio and optimal CAL for all investors under the assumption of homogeneous expectations. Note that, under this assumption, the optimal CAL for any investor is the one that is just tangent to the efficient frontier. Depending on their preferences for risk and return (their indifference curves), investors may choose different portfolio weights for the risk-free asset and the risky (tangency) portfolio. Every investor, however, will use the same risky portfolio. When this is the case, that portfolio must be the **market portfolio** of all risky assets because all investors that hold any risky assets hold the same portfolio of risky assets.

Figure 3: Determining the Optimal Risky Portfolio and Optimal CAL Assuming Homogeneous Expectations

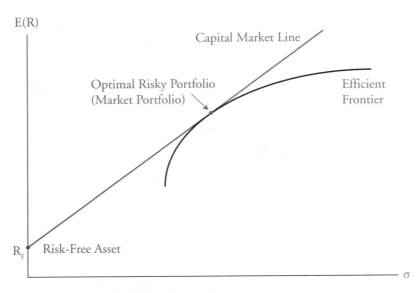

Under the assumption of homogeneous expectations, this optimal CAL for all investors is termed the **capital market line** (CML). Along this line, expected portfolio return, $E(R_P)$, is a linear function of portfolio risk, σ_P. The equation of this line is as follows:

$$E(R_P) = R_f + \left(\frac{E(R_M) - R_f}{\sigma_M} \right) \sigma_P$$

The y-intercept of this line is R_f and the slope (rise over run) of this line is as follows:

$$\left(\frac{E(R_M) - R_f}{\sigma_M} \right)$$

The intuition of this relation is straightforward. An investor who chooses to take on no risk ($\sigma_P = 0$) will earn the risk-free rate, R_f. The difference between the expected return on the market and the risk-free rate is termed the **market risk premium**. If we rewrite the CML equation as

$$E(R_P) = R_f + \left(E(R_M) - R_f \right) \left(\frac{\sigma_P}{\sigma_M} \right)$$

we can see that an investor can expect to get one unit of market risk premium in additional return (above the risk-free rate) for every unit of market risk, σ_M, that the investor is willing to accept.

If we assume that investors can both lend (invest in the risk-free asset) at the risk-free rate and borrow (as with a margin account) at the risk-free rate, they can select portfolios to the right of the market portfolio in Figure 3. An example will illustrate the calculations.

Example: Portfolio risk and return with borrowing and lending

Assume that the risk-free rate, R_f, is 5%; the expected rate of return on the market, $E(R_M)$, is 11%; and that the standard deviation of returns on the market portfolio, σ_M, is 20%. Calculate the expected return and standard deviation of returns for portfolios that are 25%, 75%, and 125% invested in the market portfolio. We will use R_M to represent these portfolio weights.

Expected portfolio returns are calculated as $E(R_P) = (1 - W_M) \times R_f + W_M \times E(R_M)$, so we have the following:

$W_M = 25\%$: $E(R_P) = 0.75 \times 5\% + 0.25 \times 11\% = 6.5\%$

$W_M = 75\%$: $E(R_P) = 0.25 \times 5\% + 0.75 \times 11\% = 9.5\%$

$W_M = 125\%$: $E(R_P) = -0.25 \times 5\% + 1.25 \times 11\% = 12.5\%$

Portfolio standard deviation is calculated as $\sigma_P = W_M \times \sigma_M$, so we have the following:

$\sigma_P = 0.25 \times 20\% = 5\%$

$\sigma_P = 0.75 \times 20\% = 15\%$

$\sigma_P = 1.25 \times 20\% = 25\%$

Figure 4: Borrowing and Lending Portfolios

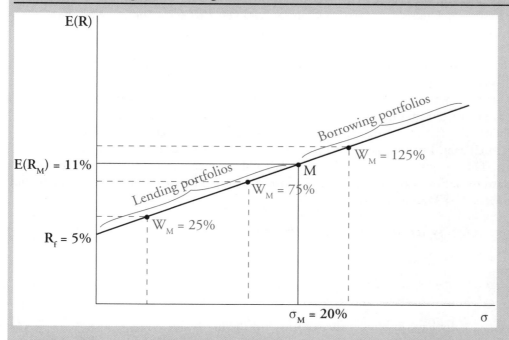

Note that with a weight (of investor assets) of 125% in the market portfolio, the investor borrows an amount equal to 25% of his portfolio assets at 5%. An investor with $10,000 would then borrow $2,500 and invest a total of $12,500 in the market portfolio. This leveraged portfolio will have an expected return of 12.5% and standard deviation of 25%.

Investors who believe market prices are informationally efficient often follow a **passive investment strategy** (i.e., invest in an index of risky assets that serves as a proxy for the market portfolio and allocate a portion of their investable assets to a risk-free asset, such as short-term government securities). In practice, many investors and portfolio managers believe their estimates of security values are correct and market prices are incorrect. Such investors will not use the weights of the market portfolio but will invest more than the market weights in securities that they believe are undervalued and less than the market weights in securities which they believe are overvalued. This is referred to as **active portfolio management** to differentiate it from a passive investment strategy that utilizes a market index for the optimal risky asset portfolio.

LOS 44.c: Explain systematic and nonsystematic risk, including why an investor should not expect to receive additional return for bearing nonsystematic risk.

CFA® Program Curriculum, Volume 4, page 338

When an investor diversifies across assets that are not perfectly correlated, the portfolio's risk is less than the weighted average of the risks of the individual securities in the portfolio. The risk that is eliminated by diversification is called **unsystematic risk** (also called *unique, diversifiable,* or *firm-specific risk*). Because the market portfolio contains *all* risky assets, it must be a well-diversified portfolio. All the risk that can be diversified away has been. The risk that remains cannot be diversified away and is called the **systematic risk** (also called *nondiversifiable risk* or *market risk*).

The concept of systematic risk applies to individual securities as well as to portfolios. Some securities' returns are highly correlated with overall market returns. Examples of firms that are highly correlated with market returns are luxury goods manufacturers such as Ferrari automobiles and Harley Davidson motorcycles. These firms have high systematic risk (i.e., they are very responsive to market, or systematic, changes). Other firms, such as utility companies, respond very little to changes in the systematic risk factors. These firms have very little systematic risk. Hence, total risk (as measured by standard deviation) can be broken down into its component parts: unsystematic risk and systematic risk. Mathematically:

total risk = systematic risk + unsystematic risk

 Professor's Note: Know this concept!

Do you actually have to buy all the securities in the market to diversify away unsystematic risk? No. Academic studies have shown that as you increase the number of stocks in a portfolio, the portfolio's risk falls toward the level of market risk. One study showed that it only took about 12 to 18 stocks in a portfolio to achieve 90% of the maximum diversification possible. Another study indicated it took 30 securities. Whatever the number, it is significantly less than *all* the securities. Figure 5 provides a general representation of this concept. Note, in the figure, that once you get to 30 or so securities in a portfolio, the standard deviation remains constant. The remaining risk is systematic, or nondiversifiable, risk. We will develop this concept later when we discuss beta, a measure of systematic risk.

Figure 5: Risk vs. Number of Portfolio Assets

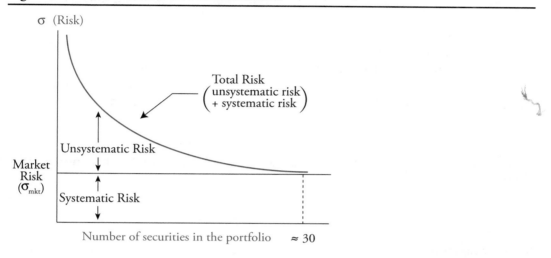

Systematic Risk is Relevant in Portfolios

One important conclusion of capital market theory is that equilibrium security returns depend on a stock's or a portfolio's systematic risk, not its total risk as measured by standard deviation. One of the assumptions of the model is that diversification is free. The reasoning is that investors will not be compensated for bearing risk that can be eliminated at no cost. If you think about the costs of a no-load index fund compared to buying individual stocks, diversification is actually very low cost if not actually free.

The implications of this conclusion are very important to asset pricing (expected returns). The riskiest stock, with risk measured as standard deviation of returns, does not necessarily have the greatest expected return. Consider a biotech stock with one new drug product that is in clinical trials to determine its effectiveness. If it turns out that the drug is effective and safe, stock returns will be quite high. If, on the other hand, the subjects in the clinical trials are killed or otherwise harmed by the drug, the stock will fall to approximately zero and returns will be quite poor. This describes a stock with high standard deviation of returns (i.e., high total risk).

The high risk of our biotech stock, however, is primarily from firm-specific factors, so its unsystematic risk is high. Because market factors such as economic growth rates have little to do with the eventual outcome for this stock, systematic risk is a small proportion of the total risk of the stock. Capital market theory says that the equilibrium return on this stock may be less than that of a stock with much less firm-specific risk but more sensitivity to the factors that drive the return of the overall market. An established manufacturer of machine tools may not be a very risky investment in terms of total risk, but may have a greater sensitivity to market (systematic) risk factors (e.g., GDP growth rates) than our biotech stock. Given this scenario, the stock with more total risk (the biotech stock) has less systematic risk and will therefore have a lower equilibrium rate of return according to capital market theory.

Note that holding many biotech firms in a portfolio will diversify away the firm-specific risk. Some will have blockbuster products and some will fail, but you can imagine that when 50 or 100 such stocks are combined into a portfolio, the uncertainty about the portfolio return is much less than the uncertainty about the return of a single biotech firm stock.

To sum up, unsystematic risk is not compensated in equilibrium because it can be eliminated for free through diversification. Systematic risk is measured by the contribution of a security to the risk of a well-diversified portfolio, and the expected equilibrium return (required return) on an individual security will depend on its systematic risk.

LOS 44.d: Explain return generating models (including the market model) and their uses.

CFA® Program Curriculum, Volume 4, page 340

Return generating models are used to estimate the expected returns on risky securities based on specific factors. For each security, we must estimate the sensitivity of its returns to each specific factor. Factors that explain security returns can be classified as macroeconomic, fundamental, and statistical factors. **Multifactor models** most commonly use macroeconomic factors such as GDP growth, inflation, or consumer confidence, along with fundamental factors such as earnings, earnings growth, firm size, and research expenditures. Statistical factors often have no basis in finance theory and are suspect in that they may represent only relations for a specific time period which have been identified by data mining (repeated tests on a single data set).

The general form of a multifactor model with *k* factors is as follows:

$$E(R_i) - R_f = \beta_{i1} \times E(\text{Factor 1}) + \beta_{i2} \times E(\text{Factor 2}) + \dots + \beta_{ik} \times E(\text{Factor k})$$

This model states that the expected excess return (above the risk-free rate) for Asset *i* is the sum of each **factor sensitivity** or **factor loading** (the *β*s) for Asset *i* multiplied by the expected value of that factor for the period. The first factor is often the expected excess return on the market, $E(R_m - R_f)$.

One multifactor model that is often used is that of Fama and French. They estimated the sensitivity of security returns to three factors: firm size, firm book value to market value ratio, and the return on the market portfolio minus the risk-free rate (excess return on the market portfolio). Carhart suggests a fourth factor that measures price momentum using prior period returns. Together, these four factors do a relatively good job of explaining returns differences for U.S. equity securities over the period for which the model has been estimated.

The simplest factor model is a single-factor model. A single-factor model with the return on the market, R_m, as its only risk factor can be written (in excess returns form) as:

$$E(R_i) - R_f = \beta_i \times [E(R_m) - R_f]$$

Here, the expected excess return (return above the risk-free rate) is the product of the factor weight or factor sensitivity, Beta i, and the risk factor, which in this model is the excess return on the market portfolio or market index, so that this is also sometimes called a **single-index model**.

A simplified form of a single-index model is the **market model**, which is used to estimate a security's (or portfolio's) beta and to estimate a security's abnormal return (return above its expected return) based on the actual market return.

The form of the market model is as follows:

$$R_i = \alpha_i + \beta_i R_m + e_i$$

where:
R_i = Return on Asset i
R_m = Market return
β_i = Slope coefficient
α_i = Intercept
e_i = Abnormal return on Asset i

The intercept α_i and slope coefficient β_i are estimated from historical return data. We can require that α_i is the risk-free rate times $(1 - \beta_i)$ to be consistent with the general form of a single-index model in excess returns form.

The expected return on Asset i is $\alpha_i + \beta_i E(R_m)$. A deviation from the expected return in a given period is the abnormal return on Asset i, e_i, or $R_i - (\alpha_i + \beta_i R_m)$.

In the market model, the factor sensitivity or beta for Asset i is a measure of how sensitive the return on Asset i is to the return on the overall market portfolio (market index).

LOS 44.e: Calculate and interpret beta.

CFA® Program Curriculum, Volume 4, page 342

The sensitivity of an asset's return to the return on the market index in the context of the market model is referred to as its **beta**. Beta is a standardized measure of the covariance of the asset's return with the market return. Beta can be calculated as follows:

$$\beta_i = \frac{\text{covariance of Asset } i\text{'s return with the market return}}{\text{variance of the market return}} = \frac{\text{Cov}_{im}}{\sigma_m^2}$$

We can use the definition of the correlation between the returns on Asset i with the returns on the market index:

$$\rho_{im} = \frac{\text{Cov}_{im}}{\sigma_i \sigma_m}$$

to get $\text{Cov}_{im} = \rho_{im}\sigma_i\sigma_m$.

Substituting for Cov_{im} in the equation for B_i, we can also calculate beta as:

$$\beta_i = \frac{\rho_{im}\sigma_i\sigma_m}{\sigma_m^2} = \rho_{im}\frac{\sigma_i}{\sigma_m}$$

Example: Calculating an asset's beta

The standard deviation of the return on the market index is estimated as 20%.

1. If Asset A's standard deviation is 30% and its correlation of returns with the market index is 0.8, what is Asset A's beta?

   Using the formula $\beta_i = \rho_{im}\dfrac{\sigma_i}{\sigma_m}$, we have: $\beta_i = 0.80\left(\dfrac{0.30}{0.20}\right) = 1.2$.

2. If the covariance of Asset A's returns with the returns on the market index is 0.048, what is the beta of Asset A?

   Using the formula $\beta_i = \dfrac{\text{Cov}_{im}}{\sigma_m^2}$, we have $\beta_i = \dfrac{0.048}{0.2^2} = 1.2$.

 Professor's Note: Candidates should be prepared to calculate beta in either of the two ways in the example.

In practice, we estimate asset betas by regressing returns on the asset on those of the market index. While regression is a Level II concept, for our purposes, you can think of it as a mathematical estimation procedure that fits a line to a data plot. In Figure 5, we represent the excess returns on Asset i as the dependent variable and the excess returns on the market index as the independent variable. The *least squares regression line* is the line that minimizes the sum of the squared distances of the points plotted from the line (this is what is meant by the line of *best fit*). The slope of this line is our estimate of beta. In Figure 6, the line is steeper than 45 degrees, the slope is greater than one, and the asset's estimated beta is greater than one. Our interpretation is that the returns on Asset i are more variable in response to systematic risk factors than is the overall market, which has a beta of one.

Figure 6: Regression of Asset Excess Returns against Market Asset Returns

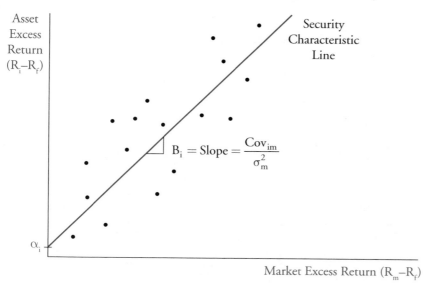

This regression line is referred to as the asset's **security characteristic line**. Mathematically, the slope of the security characteristic line is $\dfrac{Cov_{im}}{\sigma_m^2}$, which is the same formula we used earlier to calculate beta.

LOS 44.f: Explain the capital asset pricing model (CAPM), including the required assumptions, and the security market line (SML).

CFA® Program Curriculum, Volume 4, page 346

Given that the only relevant (priced) risk for an individual Asset i is measured by the covariance between the asset's returns and the returns on the market, $Cov_{i,mkt}$, we can plot the relationship between risk and return for individual assets using $Cov_{i,mkt}$ as our measure of systematic risk. The resulting line, plotted in Figure 7, is one version of what is referred to as the **security market line** (SML).

Figure 7: Security Market Line

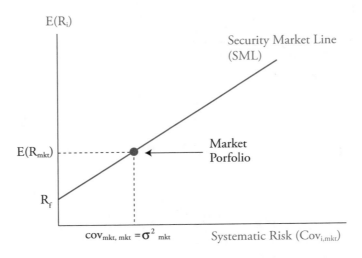

The equation of the SML is:

$$E(R_i) = RFR + \frac{E(R_{mkt}) - RFR}{\sigma^2_{mkt}}(Cov_{i,mkt})$$

which can be rearranged and stated as:

$$E(R_i) = RFR + \frac{Cov_{i,mkt}}{\sigma^2_{mkt}}[E(R_{mkt}) - RFR]$$

The line described by this last equation is presented in Figure 8, where we let the standardized covariance term, $\frac{Cov_{i,mkt}}{\sigma^2_{mkt}}$, be defined as beta, β_i.

This is the most common means of describing the SML, and this relation between beta (systematic risk) and expected return is known as the **capital asset pricing model** (CAPM).

Figure 8: The Capital Asset Pricing Model

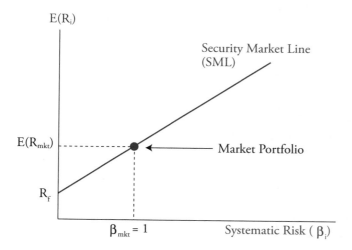

So, we can define beta, $\beta = \dfrac{Cov_{i,mkt}}{\sigma^2_{mkt}}$, as a standardized measure of systematic risk.

Beta measures the relation between a security's excess returns and the excess returns to the market portfolio.

Formally, the CAPM is stated as:

$$E(R_i) = R_f + \beta_i[E(R_{mkt}) - R_f]$$

The CAPM holds that, in equilibrium, the expected return on risky asset $E(R_i)$ is the risk-free rate (R_f) plus a beta-adjusted market risk premium, $\beta_i[E(R_{mkt}) - R_f]$. Beta measures systematic (market or covariance) risk.

Comparing the CML and the SML

It is important to recognize that the CML and SML are very different. Recall the equation of the CML:

$$E(R_P) = RFR + \sigma_P \left\{ \frac{\left[E(R_M) - RFR \right]}{\sigma_M} \right\}$$

The CML uses total risk = σ_p on the x-axis. Hence, only efficient portfolios will plot on the CML. On the other hand, the SML uses beta (systematic risk) on the x-axis. So in a CAPM world, *all properly priced securities and portfolios of securities will plot on the SML,* as shown in Figure 9.

Figure 9: Comparing the CML and the SML

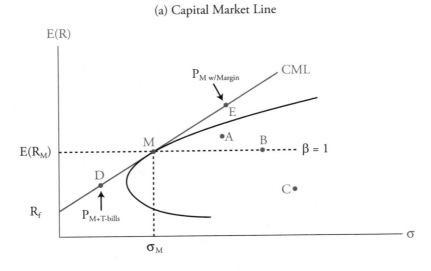

(a) Capital Market Line

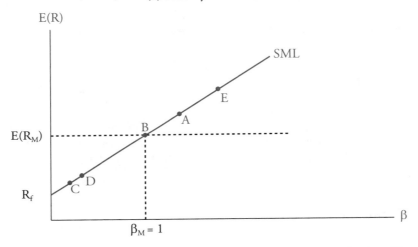

(b) Security Market Line

Portfolios that are not well diversified (efficient) plot inside the efficient frontier and are represented by risk-return combinations such as points A, B, and C in panel (a) of Figure 9. Individual securities are one example of such inefficient portfolios. According to the CAPM, the expected returns on all portfolios, well diversified or not, are determined by their systematic risk. Thus, according to the CAPM, Point A represents a high-beta stock or portfolio, Point B a stock or portfolio with a beta of one, and Point C a low-beta stock or portfolio. We know this because the expected return at Point B is equal to the expected return on the market, and the expected returns at Point A and C are greater and less than the expected return on the market (tangency) portfolio, respectively.

Note that a low-beta stock, such as represented by Point C, is not necessarily low-risk when total risk is considered. While its contribution to the risk of a well-diversified portfolio may be low, its risk when held by itself can be considered quite high. A firm whose only activity is developing a new, but as yet unproven, drug may be quite speculative with highly uncertain returns. It may also have quite low systematic risk if the uncertainty about its future returns depends primarily on firm-specific factors.

All stocks and portfolios that plot along the line labeled $\beta = 1$ in Figure 9 have the same expected return as the market portfolio and, thus, according to the CAPM, have the same systematic risk as the market portfolio (i.e., they all have betas of one).

All points on the CML (except the tangency point) represent the risk-return characteristics of portfolios formed by either combining the market portfolio with the risk-free asset or borrowing at the risk-free rate in order to invest more than 100% of the portfolio's net value in the risky market portfolio (investing on margin). Point D in Figure 8 represents a portfolio that combines the market portfolio with the risk-free asset, while points above the point of tangency, such as Point E, represent portfolios created by borrowing at the risk-free rate to invest in the market portfolio. Portfolios that do not lie on the CML are not efficient and therefore have risk that will not be rewarded with higher expected returns in equilibrium.

According to the CAPM, all securities and portfolios, diversified or not, will plot on the SML in equilibrium. In fact, all stocks and portfolios along the line labeled $\beta = 1$ in Figure 9, including the market portfolio, will plot at the same point on the SML. They will plot at the point on the SML with beta equal to one and expected return equal to the expected return on the market, regardless of their total risk.

LOS 44.g: Calculate and interpret the expected return of an asset using the CAPM.

CFA® Program Curriculum, Volume 4, page 349

The CAPM is one of the most fundamental concepts in investment theory. The CAPM is an equilibrium model that predicts the expected return on a stock, given the expected return on the market, the stock's beta coefficient, and the risk-free rate.

Example: Capital asset pricing model

The expected return on the market is 15%, the risk-free rate is 8%, and the beta for Stock A is 1.2. Compute the rate of return that would be expected (required) on this stock.

Answer:

$E(R_A) = 0.08 + 1.2 (0.15 - 0.08) = 0.164$

Note: $\beta_A > 1$, so $E(R_A) > E(R_{mkt})$

 Professor's Note: Know this calculation!

Example: Capital asset pricing model

The expected return on the market is 15%, the risk-free rate is 8%, and the beta for Stock B is 0.8. Compute the rate of return that would be expected (required) on this stock.

Answer:

$$E(R_B) = 0.08 + 0.8 (0.15 - 0.08) = 0.136$$

Note: Beta < 1 so $E(R_B) < E(R_{mkt})$

LOS 44.h: Describe and demonstrate applications of the CAPM and the SML.

CFA® Program Curriculum, Volume 4, page 351

We have used beta to estimate a security's expected return based on our estimate of the risk-free rate and the expected return on the market. In equilibrium, a security's expected return and its required return (by investors) are equal. Therefore, we can use the CAPM to estimate a security's required return, as in the following example.

Example: Using beta to estimate a required return

Acme, Inc., has a capital structure that is 40% debt and 60% equity. The expected return on the market is 12%, and the risk-free rate is 4%. What discount rate should an analyst use to calculate the NPV of a project with an equity beta of 0.9 if the firm's after-tax cost of debt is 5%?

Answer:

The required return on equity for this project is 0.04 + 0.9(0.12 − 0.04) = 11.2%.

The appropriate discount rate is a weighted average of the costs of debt and equity for this project, 0.4(5%) + 0.6(11.2%) = 8.72%.

Because the SML shows the equilibrium (required) return for any security or portfolio based on its beta (systematic risk), analysts often compare their forecast of a security's return to its required return based on its beta risk. The following example illustrates this technique.

Example: Identifying mispriced securities

The following figure contains information based on analyst's forecasts for three stocks. Assume a risk-free rate of 7% and a market return of 15%. Compute the expected and required return on each stock, determine whether each stock is undervalued, overvalued, or properly valued, and outline an appropriate trading strategy.

Forecast Data

Stock	Price Today	E(Price) in 1 Year	E(Dividend) in 1 Year	Beta
A	$25	$27	$1.00	1.0
B	40	45	2.00	0.8
C	15	17	0.50	1.2

Answer:

Expected and required returns computations are shown in the following figure.

Forecasts vs. Required Returns

Stock	Forecast Return	Required Return
A	($27 − $25 + $1) / $25 = 12.0%	0.07 + (1.0)(0.15 − 0.07) = 15.0%
B	($45 − $40 + $2) / $40 = 17.5%	0.07 + (0.8)(0.15 − 0.07) = 13.4%
C	($17 − $15 + $0.5) / $15 = 16.6%	0.07 + (1.2)(0.15 − 0.07) = 16.6%

- Stock A is *overvalued*. It is expected to earn 12%, but based on its systematic risk, it should earn 15%. It plots *below* the SML.
- Stock B is *undervalued*. It is expected to earn 17.5%, but based on its systematic risk, it should earn 13.4%. It plots *above* the SML.
- Stock C is *properly valued*. It is expected to earn 16.6%, and based on its systematic risk, it should earn 16.6%. It plots *on* the SML.

The appropriate trading strategy is:

- Short sell Stock A.
- Buy Stock B.
- Buy, sell, or ignore Stock C.

We can do this same analysis graphically. The expected return/beta combinations of all three stocks are graphed in the following figure relative to the SML.

Identifying Mispriced Securities

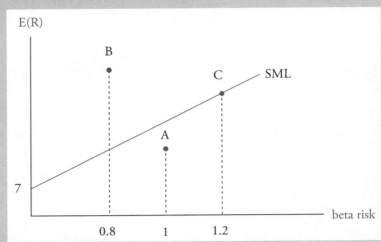

 Professor's Note: If the estimated return plots "over" the SML, the security is "under" valued. If the estimated return plots "under" the SML, the security is "over" valued.

Remember, all stocks should plot on the SML; any stock not plotting on the SML is mispriced. Notice that Stock A falls below the SML, Stock B lies above the SML, and Stock C is on the SML. If you plot a stock's expected return and it falls below the SML, the stock is overpriced. That is, the stock's expected return is too low given its systematic risk. If a stock plots above the SML, it is underpriced and is offering an expected return greater than required for its systematic risk. If it plots on the SML, the stock is properly priced.

Because the equation of the SML is the capital asset pricing model, you can determine if a stock is over- or underpriced graphically or mathematically. Your answers will always be the same.

When we evaluate the performance of a portfolio with risk that differs from that of a benchmark, we need to adjust the portfolio returns for the risk of the portfolio. There are several measures of risk-adjusted returns that are used to evaluate relative portfolio performance.

One such measure is the **Sharpe ratio** $\left(\dfrac{R_P - R_f}{\sigma_P} \right)$.

The Sharpe ratio of a portfolio is its *excess returns per unit of total portfolio risk*, and higher Sharpe ratios indicate better risk-adjusted portfolio performance. Note that this is a slope measure and, as illustrated in Figure 9, the Sharpe ratios of all portfolios along the CML are the same. Because the Sharpe ratio uses total risk, rather than systematic risk, it accounts for any unsystematic risk that the portfolio manager has taken. Note that the value of the Sharpe ratio is only useful for comparison with the Sharpe ratio of another portfolio.

In Figure 10, we illustrate that the Sharpe ratio is the slope of the CAL for the portfolio and can be compared to the slope of the CML, which is the Sharpe ratio for any portfolio along the CML.

Figure 10: Sharpe Ratios as Slopes

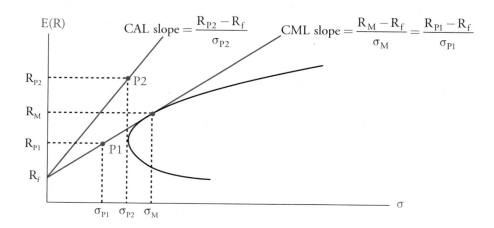

The **M-squared** (M^2) measure produces the same portfolio rankings as the Sharpe ratio but is stated in percentage terms. It is calculated as $(R_P - R_f)\dfrac{\sigma_M}{\sigma_P} - (R_M - R_f)$.

The intuition of this measure is that the first term is the excess return on a Portfolio P*, constructed by taking a leveraged position in Portfolio P so that P* has the same total risk, σ_M, as the market portfolio. As shown in Figure 11, the excess return on such a leveraged portfolio is greater than the return on the market portfolio by the vertical distance M^2.

Figure 11: M-squared for a Portfolio

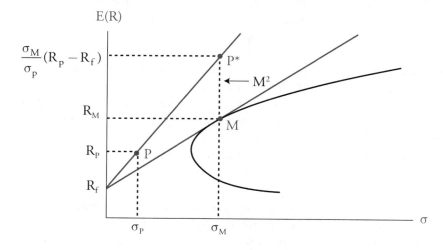

Two measures of risk-adjusted returns based on systematic risk (beta) rather than total risk are the **Treynor measure** and **Jensen's alpha**. They are similar to the Sharpe ratio and M^2 in that the Treynor measure is based on slope and Jensen's alpha is a measure of percentage returns in excess of those from a portfolio that has the same beta but lies on the SML.

The Treynor measure is calculated as $\dfrac{R_P - R_f}{\beta_P}$, interpreted as excess returns per unit of systematic risk, and represented by the slope of a line as illustrated in Figure 12. Jensen's alpha for Portfolio P is calculated as $\alpha_P = R_p - [R_f + \beta_p(R_M - R_f)]$ and is the percentage portfolio return above that of a portfolio (or security) with the same beta as the portfolio that lies on the SML, as illustrated in Figure 12.

Figure 12: Treynor Measure and Jensen's Alpha

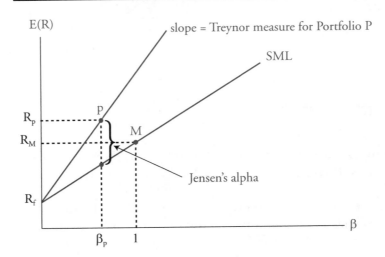

Whether risk adjustment should be based on total risk or systematic risk depends on whether a fund bears the nonsystematic risk of a manager's portfolio. If a single manager is used, then the total risk (including any nonsystematic risk) is the relevant measure and risk adjustment using total risk, as with the Sharpe and M^2 measures, is appropriate. If a fund uses multiple managers so that the overall fund portfolio is well diversified (has no nonsystematic risk), then performance measures based on systematic (beta) risk, such as the Treynor measure and Jensen's alpha, are appropriate.

These measures of risk-adjusted returns are often used to compare the performance of actively managed funds to passively managed funds. Note in Figures 9 and 10 that portfolios that lie above the CML have Sharpe ratios greater than those of any portfolios along the CML and have positive M^2 measures. Similarly, in Figure 11, we can see that portfolios that lie above the SML have Treynor measures greater than those of any security or portfolio that lies along the SML and also have positive values for Jensen's alpha.

One final note of caution is that estimating the values needed to apply these theoretical models and performance measures is often difficult and is done with error. The expected return on the market, and thus the market risk premium, may not be equal to its average historical value. Estimating security and portfolio betas is done with error as well.

KEY CONCEPTS

LOS 44.a
The availability of a risk-free asset allows investors to build portfolios with superior risk-return properties. By combining a risk-free asset with a portfolio of risky assets, the overall risk and return can be adjusted to appeal to investors with various degrees of risk aversion.

LOS 44.b
On a graph of return versus risk, the various combinations of a risky asset and the risk-free asset form the capital allocation line (CAL). In the specific case where the risky asset is the market portfolio, the combinations of the risky asset and the risk-free asset form the capital market line (CML).

LOS 44.c
Systematic (market) risk is due to factors, such as GDP growth and interest rate changes, that affect the values of all risky securities. Systematic risk cannot be reduced by diversification. Unsystematic (firm-specific) risk can be reduced by portfolio diversification.

Because one of the assumptions underlying the CAPM is that portfolio diversification to eliminate unsystematic risk is costless, investors cannot increase expected equilibrium portfolio returns by taking on unsystematic risk.

LOS 44.d
A return generating model is an equation that estimates the expected return of an investment, based on a security's exposure to one or more macroeconomic, fundamental, or statistical factors.

The simplest return generating model is the market model, which assumes the return on an asset is related to the return on the market portfolio in the following manner:

$$R_i = \alpha_i + \beta_i R_m + e_i$$

LOS 44.e
Beta can be calculated using the following equation:

$$\beta_i = \frac{[Cov(R_i, R_m)]}{\sigma_m^2} = \frac{\rho_{i,m}\sigma_i}{\sigma_m}$$

where $[Cov(R_i, R_m)]$ and $\rho_{i,m}$ are the covariance and correlation between the asset and the market, and σ_i and σ_m are the standard deviations of asset returns and market returns.

The theoretical average beta of stocks in the market is 1. A beta of zero indicates that a security's return is uncorrelated with the returns of the market.

LOS 44.f
The capital asset pricing model (CAPM) requires several assumptions:
- Investors are risk averse, utility maximizing, and rational.
- Markets are free of frictions like costs and taxes.
- All investors plan using the same time period.
- All investors have the same expectations of security returns.
- Investments are infinitely divisible.
- Prices are unaffected by an investor's trades.

The security market line (SML) is a graphical representation of the CAPM that plots expected return versus beta for any security.

LOS 44.g
The CAPM relates expected return to the market factor (beta) using the following formula:

$$E(R_i) - R_f = \beta_i [E(R_m) - R_f]$$

LOS 44.h
The CAPM and the SML indicate what a security's equilibrium required rate of return should be based on the security's exposure to market risk. An analyst can compare his expected rate of return on a security to the required rate of return indicated by the SML to determine whether the security is overvalued, undervalued, or properly valued.

The Sharpe ratio measures excess return per unit of total risk and is useful for comparing portfolios on a risk-adjusted basis. The M-squared measure provides the same portfolio rankings as the Sharpe ratio but is stated in percentage terms:

$$\text{Sharpe ratio} = \left(\frac{R_P - R_f}{\sigma_P} \right)$$

$$\text{M-squared} = (R_P - R_f)\frac{\sigma_M}{\sigma_P} - (R_M - R_f)$$

The Treynor measure measures a portfolio's excess return per unit of systematic risk. Jensen's alpha is the difference between a portfolio's return and the return of a portfolio on the SML that has the same beta:

$$\text{Treynor measure} = \frac{R_P - R_f}{\beta_P}$$

$$\text{Jensen's alpha} = \alpha_P = R_P - [R_f + \beta_P(R_M - R_f)]$$

CONCEPT CHECKERS

1. An investor put 60% of his portfolio into a risky asset offering a 10% return with a standard deviation of returns of 8% and put the balance of his portfolio in a risk-free asset offering 5%. What is the expected return and standard deviation of his portfolio?

	Expected return	Standard deviation
A.	6.0%	6.8%
B.	8.0%	4.8%
C.	10.0%	6.6%

2. What is the risk measure associated with the capital market line (CML)?
    A. Beta risk.
    B. Unsystematic risk.
    C. Total risk.

3. A portfolio to the right of the market portfolio on the CML is:
    A. a lending portfolio.
    B. a borrowing portfolio.
    C. an inefficient portfolio.

4. As the number of stocks in a portfolio increases, the portfolio's systematic risk:
    A. can increase or decrease.
    B. decreases at a decreasing rate.
    C. decreases at an increasing rate.

5. Total risk equals:
    A. unique plus diversifiable risk.
    B. market plus nondiversifiable risk.
    C. systematic plus unsystematic risk.

6. A return generating model is *least likely* to be based on a security's exposure to:
    A. statistical factors.
    B. macroeconomic factors
    C. fundamental factors.

7. The covariance of the market's returns with a stock's returns is 0.005 and the standard deviation of the market's returns is 0.05. What is the stock's beta?
    A. 1.0.
    B. 1.5.
    C. 2.0.

8. The covariance of the market's returns with the stock's returns is 0.008. The standard deviation of the market's returns is 0.08, and the standard deviation of the stock's returns is 0.11. What is the correlation coefficient of the returns of the stock and the returns of the market?
    A. 0.91.
    B. 1.00.
    C. 1.25.

9.   According to the CAPM, what is the expected rate of return for a stock with a
       beta of 1.2, when the risk-free rate is 6% and the market rate of return is 12%?
       A. 7.2%.
       B. 12.0%.
       C. 13.2%.

10.   According to the CAPM, what is the required rate of return for a stock with a
       beta of 0.7, when the risk-free rate is 7% and the expected market rate of return
       is 14%?
       A. 11.9%.
       B. 14.0%.
       C. 16.8%.

11.   The risk-free rate is 6%, and the expected market return is 15%. A stock with a
       beta of 1.2 is selling for $25 and will pay a $1 dividend at the end of the year. If
       the stock is priced at $30 at year-end, it is:
       A. overpriced, so short it.
       B. underpriced, so buy it.
       C. underpriced, so short it.

12.   A stock with a beta of 0.7 currently priced at $50 is expected to increase in price
       to $55 by year-end and pay a $1 dividend. The expected market return is 15%,
       and the risk-free rate is 8%. The stock is:
       A. overpriced, so do not buy it.
       B. underpriced, so buy it.
       C. properly priced, so buy it.

13.   Which of the following statements about the SML and the CML is *least
       accurate*?
       A. Securities that plot above the SML are undervalued.
       B. Investors expect to be compensated for systematic risk.
       C. Securities that plot on the SML have no value to investors.

ANSWERS – CONCEPT CHECKERS

1. **B**   Expected return: $(0.60 \times 0.10) + (0.40 \times 0.05) = 0.08$, or 8.0%.

   Standard deviation: $0.60 \times 0.08 = 0.048$, or 4.8%.

2. **C**   The capital market line (CML) plots return against *total risk* which is measured by standard deviation of returns.

3. **B**   A portfolio to the right of a portfolio on the CML has more risk than the market portfolio. Investors seeking to take on more risk will *borrow* at the risk-free rate to purchase more of the market portfolio.

4. **A**   When you increase the number of stocks in a portfolio, *unsystematic risk* will decrease at a decreasing rate. However, the portfolio's *systematic risk* can be increased by adding higher-beta stocks or decreased by adding lower-beta stocks.

5. **C**   Total risk equals systematic plus unsystematic risk. Unique risk is diversifiable and is unsystematic. Market (systematic) risk is nondiversifiable risk.

6 **A**   Macroeconomic, fundamental, and statistical factor exposures can be included in a return generating model to estimate the expected return of an investment. However, statistical factors may not have any theoretical basis, so analysts prefer macroeconomic and fundamental factor models.

7. **C**   Beta = covariance / market variance

   Market variance = $0.05^2 = 0.0025$

   Beta = $0.005 / 0.0025 = 2.0$

8. **A** $\rho_{1,2} = \dfrac{\text{Cov}_{1,2}}{\sigma_1 \sigma_2} = \dfrac{0.008}{(0.08)(0.11)} = 0.909$

9. **C** $6 + 1.2(12 - 6) = 13.2\%$

10. **A** $7 + 0.7(14 - 7) = 11.9\%$

11. **B**   Required rate = $6 + 1.2(15 - 6) = 16.8\%$

   Return on stock = $(30 - 25 + 1) / 25 = 24\%$

   Based on risk, the stock plots above the SML and is underpriced, so buy it.

12. **A**   Required rate = $8 + 0.7(15 - 8) = 12.9\%$

   Return on stock = $(55 - 50 + 1) / 50 = 12\%$

   The stock falls below the SML so it is *overpriced*.

13. **C**   Securities that plot on the SML are expected to earn their equilibrium rate of return and, therefore, do have value to an investor and may have diversification benefits as well. The other statements are true.

BASICS OF PORTFOLIO PLANNING AND CONSTRUCTION

Study Session 12

EXAM FOCUS

There is nothing difficult here, but the material is important because it is the foundation for the portfolio construction material at Level II and especially Level III. You should be ready to explain why investment policy statements are created and what their major components are. You should be familiar with the objectives (risk and return) and the constraints: liquidity, legal, time horizon, tax treatment, and unique circumstances. Know the difference between ability and willingness to take risk, the factors that define an asset class, and how asset allocation is used in constructing portfolios.

LOS 45.a: Describe the reasons for a written investment policy statement (IPS).

CFA® Program Curriculum, Volume 4, page 376

An investment manager is very unlikely to produce a good result for a client without understanding that client's needs, circumstances, and constraints.

A written **investment policy statement** will typically begin with the investor's goals in terms of risk and return. These should be determined jointly, as the goals of high returns and low risk (while quite popular) are likely to be mutually exclusive in practice. Investor expectations in terms of returns must be compatible with investor's tolerance for risk (uncertainty about portfolio performance).

LOS 45.b: Describe the major components of an IPS.

CFA® Program Curriculum, Volume 4, page 377

The major components of an IPS typically address the following:

- *Description of Client* circumstances, situation, and investment objectives.
- *Statement of the Purpose* of the IPS.
- *Statement of Duties and Responsibilities* of investment manager, custodian of assets, and the client.
- *Procedures* to update IPS and to respond to various possible situations.
- *Investment Objectives* derived from communications with the client.
- *Investment Constraints* that must be considered in the plan.
- *Investment Guidelines* such as how the policy will be executed, asset types permitted, and leverage to be used.
- *Evaluation of Performance,* the benchmark portfolio for evaluating investment performance, and other information on evaluation of investment results.

- *Appendices* containing information on strategic (baseline) asset allocation and permitted deviations from policy portfolio allocations, as well as how and when the portfolio allocations should be rebalanced.

In any case, the IPS will, at a minimum, contain a clear statement of client circumstances and constraints, an investment strategy based on these, and some benchmark against which to evaluate the account performance.

LOS 45.c: Describe risk and return objectives and how they may be developed for a client.

CFA® Program Curriculum, Volume 4, page 377

The **risk objectives** in an IPS may take several forms. An **absolute risk objective** might be to "have no decrease in portfolio value during any 12-month period" or to "not decrease in value by more than 2% at any point over any 12-month period." Low absolute percentage risk objectives such as these may result in portfolios made up of securities that offer guaranteed returns (e.g., U.S. Treasury bills).

Absolute risk objectives can also be stated in terms of the probability of specific portfolio results, either percentage losses or dollar losses, rather than strict limits on portfolio results. Examples are as follows:

- "No greater than a 5% probability of returns below −5% in any 12-month period."
- "No greater than a 4% probability of a loss of more than $20,000 over any 12-month period."

An absolute return objective may be stated in nominal terms, such as "an overall return of at least 6% per annum," or in real returns, such as "a return of 3% more than the annual inflation rate each year."

Relative risk objectives relate to a specific benchmark and can also be strict, such as, "Returns will not be less than 12-month euro LIBOR over any 12-month period," or stated in terms of probability, such as, "No greater than a 5% probability of returns more than 4% below the return on the MSCI World Index over any 12-month period."

Return objectives can be relative to a benchmark portfolio return, such as, "Exceed the return on the S&P 500 Index by 2% per annum." For a bank, the return objective may be relative to the bank's cost of funds (deposit rate). While it is possible for an institution to use returns on peer portfolios, such as an endowment with a stated objective to be in the top quartile of endowment fund returns, peer performance benchmarks suffer from not being *investable* portfolios. There is no way to match this investment return by portfolio construction before the fact.

In any event, the account manager must make sure that the stated risk and return objectives are compatible, given the reality of expected investment results and uncertainty over time.

LOS 45.d: Distinguish between the willingness and the ability (capacity) to take risk in analyzing an investor's financial risk tolerance.

CFA® Program Curriculum, Volume 4, page 379

An investor's **ability to bear risk** depends on financial circumstances. Longer investment horizons (20 years rather than 2 years), greater assets versus liabilities (more wealth), more insurance against unexpected occurrences, and a secure job all suggest a greater ability to bear investment risk in terms of uncertainty about periodic investment performance.

An investor's **willingness to bear risk** is based primarily on the investor's attitudes and beliefs about investments (various asset types). The assessment of an investor's attitude about risk is quite subjective and is sometimes done with a short questionnaire that attempts to categorize the investor's risk aversion or risk tolerance.

When the adviser's assessments of an investor's ability and willingness to take investment risk are compatible, there is no real problem selecting an appropriate level of investment risk. If the investor's willingness to take on investment risk is high but the investor's ability to take on risk is low, the low ability to take on investment risk will prevail in the adviser's assessment.

In situations where ability is high but willingness is low, the adviser may attempt to educate the investor about investment risk and correct any misconceptions that may be contributing to the investor's low stated willingness to take on investment risk. However, the adviser's job is not to change the investor's personality characteristics that contribute to a low willingness to take on investment risk. The approach will most likely be to conform to the lower of the investor's ability or willingness to bear risk, as constructing a portfolio with a level of risk that the client is clearly uncomfortable with will not likely lead to a good outcome in the investor's view.

LOS 45.e: Describe the investment constraints of liquidity, time horizon, tax concerns, legal and regulatory factors, and unique circumstances and their implications for the choice of portfolio assets.

CFA® Program Curriculum, Volume 4, page 384

Professor's Note: When I was studying for the CFA exams over 20 years ago, we memorized R-R-T-T-L-L-U as a checklist for addressing the important points of portfolio construction, and it still works today. Then, as now, the important points to cover in an IPS were Risk, Return, Time horizon, Tax situation, Liquidity, Legal restrictions, and the Unique constraints of a specific investor.

Investment constraints include the investor's liquidity needs, time horizon, tax considerations, legal and regulatory constraints, and unique needs and preferences.

Liquidity: Liquidity refers to the ability to turn investment assets into spendable cash in a short period of time without having to make significant price concessions to do so. Investor needs for money to pay tuition, to pay for a parent's assisted living expenses, or to fund other possible spending needs may all require that some liquid assets be held. As we noted in an earlier topic review discussing property and casualty insurance companies, claims arrive unpredictably to some extent and therefore their portfolios must hold a significant proportion of liquid (or maturing) securities in order to be prepared to honor these claims. Illiquid investments in hedge funds and private equity funds, which typically are not traded and have restrictions on redemptions, are not suitable for an investor who may unexpectedly need access to the funds.

Time horizon: In general, the longer an investor's time horizon, the more risk and less liquidity the investor can accept in the portfolio. While the expected returns on a broad equities portfolio may not be too risky for an investor with a 20-year investment horizon, they likely are too risky for an investor who must fund a large purchase at the end of this year. For such an investor, government securities or a bank certificate of deposit may be the most appropriate investments because of their low risk and high liquidity at the time when the funds will be needed.

Tax situation: Besides an individual's overall tax rate, the tax treatment of various types of investment accounts is also a consideration in portfolio construction. For a fully taxable account, investors subject to higher tax rates may prefer tax-free bonds (U.S.) to taxable bonds or prefer equities that are expected to produce capital gains, which are often taxed at a lower rate than other types of income. A focus on expected after-tax returns over time in relation to risk should correctly account for differences in tax treatments as well as investors' overall tax rates.

Some types of investment accounts, such as retirement accounts, may be tax exempt or tax deferred. Investors with such accounts may choose to put securities that generate fully taxed income, such as corporate bond interest, in accounts that are tax deferred, while seeking long-term capital gains, tax-exempt interest income, and dividend income (in jurisdictions where dividends receive preferential tax treatment) in their personal accounts, which have no tax deferral benefit.

Legal and regulatory: In addition to financial market regulations that apply to all investors, more specific legal and regulatory constraints may apply to particular investors. Trust, corporate, and qualified investment accounts may all be restricted by law from investing in particular types of securities and assets. There may also be restrictions on percentage allocations to specific types of investments in such accounts. Corporate officers and directors face legal restrictions on trading in the securities of their firms that the account manager should be aware of.

Unique circumstances: Each investor, whether individual or institutional, may have specific preferences or restrictions on which securities and assets may be purchased for the account. Ethical preferences, such as prohibiting investment in securities issued by tobacco or firearms producers, are not uncommon. Restrictions on investments in companies or countries where human rights abuses are suspected or documented would also fall into this category. Religious preferences may preclude investment in securities that make explicit interest payments. Unique investor preferences may also be based on diversification needs when the investor's income depends heavily on the prospects for one company or industry. An investor who has founded or runs a company may not want any investment in securities issued by a competitor to that company.

LOS 45.f: Explain the specification of asset classes in relation to asset allocation.

CFA® Program Curriculum, Volume 4, page 391

After having determined the investor objectives and constraints through the exercise of creating an IPS, a **strategic asset allocation** is developed which specifies the percentage allocations to the included asset classes. In choosing which asset classes to consider when developing the strategic asset allocation for the account, the correlations of returns *within* an asset class should be relatively high, indicating that the assets within the class are similar in their investment performance. On the other hand, it is low correlations of returns *between* asset classes that leads to risk reduction through portfolio diversification.

Historically, only the broad categories of equities, bonds, cash, and real estate were considered. More recently, a group of several investable asset classes, referred to collectively as alternative investments, has gained more prominence. Alternative investment asset classes include hedge funds of various types, private equity funds, managed or passively constructed commodity funds, artwork, and intellectual property rights.

We can further divide equities by whether the issuing companies are domestic or foreign, large or small, or whether they are traded in emerging or developed markets. An example of specifying asset classes is world equities. A U.S. investor may want to divide world equities into different regions. Figure 1 shows the correlation matrix, annualized returns, and volatilities among four different regions and the United States.

Figure 1: World Equities Asset Class Correlation Matrix
Monthly Index Returns from MSCI Price Returns
10 Year Period from June 28, 2001, to June 29, 2012

	1	2	3	4	5
1. MSCI USA	1.00				
2. MSCI Emerging Markets Europe	0.74	1.00			
3. MSCI Emerging Markets Asia	0.79	0.80	1.00		
4. MSCI Emerging Markets Latin America	0.79	0.85	0.82	1.00	
5. MSCI Frontier Markets Africa	0.35	0.41	0.33	0.34	1.00
Annualized Volatility	15.86%	32.52%	24.54%	28.65%	27.47%
Annualized Return	3.44%	11.20%	9.31%	17.01%	9.33%

Source: www.msci.com/products/indices/

With bonds, we can divide the overall universe of bonds into asset classes based on maturities or on criteria such as whether they are foreign or domestic, government or corporate, or investment grade or speculative (high yield). Overall, the asset classes considered should approximate the universe of permissible investments specified in the IPS.

Once the universe of asset classes has been specified, the investment manager will collect data on the returns, standard deviation of returns, and correlations of returns with those of other asset classes for each asset class.

Figure 2 illustrates the strategic asset allocation for a pension fund.

Figure 2: Strategic Asset Allocation

The Vermont Pension Investment Committee manages about $3 billion in retirement assets for various teachers and state and municipal employees in that state. VPIC's investment policy specifies the following strategic asset allocation:

Asset Class	Target
Cash	0.0%
U.S. large-cap equity	11.0%
U.S. small-/mid-cap equity	6.5%
Established international equity	10.0%
Emerging market equity	6.0%
U.S. bonds	18.0%
Global bonds	3.0%
High-yield bonds	6.0%
Emerging market debt	5.0%
Inflation-protected bonds	3.0%
Real estate	4.5%
Hedge funds	5.0%
Private equity	0.0%
Commodities	2.0%
Global asset allocation and other	20.0%
	100%

Source: State of Vermont, Office of the State Treasurer. Target allocation as of March 31, 2012. www.vermonttreasurer.gov/pension-funds.

LOS 45.g: Discuss the principles of portfolio construction and the role of asset allocation in relation to the IPS.

CFA® Program Curriculum, Volume 4, page 391

Once the portfolio manager has identified the investable asset classes for the portfolio and the risk, return, and correlation characteristics of each asset class, an *efficient frontier*,

Study Session 12
Cross-Reference to CFA Institute Assigned Reading #45 – Basics of Portfolio Planning and Construction

Study Session 12

analogous to one constructed from individual securities, can be constructed using a computer program. By combining the return and risk objectives from the IPS with the actual risk and return properties of the many portfolios along the efficient frontier, the manager can identify that portfolio which best meets the risk and return requirements of the investor. The asset allocation for the efficient portfolio selected is then the strategic asset allocation for the portfolio.

So far, we have not concerned ourselves with deviations from strategic asset allocations or with selection of individual securities within individual asset classes. These activities are referred to as active (versus passive) portfolio management strategies. A manager who varies from strategic asset allocation weights in order to take advantage of perceived short-term opportunities is adding **tactical asset allocation** to the portfolio strategy. **Security selection** refers to deviations from index weights on individual securities within an asset class. For example, a portfolio manager might overweight energy stocks and underweight financial stocks, relative to the index weights for U.S. large-cap equities as an asset class. For some asset classes, such as hedge funds, individual real estate properties, and artwork, investable indexes are not available. For these asset classes, selection of individual assets is required by the nature of the asset class.

While each of these active strategies may produce higher returns, they each also increase the risk of the portfolio compared to a passive portfolio of asset class indexes. A practice known as **risk budgeting** sets an overall risk limit for the portfolio and budgets (allocates) a portion of the permitted risk to the systematic risk of the strategic asset allocation, the risk from tactical asset allocation, and the risk from security selection.

Active portfolio management has two specific issues to consider.

1. An investor may have multiple managers actively managing to the same benchmark for the same asset class (or may have significant benchmark overlap). In this case, one manager may overweight an index stock while another may underweight the same stock. Taken together, there is no net active management risk, although each manager has reported active management risk. Overall, the risk budget is underutilized as there is less net active management than gross active management.

2. When all managers are actively managing portfolios relative to an index, trading may be excessive overall. This extra trading could have negative tax consequences, specifically potentially higher capital gains taxes, compared to an overall efficient tax strategy.

One way to address these issues is to use a **core-satellite approach**. The core-satellite approach invests the majority, or core, portion of the portfolio in passively managed indexes and invests a smaller, or satellite, portion in active strategies. This approach reduces the likelihood of excessive trading and offsetting active positions.

Clearly, the success of security selection will depend on the manager's skill and the opportunities (mispricings or inefficiencies) within a particular asset class. Similarly, the success of tactical asset allocation will depend both on the existence of short-term opportunities in specific asset classes and on the manager's ability to identify them.

KEY CONCEPTS

LOS 45.a

A written investment policy statement, the first step in the portfolio management process, is a plan for achieving investment success. An IPS forces investment discipline and ensures that goals are realistic by requiring investors to articulate their circumstances, objectives, and constraints.

LOS 45.b

Many IPS include the following sections:

- Introduction—Describes the client.
- Statement of Purpose—The intentions of the IPS.
- Statement of Duties and Responsibilities—Of the client, the asset custodian, and the investment managers.
- Procedures—Related to keeping the IPS updated and responding to unforeseen events.
- Investment Objectives—The client's investment needs, specified in terms of required return and risk tolerance.
- Investment Constraints—Factors that may hinder the ability to meet investment objectives; typically categorized as time horizon, taxes, liquidity, legal and regulatory, and unique needs.
- Investment Guidelines—For example, whether leverage, derivatives, or specific kinds of assets are allowed.
- Evaluation and Review—Related to feedback on investment results.
- Appendices—May specify the portfolio's strategic asset allocation (policy portfolio) or the portfolio's rebalancing policy.

LOS 45.c

Risk objectives are specifications for portfolio risk that are developed to embody a client's risk tolerance. Risk objectives can be either absolute (e.g., no losses greater than 10% in any year) or relative (e.g., annual return will be within 2% of FTSE return).

Return objectives are typically based on an investor's desire to meet a future financial goal, such as a particular level of income in retirement. Return objectives can be absolute (e.g., 9% annual return) or relative (e.g., outperform the S&P 500 by 2% per year).

The achievability of an investor's return expectations may be hindered by the investor's risk objectives.

LOS 45.d

Willingness to take financial risk is related to an investor's psychological factors, such as personality type and level of financial knowledge.

Ability or capacity to take risk depends on financial factors, such as wealth relative to liabilities, income stability, and time horizon.

A client's overall risk tolerance depends on both his ability to take risk and his willingness to take risk. A willingness greater than ability, or vice versa, is typically resolved by choosing the more conservative of the two and counseling the client.

Study Session 12
Cross-Reference to CFA Institute Assigned Reading #45 – Basics of Portfolio Planning and Construction

Study Session 12

LOS 45.e

Investment constraints include:

- Liquidity—The need to draw cash from the portfolio for anticipated or unexpected future spending needs. High liquidity needs often translate to a high portfolio allocation to bonds or cash.
- Time horizon—Often the period over which assets are accumulated and before withdrawals begin. Risky or illiquid investments may be inappropriate for an investor with a short time horizon.
- Tax considerations—Concerns the tax treatments of the investor's various accounts, the relative tax treatment of capital gains and income, and the investor's marginal tax bracket.
- Legal and regulatory—Constraints such as government restrictions on portfolio contents or laws against insider trading.
- Unique circumstances—Restrictions due to investor preferences (religious, ethical, etc.) or other factors not already considered.

LOS 45.f

An asset class is a group of securities with similar risk and performance characteristics. Examples of major asset classes include equity, fixed income, cash, and real estate. Portfolio managers also use more narrowly defined asset classes, such as large-cap U.S. equities or speculative international bonds, and alternative asset classes, such as commodities or investments in hedge funds.

LOS 45.g

Strategic asset allocation is a set of percentage allocations to various asset classes that is designed to meet the investor's objectives. The strategic asset allocation is developed by combining the objectives and constraints in the IPS with the performance expectations of the various asset classes. The strategic asset allocation provides the basic structure of a portfolio.

Tactical asset allocation refers to an allocation that deviates from the baseline (strategic) allocation in order to profit from a forecast of shorter-term opportunities in specific asset classes.

CONCEPT CHECKERS

1. The investment policy statement is *most accurately* considered the:
    A. starting point of the portfolio management process.
    B. key intermediate step in the portfolio management process.
    C. end product of the portfolio management process.

2. The component of an investment policy statement that defines the investment objectives is *most likely* to include information about:
    A. the investor's risk tolerance.
    B. unique needs and preferences of the investor.
    C. permitted asset types and use of leverage in the investment account.

3. A client exhibits an above-average willingness to take risk but a below-average ability to take risk. When assigning an overall risk tolerance, the investment adviser is *most likely* to assess the client's overall risk tolerance as:
    A. above average.
    B. average.
    C. below average.

4. Which of the following is *least likely* an example of a portfolio constraint?
    A. Higher tax rate on dividend income than on capital gains.
    B. Significant spending requirements in the near future.
    C. Minimum total return requirement of 8%.

5. In determining the appropriate asset allocation for a client's investment account, the manager should:
    A. consider only the investor's risk tolerance.
    B. incorporate forecasts of future economic conditions.
    C. consider the investor's risk tolerance and future needs, but not forecasts of market conditions.

ANSWERS – CONCEPT CHECKERS

1. **A**   An investment policy statement is considered to be the starting point of the portfolio management process. The IPS is a plan for achieving investment success.

2. **A**   Investment objectives are defined based on both the investor's return requirements and risk tolerance. Investment constraints include the investor's time horizon, liquidity needs, tax considerations, legal and regulatory requirements, and unique needs and preferences. Policies regarding permitted asset types and the amount of leverage to use are best characterized as investment guidelines.

3. **C**   When assigning an overall risk tolerance, the prudent approach is to use the lower of ability to take risk and willingness to take risk.

4. **C**   Return objectives are part of a policy statement's objectives, not constraints.

5. **B**   An adviser's forecasts of the expected returns and expected volatilities (risk) of different asset classes are an important part of determining an appropriate asset allocation.

6 questions: 9 minutes

1. Which of the following activities is *most likely* to be performed as part of the execution step of the portfolio management process?
    A. Completion of the investment policy statement.
    B. Top-down analysis based on macroeconomic conditions.
    C. Rebalancing the portfolio to the desired asset class exposures.

2. A manager who evaluates portfolios' investment performance adjusted for systematic risk is *most likely* to rank portfolios based on their:
    A. Sharpe ratios.
    B. Treynor measures.
    C. M-squared measures.

3. According to the capital asset pricing model:
    A. an investor who is risk averse should hold at least some of the risk-free asset in his portfolio.
    B. a stock with high risk, measured as standard deviation of returns, will have high expected returns in equilibrium.
    C. all investors who take on risk will hold the same risky-asset portfolio.

4. Beta is *best* described as the:
    A. slope of the security market line.
    B. correlation of returns with those of the market portfolio.
    C. covariance of returns with the market portfolio expressed in terms of the variance of market returns.

5. According to Markowitz portfolio theory:
    A. combining any two risky assets in a portfolio will reduce unsystematic risk compared to a portfolio holding only one of the two risky assets.
    B. adding a risky stock to a (less risky) bond portfolio can decrease portfolio risk.
    C. a portfolio with the minimum risk for its level of expected return lies on the efficient frontier.

6. An analyst has estimated that the returns for an asset, conditional on the performance of the overall economy, are:

Return	Probability	Economic Growth
5%	20%	Poor
10%	40%	Average
14%	40%	Good

The conditional expected returns on the market portfolio are:

Return	Probability	Economic Growth
2%	20%	Poor
10%	40%	Average
15%	40%	Good

According to the CAPM, if the risk-free rate is 5% and the risky asset has a beta of 1.1, with respect to the market portfolio, the analyst should:

A. sell (or sell short) the risky asset because its expected return is less than equilibrium expected return on the market portfolio.

B. buy the risky asset because the analyst expects the return on it to be higher than its required return in equilibrium.

C. sell (or sell short) the risky asset because its expected return is not sufficient to compensate for its systematic risk.

Self-Test Answers: Portfolio Management

1. **B** The execution step of the portfolio management process typically begins with a top-down analysis of economic variables. The investment policy statement is completed during the planning step. Asset class rebalancing is part of the feedback step.

2. **B** The Treynor measure is stated in terms of systematic (beta) risk. The Sharpe ratio and M-squared measure are defined in terms of total risk (standard deviation).

3. **C** One of the assumptions of the CAPM is that all investors who hold risky assets will hold the same portfolio of risky assets (the market portfolio). Risk aversion means an investor will accept more risk only if compensated with a higher expected return. In capital market theory all investors exhibit risk aversion, even an investor who is short the risk-free asset. In the CAPM, a stock's risk is measured as its beta, not its standard deviation of returns.

4. **C** A stock or portfolio's beta is its covariance with the returns of the market portfolio divided by the variance of the market portfolio.

5. **B** Because bond and stock returns are less than perfectly positively correlated, adding some of a stock to a bond portfolio will initially decrease the total portfolio risk. If two risky assets have returns that are perfectly positively correlated and have the same total risk, there is no risk-reduction benefit to combining the two. The efficient frontier consists of portfolios that have the greatest expected return for a given level of risk.

6. **C** The analyst's forecast of the expected return on the risky asset is 5(0.2) + 10(0.4) + 14(0.4) = 10.6%. The expected/equilibrium return on the market portfolio is 2(0.2) + 10(0.4) + 15(0.4) = 10.4%. The CAPM equilibrium expected return (required return in equilibrium) on the risky asset is 5 + 1.1(10.4 − 5) = 10.94%. Because the analyst's forecast return on the risky asset is less than its required return in equilibrium, the asset is overpriced and the analyst would sell if he owned it and possibly sell it short.

The following is a review of the Equity: Market Organization, Market Indices, and Market Efficiency principles designed to address the learning outcome statements set forth by CFA Institute. This topic is also covered in:

MARKET ORGANIZATION AND STRUCTURE

Study Session 13

EXAM FOCUS

There is a great deal of introductory material in this review. Almost all of the types of securities discussed are covered in detail elsewhere in the curriculum. We introduce the terminology you will need but leave many of the details to the topic reviews specific to each security type. You should understand the concept of purchasing stock on margin and be able to calculate the return on an investment using margin. Be able to differentiate between market and limit orders as well as between quote-driven, order-driven, and brokered markets. Know that market regulation should increase informational, allocational, and operational market efficiency.

LOS 46.a: Explain the main functions of the financial system.

CFA® Program Curriculum, Volume 5, page 6

The three main functions of the financial system are to:

1. Allow entities to save and borrow money, raise equity capital, manage risks, trade assets currently or in the future, and trade based on their estimates of asset values.

2. Determine the returns (i.e., interest rates) that equate the total supply of savings with the total demand for borrowing.

3. Allocate capital to its most efficient uses.

The financial system allows the transfer of assets and risks from one entity to another as well as across time. Entities who utilize the financial system include individuals, firms, governments, charities, and others.

Achievement of Purposes in the Financial System

The financial system allows entities to save, borrow, issue equity capital, manage risks, exchange assets, and to utilize information. The financial system is best at fulfilling these roles when the markets are liquid, transactions costs are low, information is readily available, and when regulation ensures the execution of contracts.

Savings. Individuals will save (e.g., for retirement) and expect a return that compensates them for risk and the use of their money. Firms save a portion of their sales to fund future expenditures. Vehicles used for saving include stocks, bonds, certificates of deposit, real assets, and other assets.

Borrowing. Individuals may borrow in order to buy a house, fund a college education, or for other purposes. A firm may borrow in order to finance capital expenditures and for other activities. Governments may issue debt to fund their expenditures. Lenders can require collateral to protect them in the event of borrower defaults, take an equity position, or investigate the credit risk of the borrower.

Issuing equity. Another method of raising capital is to issue equity, where the capital providers will share in any future profits. Investment banks help with issuance, analysts value the equity, and regulators and accountants encourage the dissemination of information.

Risk management. Entities face risks from changing interest rates, currency values, commodities values, and defaults on debt, among other things. For example, a firm that owes a foreign currency in 90 days can lock in the price of this foreign currency in domestic currency units by entering into a forward contract. Future delivery of the foreign currency is guaranteed at a domestic-currency price set at inception of the contract. In this transaction, the firm would be referred to as a *hedger*. This hedging allows the firm to enter a market that it would otherwise be reluctant to enter by reducing the risk of the transaction. Hedging instruments are available from exchanges, investment banks, insurance firms, and other institutions.

Exchanging assets. The financial system also allows entities to exchange assets. For example, Proctor and Gamble may sell soap in Europe but have costs denominated in U.S. dollars. Proctor and Gamble can exchange their euros from soap sales for dollars in the currency markets.

Utilizing information. Investors with information expect to earn a return on that information in addition to their usual return. Investors who can identify assets that are currently undervalued or overvalued in the market can earn extra returns from investing based on their information (when their analysis is correct).

Return Determination

The financial system also provides a mechanism to determine the rate of return that equates the amount of borrowing with the amount of lending (saving) in an economy. Low rates of return increase borrowing but reduce saving (increase current consumption). High rates of return increase saving but reduce borrowing. The **equilibrium interest rate** is the rate at which the amount individuals, businesses, and governments desire to borrow is equal to the amount that individuals, businesses, and governments desire to lend. Equilibrium rates for different types of borrowing and lending will differ due to differences in risk, liquidity, and maturity.

Allocation of Capital

With limited availability of capital, one of the most important functions of a financial system is to allocate capital to its most efficient uses. Investors weigh the expected risks and returns of different investments to determine their most preferred investments. As long as investors are well informed regarding risk and return and markets function well, this results in an allocation to capital to its most valuable uses.

LOS 46.b: Describe classifications of assets and markets.

CFA® Program Curriculum, Volume 5, page 14

Financial assets include securities (stocks and bonds), derivative contracts, and currencies. **Real assets** include real estate, equipment, commodities, and other physical assets.

Financial securities can be classified as debt or equity. **Debt securities** are promises to repay borrowed funds. **Equity securities** represent ownership positions.

Public (publicly traded) securities are traded on exchanges or through securities dealers and are subject to regulatory oversight. Securities that are not traded in public markets are referred to as **private securities**. Private securities are often illiquid and not subject to regulation.

Derivative contracts have values that depend on (are derived from) the values of other assets. **Financial derivative contracts** are based on equities, equity indexes, debt, debt indexes, or other financial contracts. **Physical derivative contracts** derive their values from the values of physical assets such as gold, oil, and wheat.

Markets for immediate delivery are referred to as **spot markets**. Contracts for the future delivery of physical and financial assets include forwards, futures, and options. Options provide the buyer the right, but not the obligation, to purchase (or sell) assets over some period or at some future date at predetermined prices.

The **primary market** is the market for newly issued securities. Subsequent sales of securities are said to occur in the **secondary market**.

Money markets refer to markets for debt securities with maturities of one year or less. **Capital markets** refer to markets for longer-term debt securities and equity securities that have no specific maturity date.

Traditional investment markets refer to those for debt and equity. **Alternative markets** refer to those for hedge funds, commodities, real estate, collectibles, gemstones, leases, and equipment. Alternative assets are often more difficult to value, illiquid, require investor due diligence, and therefore often sell at a discount.

LOS 46.c: Describe the major types of securities, currencies, contracts, commodities, and real assets that trade in organized markets, including their distinguishing characteristics and major subtypes.

CFA® Program Curriculum, Volume 5, page 16

Assets can be classified as securities, currencies, contracts, commodities, and real assets. Their characteristics and subtypes are as follows.

Securities

Securities can be classified as fixed income or equity securities, and individual securities can be combined in pooled investment vehicles. Corporations and governments are the most common issuers of individual securities. The initial sale of a security is called an **issue** when the security is sold to the public.

Fixed income securities typically refer to debt securities that are promises to repay borrowed money in the future. Short-term fixed income securities generally have a maturity of less than one or two years; long-term term maturities are longer than five to ten years, and intermediate term maturities fall in the middle of the maturity range.

Although the terms are used loosely, *bonds* are generally long term, whereas *notes* are intermediate term. *Commercial paper* refers to short-term debt issued by firms. Governments issue *bills* and banks issue *certificates of deposit*. In *repurchase agreements*, the borrower sells a high-quality asset and has both the right and obligation to repurchase it (at a higher price) in the future. Repurchase agreements can be for terms as short as one day.

Convertible debt is debt that an investor can exchange for a specified number of equity shares of the issuing firm.

Equity securities represent ownership in a firm and include common stock, preferred stock, and warrants.

- **Common stock** is a residual claim on a firm's assets. Common stock dividends are paid only after interest is paid to debtholders and dividends are paid to preferred stockholders. Furthermore, in the event of firm liquidation, debtholders and preferred stockholders have priority over common stockholders and are usually paid in full before common stockholders receive any payment.
- **Preferred stock** is an equity security with scheduled dividends that typically do not change over the security's life and must be paid before any dividends on common stock may be paid.
- **Warrants** are similar to options in that they give the holder the right to buy a firm's equity shares (usually common stock) at a fixed exercise price prior to the warrant's expiration.

Pooled investment vehicles include mutual funds, depositories, and hedge funds. The term refers to structures that combine the funds of many investors in a portfolio of investments. The investor's ownership interests are referred to as *shares, units, depository receipts,* or *limited partnership interests.*

- **Mutual funds** are pooled investment vehicles in which investors can purchase shares, either from the fund itself (open-end funds) or in the secondary market (closed-end funds).
- **Exchange-traded funds** (ETFs) and **exchange-traded notes** (ETNs) trade like closed-end funds but have special provisions allowing conversion into individual portfolio securities, or exchange of portfolio shares for ETF shares, that keep their market prices close to the value of their proportional interest in the overall portfolio. These funds are sometimes referred to as *depositories,* with their shares referred to as *depository receipts.*
- **Asset-backed securities** represent a claim to a portion of a pool of financial assets such as mortgages, car loans, or credit card debt. The return from the assets is passed through to investors, with different classes of claims (referred to as *tranches*) having different levels of risk.
- **Hedge funds** are organized as limited partnerships, with the investors as the limited partners and the fund manager as the general partner. Hedge funds utilize various strategies and purchase is usually restricted to investors of substantial wealth and investment knowledge. Hedge funds often use leverage. Hedge fund managers are compensated based on the amount of assets under management as well as on their investment results.

 Professor's Note: Asset-backed securities are described in more detail in the Study Session on fixed income. Mutual funds and ETFs are discussed in the Study Session on portfolio management. Hedge funds are discussed in the Study Session on alternative investments.

Currencies

Currencies are issued by a government's central bank. Some are referred to as **reserve currencies,** which are those held by governments and central banks worldwide. These include the dollar and euro and, secondarily, the British pound, Japanese yen, and Swiss franc. In spot currency markets, currencies are traded for immediate delivery.

Contracts

Contracts are agreements between two parties that require some action in the future, such as exchanging an asset for cash. Financial contracts are often based on securities, currencies, commodities, or security indexes (portfolios). They include futures, forwards, options, swaps, and insurance contracts.

A **forward contract** is an agreement to buy or sell an asset in the future at a price specified in the contract at its inception. An agreement to purchase 100 ounces of gold 90 days from now for $1,000 per ounce is a forward contract. Forward contracts are not traded on exchanges or in dealer markets.

Futures contracts are similar to forward contracts except that they are standardized as to amount, asset characteristics, and delivery time and are traded on an exchange (in a secondary market) so that they are liquid investments.

In a **swap contract**, two parties make payments that are equivalent to one asset being traded (swapped) for another. In a simple *interest rate swap*, floating rate interest payments are exchanged for fixed-rate payments over multiple settlement dates. A *currency swap* involves a loan in one currency for the loan of another currency for a period of time. An *equity swap* involves the exchange of the return on an equity index or portfolio for the interest payment on a debt instrument.

An **option contract** gives its owner the right to buy or sell an asset at a specific exercise price at some specified time in the future. A **call option** gives the option buyer the right (but not the obligation) to buy an asset. A **put option** gives the option buyer the right (but not the obligation) to sell an asset.

Sellers, or writers, of call (put) options receive a payment, referred to as the *option premium*, when they sell the options but incur the obligation to sell (buy) the asset at the specified price if the option owner chooses to exercise it.

Options on currencies, stocks, stock indexes, futures, swaps, and precious metals are traded on exchanges. Customized options contracts are also sold by dealers in the over-the-counter market.

An **insurance contract** pays a cash amount if a future event occurs. They are used to hedge against unfavorable, unexpected events. Examples include life, liability, and automobile insurance contracts. Insurance contracts can sometimes be traded to other parties and often have tax-advantaged payouts.

Credit default swaps are a form of insurance that makes a payment if an issuer defaults on its bonds. They can be used by bond investors to hedge default risk. They can also be used by parties that will experience losses if an issuer experiences financial distress and by others who are speculating that the issuer will experience more or less financial trouble than is currently expected.

Commodities

Commodities trade in spot, forward, and futures markets. They include precious metals, industrial metals, agricultural products, energy products, and credits for carbon reduction.

Futures and forwards allow both hedgers and speculators to participate in commodity markets without having to deliver or store the physical commodities.

Real Assets

Examples of **real assets** are real estate, equipment, and machinery. Although they have been traditionally held by firms for their use in production, real assets are increasingly held by institutional investors both directly and indirectly.

Buying real assets directly often provides income, tax advantages, and diversification benefits. However, they often entail substantial management costs. Furthermore, because of their heterogeneity, they usually require the investor to do substantial due diligence before investing. They are illiquid because their specialization may result in a limited pool of investors for a particular real asset.

Rather than buying real assets directly, an investor may choose to buy them indirectly through an investment such as a *real estate investment trust* (REIT) or *master limited partnership* (MLP). The investor owns an interest in these vehicles, which hold the assets directly. Indirect ownership interests are typically more liquid than ownership of the assets themselves. Another indirect ownership method is to buy the stock of firms that have large ownership of real assets.

LOS 46.d: Describe types of financial intermediaries and services that they provide.

CFA® Program Curriculum, Volume 5, page 28

Financial intermediaries stand between buyers and sellers, facilitating the exchange of assets, capital, and risk. Their services allow for greater efficiency and are vital to a well-functioning economy. Financial intermediaries include brokers and exchanges, dealers, securitizers, depository institutions, insurance companies, arbitrageurs, and clearinghouses.

Brokers, Dealers, and Exchanges

Brokers help their clients buy and sell securities by finding counterparties to trades in a cost efficient manner. They may work for large brokerage firms, for banks, or at exchanges.

Block brokers help with the placement of large trades. Typically, large trades are difficult to place without moving the market. For example, a large sell order might cause a security's price to decrease before the order can be fully executed. Block brokers help conceal their clients' intentions so that the market does not move against them.

Investment banks help corporations sell common stock, preferred stock, and debt securities to investors. They also provide advice to firms, notably about mergers, acquisitions, and raising capital.

Exchanges provide a venue where traders can meet. Exchanges sometimes act as brokers by providing electronic order matching. Exchanges regulate their members and require firms that list on the exchange to provide timely financial disclosures and to promote shareholder democratization. Exchanges acquire their regulatory power through member agreement or from their governments.

Alternative trading systems (ATS), which serve the same trading function as exchanges but have no regulatory function, are also known as **electronic communication networks** (ECNs) or **multilateral trading facilities** (MTFs). ATS that do not reveal current client orders are known as *dark pools*.

Dealers facilitate trading by buying for or selling from their own inventory. Dealers provide liquidity in the market and profit primarily from the spread (difference) between the price at which they will buy (bid price) and the price at which they will sell (ask price) the security or other asset.

Some dealers also act as brokers. **Broker-dealers** have an inherent conflict of interest. As brokers, they should seek the best prices for their clients, but as dealers, their goal is to profit through prices or spreads. As a result, traders typically place limits on how their orders are filled when they transact with broker-dealers.

Dealers that trade with central banks when the banks buy or sell government securities in order to affect the money supply are referred to as **primary dealers**.

Securitizers

Securitizers pool large amounts of securities or other assets and then sell interests in the pool to other investors. The returns from the pool, net of the securitizer's fees, are passed through to the investors. By securitizing the assets, the securitizer creates a diversified pool of assets with more predictable cash flows than the individual assets in the pool. This creates liquidity in the assets because the ownership interests are more easily valued and traded. There are also economies of scale in the management costs of large pools of assets and potential benefits from the manager's selection of assets.

Assets that are often securitized include mortgages, car loans, credit card receivables, bank loans, and equipment leases. The primary benefit of securitization is to decrease the funding costs for the assets in the pool. A firm may set up a *special purpose vehicle* (SPV) or *special purpose entity* (SPE) to buy firm assets, which removes them from the firm's balance sheet and may increase their value by removing the risk that financial trouble at the firm will give other investors a claim to the assets' cash flows.

The cash flows from securitized assets can be segregated by risk. The different risk categories are called *tranches*. The senior tranches provide the most certain cash flows, while the junior tranches have greater risk.

Depository Institutions

Examples of **depository institutions** include banks, credit unions, and savings and loans. They pay interest on customer deposits and provide transaction services such as checking accounts. These financial intermediaries then make loans with the funds, which offer diversification benefits. The intermediaries have expertise in evaluating credit quality and managing the risk of a portfolio of loans of various types.

Other intermediaries, such as payday lenders and factoring companies, lend money to firms and individuals on the basis of their wages, accounts receivable, and other future cash flows. These intermediaries often finance the loans by issuing commercial paper or other debt securities.

Securities brokers provide loans to investors who purchase securities on margin. When this margin lending is to hedge funds and other institutions, the brokers are referred to as *prime brokers*.

The equity owners (stockholders) of banks, brokers, and other intermediaries absorb any loan losses before depositors and other lenders. The more equity capital an intermediary has, the less risk for depositors. Poorly capitalized intermediaries (those with less equity) have less incentive to reduce the risk of their loan portfolios because they have less capital at risk.

Insurance Companies

Insurance companies are intermediaries, in that they collect insurance premiums in return for providing risk reduction to the insured. The insurance firm can do this efficiently because it provides protection to a diversified pool of policyholders, whose risks of loss are typically uncorrelated. This provides more predictable losses and cash flows compared to a single insurance contract, in the same way that a bank's diversified portfolio of loans diversifies the risk of loan defaults.

Insurance firms also provide a benefit to investors by managing the risks inherent in insurance: moral hazard, adverse selection, and fraud. **Moral hazard** occurs because the insured may take more risks once he is protected against losses. **Adverse selection** occurs when those most likely to experience losses are the predominant buyers of insurance. In **fraud**, the insured purposely causes damage or claims fictitious losses so he can collect on his insurance policy.

Arbitrageurs

In its pure (riskless) form, **arbitrage** refers to buying an asset in one market and reselling it in another at a higher price. By doing so, arbitrageurs act as intermediaries, providing liquidity to participants in the market where the asset is purchased and transferring the asset to the market where it is sold.

In markets with good information, pure arbitrage is rare because traders will favor the markets with the best prices. More commonly, arbitrageurs try to exploit pricing differences for similar instruments. For example, a dealer who sells a call option will often also buy the stock because the call and stock price are highly correlated. Likewise, arbitrageurs will attempt to exploit discrepancies in the pricing of the call and stock. Many (risk) arbitrageurs use complex models for valuation of related securities and for risk control. Creating similar positions using different assets is referred to as *replication*. This is also a form of intermediation because similar risks are traded in different forms and in different markets.

Clearinghouses and Custodians

Clearinghouses act as intermediaries between buyers and sellers in financial markets and provide:

- Escrow services (transferring cash and assets to the respective parties).
- Guarantees of contract completion.
- Assurance that margin traders have adequate capital.
- Limits on the aggregate net order quantity (buy orders minus sell orders) of members.

Through these activities, clearinghouses limit **counterparty risk**, the risk that the other party to a transaction will not fulfill its obligation. In some markets, the clearinghouse ensures only the trades of its member brokers and dealers, who, in turn, ensure the trades of their retail customers.

Custodians also improve market integrity by holding client securities and preventing their loss due to fraud or other events that affect the broker or investment manager.

LOS 46.e: Compare positions an investor can take in an asset.

CFA® Program Curriculum, Volume 5, page 38

An investor who owns an asset, or has the right or obligation under a contract to purchase an asset, is said to have a **long position**. A **short position** can result from borrowing an asset and selling it, with the obligation to replace the asset in the future (a short sale). The party to a contract who must sell or deliver an asset in the future is also said to have a short position. In general, investors who are long benefit from an increase in the price of an asset and those who are short benefit when the asset price declines.

Hedgers use short positions in one asset to hedge an existing risk from a long position in another asset that has returns that are strongly correlated with the returns of the asset shorted. For example, wheat farmers may take a short position in (i.e., sell) wheat futures contracts. If wheat prices fall, the resulting increase in the value of the short futures position offsets, partially or fully, the loss in the value of the farmer's crop.

 Professor's Note: As a rule of thumb, hedgers must "do in the futures market what they must do in the future." Thus, the farmer who must sell wheat in the future can reduce the risk from wheat price fluctuations by selling wheat futures.

The buyer of an option contract is said to be long the option. The seller is short the option and is said to have written the option. Note that an investor who is long (buys) a call option on an asset profits when the value of the underlying asset increases in value, while the party short the option has losses. A long position in a put option on an asset has the right to sell the asset at a specified price and profits when the price of the underlying asset falls, while the party short the option has losses.

In swaps, each party is long one asset and short the other, so the designation of the long and short side is often arbitrary. Usually, however, the side that benefits from an increase in the quoted price or rate is referred to as the long side.

In a currency contract, each party is long one currency and short the other. For example, the buyer of a euro futures contract priced in dollars is long the euro and short the dollar.

Short Sales and Positions

In a **short sale**, the short seller (1) simultaneously borrows and sells securities through a broker, (2) must return the securities at the request of the lender or when the short sale is closed out, and (3) must keep a portion of the proceeds of the short sale on deposit with the broker. Short sellers hope to profit from a fall in the price of the security or asset sold short, buying at a lower price in the future in order to repay the loan of the asset originally sold at a higher price. The repayment of the borrowed security or other asset is referred to as "covering the short position."

In a short sale, the short seller must pay all dividends or interest that the lender would have received from the security that has been loaned to the short seller. These payments are called **payments-in-lieu** of dividends or interest. The short seller must also deposit the proceeds of the short sale as collateral to guarantee the eventual repurchase of the security. The broker then earns interest on these funds and may return a portion of this interest to the short seller at a rate referred to as the **short rebate rate**. The short rebate rate is usually only provided to institutional investors and is typically 0.1% less than overnight interest rates. If the security is difficult to borrow, the short rebate rate may be lower or negative. The difference between the interest earned on the proceeds from the short sale and the short rebate paid is the return to the lender of the securities. A short sale may also require the short seller to deposit additional margin in the form of cash or short-term riskless securities.

Leveraged Positions

The use of borrowed funds to purchase an asset results in a **leveraged position** and the investor is said to be using leverage. Investors who use leverage to buy securities by borrowing from their brokers are said to buy on **margin** and the borrowed funds are referred to as a **margin loan**. The interest rate paid on the funds is the **call money rate**, which is generally higher than the government bill rate. The call money rate is lower for larger investors with better collateral.

At the time of a new margin purchase, investors are required to provide a minimum amount of equity, referred to as the **initial margin requirement**. This requirement may be set by the government, exchange, clearinghouse, or broker. Lower risk in an investor's portfolio will often result in the broker lending more funds.

The use of leverage magnifies both the gains and losses from changes in the value of the underlying asset. The additional risk from the use of borrowed funds is referred to as risk from **financial leverage**.

LOS 46.f: Calculate and interpret the leverage ratio, the rate of return on a margin transaction, and the security price at which the investor would receive a margin call.

CFA® Program Curriculum, Volume 5, page 41

The **leverage ratio** of a margin investment is the value of the asset divided by the value of the equity position. For example, an investor who satisfies an initial margin requirement of 50% equity has a 2-to-1 leverage ratio so that a 10% increase (decrease) in the price of the asset results in a 20% increase (decrease) in the investor's equity amount.

Example: Margin transaction

Given the following information:

Shares purchased	1,000
Purchase price per share	$100
Annual dividend per share	$2.00
Initial margin requirement	40%
Call money rate	4%
Commission per share	$0.05
Stock price after one year	$110

Calculate (1) the leverage ratio and (2) the investor's return on the margin transaction (return on equity) if the stock is sold at the end of one year.

Answer:

1. The leverage ratio = 1 / 0.40 = 2.5.

2. The total purchase price is 1,000 × $100 = $100,000. The investor must post initial margin of 40% × $100,000 = $40,000. The remaining $60,000 is borrowed. The commission on the purchase is 1,000 × $0.05 = $50. Thus, the total initial equity investment is $40,050.

At the end of one year, the stock value is 1,000 × $110 = $110,000, for a gain of $9,950. Dividends received are 1,000 × $2.00 = $2,000. Interest paid is $60,000 × 4% = $2,400. The commission on the sale is 1,000 × $0.05 = $50.

The gain on the transaction in one year is $9,950 + $2,000 – $2,400 – $50 = $9,500. The return on the equity investment is $9,500 / $40,050 = 23.72%. The investor's net return is less than the asset total return (10% price appreciation + 2% dividend = 12%) multiplied by the leverage ratio (12% × 2.5 = 30%) because of the loan interest and commissions.

We can also solve for the return on the margin transaction with the cash flow functions on a financial calculator. The initial cash outflow is the $40,000 initial margin + $50 purchase commission = $40,050. The inflow after one year is the $110,000 stock value + $2,000 dividends – $60,000 margin repayment – $2,400 margin interest – $50 sale commission = $49,550. Using the cash flow functions: CF_0 = –40,050; CF_1 = 49,550; CPT IRR = 23.72%.

To ensure that the loan is covered by the value of the asset, an investor must maintain a minimum equity percentage, called the **maintenance margin requirement**, in the account. This minimum is typically 25% of the current position value, but brokers may require a greater minimum equity percentage for volatile stocks.

If the percentage of equity in a margin account falls below the maintenance margin requirement, the investor will receive a **margin call**, a request to bring the equity percentage in the account back up to the maintenance margin percentage. An investor can satisfy this request by depositing additional funds or depositing other unmargined securities that will bring the equity percentage up to the minimum requirement. If the investor does not meet the margin call, the broker must sell the position.

The stock price which results in a margin call can be calculated by using the following formula:

$$\text{margin call price} = P_0 \left(\frac{1 - \text{initial margin}}{1 - \text{maintenance margin}} \right)$$

where:
P_0 = initial purchase price

Example: Margin call price

If an investor purchases a stock for $40 per share with an initial margin requirement of 50% and the maintenance margin requirement is 25%, at what price will the investor get a margin call?

Answer:

$$\frac{\$40(1 - 0.5)}{1 - 0.25} = \$26.67$$

A margin call is triggered at a price below $26.67.

In a short sale, the investor must deposit initial margin equal to a percentage of the value of the shares sold short to protect the broker in case the share price increases. An increase in the share price can decrease the margin percentage below the maintenance margin percentage and generate a margin call.

LOS 46.g: Compare execution, validity, and clearing instructions.

LOS 46.h: Compare market orders with limit orders.

CFA® Program Curriculum, Volume 5, page 44

Securities dealers provide prices at which they will buy and sell shares. The **bid price** is the price at which a dealer will buy a security. The **ask** or **offer price** is the price at which a dealer will sell a security. The difference between the bid and ask prices is referred to as the **bid-ask spread** and is the source of a dealer's compensation. The bid and ask are quoted for specific trade sizes (**bid size** and **ask size**).

The quotation in the market is the highest dealer bid and lowest dealer ask from among all dealers in a particular security. More liquid securities have market quotations with bid-ask spreads that are lower (as a percentage of share price) and therefore have lower transactions costs for investors. Traders who post bids and offers are said to *make a market*, while those who trade with them at posted prices are said to *take the market*.

When investors want to buy or sell, they must enter orders that specify the size of the trade and whether to buy or sell. The order can also include *execution instructions* that specify how to trade, *validity instructions* that specify when the order can be filled, and *clearing instructions* that specify how to settle the trade.

Execution Instructions

The most common orders, in terms of execution instructions, are market or limit orders. A **market order** instructs the broker to execute the trade immediately at the best possible price. A **limit order** places a minimum execution price on sell orders and a maximum execution price on buy orders. For example, a buy order with a limit of $6 will be executed immediately as long as the shares can be purchased for $6 or less.

A market order is often appropriate when the trader wants to execute quickly, as when the trader has information she believes is not yet reflected in market prices. The disadvantage of market orders is that they may execute at unfavorable prices, especially if the security has low trading volume relative to the order size. A market buy order may execute at a high price or a market sell order may execute at a low price. Executing at an unfavorable price represents a concession by the trader for immediate liquidity. Unfortunately, these price concessions are unpredictable.

To avoid price execution uncertainty, a trader can place a limit order instead of the market order. The disadvantage of the limit order is that it might not be filled. For example, if a trader places a limit buy order of $50 and no one is willing to sell at $50, the order will not be filled. Furthermore, if the stock price rises over time, the trader misses out on the gains.

A limit buy order above the best ask or a limit sell order below the best bid are said to be *marketable* or *aggressively priced* because at least part of the order is likely to execute immediately. If the limit price is between the best bid and the best ask, a limit order is said to be *making a new market* or *inside the market*. Limit orders waiting to execute are called **standing limit orders**.

A limit buy order at the best bid or a limit sell order at the best ask are said to *make the market*. Again, the order might not be filled. A buy order with a limit price below the best bid, or a sell order with a limit price above the best ask, is said to be *behind the market*. It will likely not execute until security prices move toward the limit price. A limit buy order with a price considerably lower than the best bid, or a limit sell order with a price significantly higher than the best ask, is said to be *far from the market*.

Other execution instructions concern the volume of the trade. **All-or-nothing orders** execute only if the whole order can be filled. Orders can specify the minimum size of a trade, which is beneficial when trading costs depend on the number of executed trades rather than the size of the order.

Trade visibility can also be specified. **Hidden orders** are those for which only the broker or exchange knows the trade size. These are useful for investors that have a large amount to trade and do not want to reveal their intentions. Traders can also specify **display size**, where some of the trade is visible to the market, but the rest is not. These are also referred to as **iceberg orders** because part of most of the order is hidden from view. They allow the investor to advertise some of the trade, with the rest of the trade potentially executed once the visible part has executed. Sometimes entering trades for part of the position the trader wishes to establish is a way to estimate the liquidity of, or the buying interest in, the security in question.

Validity Instructions

Validity instructions specify when an order should be executed. Most orders are **day orders**, meaning they expire if unfilled by the end of the trading day. **Good-till-cancelled** orders last until they are filled. **Immediate-or-cancel** orders are cancelled unless they can be filled immediately. They are also known as **fill-or-kill** orders. **Good-on-close** orders are only filled at the end of the trading day. If they are market orders, they are referred to as **market-on-close** orders. These are often used by mutual funds because their portfolios are valued using closing prices. There are also **good-on-open** orders.

Stop Orders

Stop orders are those that are not executed unless the stop price has been met. They are often referred to as **stop loss orders** because they can be used to prevent losses or to protect profits. Suppose an investor purchases a stock for $50. If the investor wants to sell out of the position if the price falls 10% to $45, he can enter a **stop-sell order** at $45. If the stock trades down to $45 or lower, this *triggers* a market order to sell. There is no guarantee that the order will execute at $45, and a rapidly falling stock could be sold at a price significantly lower than $45.

A **stop-buy** is entered with at stop (trigger) above the current market price. There are two primary reasons a trader would enter a stop-buy order. (1) A trader with a short position could attempt to limit losses from an increasing stock price with a stop-buy order. (2) It is often said, "You don't get paid for being right until the market agrees with you." With this in mind, an investor who believes a stock is undervalued, but does not wish to own it until there are signs that market participants are being convinced of this undervaluation, may place a stop-buy order at a price some specific percentage above the current price.

Note that stop orders reinforce market momentum. Stop-sell orders execute when market prices are falling, and stop-buy orders execute when the market is rising. Execution prices for stop orders are therefore often unfavorable.

Example: Using stop orders

Raymond Flowers believes that the shares of Acme Corp. that he owns are overvalued currently but knows that stocks often continue to increase above their intrinsic values for some time before correcting. What type of order should Flowers place if he wants to sell his shares when the price begins to fall a significant amount?

Answer:

Flowers should enter a good-till-cancelled stop-sell order at a price some percentage below the current level. If, for example, the shares are trading at 40, he could enter a stop-sell order at 36, 10% below the current level. Investors sometimes move these stops up as a stock continues to increase in price. In response to a price increase to 42, Flowers might move his stop-sell order up to 37.80, 10% below the new price. Note that a limit order to sell with a limit price below the current market price would likely execute immediately.

Clearing Instructions

Clearing instructions tell the trader how to clear and settle a trade. They are usually standing instructions and not attached to an order. Retail trades are typically cleared and settled by the broker, whereas institutional trades may be settled by a custodian or another broker, which might be the trader's prime broker. Using two brokers allows the investor to keep one broker as her prime broker for margin and custodial services while using a variety of other brokers for specialized execution.

One important clearing instruction is whether a sell order is a short sale or long sale. In the former, the broker must confirm that the security can be borrowed and in the latter, that the security can be delivered.

LOS 46.i: Define primary and secondary markets and explain how secondary markets support primary markets.

CFA® Program Curriculum, Volume 5, page 50

Primary capital markets refer to the sale of newly issued securities. New equity issues involve either:

- New shares issued by firms whose shares are already trading in the marketplace. These issues are called **seasoned offerings** or **secondary issues**.
- First-time issues by firms whose shares are not currently publicly traded. These are called **initial public offerings** (IPOs).

Secondary financial markets are where securities trade after their initial issuance. Placing a buy order on the London Stock Exchange is an order in the secondary market and will result in purchase of existing shares from their current owner.

Primary Market: Public Offerings

Corporate stock or bond issues are almost always sold with the assistance of an investment banking firm. The investment bank finds investors who agree to buy part of the issue. These are not actual orders but are referred to as **indications of interest**. When the number of shares covered by indications of interest are greater (less) than the number of shares to be offered, the offering price may be adjusted upward (downward). This process of gathering indications of interest is referred to as **book building**. In London, the book builder is referred to as the **book runner**. In Europe, an **accelerated book build** occurs when securities must be issued quickly. To build a book, the investment bank disseminates information about the firm's financials and prospects. The issuer must also make disclosures including how the funds will be used.

The most common way an investment bank assists with a security issuance is through an **underwritten offering**. Here, the investment bank agrees to purchase the entire issue at a price that is negotiated between the issuer and bank. If the issue is undersubscribed, the investment bank must buy the unsold portion. In the case of an IPO, the investment bank also agrees to make a market in the stock for a period after the issuance to provide price support for the issue.

An investment bank can also agree to distribute shares of an IPO on a **best efforts** basis, rather than agreeing to purchase the whole issue. If the issue is undersubscribed, the bank is not obligated to buy the unsold portion.

Note that investment banks have a conflict of interest in an underwritten offer. As the issuer's agents, they should set the price high to raise the most funds for the issuer. But, as underwriters, they would prefer that the price be set low enough that the whole issue sells. This also allows them to allocate portions of an undervalued IPO to their clients. This results in IPOs typically being underpriced. Issuers also could have an interest in underpricing the IPO because of the negative publicity when an undersubscribed IPO initially trades at a price below the IPO price investors pay. An IPO that is oversubscribed and has the expectation of trading significantly above its IPO price is referred to as a hot issue.

Primary Market: Private Placements and Other Transactions

In a **private placement**, securities are sold directly to qualified investors, typically with the assistance of an investment bank. Qualified investors are those with substantial wealth and investment knowledge. Private placements do not require the issuer to disclose as much information as they must when the securities are being sold to the public. The issuance costs are less with a private placement and the offer price is also lower because the securities cannot be resold in public markets, making them less valuable than shares registered for public trading.

In a **shelf registration**, a firm makes its public disclosures as in a regular offering but then issues the registered securities over time when it needs capital and when the markets are favorable.

A **dividend reinvestment plan** (DRP or DRIP) allows existing shareholders to use their dividends to buy new shares from the firm at a slight discount.

In a **rights offering**, existing shareholders are given the right to buy new shares at a discount to the current market price. Shareholders tend to dislike rights offerings because their ownership is diluted unless they exercise their rights and buy the additional shares. However, rights can be traded separately from the shares themselves in some circumstances.

In addition to firms issuing securities, governments issue short-term and long-term debt, either by auction or through investment banks.

Importance of the Secondary Market

Secondary markets are important because they provide liquidity and price/value information. Liquid markets are those in which a security can be sold quickly without incurring a discount from the current price. The better the secondary market, the easier it is for firms to raise external capital in the primary market, which results in a lower cost of capital for firms with shares that have adequate liquidity.

LOS 46.j: Describe how securities, contracts, and currencies are traded in quote-driven, order-driven, and brokered markets.

CFA® Program Curriculum, Volume 5, page 54

The trading of securities in the secondary market has encouraged the development of market structures to facilitate trading. Trading can be examined according to when securities are traded and how they are traded.

Securities markets may be structured as call markets or continuous markets. In **call markets**, the stock is only traded at specific times. Call markets are potentially very liquid when in session because all traders are present, but they are obviously illiquid between sessions. In a call market, all trades, bids, and asks are declared, and then one negotiated price is set that clears the market for the stock. This method is used in smaller markets but is also used to set opening prices and prices after trading halts on major exchanges.

In **continuous markets**, trades occur at any time the market is open. The price is set by either the auction process or by dealer bid-ask quotes.

Market Structures

There are three main categories of securities markets: *quote-driven markets* where investors trade with dealers, *order-driven markets* where rules are used to match buyers and sellers, and *brokered markets* where investors use brokers to locate a counterparty to a trade.

Quote-Driven Markets

In **quote-driven markets**, traders transact with dealers (market makers) who post bid and ask prices. Dealers maintain an inventory of securities. Quote-driven markets are thus sometimes called **dealer markets**, **price-driven markets**, or **over-the-counter markets**. Most securities other than stocks trade in quote-driven markets. Trading often takes place electronically.

Order-Driven Markets

In **order-driven markets**, orders are executed using trading rules, which are necessary because traders are usually anonymous. Exchanges and automated trading systems are examples of order-driven markets. Two sets of rules are used in these markets: order matching rules and trade pricing rules.

Order matching rules establish an *order precedence hierarchy*. **Price priority** is one criteria, where the trades given highest priority are those at the highest bid (buy) and lowest ask (sell). If orders are at the same prices, a **secondary precedence rule** gives priority to non-hidden orders and earliest arriving orders. These rules encourage traders to price their trades aggressively, display their entire orders, and trade earlier, thereby improving liquidity.

After orders are created using order matching rules, **trade pricing rules** are used to determine the price. Under the *uniform pricing rule*, all orders trade at the same price, which is the price that results in the highest volume of trading. The *discriminatory pricing rule* uses the limit price of the order that arrived first as the trade price.

In an electronic crossing network, the typical trader is an institution. Orders are batched together and crossed (matched) at fixed points in time during the day at the average of the bid and ask quotes from the exchange where the stock primarily trades. This pricing rule is referred to as the *derivative pricing rule* because it is derived from the security's main market. The price is not determined by orders in the crossing network.

Brokered Markets

In **brokered markets**, brokers find the counterparty in order to execute a trade. This service is especially valuable when the trader has a security that is unique or illiquid. Examples are large blocks of stock, real estate, and artwork. Dealers typically do not carry an inventory of these assets and there are too few trades for these assets to trade in order-driven markets.

Market Information

A market is said to be **pre-trade transparent** if investors can obtain pre-trade information regarding quotes and orders. A market is **post-trade transparent** if investors can obtain post-trade information regarding completed trade prices and sizes.

Buy-side traders value transparency because it allows them to better understand security values and trading costs. Dealers, on the other hand, prefer opaque markets because this provides them with an informational advantage over traders who trade less frequently in the security. Transactions costs and bid-ask spreads are larger in opaque markets.

LOS 46.k: Describe characteristics of a well-functioning financial system.

CFA® Program Curriculum, Volume 5, page 58

A well-functioning financial system allows entities to achieve their purposes. More specifically, **complete markets** fulfill the following:

- Investors can save for the future at fair rates of return.
- Creditworthy borrowers can obtain funds.
- Hedgers can manage their risks.
- Traders can obtain the currencies, commodities, and other assets they need.

If a market can perform these functions at low trading costs (including commissions, bid-ask spreads, and price impacts), it is said to be **operationally efficient**. If security prices reflect all the information associated with fundamental value in a timely fashion, then the financial system is **informationally efficient**. A well-functioning financial system has complete markets that are operationally and informationally efficient, with prices that reflect fundamental values.

A well-functioning financial system has financial intermediaries that:

- Organize trading venues, including exchanges, brokerages, and alternative trading systems.
- Supply liquidity.
- Securitize assets so that borrowers can obtain funds inexpensively.
- Manage banks that use depositor capital to fund borrowers.
- Manage insurance firms that pool unrelated risks.
- Manage investment advisory services that assist investors with asset management inexpensively.
- Provide clearinghouses that settle trades.
- Manage depositories that provide for asset safety.

The benefits of a well-functioning financial system are tremendous. Savers can fund entrepreneurs who need capital to fund new companies. Company risks can be shared so that risky companies can be funded. These benefits are enhanced because the transactions occur among strangers, widening the opportunities for capital formation and risk sharing in the economy.

Furthermore, in informationally efficiently markets, capital is allocated to its most productive use. That is, they are **allocationally efficient**. Informational efficiency is brought about by traders who bid prices up and down in response to new information that changes estimates of securities' fundamental values. If markets are operationally efficient, security prices will be more informationally efficient because low trading costs encourage trading based on new information. The existence of accounting standards and financial reporting requirements also reduces the costs of obtaining information and increases security values.

LOS 46.l: Describe objectives of market regulation.

CFA® Program Curriculum, Volume 5, page 60

Without market regulation, many problems could persist in financial markets:

- *Fraud and theft*: In complex financial markets, the potential for theft and fraud increases because investment managers and others can take advantage of unsophisticated investors. Furthermore, if returns are often random, it is difficult for investors to determine if their agents (e.g., investment managers and brokers) are performing well.
- *Insider trading*: If investors believe traders with inside information will exploit them, they will exit the market and liquidity will be reduced.
- *Costly information*: If obtaining information is relatively expensive, markets will not be as informationally efficient and investors will not invest as much.
- *Defaults:* Parties might not honor their obligations in markets.

To solve these problems, market regulation should:

- Protect unsophisticated investors so that trust in the markets is preserved.
- Require minimum standards of competency and make it easier for investors to evaluate performance. The CFA Program and the Global Investment Performance Standards are part of this effort.
- Prevent insiders from exploiting other investors.
- Require common financial reporting requirements (e.g., those of the International Accounting Standards Board) so that information gathering is less expensive.
- Require minimum levels of capital so that market participants will be able to honor their long-term commitments. This is especially important for insurance companies and pension funds that individuals depend on for their financial future. With capital at stake, market participants have more incentive to be careful about the risks they take.

Regulation can be provided by governments as well as industry groups. For example, most exchanges, clearinghouses, and dealer trade organizations are self-regulating organizations (SROs), meaning that they regulate their members. Governments sometimes delegate regulatory authority to SROs.

When they fail to address the problems mentioned above, financial markets do not function well. Liquidity declines, firms shun risky projects, new ideas go unfunded, and economic growth slows.

KEY CONCEPTS

LOS 46.a
The three main functions of the financial system are to:
1. Allow entities to save, borrow, issue equity capital, manage risks, exchange assets, and utilize information.

2. Determine the return that equates aggregate savings and borrowing.

3. Allocate capital efficiently.

LOS 46.b
Assets and markets can be classified as:
- Financial assets (e.g., securities, currencies, derivatives) versus real assets (e.g., real estate, equipment).
- Debt securities versus equity securities.
- Public securities that trade on exchanges or through dealers versus private securities.
- Physical derivative contracts (e.g., on grains or metals) versus financial derivative contracts (e.g., on bonds or equity indexes).
- Spot versus future delivery markets.
- Primary markets (issuance of new securities) versus secondary markets (trading of previously issued securities).
- Money markets (short-term debt instruments) versus capital markets (longer-term debt instruments and equities).
- Traditional investment markets (bonds, stocks) versus alternative investment markets (e.g., real estate, hedge funds, fine art).

LOS 46.c
The major types of assets are securities, currencies, contracts, commodities, and real assets.

Securities include fixed income (e.g., bonds, notes, commercial paper), equity (common stock, preferred stock, warrants), and pooled investment vehicles (mutual funds, exchange-traded funds, hedge funds, asset-backed securities).

Contracts include futures, forwards, options, swaps, and insurance contracts.

Commodities include agricultural products, industrial and precious metals, and energy products and are traded in spot, forward, and futures markets.

Most national currencies are traded in spot markets and some are also traded in forward and futures markets.

LOS 46.d
Financial intermediaries perform the following roles:

- Brokers, exchanges, and alternative trading systems connect buyers and sellers of the same security at the same location and time. They provide a centralized location for trading.
- Dealers match buyers and sellers of the same security at different points in time.
- Arbitrageurs connect buyers and sellers of the same security at the same time but in different venues. They also connect buyers and sellers of non-identical securities of similar risk.
- Securitizers and depository institutions package assets into a diversified pool and sell interests in it. Investors obtain greater liquidity and choose their desired risk level.
- Insurance companies create a diversified pool of risks and manage the risk inherent in providing insurance.
- Clearinghouses reduce counterparty risk and promote market integrity.

LOS 46.e
A long position in an asset represents current or future ownership. A long position benefits when the asset increases in value.

A short position represents an agreement to sell or deliver an asset or results from borrowing an asset and selling it (i.e., a short sale). A short position benefits when the asset decreases in value.

When an investor buys a security by borrowing from a broker, the investor is said to buy on margin and has a leveraged position. The risk of investing borrowed funds is referred to as financial leverage. More leverage results in greater risk.

LOS 46.f
The leverage ratio is the value of the asset divided by the value of the equity position. Higher leverage ratios indicate greater risk.

The return on a margin transaction is the increase in the value of the position after deducting selling commissions and interest charges, divided by the amount of funds initially invested, including purchase commissions.

The maintenance margin is the minimum percentage of equity that a margin investor is required to maintain in his account. If the investor's equity falls below the maintenance margin, the investor will receive a margin call. The stock price that will result in a margin call is:

$$\text{margin call price} = P_0 \left(\frac{1 - \text{initial margin}}{1 - \text{maintenance margin}} \right)$$

where:
P_0 = initial purchase price

LOS 46.g

Execution instructions specify how to trade. Market orders and limit orders are examples of execution instructions.

Validity instructions specify when an order can be filled. Day orders, good-til-cancelled orders, and stop orders are examples of validity instructions.

Clearing instructions specify how to settle a trade.

LOS 46.h

A market order is an order to execute the trade immediately at the best possible price. A market order is appropriate when the trader wants to execute a transaction quickly. The disadvantage of a market order is that it may execute at an unfavorable price.

A limit order is an order to trade at the best possible price, subject to the price satisfying the limit condition. A limit order avoids price execution uncertainty. The disadvantage of a limit order is that it may not be filled. A buy (sell) order with a limit of $18 will only be executed if the security can be bought (sold) at a price of $18 or less (more).

LOS 46.i

New issues of securities are sold in primary capital markets. Secondary financial markets are where securities trade after their initial issuance.

In an underwritten offering, the investment bank guarantees that the issue will be sold at a price that is negotiated between the issuer and bank. In a best efforts offering, the bank acts only as a broker.

In a private placement, a firm sells securities directly to qualified investors, without the disclosures of a public offering.

A liquid secondary market makes it easier for firms to raise external capital in the primary market, which results in a lower cost of capital for firms.

LOS 46.j

There are three main categories of securities markets:

1. Quote-driven markets: Investors trade with dealers that maintain inventories of securities, currencies, or contracts.

2. Order-driven markets: Order-matching and trade-pricing rules are used to match the orders of buyers and sellers.

3. Brokered markets: Brokers locate a counterparty to take the other side of a buy or sell order.

In call markets, securities are only traded at specific times. In continuous markets, trades occur at any time the market is open.

LOS 46.k

A well-functioning financial system has the following characteristics:

- Complete markets: Savers receive a return, borrowers can obtain capital, hedgers can manage risks, and traders can acquire needed assets.
- Operational efficiency: Trading costs are low.
- Informational efficiency: Prices reflect fundamental information quickly.
- Allocational efficiency: Capital is directed to its highest valued use.

LOS 46.l

The objectives of market regulation are to:

- Protect unsophisticated investors.
- Establish minimum standards of competency.
- Help investors to evaluate performance.
- Prevent insiders from exploiting other investors.
- Promote common financial reporting requirements so that information gathering is less expensive.
- Require minimum levels of capital so that market participants will be able to honor their commitments and be more careful about their risks.

CONCEPT CHECKERS

1. Daniel Ferramosco is concerned that a long-term bond he holds might default. He therefore buys a contract that will compensate him in the case of default. What type of contract does he hold?
    A. Physical derivative contract.
    B. Primary derivative contract.
    C. Financial derivative contract.

2. A financial intermediary buys a stock and then resells it a few days later at a higher price. Which intermediary would this *most likely* describe?
    A. Broker.
    B. Dealer.
    C. Arbitrageur.

3. Which of the following is *most* similar to a short position in the underlying asset?
    A. Buying a put.
    B. Writing a put.
    C. Buying a call.

4. An investor buys 1,000 shares of a stock on margin at a price of $50 per share. The initial margin requirement is 40% and the margin lending rate is 3%. The investor's broker charges a commission of $0.01 per share on purchases and sales. The stock pays an annual dividend of $0.30 per share. One year later, the investor sells the 1,000 shares at a price of $56 per share. The investor's rate of return is *closest* to:
    A. 12%.
    B. 27%.
    C. 36%.

5. A stock is selling at $50. An investor's valuation model estimates its intrinsic value to be $40. Based on her estimate, she would *most likely* place a:
    A. short-sale order.
    B. stop order to buy.
    C. market order to buy.

6. Which of the following limit buy orders would be the *most likely* to go unexecuted?
    A. A marketable order.
    B. An order behind the market.
    C. An order making a new market.

7. New issues of securities are transactions in the:
    A. primary market.
    B. secondary market.
    C. seasoned market.

8.   In which of the following types of markets do stocks trade any time the market is open?
      A. Exchange markets.
      B. Call markets.
      C. Continuous markets.

9.   A market is said to be informationally efficient if it features:
      A. market prices that reflect all available information about the value of the securities traded.
      B. timely and accurate information about current supply and demand conditions.
      C. many buyers and sellers that are willing to trade at prices above and below the prevailing market price.

10.   Which of the following would *least likely* be an objective of market regulation?
      A. Reduce burdensome accounting standards.
      B. Make it easier for investors to evaluate performance.
      C. Prevent investors from using inside information in securities trading.

Study Session 13

ANSWERS – CONCEPT CHECKERS

1. **C**   Daniel holds a derivative contract that has a value determined by another financial contract; in this case, the long-term bond.

2. **B**   This situation best describes a dealer. A dealer buys an asset for its inventory in the hopes of reselling it later at a higher price. Brokers stand between buyers and sellers of the same security at the same location and time. Arbitrageurs trade in the same security simultaneously in different markets.

3. **A**   Buying a put is most similar to a short position in the underlying asset because the put increases in value if the underlying asset value decreases. The writer of a put and the holder of a call have a long exposure to the underlying asset because their positions increase in value if the underlying asset value increases.

4. **B**   The total purchase price is 1,000 × $50 = $50,000. The investor must post initial margin of 40% × $50,000 = $20,000. The remaining $30,000 is borrowed. The commission on the purchase is 1,000 × $0.01 = $10. Thus, the initial equity investment is $20,010.

    In one year, the sales price is 1,000 × $56 = $56,000, so the capital gain is $56,000 – $50,000 = $6,000. Dividends received are 1,000 × $0.30 = $300. Interest paid is $30,000 × 3% = $900. The commission on the sale is 1,000 × $0.01 = $10.

    The gain on the transaction in one year is $6,000 + $300 – $900 – $10 = $5,390. The return on the equity investment is $5,390 / $20,010 = 26.94%.

5. **A**   If the investor believes the stock is overvalued in the market, the investor should place a short-sale order, which would be profitable if the stock moves toward her value estimate.

6. **B**   A behind-the-market limit order would be least likely executed. In the case of a buy, the limit buy order price is below the best bid. It will likely not execute until security prices decline. A marketable buy order is the most likely to trade because it is close to the best ask price. In an order that is making a new market or inside the market, the limit buy order price is between the best bid and ask.

7. **A**   The primary market refers to the market for newly issued securities.

8. **C**   Continuous markets are defined as markets where stocks can trade any time the market is open. Some exchange markets are call markets where orders are accumulated and executed at specific times.

9. **A**   Informational efficiency means the prevailing price reflects all available information about the value of the asset, and the price reacts quickly to new information.

10. **A**   Market regulation should require financial reporting standards so that information gathering is less expensive and the informational efficiency of the markets is enhanced.

The following is a review of the Equity: Market Organization, Market Indices, and Market Efficiency principles designed to address the learning outcome statements set forth by CFA Institute. This topic is also covered in:

SECURITY MARKET INDICES

EXAM FOCUS

Security market indexes are used to measure the performance of markets and investment managers. Understand the construction, calculation, and weaknesses of price-weighted, market capitalization-weighted, and equal-weighted indexes. Be familiar with the various security indexes and their potential weaknesses.

LOS 47.a: Describe a security market index.

CFA® Program Curriculum, Volume 5, page 78

A **security market index** is used to represent the performance of an asset class, security market, or segment of a market. They are usually created as portfolios of individual securities, which are referred to as the **constituent securities** of the index. An index has a numerical value that is calculated from the market prices (actual when available, or estimated) of its constituent securities at a point in time. An index return is the percentage change in the index's value over a period of time.

LOS 47.b: Calculate and interpret the value, price return, and total return of an index.

CFA® Program Curriculum, Volume 5, page 79

An index return may be calculated using a **price index** or a **return index**. A price index uses only the prices of the constituent securities in the return calculation. A rate of return that is calculated based on a price index is referred to as a **price return**.

A return index includes both prices and income from the constituent securities. A rate of return that is calculated based on a return index is called a **total return**. If the assets in an index produce interim cash flows such as dividends or interest payments, the total return will be greater than the price return.

Once returns are calculated for each period, they then can be compounded together to arrive at the return for the measurement period:

$$R_P = (1 + R_{S1})(1 + R_{S2})(1 + R_{S3})(1 + R_{S4})...(1 + R_{Sk}) - 1$$

where:
R_P = portfolio return during the measurement period
k = total number of subperiods
R_{Sk} = portfolio return during the subperiod k

For example, if the returns for the first two periods were 0.50% and 1.04%, they would be geometrically linked to produce 1.55%:

$$R_P = (1 + R_{S1})(1 + R_{S2}) - 1 = (1.005)(1.0104) - 1 = 0.0155 \text{ or } 1.55\%$$

If the starting index value is 100, its value after two periods would be $100 \times 1.0155 = 101.55$.

LOS 47.c: Describe the choices and issues in index construction and management.

CFA® Program Curriculum, Volume 5, page 82

Index providers must make several decisions:

- What is the *target market* the index is intended to measure?
- Which securities from the target market should be included?
- How should the securities be weighted in the index?
- How often should the index be rebalanced?
- When should the selection and weighting of securities be re-examined?

The target market may be defined very broadly (e.g., stocks in the United States) or narrowly (e.g., small-cap value stocks in the United States). It may also be defined by geographic region or by economic sector (e.g., cyclical stocks). The constituent stocks in the index could be all the stocks in that market or just a representative sample. The selection process may be determined by an objective rule or subjectively by a committee.

LOS 47.d: Compare the different weighting methods used in index construction.

CFA® Program Curriculum, Volume 5, page 83

Weighting schemes for stock indexes include price weighting, equal weighting, market capitalization weighting, float-adjusted market capitalization weighting, and fundamental weighting.

A **price-weighted index** is simply an arithmetic average of the prices of the securities included in the index. The divisor of a price-weighted index is adjusted for stock splits and changes in the composition of the index when securities are added or deleted, such that the index value is unaffected by such changes.

The advantage of a price-weighted index is that its computation is simple. One disadvantage is that a given percentage change in the price of a higher priced stock has a greater impact on the index's value than does an equal percentage change in the price of a lower priced stock. Put another way, higher priced stocks have more weight in the calculation of a price-weighted index. Additionally, a stock's weight in the index going forward changes if the firm splits its stock, repurchases stock, or issues stock dividends, as all of these actions will affect the price of the stock and therefore its weight in the index. A portfolio that has an equal number of shares in each of the constituent stocks will have price returns (ignoring dividends) that will match the returns of a price-weighted index.

Two major price-weighted indexes are the Dow Jones Industrial Average (DJIA) and the Nikkei Dow Jones Stock Average. The DJIA is a price-weighted index based on 30 U.S. stocks. The Nikkei Dow is constructed from the prices of 225 stocks that trade in the first section of the Tokyo Stock Exchange.

An **equal-weighted index** is calculated as the arithmetic average return of the index stocks and, for a given time period, would be matched by the returns on a portfolio that had equal dollar amounts invested in each index stock. As with a price-weighted index, an advantage of an equal-weighted index is its simplicity.

One complication with an equal-weighted index return is that a matching portfolio would have to be adjusted periodically (rebalanced) as prices change so that the values of all security positions are made equal each period. The portfolio rebalancing required to match the performance of an equal-weighted index creates high transactions costs that would decrease portfolio returns.

Another concern with an equal-weighted index is that the weights placed on the returns of the securities of smaller capitalization firms are greater than their proportions of the overall market value of the index stocks. Conversely, the weights on the returns of large capitalization firms in the index are smaller than their proportions of the overall market value of the index stocks.

The Value Line Composite Average and the Financial Times Ordinary Share Index are well-known examples of equal-weighted indexes.

A **market capitalization-weighted index** (or **value-weighted index**) has weights based on the market capitalization of each index stock (current stock price multiplied by the number of shares outstanding) as a proportion of the total market capitalization of all the stocks in the index. A market capitalization-weighted index return can be matched with a portfolio in which the value of each security position in the portfolio is the same proportion of the total portfolio value as the proportion of that security's market capitalization to the total market capitalization of all of the securities included in the index. This weighting method more closely represents changes in aggregate investor wealth than price weighting. Because the weight of an index stock is based on its market capitalization, a market capitalization-weighted index does not need to be adjusted when a stock splits or pays a stock dividend.

An alternative to using a firm's market capitalization to calculate its weight in an index is to use its **market float**. A firm's market float is the total value of the shares that are actually available to the investing public and excludes the value of shares held by controlling stockholders because they are unlikely to sell their shares. For example, the float for Microsoft would exclude shares owned by Bill Gates and Paul Allen (the founders) and those of certain other large shareholders as well. The market float is often calculated excluding those shares held by corporations or governments as well. Sometimes the market float calculation excludes shares that are not available to foreign buyers and is then referred to as the **free float**. The reason for this is to better match the index weights of stocks to their proportions of the total value of all the shares of index stocks that are actually available to investors.

A **float-adjusted market capitalization-weighted index** is constructed like a market capitalization-weighted index. The weights, however, are based on the proportionate value of each firm's shares that are available to investors to the total market value of the shares of index stocks that are available to investors. Firms with relatively large percentages of their shares held by controlling stockholders will have less weight than they have in an unadjusted market-capitalization index.

The advantage of market capitalization-weighted indexes of either type is that index security weights represent proportions of total market value. The primary disadvantage of value-weighted indexes is that the relative impact of a stock's return on the index increases as its price rises and decreases as its price falls. This means that stocks that are possibly overvalued are given disproportionately high weights in the index and stocks that are possibly undervalued are given disproportionately low weights. Holding a value-weighted portfolio is, therefore, similar to following a momentum strategy, under which the most successful stocks are given the greatest weights and poor performing stocks are underweighted.

The Standard and Poor's 500 (S&P 500) Index Composite is an example of a market capitalization-weighted index.

An index that uses **fundamental weighting** uses weights based on firm fundamentals, such as earnings, dividends, or cash flow. In contrast to market capitalization index weights, these weights are unaffected by the share prices of the index stocks (although related to them over the long term). Fundamental weights can be based on a single measure or some combination of fundamental measures.

An advantage of a fundamental-weighted index is that it avoids the bias of market capitalization-weighted indexes toward the performance of the shares of overvalued firms and away from the performance of the shares of undervalued firms. A fundamental-weighted index will actually have a value tilt, overweighting firms with high value-based metrics such as book-to-market ratios or earnings yields. Note that a firm with a high earnings yield (total earnings to total market value) relative to other index firms will by construction have a higher weight in an earnings-weighted index because, among index stocks, its earnings are high relative to its market value.

LOS 47.e: Calculate and analyze the value and return of an index on the basis of its weighting method.

CFA® Program Curriculum, Volume 5, page 83

Price Weighting

A price-weighted index adds the market prices of each stock in the index and divides this total by the number of stocks in the index. The divisor, however, must be adjusted for stock splits and other changes in the index portfolio to maintain the continuity of the series over time.

$$\text{price-weighted index} = \frac{\text{sum of stock prices}}{\text{number of stocks in index adjusted for splits}}$$

Example: Price-weighted index

Given the information for the three stocks presented in the following figure, calculate a price-weighted index return over a 1-month period.

Index Firm Data

	Share Price *December 31, 20X6*	Share Price *January 31, 20X7*
Stock X	$10	$20
Stock Y	$20	$15
Stock Z	$60	$40

Answer:

The price-weighted index is (10 + 20 + 60) / 3 = 30 as of December 31 and (20 + 15 + 40) / 3 = 25 as of January 31. Hence, the price-weighted 1-month percentage return is:

$$\frac{25}{30} - 1 = -16.7\%$$

Example: Adjusting a price-weighted index for stock splits

At the market close on day 1, Stock A has a price of $10, Stock B has a price of $20, and Stock C has a price of $90. The value of a price-weighted index of these three stocks is (10 + 20 + 90) / 3 = 40 at the close of trading. If Stock C splits 2-for-1, effective on day 2, what is the new denominator for the index?

Answer:

The effect of the split on the price of Stock C, in the absence of any change from the price at the end of day 1, would be to reduce it to $90 / 2 = $45. The index denominator will be adjusted so that the index value would remain at 40 if there were no changes in the stock prices other than to adjust for the split. The new denominator, d, must satisfy (10 + 20 + 45) / d = 40 and equals 1.875.

The returns on a price-weighted index could be matched by purchasing an equal number of shares of each stock represented in the index. Because the index is price weighted, a percentage change in a high-priced stock will have a relatively greater effect on the index than the same percentage change in a low-priced stock.

Market Capitalization Weighting

A market capitalization-weighted index is calculated by summing the total value (current stock price multiplied by the number of shares outstanding) of all the stocks in the index. This sum is then divided by a similar sum calculated during the selected base period. The ratio is then multiplied by the index's base value (typically 100).

For example, if the total market values of the index portfolio on December 31 and January 31 are $80 million and $95 million, respectively, the index value at the end of January is:

$$\text{current index value} = \frac{\text{current total market value of index stocks}}{\text{base year total market value of index stocks}} \times \text{base year index value}$$

$$\text{current index value} = \frac{\$95 \text{ million}}{\$80 \text{ million}} \times 100 = 118.75$$

Thus, the market capitalization-weighted index percentage return is:

(118.75 / 100) − 1 = 18.75%

The following example of price-weighting versus market value-weighting shows how these two indexes are calculated and how they differ.

Example: Price-weighted vs. market capitalization-weighted indexes

Consider the three firms described below. Compare the effects on a price-weighted index and a market capitalization-weighted index if Stock A doubles in price or if Stock C doubles in price. Assume the period shown in the table is the base period for the market capitalization-weighted index and that its base value is 100.

Index Firm Data

Company	Number of Shares Outstanding (000s)	Stock Price	Capitalization (000s)
A	100	$100	$10,000
B	1,000	$10	$10,000
C	20,000	$1	$20,000

Answer:

The price-weighted index equals:

$$\frac{100+10+1}{3} = 37$$

If Stock A doubles in price to $200, the price-weighted index value is:

$$\frac{200+10+1}{3} = 70.33$$

If Stock C doubles in price to $2, the price-weighted index value is:

$$\frac{100+10+2}{3} = 37.33$$

If Stock A doubles in value, the index goes up 33.33 points, while if Stock C doubles in value, the index only goes up 0.33 points. Changes in the value of the firm with the highest stock price have a disproportionately large influence on a price-weighted index.

For a market capitalization-weighted index, the base period market capitalization is $(100,000 \times \$100) + (1,000,000 \times \$10) + (20,000,000 \times \$1) = \$40,000,000$.

If Stock A doubles in price to $200, the index goes to:

$$\frac{100,000 \times \$200 + 1,000,000 \times \$10 + 20,000,000 \times \$1}{\$40,000,000} \times 100 = 125$$

If Stock C doubles in price to $2, the index goes to:

$$\frac{100,000 \times \$100 + 1,000,000 \times \$10 + 20,000,000 \times \$2}{\$40,000,000} \times 100 = 150$$

In the market capitalization-weighted index, the returns on Stock C have the greatest influence on the index return because Stock C's market capitalization is larger than that of Stock A or Stock B.

Equal Weighting

An equal-weighted index places an equal weight on the returns of all index stocks, regardless of their prices or market values. A $2 change in the price of a $20 stock has the same effect on the index as a $30 change in the price of a $300 stock regardless of the size of the company. The return of an equal-weighted index over a given period is often calculated as a simple average of the returns of the index stocks.

Example: Equally weighted index

Calculate the equal-weighted index value for the three stocks described below, assuming an initial index value of 131.

Equal-Weighted Index Data

Stock	Initial Price	Current Price	Price Change
A	$12	$15	+25.0%
B	$52	$48	–7.7%
C	$38	$45	+18.4%

Answer:

$$\text{change in index} = \frac{25\% - 7.7\% + 18.4\%}{3} = 11.9\%$$

new index value = 131(1 + 0.119) = 146.59

Note that for a total return index, period returns would include any dividends paid over the period.

LOS 47.f: Describe rebalancing and reconstitution of an index.

CFA® Program Curriculum, Volume 5, page 91

Rebalancing refers to adjusting the weights of securities in a portfolio to their target weights after price changes have affected the weights. For index calculations, rebalancing to target weights on the index securities is done on a periodic basis, usually quarterly. Because the weights in price- and value-weighted indexes (portfolios) are adjusted to their correct values by changes in prices, rebalancing is an issue primarily for equal-weighted indexes. As noted previously, the weights on security returns in an (initially) equal-weighted portfolio are not equal as securities prices change over time. Therefore, rebalancing the portfolio at the end of each period used to calculate index returns is necessary for the portfolio return to match the index return.

Index **reconstitution** refers to periodically adding and deleting securities that make up an index. Securities are deleted if they no longer meet the index criteria and are replaced by other securities that do. Indexes are reconstituted to reflect corporate events such as bankruptcy or delisting of index firms and are at the subjective judgment of a committee.

When a security is added to an index, its price tends to rise as portfolio managers seeking to track that index in a portfolio buy the security. The prices of deleted securities tend to fall as portfolio managers sell them. Note that additions and deletions also require that the weights on the returns of other index stocks be adjusted to conform to the desired weighting scheme.

LOS 47.g: Describe uses of security market indices.

CFA® Program Curriculum, Volume 5, page 93

Security market indexes have several uses:

- *Reflection of market sentiment.* Indexes provide a representative market return and thus reflect investor confidence. Although the Dow Jones Industrial Average is a popular index, it reflects the performance of only 30 stocks and thus may not be a good measure of sentiment with regard to the broader market.
- *Benchmark of manager performance.* An index can be used to evaluate the performance of an active manager. Because portfolio performance depends to a large degree on its chosen style, the benchmark should be consistent with the manager's investment approach and style to assess the manager's skill accurately. The index stocks should be those that the manager will actually choose from. For example, a value manager should be compared against a value index, not a broad market index, because portfolio securities will be selected from among value stocks.
- *Measure of market return and risk.* In asset allocation, estimates of the expected return and standard deviation of returns for various asset classes are based on historical returns for an index of securities representing that asset class.
- *Measure of beta and risk-adjusted return.* The use of the capital asset pricing model (CAPM) to determine a stock's expected return requires an estimate of its beta and the return on the market. Index portfolio returns are used as a proxy for the returns on the market portfolio, both in estimating a stock's beta, and then again in calculating its expected return based on its systematic (beta) risk. Expected returns can then be compared to actual stock returns to determine systematic risk-adjusted returns.
- *Model portfolio for index funds.* Investors who wish to invest passively can invest in an index fund, which seeks to replicate the performance of a market index. There are index mutual funds and index exchange-traded funds, as well as private portfolios that are structured to match the return of an index.

LOS 47.h: Describe types of equity indices.

CFA® Program Curriculum, Volume 5, page 94

Investors can use a variety of equity market indexes. These equity indexes can be classified as follows:

- *Broad market index.* Provides a measure of a market's overall performance and usually contains more than 90% of the market's total value. For example, the Wilshire 5000 Index contains more than 6,000 equity securities and is, therefore, a good representation of the overall performance of the U.S. equity market.
- *Multi-market index.* Typically constructed from the indexes of markets in several countries and is used to measure the equity returns of a geographic region (e.g., Latin America indexes), markets based on their stage of economic development (e.g., emerging markets indexes), or the entire world (e.g., MSCI World Index).
- *Multi-market index with fundamental weighting.* Uses market capitalization-weighting for the country indexes but then weights the country index returns in the global index by a fundamental factor (e.g., GDP). This prevents a country with previously high stock returns from being overweighted in a multi-market index.

- *Sector index.* Measures the returns for an industry sector such as health care, financial, or consumer goods firms. Investors can use these indexes in cyclical analysis because some sectors do better than others in various phases of the business cycle. Sector indexes can be for a particular country or global. These indexes are used to evaluate portfolio managers and to construct index portfolios.

- *Style index.* Measures the returns to market capitalization and value or growth strategies. Some indexes reflect a combination of the two (e.g., small-cap value fund). Because there is no widely accepted definition of large-cap, mid-cap, or small-cap stocks, different indexes use different definitions. These definitions may be specified values of market capitalization or relative definitions, such as defining large-cap stocks as the largest 500 firms in a given market. In constructing value stock and growth stock indexes, price-to-earnings ratios or dividend yields are often used to identify value and growth stocks. Over time, stocks can migrate from one classification to another. For example, a successful small-cap company might grow to become a mid-cap or large-cap company. This causes style indexes to typically have higher turnover of constituent firms than broad market indexes.

LOS 47.i: Describe types of fixed-income indices.

CFA® Program Curriculum, Volume 5, page 97

Many different fixed income indexes are available to investors. Investors should be aware of several issues with the construction of fixed income indexes:

- *Large universe of securities.* The fixed income security universe is much broader than the universe of stocks. Fixed income securities are issued not just by firms, but also by governments and government agencies. Each of these entities may also issue various types of fixed income securities. Also, unlike stocks, bonds mature and must be replaced in fixed income indexes. As a result, turnover is high in fixed income indexes.

- *Dealer markets and infrequent trading.* Fixed income securities are primarily traded by dealers, so index providers must depend on dealers for recent prices. Because fixed income securities are typically illiquid, a lack of recent trades may require index providers to estimate the value of index securities from recent prices of securities with similar characteristics.

The large number of fixed income securities results in large differences in the number of index securities among fixed income indexes. Illiquidity, transactions costs, and high turnover of constituent securities make it both difficult and expensive for fixed income portfolio managers to replicate a fixed income index.

Fixed income securities vary widely with respect to their coupon rates, ratings, maturities, and embedded options such as convertibility to common stock. Consequently, a wide variety of fixed income indexes is available. Like equity indexes, fixed income indexes are created for various sectors, geographic regions, and levels of country economic development. They can also be constructed based on type of issuer or collateral, coupon, maturity, default risk, or inflation protection. Broad market indexes, sector indexes, style indexes, and other specialized indexes are available.

LOS 47.j: Describe indices representing alternative investments.

CFA® Program Curriculum, Volume 5, page 100

Alternative assets are of interest to investors because of their potential diversification benefits. Three of the most widely held alternative assets are commodities, real estate, and hedge funds.

Commodity indexes represent futures contracts on commodities such as grains, livestock, metals, and energy. Examples include the Commodity Research Bureau Index and the S&P GSCI (previously the Goldman Sachs Commodity Index).

The issues in commodity indexes relevant for investors are as follows:

- *Weighting method.* Commodity index providers use a variety of weighting schemes. Some use equal weighting, others weight commodities by their global production values, and others use fixed weights that the index provider determines. As a result, different indexes have significantly different commodity exposures and risk and return characteristics. For example, one index may have a large exposure to the prices of energy commodities while another has a large exposure to the prices of agricultural products.
- *Futures vs. actual.* Commodity indexes are based on the prices of commodity futures contracts, not the spot prices of commodities. Commodity futures contracts reflect the risk-free rate of return, changes in futures prices, and the roll yield. Furthermore, the contracts mature and must be replaced over time by other contracts. For these reasons, the return on commodity futures differs from the returns on a long position in the commodity itself.

Real estate indexes can be constructed using returns based on appraisals of properties, repeat property sales, or the performance of Real Estate Investment Trusts (REITs). REITs are similar to closed-end mutual funds in that they invest in properties or mortgages and then issue ownership interests in the pool of assets to investors. While real properties are quite illiquid, REIT shares trade like any common shares and many offer very good liquidity to investors. FTSE International produces a family of REIT indexes.

Hedge funds pool investor money and invest in nontraditional assets, using leverage (borrowed money or derivative contracts) and both long and short positions. Most **hedge fund indexes** equally weight the returns of the hedge funds included in the index.

Hedge funds are largely unregulated and are not required to report their performance to index providers. Consequently, some funds will report to one index but not another. The performance of different indexes can thus vary substantially.

Furthermore, it is often the case that those funds that report are the funds that have been successful, as the poorly performing funds do not want to publicize their performance. Funds that have reported in the past but have recently had poor returns may stop reporting their performance. The result is an upward bias in index returns, with hedge funds appearing to be better investments than they actually are.

Professor's Note: Commodities (including the components of return on a commodity investment), real estate, and hedge funds (including hedge fund performance biases) are discussed further in the Study Session on alternative investments.

LOS 47.k: Compare types of security market indices.

CFA® Program Curriculum, Volume 5, page 102

The following table summarizes some of the noteworthy characteristics of various global indexes. Notice from the table that most security market indexes are market capitalization-weighted and often adjusted for the float (securities actually available for purchase). The number of securities in many of these indexes can vary.

Index	Reflects	Number of Constituent Securities	Weighting Method	Notes
Dow Jones Industrial Average	Large U.S. stocks	30	Price	Stocks are chosen by Wall Street Journal editors
Nikkei Stock Average	Large Japanese stocks	225	Modified price	Contains some illiquid stocks, price weighting and adjusted for high-priced shares
TOPIX	All stocks on the Tokyo Stock Exchange First Section	Variable	Market capitalization, adjusted for float	Has a large number of small illiquid stocks making it hard to replicate. Contains 93% of the market cap of Japanese equities
MSCI All Country World Index	Stocks in 23 developed and 22 emerging markets	Variable	Market capitalization, adjusted for float	Available in both U.S. dollars and local currency
S&P Developed Ex-U.S. BMI Energy Sector Index	Global energy stocks outside the United States	Variable	Market capitalization, adjusted for float	Is the model portfolio for an ETF
Barclays Capital Global Aggregate Bond Index	Global investment-grade bonds	Variable	Market capitalization	Formerly compiled by Lehman Brothers
Markit iBoxx Euro High-Yield Bond Indexes	Below investment-grade bonds	Variable	Market capitalization	Represents liquid portion of market and rebalanced monthly
FTSE EPRA/ NAREIT Global Real Estate Index	Global real estate	335	Market capitalization, adjusted for float	Represents publicly traded REITs

Index	Reflects	Number of Constituent Securities	Weighting Method	Notes
HFRX Global Hedge Fund Index	Global hedge funds	Variable	Asset weighted	Contains a variety of hedge fund strategies and is weighted based on the amount invested in each hedge fund
HFRX Equal Weighted Strategies EUR Index	Global hedge funds	Variable	Equal weighted	Contains same strategy funds as HFRX Global Hedge Fund Index and is equal weighted
Morningstar Style Indexes	U.S. stocks grouped by value/growth and market cap	Variable	Market capitalization, adjusted for float	Nine categories classified by combinations of three cap categories and three value/growth categories

KEY CONCEPTS

LOS 47.a
A security market index represents the performance of an asset class, security market, or segment of a market. The performance of the market or segment over a period of time is represented by the percentage change in (i.e., the return on) the value of the index.

LOS 47.b
A price index uses only the prices of the constituent securities in the return calculation. The rate of return is called a price return.

A total return index uses both the price of and the income from the index securities in the return calculation.

LOS 47.c
Decisions that index providers must make when constructing and managing indexes include:
- The target market the index will measure.
- Which securities from the target market to include.
- The appropriate weighting method.
- How frequently to rebalance the index to its target weights.
- How frequently to re-examine the selection and weighting of securities.

LOS 47.d
A price-weighted index is the arithmetic mean of the prices of the index securities. The divisor, which is initially equal to the number of securities in the index, must be adjusted for stock splits and changes in the composition of the index over time.

An equal-weighted index assigns the same weight to each of its constituent securities.

A market capitalization-weighted index gives each constituent security a weight equal to its proportion of the total market value of all securities in the index. Market capitalization can be adjusted for a security's market float or free float to reflect the fact that not all outstanding shares are available for purchase.

A fundamental-weighted index uses weights that are independent of security prices, such as company earnings, revenue, assets, or cash flow.

LOS 47.e

$$\text{Price-weighted index} = \frac{\text{sum of stock prices}}{\text{number of stocks in index adjusted for splits}}.$$

Market capitalization-weighted index =

$$\frac{\text{current total market value of index stocks}}{\text{base year total market value of index stocks}} \times \text{base year index value}.$$

$$\text{Equal-weighted index} = (1 + \text{average percentage change in index stocks}) \times \text{initial index value}.$$

LOS 47.f
Index providers periodically rebalance the weights of the constituent securities. This is most important for equal-weighted indexes.

Reconstitution refers to changing the securities that are included in an index. This is necessary when securities mature or when they no longer have the required characteristics to be included.

LOS 47.g
Indexes are used for the following purposes:
- Reflection of market sentiment.
- Benchmark of manager performance.
- Measure of market return.
- Measure of beta and excess return.
- Model portfolio for index funds.

LOS 47.h
Broad market equity indexes represent the majority of stocks in a market.

Multi-market equity indexes contain the indexes of several countries. Multi-market equity indexes with fundamental weighting use market capitalization weighting for the securities within a country's market but then weight the countries within the global index by a fundamental factor.

Sector indexes measure the returns for a sector (e.g., health care) and are useful because some sectors do better than others in certain business cycle phases. These indexes are used to evaluate portfolio managers and as models for sector investment funds.

Style indexes measure the returns to market capitalization and value or growth strategies. Stocks tend to migrate among classifications, which causes style indexes to have higher constituent turnover than broad market indexes.

LOS 47.i
Fixed income indexes can be classified by issuer, collateral, coupon, maturity, credit risk (e.g., investment grade versus high-yield), and inflation protection. They can be delineated as broad market, sector, style, or other specialized indexes. Indexes exist for various sectors, regions, and levels of development.

The fixed income security universe is much broader than the equity universe, and fixed income indexes have higher turnover. Index providers must depend on dealers for fixed income security prices, and the securities are often illiquid. Fixed income security indexes vary widely in their numbers of constituent securities and can be difficult and expensive to replicate.

LOS 47.j

Indexes have been developed to represent markets for alternative assets such as commodities, real estate, and hedge funds.

Issues in creating commodity indexes include the weighting method (different indexes can have vastly different commodity weights and resulting risk and return) and the fact that commodity indexes are based on the performance of commodity futures contracts, not the actual commodities, which can result in different performance for a commodity index versus the actual commodity.

Real estate indexes include appraisal indexes, repeat property sales indexes, and indexes of real estate investment trusts.

Because hedge funds report their performance to index providers voluntarily, the performance of different hedge fund indexes can vary substantially and index returns have an upward bias.

LOS 47.k

Security market indexes available from commercial providers represent a variety of asset classes and reflect target markets that can be classified by:

- Geographic location, such as country, regional, or global indexes.
- Sector or industry, such as indexes of energy producers.
- Level of economic development, such as emerging market indexes.
- Fundamental factors, such as indexes of value stocks or growth stocks.

CONCEPT CHECKERS

Use the information in the following table to answer Questions 1 through 3.

	As of January 1		As of December 31	
	Share Price	Number of Shares Outstanding (thousands)	Share Price	Number of Shares Outstanding (thousands)
Stock A	$22	1,500	$28	1,500
Stock B	$40	10,000	$50	10,000
Stock C	$34	3,000	$30	3,000

1.   The 1-year return on a price-weighted index of these three stocks is *closest* to:
     A. 12.5%.
     B. 13.5%.
     C. 18.0%.

2.   The 1-year return on an equal-weighted index of these three stocks is *closest* to:
     A. 12.0%.
     B. 12.5%.
     C. 13.5%.

3.   The 1-year return on a market capitalization-weighted index of these stocks is *closest* to:
     A. 12.5%.
     B. 13.5%.
     C. 18.0%.

4.   Market float of a stock is *best* described as its:
     A. total outstanding shares.
     B. shares that are available to domestic investors.
     C. outstanding shares excluding those held by controlling shareholders.

5.   For which of the following indexes will rebalancing occur *most* frequently?
     A. A price-weighted index.
     B. An equal-weighted index.
     C. A market capitalization-weighted index.

6.   Which of the following would *most likely* represent an inappropriate use of an index?
     A. As a reflection of market sentiment.
     B. Comparing a small-cap manager against a broad market.
     C. Using the CAPM to determine the expected return and beta.

7.   Which of the following is *least accurate* regarding fixed income indexes?
     A. Replicating the return on a fixed income security index is difficult for investors.
     B. There is a great deal of heterogeneity in the composition of fixed income security indexes.
     C. Due to the large universe of fixed income security issues, data for fixed income securities are relatively easy to obtain.

8.   Most of the widely used global security indexes are:
     A. price-weighted.
     B. equal-weighted.
     C. market capitalization-weighted.

ANSWERS – CONCEPT CHECKERS

1. **A** $\dfrac{22+40+34}{3}=32,\ \dfrac{28+50+30}{3}=36,\ \dfrac{36}{32}-1=0.125=12.5\%$

2. **C** $\left[\left(\dfrac{28}{22}-1\right)+\left(\dfrac{50}{40}-1\right)+\left(\dfrac{30}{34}-1\right)\right]\left(\dfrac{1}{3}\right)=0.135=13.5\%$

3. **C**   Total portfolio value January 1:

$$\left[22(1,500)+40(10,000)+34(3,000)\right](1,000)=\$535,000,000$$

Total portfolio value December 31:

$$\left[28(1,500)+50(10,000)+30(3,000)\right](1,000)=\$632,000,000$$

$$\dfrac{632}{535}-1=0.1813\approx18\%$$

From a base value of 100, the December 31 index value would be $\dfrac{632}{535}\times100=118.13$.

4. **C**   Market float represents shares available to the investing public and excludes shares held by controlling shareholders. Free float is a narrower measure that also excludes shares that are not available to foreign investors.

5. **B**   An equal-weighted index will be rebalanced most frequently because as stock prices change, their representation in the index needs to be adjusted. Price-weighted and market capitalization-weighted indexes do not usually need rebalancing.

6. **B**   Comparing a small-cap manager against a broad market would be an inappropriate use of an index. A benchmark should be consistent with the manager's investment approach and style. A manager's performance will depend to a large degree on its chosen style.

7. **C**   Fixed income securities are largely traded by dealers and trade infrequently. Data are therefore difficult to obtain.

8. **C**   Most global security indexes are market capitalization-weighted with a float adjustment to reflect the amount of shares available to investors.

MARKET EFFICIENCY

EXAM FOCUS

The informational efficiency of market prices is a very important concept to a portfolio manager. When markets are truly efficient, careful analysis and security selection using publicly available information will not lead to positive risk-adjusted returns on average. For the exam, you must understand the three forms of market efficiency and know the evidence from tests of each form of market efficiency. Focus your attention on the implications of this evidence about the value of technical and fundamental analysis and about the role of portfolio managers in the investment process. Finally, be familiar with market anomalies listed and the perspective provided by behavioral finance.

LOS 48.a: Describe market efficiency and related concepts, including their importance to investment practitioners.

CFA® Program Curriculum, Volume 5, page 116

An **informationally efficient capital market** is one in which the current price of a security fully, quickly, and rationally reflects all available information about that security. This is really a statistical concept. An academic might say, "Given all available information, current securities prices are unbiased estimates of their values, so that the expected return on any security is just the equilibrium return necessary to compensate investors for the risk (uncertainty) regarding its future cash flows." This concept is often put more intuitively as, "You can't beat the market."

In a perfectly efficient market, investors should use a **passive investment** strategy (i.e., buying a broad market index of stocks and holding it) because **active investment** strategies will underperform due to transactions costs and management fees. However, to the extent that market prices are inefficient, active investment strategies can generate positive risk-adjusted returns.

One method of measuring a market's efficiency is to determine the time it takes for trading activity to cause information to be reflected in security prices (i.e., the lag from the time information is disseminated to the time prices reflect the value implications of that information). In some very efficient markets, such as foreign currency markets, this lag can be as short as a minute. If there is a significant lag, informed traders can use the information to potentially generate positive risk-adjusted returns.

Note that market prices should not be affected by the release of information that is well anticipated. Only new information (information that is unexpected and changes expectations) should move prices. The announcement that a firm's earnings were up 45% over the last quarter may be good news if the expected increase was 20%. On the other hand, this may be bad news if a 70% increase was anticipated or no news at all if market participants correctly anticipated quarterly earnings.

LOS 48.b: Distinguish between market value and intrinsic value.

CFA® Program Curriculum, Volume 5, page 118

The **market value** of an asset is its current price. The **intrinsic value** or **fundamental value** of an asset is the value that a rational investor with full knowledge about the asset's characteristics would willingly pay. For example, a bond investor would fully know and understand a bond's coupon, maturity, default risk, liquidity, and other characteristics and would use these to estimate its intrinsic value.

In markets that are highly efficient, investors can typically expect market values to reflect intrinsic values. If markets are not completely efficient, active managers will buy assets for which they think intrinsic values are greater than market values and sell assets for which they think intrinsic values are less than market values.

Intrinsic values cannot be known with certainty and are estimated by investors who will have differing estimates of an asset's intrinsic value. The more complex an asset, the more difficult it is to estimate its intrinsic value. Furthermore, intrinsic value is constantly changing as new (unexpected) information becomes available.

LOS 48.c: Explain factors that affect a market's efficiency.

CFA® Program Curriculum, Volume 5, page 120

Markets are generally neither perfectly efficient nor completely inefficient. The degree of informational efficiency varies across countries, time, and market types. The following factors affect the degree of market efficiency.

Number of market participants. The larger the number of investors, analysts, and traders who follow an asset market, the more efficient the market. The number of participants can vary through time and across countries. For example, some countries prevent foreigners from trading in their markets, reducing market efficiency.

Availability of information. The more information is available to investors, the more efficient the market. In large, developed markets such as the New York Stock Exchange, information is plentiful and markets are quite efficient. In emerging markets, the availability of information is lower, and consequently, market prices are relatively less efficient. Some assets, such as bonds, currencies, swaps, forwards, mortgages, and money market securities that trade in over-the-counter (OTC) markets, may have less available information.

Access to information should not favor one party over another. Therefore, regulations such as the U.S. Securities and Exchange Commission's Regulation FD (fair disclosure) require that firms disclose the same information to the public that they disclose to stock analysts. Traders with material inside information about a firm are prohibited from trading on that information.

Impediments to trading. **Arbitrage** refers to buying an asset in one market and simultaneously selling it at a higher price in another market. This buying and selling of assets will continue until the prices in the two markets are equal. Impediments to arbitrage, such as high transactions costs or lack of information, will limit arbitrage activity and allow some price inefficiencies (i.e., mispricing of assets) to persist.

Short selling improves market efficiency. The sales pressure from short selling prevents assets from becoming overvalued. Restrictions on short selling, such as an inability to borrow stock cheaply, can reduce market efficiency.

Transaction and information costs. To the extent that the costs of information, analysis, and trading are greater than the potential profit from trading misvalued securities, market prices will be inefficient. It is generally accepted that markets are efficient if, after deducting costs, there are no risk-adjusted returns to be made from trading based on publicly available information.

LOS 48.d: Contrast weak-form, semi-strong-form, and strong-form market efficiency.

CFA® Program Curriculum, Volume 5, page 123

Professor Eugene Fama originally developed the concept of market efficiency and identified three forms of market efficiency. The difference among them is that each is based on a different set of information.

1. **Weak-form market efficiency**. The weak form of the efficient markets hypothesis (EMH) states that current security prices *fully reflect all currently available security market data*. Thus, past price and volume (market) information will have no predictive power about the future direction of security prices because price changes will be independent from one period to the next. In a weak-form efficient market, an investor cannot achieve positive risk-adjusted returns on average by using technical analysis.

2. **Semi-strong form market efficiency**. The semi-strong form of the EMH holds that security prices rapidly adjust without bias to the arrival of all new public information. As such, current security prices *fully reflect all publicly available information*. The semi-strong form says security prices include all past security market information and nonmarket information available to the public. The implication is that an investor cannot achieve positive risk-adjusted returns on average by using fundamental analysis.

3. **Strong-form market efficiency**. The strong form of the EMH states that security prices *fully reflect all information from both public and private sources*. The strong form includes all types of information: past security market information, public, and private (inside) information. This means that no group of investors has monopolistic access to information relevant to the formation of prices, and none should be able to consistently achieve positive abnormal returns.

    Given the prohibition on insider trading in most markets, it would be unrealistic to expect markets to reflect all private information. The evidence supports the view that markets are not strong-form efficient.

Professor's Note: As a base level knowledge of the EMH, you should know that the weak form is based on past security market information; the semi-strong form is based on all public information (including market information); and the strong form is based on both public information and inside or private information.

LOS 48.e: Explain the implications of each form of market efficiency for fundamental analysis, technical analysis, and the choice between active and passive portfolio management.

CFA® Program Curriculum, Volume 5, page 128

Abnormal profit (or **risk-adjusted returns**) calculations are often used to test market efficiency. To calculate abnormal profits, the expected return for a trading strategy is calculated given its risk, using a model of expected returns such as the CAPM or a multifactor model. If returns are, on average, greater than equilibrium expected returns, we can reject the hypothesis of efficient prices with respect to the information on which the strategy is based.

The results of tests of the various forms of market efficiency have implications about the value of technical analysis, fundamental analysis, and portfolio management in general.

Technical analysis seeks to earn positive risk-adjusted returns by using historical price and volume (trading) data. Tests of weak-form market efficiency have examined whether technical analysis produces abnormal profits. Generally, the evidence indicates that technical analysis does not produce abnormal profits, so we cannot reject the hypothesis that markets are weak-form efficient. However, technical analysis has been shown to have success in emerging markets, and there are so many possible technical analysis trading strategies that they cannot all be tested. As noted previously, the success of any technical analysis strategy should be evaluated considering the costs of information, analysis, and trading.

Fundamental analysis is based on public information such as earnings, dividends, and various accounting ratios and estimates. The semi-strong form of market efficiency suggests that all public information is already reflected in stock prices. As a result, investors should not be able to earn abnormal profits by trading on this information.

One method of testing the semi-strong form is an **event study**. Event studies examine abnormal returns before and after the release of new information that affects a firm's intrinsic value, such as earnings announcements or dividend changes. The null hypothesis is that investors should not be able to earn positive abnormal returns on average by trading based on firm events because prices will rapidly reflect news about a firm's prospects. The evidence in developed markets indicates that markets are generally semi-strong form efficient. However, there is evidence of semi-strong form inefficiency in some emerging markets.

The evidence that developed markets are generally semi-strong form efficient raises questions about the usefulness of fundamental analysis. It must be fundamental analysis, however, that results in informationally efficient market prices. Fundamental analysis can also be of use to those exceptionally skilled investors who can generate abnormal profits through its use and to those who act rapidly before new information is reflected in prices.

 Professor's Note: Markets can be weak-form efficient without being semi-strong or strong-form efficient. If markets are semi-strong form efficient, they must be weak-form efficient because public information includes market information, but semi-strong form efficient markets need not be strong-form efficient.

Active vs. Passive Portfolio Management

If markets are semi-strong form efficient, investors should invest passively (i.e., invest in an index portfolio that replicates the returns on a market index). Indeed, the evidence shows that most mutual fund managers cannot outperform a passive index strategy over time.

If so, what is the role of a portfolio manager? Even if markets are efficient, portfolio managers can add value by establishing and implementing portfolio risk and return objectives and by assisting clients with portfolio diversification, asset allocation, and tax management.

LOS 48.f: Describe selected market anomalies.

CFA® Program Curriculum, Volume 5, page 129

An anomaly is something that deviates from the common rule. Tests of the EMH are frequently called *anomaly studies*, so in the efficient markets literature, a **market anomaly** is something that would lead us to reject the hypothesis of market efficiency.

Just by chance, some variables will be related to abnormal returns over a given period, although in fact these relationships are unlikely to persist over time. Thus, analysts using historical data can find patterns in security returns that appear to violate market efficiency but are unlikely to recur in the future. If the analyst uses a 5% significance level and examines the relationship between stock returns and 40 variables, two of the variables are expected to show a statistically significant relationship with stock returns by random chance. Recall that the significance level of a hypothesis test is the probability that the null hypothesis (efficiency here) will be rejected purely by chance, even when it is true. Investigating data until a statistically significant relation is found is referred to as **data mining** or **data snooping**. Note that 1,000 analysts, each testing different hypotheses on the same data set, could produce the same results as a single researcher who performed 1,000 hypothesis tests.

To avoid data-mining bias, analysts should first ask if there is an economic basis for the relationships they find between certain variables and stock returns and then test the discovered relationships with a large sample of data to determine if the relationships are persistent and present in various subperiods.

Anomalies in Time-Series Data

Calendar anomalies. The **January effect** or **turn-of-the-year effect** is the finding that during the first five days of January, stock returns, especially for small firms, are significantly higher than they are the rest of the year. In an efficient market, traders would exploit this profit opportunity in January, and in so doing, eliminate it.

Possible explanations for the January effect are **tax-loss selling**, as investors sell losing positions in December to realize losses for tax purposes and then repurchase stocks in January, pushing their prices up, and **window dressing**, as portfolio managers sell risky stocks in December to remove them from their year-end statements and repurchase them in January. Evidence indicates that each of these explains only a portion of the January effect. However, after adjustments are made for risk, the January effect does not appear to persist over time.

Other calendar anomalies that were found at one time but no longer appear to persist are the *turn-of-the-month effect* (stock returns are higher in the days surrounding month end), the *day-of-the-week effect* (average Monday returns are negative), the *weekend effect* (positive Friday returns are followed by negative Monday returns), and the *holiday effect* (pre-holiday returns are higher).

Overreaction and momentum anomalies. The **overreaction effect** refers to the finding that firms with poor stock returns over the previous three or five years (losers) have better subsequent returns than firms that had high stock returns over the prior period. This pattern has been attributed to investor overreaction to both unexpected good news and unexpected bad news. This pattern is also present for bonds and in some international markets. **Momentum effects** have also been found where high short-term returns are followed by continued high returns. This pattern is present in some international markets as well.

Both the overreaction and momentum effects violate the weak form of market efficiency because they provide evidence of a profitable strategy based only on market data. Some researchers argue that the evidence of overreaction to new information is due to the nature of the statistical tests used and that evidence of momentum effects in securities prices reflects rational investor behavior.

Anomalies in Cross-Sectional Data

The **size effect** refers to initial findings that small-cap stocks outperform large-cap stocks. This effect could not be confirmed in later studies, suggesting that either investors had traded on, and thereby eliminated, this anomaly or that the initial finding was simply a random result for the time period examined.

The **value effect** refers to the finding that **value stocks** [those with lower price-to-earnings (P/E), lower market-to-book (M/B), and higher dividend yields] have outperformed **growth stocks** (those with higher P/E, higher M/B, and lower dividend yields). This violates the semi-strong form of market efficiency because the information necessary to classify stocks as value or growth is publicly available. However, some researchers attribute the value effect to greater risk of value stocks that is not captured in the risk adjustment procedure used in the studies.

Other Anomalies

Closed-end investment funds. The shares of **closed-end investment funds** trade at prices that sometimes deviate from the **net asset value** (NAV) of the fund shares, often trading at large discounts to NAV. Such large discounts are an anomaly because, by arbitrage, the value of the pool of assets should be the same as the market price for closed-end shares. Various explanations have been put forth to explain this anomaly, including management fees, taxes on future capital gains, and share illiquidity. None of these explanations fully explains the pricing discrepancy. However, transactions costs would eliminate any profits from exploiting the unexplained portion of closed-end fund discounts.

Earnings announcements. An **earnings surprise** is that portion of announced earnings that was not expected by the market. Positive earnings surprises (earnings higher than expected) precede periods of positive risk-adjusted post-announcement stock returns, and negative surprises lead to predictable negative risk-adjusted returns. The anomaly is that the adjustment process does not occur entirely on the announcement day. Investors could exploit this anomaly by buying positive earnings surprise firms and selling negative earnings surprise firms. Some researchers argue that evidence of predictable abnormal returns after earnings surprises is a result of estimating risk-adjusted returns incorrectly in the tests and that transactions costs would eliminate any abnormal profits from attempting to exploit this returns anomaly.

Initial public offerings. IPOs are typically underpriced, with the offer price below the market price once trading begins. However, the long-term performance of IPO shares as a group is below average. This suggests that investors overreact, in that they are too optimistic about a firm's prospects on the offer day. Some believe this is not an anomaly, but rather a result of the statistical methodologies used to estimate abnormal returns.

 Professor's Note: The initial underpricing of IPOs is also discussed in the topic review of Market Organization and Structure.

Economic fundamentals. Research has found that stock returns are related to known economic fundamentals such as dividend yields, stock volatility, and interest rates. However, we would expect stock returns to be related to economic fundamentals in efficient markets. The relationship between stock returns and dividend yields is also not consistent over all time periods.

Implications for Investors

The majority of the evidence suggests that reported anomalies are not violations of market efficiency but are due to the methodologies used in the tests of market efficiency. Furthermore, both underreaction and overreaction have been found in the markets, meaning that prices are efficient on average. Other explanations for the evidence of anomalies are that they are transient relations, too small to profit from, or simply reflect returns to risk that the researchers have failed to account for.

The bottom line for investors is that portfolio management based on previously identified anomalies will likely be unprofitable. Investment management based solely on anomalies has no sound economic basis.

LOS 48.g: Contrast the behavioral finance view of investor behavior to that of traditional finance.

CFA® Program Curriculum, Volume 5, page 136

Behavioral finance examines investor behavior, its effect on financial markets, how cognitive biases may result in anomalies, and whether investors are rational. Traditional finance models, including efficient markets, are based on an assumption that the market as a whole acts rationally, although some individual investors may not.

Behavioralists argue that investors, while risk averse, have risk preferences that are asymmetric. **Loss aversion** refers to the tendency for investors to be more risk averse when faced with potential losses and less risk averse when faced with potential gains. Put another way, investors dislike losses more than they like gains of an equal amount. Dislike of losses may explain investor overreaction. However, investor underreaction is just as common as overreaction, and loss aversion does not explain underreaction.

Investors sometimes overestimate their ability to value securities. If there is a prevalence of **investor overconfidence**, securities will be mispriced. However, it appears that this mispricing may be hard to predict, may only be temporary, may not be exploitable for abnormal profits, and may only exist for high-growth firms. Overconfidence in their estimates also causes investors to hold portfolios that are not well diversified, increasing their portfolio risk but not overall market risk.

Other behavioral biases that have been identified include:

- **Representativeness**. Investors assume good companies or good markets are good investments.
- **Gambler's fallacy**. Recent results affect investor estimates of future probabilities.
- **Mental accounting**. Investors classify different investments into separate mental accounts instead of viewing them as a total portfolio.
- **Conservatism**. Investors react slowly to changes.
- **Disposition effect**. Investors are willing to realize gains but unwilling to realize losses.
- **Narrow framing**. Investors view events in isolation.

Although investor biases may help explain the existence of security mispricing and anomalies, it is not clear that they are predictable enough so that abnormal profits could be earned by exploiting them.

One explanation for the evidence of the slow adjustment of security prices to new information is the concept of **information cascades**. This refers to the idea that uninformed traders, when faced with unclear information, watch the actions of informed traders to make their decisions. Recall the earnings surprise anomaly, in which prices were slow to adjust to earnings surprises. Information cascades can explain this occurrence. Information cascades are somewhat similar to investor **herding behavior**, a term to describe trading that occurs in clusters and is not necessarily driven by information.

Information cascades are consistent with investor rationality and improved market efficiency if they result from uninformed traders who are imitating informed traders. Information cascades do not necessarily tend toward correct security pricing, in which case the cascade is said to be fragile and likely to be corrected as investors react to public information. The existence of securities pricing consistent with the idea of information cascades does not necessarily present an opportunity to earn abnormal profits.

Behavioral finance can account for how securities prices can deviate from their rational levels and be biased estimates of intrinsic value. If investor rationality is viewed as a prerequisite for market efficiency, then markets are not efficient. If market efficiency only requires that investors cannot consistently earn abnormal risk-adjusted returns, then the research supports the belief that markets are efficient.

KEY CONCEPTS

LOS 48.a

In an informationally efficient capital market, security prices reflect all available information fully, quickly, and rationally. The more efficient a market is, the quicker its reaction will be to new information. Only unexpected information should elicit a response from traders.

If the market is fully efficient, active investment strategies cannot earn positive risk-adjusted returns consistently, and investors should therefore use a passive strategy.

LOS 48.b

An asset's market value is the price at which it can currently be bought or sold.

An asset's intrinsic value is the price that investors with full knowledge of the asset's characteristics would place on the asset.

LOS 48.c

Large numbers of market participants and greater information availability tend to make markets more efficient.

Impediments to arbitrage and short selling and high costs of trading and gathering information tend to make markets less efficient.

LOS 48.d

The weak form of the efficient markets hypothesis (EMH) states that security prices fully reflect all past price and volume information.

The semi-strong form of the EMH states that security prices fully reflect all publicly available information.

The strong form of the EMH states that security prices fully reflect all public and private information.

LOS 48.e

If markets are weak-form efficient, technical analysis does not consistently result in abnormal profits.

If markets are semi-strong form efficient, fundamental analysis does not consistently result in abnormal profits. However, fundamental analysis is necessary if market prices are to be semi-strong form efficient.

If markets are strong-form efficient, active investment management does not consistently result in abnormal profits.

Even if markets are strong-form efficient, portfolio managers can add value by establishing and implementing portfolio risk and return objectives and assisting with portfolio diversification, asset allocation, and tax minimization.

©2012 Kaplan, Inc.

LOS 48.f

A market anomaly is something that deviates from the efficient market hypothesis. Most evidence suggests anomalies are not violations of market efficiency but are due to the methodologies used in anomaly research, such as data mining or failing to adjust adequately for risk.

Anomalies that have been identified in time-series data include calendar anomalies such as the January effect (small firm stock returns are higher at the beginning of January), overreaction anomalies (stock returns subsequently reverse), and momentum anomalies (high short-term returns are followed by continued high returns).

Anomalies that have been identified in cross-sectional data include a size effect (small-cap stocks outperform large-cap stocks) and a value effect (value stocks outperform growth stocks).

Other identified anomalies involve closed-end investment funds selling at a discount to NAV, slow adjustments to earnings surprises, investor overreaction to and long-term underperformance of IPOs, and a relationship between stock returns and prior economic fundamentals.

LOS 48.g

Behavioral finance examines whether investors behave rationally, how investor behavior affects financial markets, and how cognitive biases may result in anomalies. Behavioral finance describes investor irrationality but does not necessarily refute market efficiency as long as investors cannot consistently earn abnormal risk-adjusted returns.

CONCEPT CHECKERS

1. In an informationally efficient capital market:
   A. active managers can generate abnormal profits.
   B. security prices quickly reflect new information.
   C. investors react to all information releases rapidly.

2. In terms of market efficiency, short selling *most likely*:
   A. leads to excess volatility, which reduces market efficiency.
   B. promotes market efficiency by making assets less likely to become overvalued.
   C. has little effect on market efficiency because short sellers face the risk of unlimited losses.

3. The intrinsic value of an asset:
   A. changes through time as new information is released.
   B. is the price at which the asset can be bought or sold at a given point in time.
   C. can be easily determined with a financial calculator, given investor risk preferences.

4. The weak-form EMH asserts that stock prices fully reflect which of the following types of information?
   A. Market only.
   B. Market and public.
   C. Public and private.

5. Research has revealed that the performance of professional money managers tends to be:
   A. equal to the performance of a passive investment strategy.
   B. inferior to the performance of a passive investment strategy.
   C. superior to the performance of a passive investment strategy.

6. Which of the following *best* describes the majority of the evidence regarding anomalies in stock returns?
   A. Weak-form market efficiency holds but semi-strong form efficiency does not.
   B. Neither weak-form nor semi-strong form market efficiency holds.
   C. Reported anomalies are not violations of market efficiency but are the result of research methodologies.

7. Investors who exhibit loss aversion *most likely*:
   A. have symmetric risk preferences.
   B. are highly risk averse.
   C. dislike losses more than they like an equal gain.

ANSWERS – CONCEPT CHECKERS

1. **B** In informationally efficient capital markets, new information is quickly reflected in security prices. Investors react only to unexpected information releases because information releases that are expected will already be reflected in securities prices. Active strategies will underperform in an efficient market because they have greater transactions and management costs than passive strategies and will not consistently create positive abnormal returns after adjusting for risk.

2. **B** Short selling promotes market efficiency because the sales pressure from short selling can reduce the prices of assets that have become overvalued.

3. **A** Intrinsic value changes as new information arrives in the marketplace. It cannot be known with certainty and can only be estimated. The price of an asset at a given point in time is its market value, which will differ from its intrinsic value if markets are not fully efficient.

4. **A** Weak-form EMH states that stock prices fully reflect all market (i.e., price and volume) information.

5. **B** Tests indicate that mutual fund performance has been inferior to that of a passive index strategy.

6. **C** The majority of evidence is that anomalies are not violations of market efficiency but are due to the research methodologies used. Portfolio management based on anomalies will likely be unprofitable after transactions costs are considered.

7. **C** Loss aversion refers to the tendency of investors to be more risk averse when faced with potential losses and less risk averse when faced with potential gains. That is, they dislike losses more than they like gains of an equal amount. Their risk preferences are asymmetric.

OVERVIEW OF EQUITY SECURITIES

EXAM FOCUS

Equities have higher returns than bonds and bills, but also higher risk. Know the characteristics of common and preferred equity types, as well as the methods of investing in foreign stock. Understand the difference between the book value of equity and market value of equity and what this difference represents.

LOS 49.a: Describe characteristics of types of equity securities.

CFA® Program Curriculum, Volume 5, page 156

Common shares are the most common form of equity and represent an ownership interest. Common shareholders have a residual claim (after the claims of debtholders and preferred stockholders) on firm assets if the firm is liquidated and govern the corporation through voting rights. Firms are under no obligation to pay dividends on common equity; the firm determines what dividend will be paid periodically. Common stockholders are able to vote for the board of directors, on merger decisions, and on the selection of auditors. If they are unable to attend the annual meeting, shareholders can vote by **proxy** (having someone else vote as they direct them, on their behalf).

In a **statutory voting** system, each share held is assigned one vote in the election of each member of the board of directors. Under **cumulative voting**, shareholders can allocate their votes to one or more candidates as they choose. For example, consider a situation where a shareholder has 100 shares and three directors will be elected. Under statutory voting, the shareholder can vote 100 shares for his director choice in each election. Under cumulative voting, the shareholder has 300 votes, which can be cast for a single candidate or spread across multiple candidates. The three receiving the greatest number of votes are elected. Cumulative voting makes it possible for a minority shareholder to have more proportional representation on the board. The way the math works, a holder of 30% of the firm's shares could choose three of ten directors with cumulative voting but could elect no directors under statutory voting.

Callable common shares give the firm the right to repurchase the stock at a pre-specified call price. Investors receive a fixed amount when the firm calls the stock. The call feature benefits the firm because when the stock's market price is greater than the call price, the firm can call the shares and reissue them later at a higher price. Calling the shares, similarly to the repurchase of shares, allows the firm to reduce its dividend payments without changing its per-share dividend.

Putable common shares give the shareholder the right to sell the shares back to the firm at a specific price. A put option on the shares benefits the shareholder because it effectively places a floor under the share value. Shareholders pay for the put option because other things equal, putable shares are sold for higher prices than non-putable shares and raise more capital for the firm when they are issued.

Preference shares (or **preferred stock**) have features of both common stock and debt. As with common stock, preferred stock dividends are not a contractual obligation, the shares usually do not mature, and the shares can have put or call features. Like debt, preferred shares typically make fixed periodic payments to investors and do not usually have voting rights.

Cumulative preference shares are usually promised fixed dividends, and any dividends that are not paid must be made up before common shareholders can receive dividends. The dividends of **non-cumulative preference shares** do not accumulate over time when they are not paid, but dividends for any period must be paid before common shareholders can receive dividends.

Preferred shares have a stated par value and pay a percentage dividend based on the par value of the shares. An $80 par value preferred with a 10% dividend pays a dividend of $8 per year. Investors in **participating preference shares** receive extra dividends if firm profits exceed a predetermined level and may receive a value greater than the par value of the preferred stock if the firm is liquidated. **Non-participating preference shares** have a claim equal to par value in the event of liquidation and do not share in firm profits. Smaller and riskier firms whose investors may be concerned about the firm's future often issue participating preferred stock so investors can share in the upside potential of the firm.

Convertible preference shares can be exchanged for common stock at a conversion ratio determined when the shares are originally issued. It has the following advantages:

- The preferred dividend is higher than a common dividend.
- If the firm is profitable, the investor can share in the profits by converting his shares into common stock.
- The conversion option becomes more valuable when the common stock price increases.
- Preferred shares have less risk than common shares because the dividend is stable and they have priority over common stock in receiving dividends and in the event of liquidation of the firm.

Because of their upside potential, convertible preferred shares are often used to finance risky venture capital and private equity firms. The conversion feature compensates investors for the additional risk they take when investing in such firms.

LOS 49.b: Describe differences in voting rights and other ownership characteristics among different equity classes.

CFA® Program Curriculum, Volume 5, page 157

A firm may have different classes of common stock (e.g., "Class A" and "Class B" shares). One class may have greater voting power and seniority if the firm's assets are liquidated. The classes may also be treated differently with respect to dividends, stock splits, and other transactions with shareholders. Information on the ownership and voting rights of different classes of equity shares can be found in the company's filings with securities regulators, such as the Securities and Exchange Commission in the United States.

LOS 49.c: Distinguish between public and private equity securities.

CFA® Program Curriculum, Volume 5, page 163

The discussion so far has centered on equity that is publicly traded. **Private equity** is usually issued to institutional investors via private placements. Private equity markets are smaller than public markets but are growing rapidly.

Compared to public equity, private equity has the following characteristics:

- Less liquidity because no public market for the shares exists.
- Share price is negotiated between the firm and its investors, not determined in a market.
- More limited firm financial disclosure because there is no government or exchange requirement to do so.
- Lower reporting costs because of less onerous reporting requirements.
- Potentially weaker corporate governance because of reduced reporting requirements and less public scrutiny.
- Greater ability to focus on long-term prospects because there is no public pressure for short-term results.
- Potentially greater return for investors once the firm goes public.

The three main types of private equity investments are venture capital, leveraged buyouts, and private investments in public equity.

Venture capital refers to the capital provided to firms early in their life cycles to fund their development and growth. Venture capital financing at various stages of a firm's development is referred to as *seed* or *start-up*, *early stage*, or *mezzanine* financing. Investors can be family, friends, wealthy individuals, or private equity funds. Venture capital investments are illiquid and investors often have to commit funds for three to ten years before they can cash out (exit) their investment. Investors hope to profit when they can sell their shares after (or as part of) an initial public offering or to an established firm.

In a **leveraged buyout** (LBO), investors buy all of a firm's equity using debt financing (leverage). If the buyers are the firm's current management, the LBO is referred to as a **management buyout** (MBO). Firms in LBOs usually have cash flow that is adequate to service the issued debt or have undervalued assets that can be sold to pay down the debt over time.

In a **private investment in public equity** (PIPE), a public firm that needs capital quickly sells private equity to investors. The firm may have growth opportunities, be in distress, or have large amounts of debt. The investors can often buy the stock at a sizeable discount to its market price.

LOS 49.d: Describe methods for investing in non-domestic equity securities.

CFA® Program Curriculum, Volume 5, page 165

When capital flows freely across borders, markets are said to be *integrated*. The world's financial markets have become more integrated over time, especially as a result of improved communications and trading technologies. However, barriers to global capital flows still exist. Some countries restrict foreign ownership of their domestic stocks, primarily to prevent foreign control of domestic companies and to reduce the variability of capital flows in and out of their countries.

An increasing number of countries have dropped foreign capital restrictions. Studies have shown that reducing capital barriers improves equity market performance. Furthermore, companies are increasingly turning to foreign investors for capital by listing their stocks on foreign stock exchanges or by encouraging foreign ownership of shares.

From the firm's perspective, listing on foreign stock exchanges increases publicity for the firm's products and the liquidity of the firm's shares. Foreign listing also increases firm transparency due to the stricter disclosure requirements of many foreign markets.

Direct investing in the securities of foreign companies simply refers to buying a foreign firm's securities in foreign markets. Some obstacles to direct foreign investment are that:

- The investment and return are denominated in a foreign currency.
- The foreign stock exchange may be illiquid.
- The reporting requirements of foreign stock exchanges may be less strict, impeding analysis.
- Investors must be familiar with the regulations and procedures of each market in which they invest.

Other methods for investing in foreign companies are provided by global depository receipts (GDRs), American depository receipts (ADRs), global registered shares (GRSs), and baskets of listed depository receipts (BLDRs).

Depository receipts (DRs) represent ownership in a foreign firm and are traded in the markets of other countries in local market currencies. A bank deposits shares of the foreign firm and then issues receipts representing ownership of a specific number of the foreign shares. The **depository bank** acts as a custodian and manages dividends, stock splits, and other events. Although the investor does not have to convert to the foreign currency, the value of the DR is affected by exchange rate changes, as well as firm fundamentals, economic events, and any other factors that affect the value of any stock.

If the firm is involved with the issue, the depository receipt is a **sponsored DR**; otherwise, it is an **unsponsored DR**. A sponsored DR provides the investor voting rights and is usually subject to greater disclosure requirements. In an unsponsored DR, the depository bank retains the voting rights.

Global depository receipts (GDRs) are issued outside the United States and the issuer's home country. Most GDRs are traded on the London and Luxembourg exchanges. Although not listed on U.S. exchanges, they are usually denominated in U.S. dollars and can be sold to U.S. institutional investors. GDRs are not subject to the capital flow restrictions imposed by governments and thus offer the firm and the investor greater opportunities for foreign investment. The firm usually chooses to list the GDR in a market where many investors are familiar with the firm.

American depository receipts (ADRs) are denominated in U.S. dollars and trade in the United States. The security on which the ADR is based is the **American depository share** (ADS), which trades in the firm's domestic market. Some ADRs allow firms to raise capital in the United States or use the shares to acquire other firms. Most require U.S. Securities and Exchange Commission (SEC) registration, but some are privately placed (Rule 144A or Regulation S receipts).

The four types of ADRs, with different levels of trading availability and firm requirements, are summarized in Figure 1.

Figure 1: Types of ADRs

	Level I	*Level II*	*Level III*	*Rule 144A*
Trading location	Over-the-counter (OTC)	NYSE, Nasdaq, and AMEX	NYSE, Nasdaq, and AMEX	Private
SEC registration required	Yes	Yes	Yes	No
Ability to raise capital in United States	No	No	Yes	Yes
Firm listing expenses	Low	High	High	Low

Global registered shares (GRS) are traded in different currencies on stock exchanges around the world.

A **basket of listed depository receipts** (BLDR) is an exchange-traded fund (ETF) that is a collection of DRs. ETF shares trade in markets just like common stocks.

LOS 49.e: Compare the risk and return characteristics of types of equity securities.

CFA® Program Curriculum, Volume 5, page 170

The returns on equity investments consist of price changes, dividend payments, and, in the case of equities denominated in a foreign currency, gains or losses from changes in exchange rates. A Japanese investor who invests in euro-denominated shares will have greater yen-based returns if the euro appreciates relative to the yen.

Gains from dividends and the reinvestment of dividends have been an important part of equity investors' long-term returns. For example, $1 invested in U.S. stocks in 1900 would have been worth $582 in real terms in 2008 with dividends reinvested but only

$6 with price appreciation alone. Over the same time period, the terminal wealth for bonds and bills would have been $9.90 and $2.90, respectively.[1]

The risk of equity securities is most commonly measured as the standard deviation of returns. Preferred stock is less risky than common stock because preferred stock pays a known, fixed dividend to investors that is a large part of the return, whereas common dividends are variable and can vary with earnings. Also, preferred stockholders receive their distributions before common shareholders and have a claim in liquidation equal to the par value of their shares that has priority over the claims of common stock owners. Because it is less risky, preferred stock has a lower average return than common stock.

Cumulative preferred shares have less risk than non-cumulative preferred shares because they retain the right to receive any missed dividends before any common stock dividends can be paid.

For both common and preferred shares, putable shares are less risky and callable shares are more risky compared to shares with neither option. Putable shares are less risky because if the market price drops, the investor can put the shares back to the firm at a fixed price (assuming the firm has the capital to honor the put). Because of this feature, putable shares usually pay a lower dividend yield than non-putable shares.

Callable shares are the most risky because if the market price rises, the firm can call the shares, limiting the upside potential of the shares. Callable shares, therefore, usually have higher dividend yields than non-callable shares.

LOS 49.f: Explain the role of equity securities in the financing of a company's assets.

CFA® Program Curriculum, Volume 5, page 173

Equity capital is used for the purchase of long-term assets, equipment, research and development, and expansion into new businesses or geographic areas. Equity securities provide the firm with "currency" that can be used to buy other companies or that can be offered to employees as incentive compensation. Having publicly traded equity securities provides liquidity, which may be especially important to firms that need to meet regulatory requirements, capital adequacy ratios, and liquidity ratios.

LOS 49.g: Distinguish between the market value and book value of equity securities.

CFA® Program Curriculum, Volume 5, page 173

The primary goal of firm management is to increase the book value of the firm's equity and thereby increase the market value of its equity. The **book value of equity** is the value of the firm's assets on the balance sheet minus its liabilities. It increases when the firm has positive net income and retained earnings that flow into the equity account. When

---

1. Ryan C. Fuhrmann, CFA, and Asjeet S. Lamba, CFA, *Overview of Equity Securities*, CFA Program Curriculum, Volume 5, Level I, 2013, p. 171.

management makes decisions that increase income and retained earnings, they increase the book value of equity.

The **market value of equity** is the total value of a firm's outstanding equity shares based on market prices and reflects the expectations of investors about the firm's future performance. Investors use their perceptions of the firm's risk and the amounts and timing of future cash flows to determine the market value of equity. The market value and book value of equity are seldom equal. Although management may be maximizing the book value of equity, this may not be reflected in the market value of equity because book value does not reflect investor expectations about future firm performance.

LOS 49.h: Compare a company's cost of equity, its (accounting) return on equity, and investors' required rates of return.

CFA® Program Curriculum, Volume 5, page 178

A key ratio used to determine management efficiency is the **accounting return on equity**, usually referred to simply as the **return on equity** (ROE). ROE is calculated as net income available to common (net income minus preferred dividends) divided by the average book value of common equity over the period:

$$\text{ROE}_t = \frac{\text{NI}_t}{\text{average BV}_t} = \frac{\text{NI}_t}{(\text{BV}_t + \text{BV}_{t-1})\,/\,2}$$

Alternatively, ROE is often calculated using only beginning-of-year book value of equity (i.e., book value of equity for end of year t – 1):

$$\text{ROE}_t = \frac{\text{NI}_t}{\text{BV}_{t-1}}$$

The first method is more appropriate when it is the industry convention or when book value is volatile. The latter method is more appropriate when examining ROE for a number of years or when book value is stable.

Higher ROE is generally viewed as a positive for a firm, but the reason for an increase should be examined. For example, if book value is decreasing more rapidly than net income, ROE will increase. This is not, however, a positive for the firm. A firm can also issue debt to repurchase equity, thereby decreasing the book value of equity. This would increase the ROE but also make the firm's shares riskier due to the increased financial leverage (debt).

 Professor's Note: The DuPont formula discussed in the topic review of Financial Analysis Techniques can help the analyst determine the reasons for changes in ROE.

The book value of equity reflects a firm's financial decisions and operating results since its inception, whereas the market value of equity reflects the market's consensus view of a firm's future performance. The **price-to-book ratio** (also called the **market-to-book ratio**) is the market value of a firm's equity divided by the book value of its equity. The more optimistic investors are about the firm's future growth, the greater its price-to-book ratio. The price-to-book ratio is used as a measure of relative value. Often, firms with low price-to-book ratios are considered *value stocks*, while firms with high price-to-book ratios are considered *growth stocks*.

Example: ROE, market, and book value of equity calculations

Given the figures below for O'Grady Industries, calculate the return on average equity for 20X9 and the total market value of equity, the book value per share, and the price-to-book ratio at the end of 20X9.

Index Firm Data

Fiscal Year-End Dec. 31	20X9	20X8
Total stockholder's equity	18,503	17,143
Net income available to common	3,526	3,056
Stock price	$16.80	$15.30
Shares outstanding	3,710	2,790

Answer:

The return on average equity for 20X9 is:

$$ROE_t = \frac{NI_t}{average\ BV_t} = \frac{NI_t}{(BV_t + BV_{t-1})/2} = \frac{\$3,526}{(\$18,503 + \$17,143)/2} = 19.78\%$$

The total market value of the firm's equity at the end of 20X9 is:

$16.80 \times 3,710 = \$62,328$

The book value per share at the end of 20X9 is:

$$= \frac{\$18,503}{3,710} = \$4.99$$

The price-to-book ratio at the end of 20X9 is:

$$= \frac{\$16.80}{\$4.99} = 3.37$$

Investors' Required Return and the Cost of Equity

A firm's **cost of equity** is the expected equilibrium total return (including dividends) on its shares in the market. It is usually estimated in practice using a dividend-discount model or the capital asset pricing model. At any point in time, a decrease in share price will increase the expected return on the shares and an increase in share price will decrease expected returns, other things equal. Because the intrinsic value of a firm's shares is the discounted present value of its future cash flows, an increase (decrease) in the required return used to discount future cash flows will decrease (increase) intrinsic value.

Investors also estimate the expected market returns on equity shares and compare this to the minimum return they will accept for bearing the risk inherent in a particular stock.

If an investor estimates the expected return on a stock to be greater than her minimum required rate of return on the shares, given their risk, then the shares are an attractive investment. Investors can have different required rates of return for a given risk, different estimates of a firm's future cash flows, and different estimates of the risk of a firm's equity shares. A firm's cost of equity can be interpreted as the minimum rate of return required by investors (in the aggregate) to compensate them for the risk of the firm's equity shares.

KEY CONCEPTS

LOS 49.a

Common shareholders have a residual claim on firm assets and govern the corporation through voting rights. Common shares have variable dividends which the firm is under no legal obligation to pay.

Callable common shares allow the firm the right to repurchase the shares at a pre-specified price. Putable common shares give the shareholder the right to sell the shares back to the firm at a pre-specified price.

Preferred stock typically does not mature, does not have voting rights, and has dividends that are fixed in amount but are not a contractual obligation of the firm.

Cumulative preferred shares require any dividends that were missed in the past (dividends in arrears) to be paid before common shareholders receive any dividends. Participating preferred shares receive extra dividends if firm profits exceed a pre-specified level and a value greater than the par value if the firm is liquidated. Convertible preferred stock can be converted to common stock at a pre-specified conversion ratio.

LOS 49.b

Some companies' equity shares are divided into different classes, such as Class A and Class B shares. Different classes of common equity may have different voting rights and priority in liquidation.

LOS 49.c

Compared to publicly traded firms, private equity firms have lower reporting costs, greater ability to focus on long-term prospects, and potentially greater return for investors once the firm goes public. However, private equity investments are illiquid, firm financial disclosure may be limited, and corporate governance may be weaker.

LOS 49.d

Investors who buy foreign stock directly on a foreign stock exchange receive a return denominated in a foreign currency, must abide by the foreign stock exchange's regulations and procedures, and may be faced with less liquidity and less transparency than is available in the investor's domestic markets. Investors can often avoid these disadvantages by purchasing depository receipts for the foreign stock that trade on their domestic exchange.

Global depository receipts are issued outside the United States and outside the issuer's home country. American depository receipts are denominated in U.S. dollars and are traded on U.S. exchanges.

Global registered shares are common shares of a firm that trade in different currencies on stock exchanges throughout the world.

Baskets of listed depository receipts are exchange-traded funds that invest in depository receipts.

LOS 49.e

Equity investor returns consist of dividends, capital gains or losses from changes in share prices, and any foreign exchange gains or losses on shares traded in a foreign currency. Compounding of reinvested dividends has been an important part of an equity investor's long-term return.

Preferred stock is less risky than common stock because preferred stock pays a known, fixed dividend to investors; preferred stockholders must receive dividends before common stock dividends can be paid; and preferred stockholders have a claim equal to par value if the firm is liquidated. Putable shares are the least risky and callable shares are the most risky. Cumulative preferred shares are less risky than non-cumulative preferred shares, as any dividends missed must be paid before a common stock dividend can be paid.

LOS 49.f

Equity securities provide funds to the firm to buy productive assets, to buy other companies, or to offer to employees as compensation. Equity securities provide liquidity that may be important when the firm must raise additional funds.

LOS 49.g

The book value of equity is the difference between the financial statement value of the firm's assets and liabilities. Positive retained earnings increase the book value of equity. Book values reflect the firm's past operating and financing choices.

The market value of equity is the share price multiplied by the number of shares outstanding. Market value reflects investors' expectations about the timing, amount, and risk of the firm's future cash flows.

LOS 49.h

The accounting return on equity (ROE) is calculated as the firm's net income divided by the book value of common equity. ROE measures whether management is generating a return on common equity but is affected by the firm's accounting methods.

The firm's cost of equity is the minimum rate of return that investors in the firm's equity require. Investors' required rates of return are reflected in the market prices of the firm's shares.

CONCEPT CHECKERS

1. Which of the following *best* describes the benefit of cumulative share voting?
    A. It provides significant minority shareholders with proportional representation on the board.
    B. It prevents minority shareholders from exercising excessive control.
    C. If cumulative dividends are not paid, preferred shareholders are given voting rights.

2. The advantage of participating preferred shares versus non-participating preferred shares is that participating preferred shares can:
    A. obtain voting rights.
    B. receive extra dividends.
    C. be converted into common stock.

3. Compared to public equity, which of the following is *least likely* to characterize private equity?
    A. Lower reporting costs.
    B. Potentially weaker corporate governance.
    C. Lower returns because of its less liquid market.

4. Global depository receipts are most often denominated in:
    A. the currency of the country where they trade and issued outside the United States.
    B. U.S. dollars and issued in the United States.
    C. U.S. dollars and issued outside the United States.

5. Which of the following types of preferred shares has the *most* risk for investors?
    A. Putable shares.
    B. Callable shares.
    C. Non-putable, non-callable shares.

6. Which of the following *best* describes the book value of equity?
    A. Management should attempt to maximize book value of equity.
    B. Book value of equity decreases when retained earnings increase.
    C. Book value of equity reflects investors' perceptions of the firm's future.

7. Which of the following causes of an increase in return on equity is *most likely* a positive sign for a firm's equity investors?
    A. A firm issues debt to repurchase equity.
    B. Net income is increasing at a faster rate than book value of equity.
    C. Net income is decreasing at a slower rate than book value of equity.

ANSWERS – CONCEPT CHECKERS

1. **A** Cumulative voting allows minority shareholders to gain representation on the board because they can use all of their votes for specific board members.

2. **B** Participating preferred shares can receive extra dividends if firm profits exceed a pre-specified level and a value greater than the par value if the firm is liquidated.

3. **C** Private equity has less liquidity because no public market for it exists. The lower liquidity of private equity would increase required returns.

4. **C** Global Depository Receipts are not listed on U.S. exchanges and are most often denominated in U.S. dollars. They are not issued in the United States.

5. **B** Callable shares are the most risky because if the market price rises, the firm can call in the shares, limiting the investor's potential gains. Putable shares are the least risky because if the market price drops, the investor can put the shares back to the firm at a predetermined price. The risk of non-putable, non-callable shares falls in between.

6. **A** The primary goal of firm management is to increase the book value of equity. It *increases* when retained earnings are positive. The *market* value of equity reflects the collective expectations of investors about the firm's future performance.

7. **B** Net income increasing at a faster rate than book value of equity generally would be a positive sign. If a firm issues debt to repurchase equity, this decreases the book value of equity and increases the ROE. However, now the firm becomes riskier due to the increased debt. Net income decreasing at a slower rate than book value of equity would increase ROE, but decreasing net income is not a positive sign.

INTRODUCTION TO INDUSTRY AND COMPANY ANALYSIS

Study Session 14

EXAM FOCUS

This topic provides a great deal of material on industry analysis. Understand the effects of business cycles and the stage of an industry's life cycle. Porter's five forces and two competitive strategies are very important to know. Beyond these, make sure that you know the effects on price competition and profitability of the items considered in industry analysis and of the various firm characteristics discussed.

LOS 50.a: Explain the uses of industry analysis and the relation of industry analysis to company analysis.

CFA® Program Curriculum, Volume 5, page 188

Industry analysis is important for company analysis because it provides a framework for understanding the firm. Analysts will often focus on a group of specific industries so that they can better understand the business conditions the firms in those industries face.

Understanding a firm's business environment can provide insight about the firm's potential growth, competition, and risks. For a credit analyst, industry conditions can provide important information about whether a firm will be able to meet its obligations during the next recession.

In an active management strategy, industry analysis can identify industries that are undervalued or overvalued in order to weight them appropriately. Some investors engage in **industry rotation**, which is overweighting or underweighting industries based on the current phase of the business cycle. A firm's industry has been found to be as important as its home country in determining its performance.

In performance attribution analysis, the sources of portfolio return are determined relative to a benchmark. The industry representation within a portfolio is often a significant component of attribution analysis.

LOS 50.b: Compare methods by which companies can be grouped, current industry classification systems, and classify a company, given a description of its activities and the classification system.

CFA® Program Curriculum, Volume 5, page 189

One way to group companies into an industry is by the *products and services* they offer. For example, the firms that produce automobiles constitute the auto industry. A **sector** is a group of similar industries. Hospitals, doctors, pharmaceutical firms, and other industries are included in the health care sector. Systems that are grouped by products and services usually use a firm's **principal business activity** (the largest source of sales or earnings) to classify firms. Examples of these systems are discussed in the following and include the Global Industry Classification Standard (GICS), Russell Global Sectors (RGS), and Industry Classification Benchmark.

Firms can also be classified by their *sensitivity to business cycles*. This system has two main classifications: cyclical and non-cyclical firms.

Statistical methods, such as cluster analysis, can also be used. This method groups firms that historically have had highly correlated returns. The groups (i.e., industries) formed will then have lower returns correlations between groups.

This method has several limitations:

- Historical correlations may not be the same as future correlations.
- The groupings of firms may differ over time and across countries.
- The grouping of firms is sometimes non-intuitive.
- The method is susceptible to statistical error (i.e., firms can be grouped by a relationship that occurs by chance, or not grouped together when they should be).

Industry Classification Systems

Classifying firms by industry provides a method of examining trends and firm valuations. It also allows analysts to compare firms in different countries on a similar basis. The following are the industry classification systems currently available to investors.

Commercial Classifications

Several index providers classify firms. Some use three levels of classification, while others use four levels. The providers generally use firm fundamentals such as revenue to classify firms. Although the nomenclature differs among providers, the broadest category is generally the sector level, followed by industry and sub-industry.

Commercial industry classifications include the Global Industry Classification Standard developed by Standard & Poor's and MSCI Barra, Russell Global Sectors, and the Industry Classification Benchmark developed by Dow Jones and FTSE.

Sectors and firm compositions representative of those used by commercial providers are as follows.

Basic materials and processing firms produce:

- Building materials.
- Chemicals.
- Paper and forest products.
- Containers and packaging.
- Metals, minerals, and mining.

Consumer discretionary firms are cyclical and sell goods and services in industries such as:

- Automotive.
- Apparel.
- Hotels and restaurants.

Consumer staples firms are less cyclical and sell goods and services in industries such as:

- Food.
- Beverage.
- Tobacco.
- Personal care products.

Energy firms are involved in:

- Energy exploration.
- Refining.
- Production.
- Energy equipment.
- Energy services.

Financial services firms include firms involved in:

- Banking.
- Insurance.
- Real estate.
- Asset management.
- Brokerage.

Health care includes:

- Pharmaceuticals.
- Biotech.
- Medical devices.
- Health care equipment.
- Medical supplies.
- Health care services.

Industrial and producer durables firms produce capital goods for commercial services industries including:

- Heavy machinery and equipment.
- Aerospace.
- Defense.
- Transportation.
- Commercial services and supplies.

Technology firms sell or produce:

- Computers.
- Software.
- Semiconductors.
- Communications equipment.
- Internet services.
- Electronic entertainment.
- Consulting and services.

Telecommunications firms include wired and wireless service providers. *Utilities* includes electric, gas, and water utilities. Some industry classification providers include telecommunication and utilities in the same group, while others separate them.

To classify a firm accurately, an analyst should have detailed knowledge about the firm and the delineation of industry classifications.

Government Classifications

Several government bodies also provide industry classification of firms. They frequently do so to organize the economic data they publish. A main thrust of their systems is to make comparisons of industries consistent across time and country. The main systems are similar to each other.

- *International Standard Industrial Classification of All Economic Activities* (ISIC) was produced by the United Nations in 1948 to increase global comparability of data.
- *Statistical Classification of Economic Activities in the European Community* is similar to the ISIC but is designed for Europe.
- *Australian and New Zealand Standard Industrial Classification* was jointly developed by those countries.
- *North American Industry Classification System* (NAICS) was jointly developed by the United States, Canada, and Mexico.

The methodologies that government providers use in their compilation of industry groups differ from those used by commercial providers. Most governments do not identify individual firms in a group, so an analyst cannot know the groups' exact composition. Commercial providers identify the constituent firms. Government systems are updated less frequently; for example, the NAICS is updated every five years. Governments do not distinguish between small and large firms, for-profit and not-for-profit organizations, or private and public firms. Commercial providers only include for-profit and public firms and can delineate by the size of the firm.

An analyst should not assume that two firms in the same narrowest industry classification can be compared with each other for fundamental analysis and valuation. Instead, the analyst should construct *peer groups*, as described later in this topic review.

LOS 50.c: Explain the factors that affect the sensitivity of a company to the business cycle and the uses and limitations of industry and company descriptors such as "growth," "defensive," and "cyclical".

CFA® Program Curriculum, Volume 5, page 190

A **cyclical firm** is one whose earnings are highly dependent on the stage of the business cycle. These firms have high earnings volatility and high operating leverage. Their products are often expensive, non-necessities whose purchase can be delayed until the economy improves. Examples of cyclical industries include basic materials and processing, consumer discretionary, energy, financial services, industrial and producer durables, and technology.

In contrast, a **non-cyclical firm** produces goods and services for which demand is relatively stable over the business cycle. Examples of non-cyclical industries include health care, utilities, telecommunications, and consumer staples.

Sectors can also be classified by their sensitivity to the phase of the business cycle. Cyclical sector examples include energy, financials, technology, materials, and consumer discretionary. Non-cyclical sector examples include health care, utilities, and consumer staples.

Non-cyclical industries can be further separated into defensive (stable) or growth industries. **Defensive industries** are those that are least affected by the stage of the business cycle and include utilities, consumer staples (such as food producers), and basic services (such as drug stores). **Growth industries** have demand so strong they are largely unaffected by the stage of the business cycle.

Descriptors such as "growth," "defensive," and "cyclical" should be used with caution. Cyclical industries, which are supposed to be dependent on the business cycle, often include growth firms that are less dependent on the business cycle. Non-cyclical industries can be affected by severe recessions, as was the case in the 2008–09 downturn. Defensive industries may not always be safe investments. For example, grocery stores are classified as defensive, but they are subject to intense price competition that reduces earnings. Defensive industries may also contain some truly defensive and some growth firms. Because business cycle phases differ across countries and regions, two cyclical firms operating in different countries may be simultaneously experiencing different cyclical effects on earnings growth.

LOS 50.d: Explain the relation of "peer group," as used in equity valuation, to a company's industry classification.

CFA® Program Curriculum, Volume 5, page 197

A **peer group** is a set of similar companies an analyst will use for valuation comparisons. More specifically, a peer group will consist of companies with similar business activities, demand drivers, cost structure drivers, and availability of capital.

To form a peer group, an analyst will often start by identifying companies in the same industry classification, using the commercial classification providers previously described. Usually, the analyst will use other information to verify that the firms in an industry are indeed peers. An analyst might include a company in more than one peer group.

The following are steps an analyst would use to form a peer group:

- Use commercial classification providers to determine which firms are in the same industry.
- Examine firms' annual reports to see if they identify key competitors.
- Examine competitors' annual reports to see if other competitors are named.
- Use industry trade publications to identify competitors.

- Confirm that comparable firms have similar sources of sales and earnings, have similar sources of demand, and are in similar geographic markets.
- Adjust financial statements of non-financial companies for any financing subsidiary data they include.

LOS 50.e: Describe the elements that need to be covered in a thorough industry analysis.

CFA® Program Curriculum, Volume 5, page 202

A thorough industry analysis should include the following elements:

- Evaluate the relationships between macroeconomic variables and industry trends using information from industry groups, firms in the industry, competitors, suppliers, and customers.
- Estimate industry variables using different approaches and scenarios.
- Compare with other analysts' forecasts of industry variables to confirm the validity of the analysis and potentially find industries that are misvalued as a result of consensus forecasts.
- Determine the relative valuation of different industries.
- Compare the valuations of industries across time to determine the volatility of their performance over the long run and during different phases of the business cycle. This is useful for long-term investing as well as short-term industry rotation based on the current economic environment.
- Analyze industry prospects based on **strategic groups**, which are groups of firms that are distinct from the rest of the industry due to the delivery or complexity of their products or barriers to entry. For example, full-service hotels are a distinct market segment within the hotel industry.
- Classify industries by **life-cycle stage**, whether it is embryonic, growth, shakeout, mature, or declining.
- Position the industry on the **experience curve**, which shows the cost per unit relative to output. The curve declines because of increases in productivity and economies of scale, especially in industries with high fixed costs.
- Consider the forces that affect industries, which include demographic, macroeconomic, governmental, social, and technological influences.
- Examine the forces that determine competition within an industry.

LOS 50.f: Describe the principles of strategic analysis of an industry.

CFA® Program Curriculum, Volume 5, page 204

Industries differ markedly in profitability because of differences in economic fundamentals, industry structure, and degree of competition. In some industries, competition is intense and few firms earn economic profits. **Economic profits**, the return on invested capital minus its cost, are greater than 20% in some industries and negative in others. The degree of economic profits depends in part on pricing power (elasticity of demand for the firm's products). An analyst should understand that industry conditions and profits can change dramatically over time, so industry analysis should be forward-looking.

One component of an analyst's industry analysis should be **strategic analysis**, which examines how an industry's competitive environment influences a firm's strategy. The analysis framework developed by Michael Porter[1] delineates five forces that determine industry competition.

1. *Rivalry among existing competitors.* Rivalry increases when many firms of relatively equal size compete within an industry. Slow growth leads to competition as firms fight for market share, and high fixed costs lead to price decreases as firms try to operate at full capacity. For example, the high fixed costs in the auto industry from capital investments and labor contracts force firms to produce a large number of vehicles that they can only sell at low margins. Industries with products that are undifferentiated or have barriers (are costly) to exit tend to have high levels of competition.

2. *Threat of new entrants.* Industries that have significant barriers to entry (e.g., large capital outlays for facilities) will find it easier to maintain premium pricing. It is costly to enter the steel or oil production industries. Those industries have large barriers to entry and thus less competition from newcomers. An analyst should identify factors that discourage new entrants, such as economies of scale.

3. *Threat of substitute products.* Substitute products limit the profit potential of an industry because they limit the prices firms can charge by increasing the elasticity of demand. Commodity-like products have high levels of competition and low profit margins. The more differentiated the products are within an industry, the less price competition there will be. For example, in the pharmaceutical industry, patents protect a producer from competition in the markets for patented drugs.

4. *Bargaining power of buyers.* Buyers' ability to bargain for lower prices or higher quality influences industry profitability. Bargaining by governments and ever-larger health care providers have put downward pressure even on patented drugs.

5. *Bargaining power of suppliers.* Suppliers' ability to raise prices or limit supply influences industry profitability. Suppliers are more powerful if there are just a few of them and their products are scarce. For example, Microsoft is one of the few suppliers of operating system software and thus has pricing power.

The first two forces deserve further attention because almost all firms must be concerned about the threat of new entrants and competition that would erode profits. Studying these forces also helps the analyst better understand the subject firm's competitors and prospects. The following summary describes how these two factors influence the competitive environment in an industry:

- Higher barriers to entry reduce competition.
- Greater concentration (a small number of firms control a large part of the market) reduces competition, whereas market fragmentation (a large number of firms, each with a small market share) increases competition.
- Unused capacity in an industry, especially if prolonged, results in intense price competition. For example, underutilized capacity in the auto industry has resulted in very competitive pricing.

---

1. Michael Porter, "The Five Competitive Forces That Shape Strategy," *Harvard Business Review,* Volume 86, No. 1: pp. 78–93.

- Stability in market share reduces competition. For example, loyalty of a firm's customers tends to stabilize market share and profits.
- More price sensitivity in customer buying decisions results in greater competition.
- Greater maturity of an industry results in slowing growth.

LOS 50.g: Explain the effects of barriers to entry, industry concentration, industry capacity, and market share stability on pricing power and return on capital.

CFA® Program Curriculum, Volume 5, page 206

Barriers to Entry

High barriers to entry benefit existing industry firms because they prevent new competitors from competing for market share and reducing the existing firms' return on capital. In industries with low barriers to entry, firms have little pricing power and competition reduces existing firms' return on capital. To assess the ease of entry, the analyst should determine how easily a new entrant to the industry could obtain the capital, intellectual property, and customer base needed to be successful. One method of determining the ease of entry is to examine the composition of the industry over time. If the same firms dominate the industry today as ten years ago, entry is probably difficult.

High barriers to entry do not necessarily mean firm pricing power is high. Industries with high barriers to entry may have strong competition among existing firms. This is more likely when the products sold are undifferentiated and commodity-like or when high barriers to exit result in overcapacity. For example, an automobile factory may have a low value in an alternative use, making firm owners less likely to exit the industry. They continue to operate even when losing money, hoping to turn things around, which can result in industry overcapacity and intense price competition.

Low barriers to entry do not ensure success for new entrants. Barriers to entry may change over time, and so might the competitive environment.

Industry Concentration

High industry concentration does not guarantee pricing power.

- Absolute market share may not matter as much as a firm's market share relative to its competitors. A firm may have a 50% market share, but if a single competitor has the other 50%, their 50% share would not result in a great degree of pricing power. Return on capital is limited by intense competition between the two firms.
- Conversely, a firm that has a 10% market share when no competitor has more than 2% may have a good degree of pricing power and high return on capital.
- If industry products are undifferentiated and commodity-like, then consumers will switch to the lowest-priced producer. The more importance consumers place on price, the greater the competition in an industry. Greater competition leads to lower return on capital.

- Industries with greater product differentiation in regard to features, reliability, and service after the sale will have greater pricing power. Return on capital can be higher for firms that can better differentiate their products.
- If the industry is capital intensive, and therefore costly to enter or exit, overcapacity can result in intense price competition.

Tobacco, alcohol, and confections are examples of highly concentrated industries in which firms' pricing power is relatively strong. Automobiles, aircraft, and oil refining are examples of highly concentrated industries with relatively weak pricing power.

Although industry concentration does not guarantee pricing power, a fragmented market does usually result in strong competition. When there are many industry members, firms cannot coordinate pricing, firms will act independently, and because each member has such a small market share, any incremental increase in market share may make a price decrease profitable.

Industry Capacity

Industry capacity has a clear impact on pricing power. Undercapacity, a situation in which demand exceeds supply at current prices, results in pricing power and higher return on capital. Overcapacity, with supply greater than demand at current prices, will result in downward pressure on price and lower return on capital.

An analyst should be familiar with the industry's current capacity and its planned investment in additional capacity. Capacity is fixed in the short run and variable in the long run. In other words, given enough time, producers will build enough factories and raise enough capital to meet demand at a price close to minimum average cost. However, producers may overshoot the optimal industry capacity, especially in cyclical markets. For example, producers may start to order new equipment during an economic expansion to increase capacity. By the time they bring the additional production on to the market, the economy may be in a recession with decreased demand. A diligent analyst can look for signs that the planned capacity increases of all producers (who may not take into account the capacity increases of other firms) sum to more output than industry demand will support.

Capacity is not necessarily physical. For example, an increase in demand for insurance can be more easily and quickly met than an increase in demand for a product requiring physical capacity, such as electricity or refined petroleum products.

If capacity is physical and specialized, overcapacity can exist for an extended period if producers expand too much over the course of a business cycle. Specialized physical capacity may have a low liquidation value and be costly to reallocate to a different product. Non-physical capacity (e.g., financial capital) can be reallocated more quickly to new industries than physical capacity.

Market Share Stability

An analyst should examine whether firms' market shares in an industry have been stable over time. Market shares that are highly variable likely indicate a highly competitive industry in which firms have little pricing power. More stable market shares likely indicate less intense competition in the industry.

Factors that affect market share stability include barriers to entry, introductions of new products and innovations, and the **switching costs** that customers face when changing from one firm's products to another. Switching costs, such as the time and expense of learning to use a competitor's product, tend to be higher for specialized or differentiated products. High switching costs contribute to market share stability and pricing power.

LOS 50.h: Describe product and industry life cycle models, classify an industry as to life cycle phase (e.g., embryonic, growth, shakeout, maturity, and decline) based on a description of it, and describe the limitations of the life-cycle concept in forecasting industry performance.

CFA® Program Curriculum, Volume 5, page 213

Industry life cycle analysis should be a component of an analyst's strategic analysis. An industry's stage in the cycle has an impact on industry competition, growth, and profits. An industry's stage will change over time, so the analyst must monitor the industry on an ongoing basis. The five phases of the industry life-cycle model are illustrated in Figure 1.

Figure 1: Stages of the Industry Life Cycle

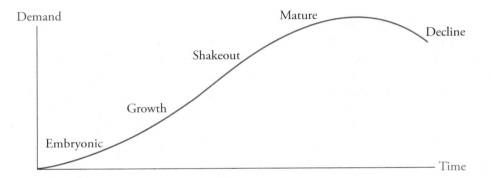

In the **embryonic stage**, the industry has just started. The characteristics of this stage are as follows:

- *Slow growth:* customers are unfamiliar with the product.
- *High prices:* the volume necessary for economies of scale has not been reached.
- *Large investment required:* to develop the product.
- *High risk of failure:* most embryonic firms fail.

In the **growth stage**, industry growth is rapid. The characteristics of this stage are as follows:

- *Rapid growth:* new consumers discover the product.
- *Limited competitive pressures:* the threat of new firms coming into the market peaks during the growth phase, but rapid growth allows firms to grow without competing on price.
- *Falling prices:* economies of scale are reached and distribution channels increase.
- *Increasing profitability:* due to economies of scale.

In the **shakeout stage**, industry growth and profitability are slowing due to strong competition. The characteristics of this stage are as follows:

- *Growth has slowed:* demand reaches saturation level with few new customers to be found.
- *Intense competition:* industry growth has slowed, so firm growth must come at the expense of competitors.
- *Increasing industry overcapacity:* firm investment exceeds increases in demand.
- *Declining profitability:* due to overcapacity.
- *Increased cost cutting:* firms restructure to survive and attempt to build brand loyalty.
- *Increased failures:* weaker firms liquidate or are acquired.

In the **mature stage**, there is little industry growth and firms begin to consolidate. The characteristics of this stage are as follows:

- *Slow growth:* market is saturated and demand is only for replacement.
- *Consolidation:* market evolves to an oligopoly.
- *High barriers to entry:* surviving firms have brand loyalty and low cost structures.
- *Stable pricing:* firms try to avoid price wars, although periodic price wars may occur during recessions.
- *Superior firms gain market share:* the firms with better products may grow faster than the industry average.

In the **decline stage**, industry growth is negative. The characteristics of this stage are as follows:

- *Negative growth:* due to development of substitute products, societal changes, or global competition.
- *Declining prices:* competition is intense and there are price wars due to overcapacity.
- *Consolidation:* failing firms exit or merge.

An analyst should determine whether a firm is "acting its age" or stage of industry development. Growth firms should be reinvesting in operations in an attempt to increase product offerings, increase economies of scale, and build brand loyalty. They are not yet worried about cost efficiency. They should not pay out cash flows to investors but save them for internal growth. On the other hand, mature firms focus on cost efficiency because demand is largely from replacement. They find few opportunities to introduce new products. These firms should typically pay out cash to investors as dividends or stock repurchases because cash flows are strong but internal growth is limited. An analyst should be concerned about firms that do not act their stage, such as a mature firm that is investing in low-return projects for the sake of increasing firm size.

Although life-cycle analysis is a useful tool, industries do not always conform to its framework. Life-cycle stages may not be as long or short as anticipated, or they might be skipped altogether. An industry's product may become obsolete quickly due to technological change, government regulation, societal change, or demographics. Life-cycle analysis is likely most useful during stable periods, not during periods of upheaval when conditions are changing rapidly. Furthermore, some firms will experience growth and profits that are dissimilar to others in their industries due to competitive advantages or disadvantages.

LOS 50.i: Compare characteristics of representative industries from the various economic sectors.

CFA® Program Curriculum, Volume 5, page 219

To illustrate the long list of factors to be considered in industry analysis, we use the following strategic analysis of the candy/confections industry.

- *Major firms*: Cadbury, Hershey, Mars, and Nestle.
- *Barriers to entry and success*: Very high. Low capital and technological barriers, but consumers have strong brand loyalty.
- *Industry concentration*: Very concentrated. Largest four firms dominate global market share.
- *Influence of industry capacity on pricing*: None. Pricing is determined by strength of brand, not production capacity.
- *Industry stability*: Very stable. Market share changes slowly.
- *Life cycle*: Very mature. Growth is driven by population changes.
- *Competition*: Low. Lack of unbranded candy makers in market reduces competition. Consumer decision is based on brand awareness, not price.
- *Demographic influences*: Not applicable.
- *Government influence*: Low. Industry is largely unregulated, but regulation arising from concerns about obesity is possible.
- *Social influence*: Not applicable.
- *Technological influence*: Very low. Limited impact from technology.
- *Business cycle sensitivity*: Non-cyclical and defensive. Demand for candy is very stable.

LOS 50.j: Describe demographic, governmental, social and technological influences on industry growth, profitability and risk.

CFA® Program Curriculum, Volume 5, page 221

The external influences on industry growth, profitability, and risk should be a component of an analyst's strategic analysis. These external factors include macroeconomic, technological, demographic, governmental, and social influences.

Macroeconomic factors can be yclical or structural (longer-term) trends, most notably economic output as measured by GDP or some other measure. Interest rates affect financing costs for firms and individuals, as well as financial institution profitability. Credit availability affects consumer and business expenditures and funding. Inflation affects costs, prices, interest rates, and business and consumer confidence. An example of a structural economic factor is the education level of the work force. More education can increase workers' productivity and real wages, which in turn can increase their demand for consumer goods.

Technology can change an industry dramatically through the introduction of new or improved products. Computer hardware is an example of an industry that has undergone dramatic transformation. Radical improvements in circuitry were assisted by transformations in other industries, including the computer software and telecommunications industries. Another example of an industry that has been changed by technology is photography, which has largely moved from film to digital media.

Demographic factors include age distribution and population size, as well as other changes in the composition of the population. As a large segment of the population reaches their twenties, residential construction, furniture, and related industries see increased demand. An aging of the overall population can mean significant growth for the health care industry and developers of retirement communities. For example, the aging of the post-World War II Baby Boomers is an example of demographics that will increase demand in these industries.

Governments have an important and widespread effect on businesses through various channels, including taxes and regulation. The level of tax rates certainly affects industries, but analysts should also be aware of the differential taxation applied to some goods. For example, tobacco is heavily taxed in the United States. Specific regulations apply to many industries. Entry into the health care industry, for example, is controlled by governments that license doctors and other providers. Governments can also empower self-regulatory organizations, such as stock exchanges that regulate their members. Some industries, such as the U.S. defense industry, depend heavily on government purchases of goods and services.

Social influences relate to how people work, play, spend their money, and conduct their lives; these factors can have a large impact on industries. For example, when women entered the U.S. workforce, the restaurant industry benefitted because there was less cooking at home. Child care, women's clothing, and other industries were also dramatically affected.

LOS 50.k: Describe the elements that should be covered in a thorough company analysis.

CFA® Program Curriculum, Volume 5, page 227

Having gained understanding of an industry's external environment, an analyst can then focus on **company analysis**. This involves analyzing the firm's financial condition, products and services, and **competitive strategy**. Competitive strategy is how a firm responds to the opportunities and threats of the external environment. The strategy may be defensive or offensive.

Porter has identified two important competitive strategies that can be employed by firms within an industry: a **cost leadership (low-cost) strategy** or a **product or service differentiation strategy**. According to Porter, a firm must decide to focus on one of these two areas to compete effectively.

In a *low-cost strategy*, the firm seeks to have the lowest costs of production in its industry, offer the lowest prices, and generate enough volume to make a superior return. The strategy can be used defensively to protect market share or offensively to gain market share. If industry competition is intense, pricing can be aggressive or even predatory. In **predatory pricing**, the firm hopes to drive out competitors and later increase prices. Although there are often laws prohibiting predatory pricing, it can be hard to prove if the firm's costs are not easily traced to a particular product. A low-cost strategy firm should have managerial incentives that are geared toward improving operating efficiency.

In a *differentiation strategy*, the firm's products and services should be distinctive in terms of type, quality, or delivery. For success, the firm's cost of differentiation must be less than the price premium buyers place on product differentiation. The price premium should also be sustainable over time. Successful differentiators will have outstanding marketing research teams and creative personnel.

A company analysis should include the following elements:

- Firm overview, including information on operations, governance, and strengths and weaknesses.
- Industry characteristics.
- Product demand.
- Product costs.
- Pricing environment.
- Financial ratios, with comparisons to other firms and over time.
- Projected financial statements and firm valuation.

A firm's return on equity (ROE) should be part of the financial analysis. The ROE is a function of profitability, total asset turnover, and financial leverage (debt).

 Professor's Note: The DuPont formula discussed in the topic review of Financial Analysis Techniques can help an analyst understand what drives ROE.

Analysts often use **spreadsheet modeling** to analyze and forecast company fundamentals. The problem with this method is that the models' complexity can make their conclusions seem precise. However, estimation is performed with error that can compound over time. As a check on a spreadsheet model's output, an analyst should consider which factors are likely to be different going forward and how this will affect the firm. Analysts should also be able to explain the assumptions of a spreadsheet model.

KEY CONCEPTS

LOS 50.a

Industry analysis is necessary for understanding a company's business environment before engaging in analysis of the company. The industry environment can provide information about the firm's potential growth, competition, risks, appropriate debt levels, and credit risk.

Industry valuation can be used in an active management strategy to determine which industries to overweight or underweight in a portfolio.

Industry representation is often a component in a performance attribution analysis of a portfolio's return.

LOS 50.b

Firms can be grouped into industries according to their products and services or business cycle sensitivity, or through statistical methods that group firms with high historical correlation in returns.

Industry classification systems from commercial providers include the Global Industry Classification Standard (Standard & Poor's and MSCI Barra), Russell Global Sectors, and the Industry Classification Benchmark (Dow Jones and FTSE).

Industry classification systems developed by government agencies include the International Standard Industrial Classification (ISIC), the North American Industry Classification System (NAICS), and systems designed for the European Union and Australia/New Zealand.

LOS 50.c

A cyclical firm has earnings that are highly dependent on the business cycle. A non-cyclical firm has earnings that are less dependent on the business cycle. Industries can also be classified as cyclical or non-cyclical. Non-cyclical industries or firms can be classified as defensive (demand for the product tends not to fluctuate with the business cycle) or growth (demand is so strong that it is largely unaffected by the business cycle).

Limitations of descriptors such as growth, defensive, and cyclical include the facts that cyclical industries often include growth firms; even non-cyclical industries can be affected by severe recessions; defensive industries are not always safe investments; business cycle timing differs across countries and regions; and the classification of firms is somewhat arbitrary.

LOS 50.d

A peer group should consist of companies with similar business activities, demand drivers, cost structure drivers, and availability of capital. To form a peer group, the analyst will often start by identifying companies in the same industry, but the analyst should use other information to verify that the firms in an industry are comparable.

LOS 50.e

A thorough industry analysis should:

- Evaluate the relationships between macroeconomic variables and industry trends.
- Estimate industry variables using different approaches and scenarios.
- Check estimates against those from other analysts.
- Compare the valuation for different industries.
- Compare the valuation for industries across time to determine risk and rotation strategies.
- Analyze industry prospects based on strategic groups.
- Classify industries by their life-cycle stage.
- Position the industry on the experience curve.
- Consider demographic, macroeconomic, governmental, social, and technological influences.
- Examine the forces that determine industry competition.

LOS 50.f

Strategic analysis of an industry involves analyzing the competitive forces that determine the possibility of economic profits.

Porter's five forces that determine industry competition are:

1. Rivalry among existing competitors.
2. Threat of new entrants.
3. Threat of substitute products.
4. Bargaining power of buyers.
5. Bargaining power of suppliers.

LOS 50.g

High barriers to entry prevent new competitors from taking away market share, but they do not guarantee pricing power or high return on capital, especially if the products are undifferentiated or barriers to exit result in overcapacity. Barriers to entry may change over time.

While market fragmentation usually results in strong competition and low return on capital, high industry concentration may not guarantee pricing power. If industry products are undifferentiated, consumers will switch to the cheapest producer. Overcapacity may result in price wars.

Capacity is fixed in the short run and variable in the long run. Undercapacity typically results in pricing power. Producers may overinvest in new capacity, especially in cyclical industries or if the capacity is physical and specialized. Non-physical capacity comes into production and can be reallocated more quickly than physical capacity.

Highly variable market shares indicate a highly competitive industry. Stable market shares suggest less intense competition. High switching costs contribute to market share stability.

LOS 50.h
Phases of the industry life-cycle model are the embryonic, growth, shakeout, maturity, and decline stages.

- Embryonic stage: Slow growth; high prices; large investment required; high risk of failure.
- Growth stage: Rapid growth; little competition; falling prices; increasing profitability.
- Shakeout stage: Slowing growth; intense competition; industry overcapacity; declining profitability; cost cutting; increased failures.
- Mature stage: Slow growth; consolidation; high barriers to entry; stable pricing; superior firms gain market share.
- Decline stage: Negative growth; declining prices; consolidation.

A limitation of life-cycle analysis is that life-cycle stages may not be as long or short as anticipated or might be skipped altogether due to technological change, government regulation, societal change, or demographics. Firms in the same life-cycle stage will experience dissimilar growth and profits due to their competitive positions.

LOS 50.i
The elements of an industry strategic analysis are the major firms, barriers to entry, industry concentration, influence of industry capacity on pricing, industry stability, life cycle, competition, demographic influences, government influence, social influence, technological influence, and whether the industry is growth, defensive, or cyclical.

LOS 50.j
Demographic influences on industries include the size and age distribution of the population.

Government factors include tax rates, regulations, empowerment of self-regulatory organizations, and government purchases of goods and services.

Social influences relate to how people interact and conduct their lives.

Technology can dramatically change an industry through the introduction of new or improved products.

LOS 50.k
Company analysis should include an overview of the firm, industry characteristics, and analysis of product demand, product costs, the pricing environment, the firm's financial ratios, and projected financial statements and firm valuation. The analysis should describe the company's competitive strategy.

Companies can employ a cost leadership (low-cost) strategy or a product or service differentiation strategy. A cost leadership firm seeks to have the lowest costs of production in its industry, offer the lowest prices, and generate enough volume to make a superior return. A differentiating firm's products and services should be distinctive in terms of type, quality, or delivery.

CONCEPT CHECKERS

1. Industry classification systems from commercial index providers typically classify firms by:
   A. statistical methods.
   B. products and services.
   C. business cycle sensitivity.

2. Firms and industries are *most appropriately* classified as cyclical or non-cyclical based on:
   A. their stock price fluctuations relative to the market.
   B. the sensitivity of their earnings to the business cycle.
   C. the volatility of their earnings relative to a peer group.

3. An analyst should *most likely* include two firms in the same peer group for analysis if the firms:
   A. are both grouped in the same industry classification.
   B. are similar in size, industry life-cycle stage, and cyclicality.
   C. derive their revenue and earnings from similar business activities.

4. The industry experience curve shows the cost per unit relative to:
   A. output.
   B. age of firms.
   C. industry life-cycle stage.

5. Greater pricing power is *most likely* to result from greater:
   A. unused capacity.
   B. market concentration.
   C. volatility in market share.

6. Which of the following statements *best* describes the relationship between pricing power and ease of entry and exit? Greater ease of entry:
   A. and greater ease of exit decrease pricing power.
   B. and greater ease of exit increase pricing power.
   C. decreases pricing power and greater ease of exit increases pricing power.

7. Industry overcapacity and increased cost cutting characterize which stage of the industry life cycle?
   A. Growth.
   B. Shakeout.
   C. Maturity.

8. Which of the following is *least likely* a significant external influence on industry growth?
   A. Social influences.
   B. Macroeconomic factors.
   C. Supplier bargaining power.

©2012 Kaplan, Inc.

9.   Which of the following is *least likely* an element of an industry strategic analysis?
      A. Market correlations.
      B. Demographic influences.
      C. Influence of industry capacity on pricing.

10.   Which of the following *best* describes a low-cost competitive strategy?
      A. Volume sold is typically modest.
      B. Managerial incentives promote operational efficiency.
      C. Success depends heavily on creative marketing and product development.

ANSWERS – CONCEPT CHECKERS

1. **B**   The classification systems provided by S&P/MSCI Barra, Russell, and Dow Jones/FTSE classify firms according to the product or service they produce.

2. **B**   For industry analysis, cyclical firms and industries are those with earnings that are highly dependent on the business cycle, while non-cyclical firms and industries are those with earnings that are relatively less sensitive to the business cycle.

3. **C**   Firms should be included in a peer group if their business activities are comparable. An analyst may begin with available industry classifications when forming peer groups but should refine them based on factors including the firms' sources of demand and earnings and the geographic markets in which they operate.

4. **A**   The experience curve shows the cost per unit relative to output. Unit cost declines at higher output volume because of increases in productivity and economies of scale, especially in industries with high fixed costs.

5. **B**   Greater concentration (a small number of firms control a large part of the market) typically reduces competition and results in greater pricing power. Greater unused capacity in an industry, especially if chronic, results in greater price competition and less pricing power. Greater stability in market share is typically associated with greater pricing power.

6. **C**   In industries with greater ease of entry, firms have little pricing power because new competitors can take away market share. High costs of exiting result in overcapacity and likely price wars. Greater ease of exit (i.e., low costs of exit) increases pricing power.

7. **B**   The shakeout stage is characterized by slowed growth, intense competition, industry overcapacity, increased cost cutting, declining profitability, and increased failures.

8. **C**   Supplier bargaining power is best characterized as a force internal to the industry. External influences on industry growth, profitability, and risk include macroeconomic, technological, demographic, governmental, and social influences.

9. **A**   Elements of an industry strategic analysis include the major firms, barriers to entry/ success, industry concentration, influence of industry capacity on pricing, industry stability, life cycle, competition, demographic influences, government influence, social influence, technological influence, and whether the industry is growth, defensive, or cyclical.

10. **B**   Firms that use a low-cost strategy should have managerial incentives suitable to create efficient operations. In a low-cost strategy, the firm seeks to generate high enough sales volume to make a superior return. Marketing and product development are key elements of a differentiation strategy.

EQUITY VALUATION: CONCEPTS AND BASIC TOOLS

Study Session 14

EXAM FOCUS

This topic review discusses the use of discounted cash flow models, price multiples, and asset-based models for stock valuation. Know when the various models are appropriate, how to apply them, and their advantages and disadvantages. This topic is foundational material for all three levels of the CFA exams. Be sure you understand these fundamental concepts.

LOS 51.a: Evaluate whether a security, given its current market price and a value estimate, is overvalued, fairly valued, or undervalued by the market.

CFA® Program Curriculum, Volume 5, page 244

Recall from the topic review of Market Efficiency that **intrinsic value** or **fundamental value** is defined as the rational value investors would place on the asset if they had full knowledge of the asset's characteristics. Analysts use valuation models to estimate the intrinsic values of stocks and compare them to the stocks' market prices to determine whether individual stocks are overvalued, undervalued, or fairly valued. In doing valuation analysis for stocks, analysts are assuming that some stocks' prices deviate significantly from their intrinsic values.

To the extent that market prices deviate from intrinsic values, analysts who can estimate a stock's intrinsic value better than the market can earn abnormal profits if the stock's market price moves toward its intrinsic value over time. There are several things to consider, however, in deciding whether to invest based on differences between market prices and estimated intrinsic values.

1. The larger the percentage difference between market prices and estimated values, the more likely the investor is to take a position based on the estimate of intrinsic value. Small differences between market prices and estimates of intrinsic values are to be expected.

2. The more confident the investor is about the appropriateness of the valuation model used, the more likely the investor is to take an investment position in a stock that is identified as overvalued or undervalued.

3. The more confident the investor is about the estimated inputs used in the valuation model, the more likely the investor is to take an investment position in a stock that is identified as overvalued or undervalued. Analysts must also consider the sensitivity of a model value to each of its inputs in deciding whether to act on a difference between model values and market prices. If a decrease of one-half percent in the long-term growth rate used in the valuation model would produce an estimated value equal to the market price, an analyst would have to be quite sure of the model's growth estimate to take a position in the stock based on its estimated value.

4. Even if we assume that market prices sometimes deviate from intrinsic values, market prices must be treated as fairly reliable indications of intrinsic value. Investors must consider why a stock is mispriced in the market. Investors may be more confident about estimates of value that differ from market prices when few analysts follow a particular security.

5. Finally, to take a position in a stock identified as mispriced in the market, an investor must believe that the market price will actually move toward (and certainly not away from) its estimated intrinsic value and that it will do so to a significant extent within the investment time horizon.

LOS 51.b: Describe major categories of equity valuation models.

CFA® Program Curriculum, Volume 5, page 246

Analysts use a variety of models to estimate the value of equities. Usually, an analyst will use more than one model with several different sets of inputs to determine a range of possible stock values.

In **discounted cash flow models** (or **present value models**), a stock's value is estimated as the present value of cash distributed to shareholders (*dividend discount models*) or the present value of cash available to shareholders after the firm meets its necessary capital expenditures and working capital expenses (*free cash flow to equity models*).

There are two basic types of **multiplier models** (or **market multiple models**) that can be used to estimate intrinsic values. In the first type, the ratio of stock price to such fundamentals as earnings, sales, book value, or cash flow per share is used to determine if a stock is fairly valued. For example, the price to earnings (P/E) ratio is frequently used by analysts.

The second type of multiplier model is based on the ratio of **enterprise value** to either earnings before interest, taxes, depreciation, and amortization (EBITDA) or revenue. Enterprise value is the market value of all a firm's outstanding securities minus cash and short-term investments. Common stock value can be estimated by subtracting the value of liabilities and preferred stock from an estimate of enterprise value.

In **asset-based models**, the intrinsic value of common stock is estimated as total asset value minus liabilities and preferred stock. Analysts typically adjust the book values of the firm's assets and liabilities to their fair values when estimating the market value of its equity with an asset-based model.

LOS 51.c: Explain the rationale for using present-value of cash flow models to value equity and describe the dividend discount and free-cash-flow-to-equity models.

CFA® Program Curriculum, Volume 5, page 248

The **dividend discount model** (DDM) is based on the rationale that the intrinsic value of stock is the present value of its future dividends.

The most general form of the model is as follows:

$$V_0 = \sum_{t=1}^{\infty} \frac{D_t}{(1 + k_e)^t}$$

where:
V_0 = current stock value
D_t = dividend at time t
k_e = required rate of return on common equity

One-year holding period DDM. For a holding period of one year, the value of the stock today is the present value of any dividends during the year plus the present value of the expected price of the stock at the end of the year (referred to as its **terminal value**).

The one-year holding period DDM is simply:

$$\text{value} = \frac{\text{dividend to be received}}{(1 + k_e)} + \frac{\text{year-end price}}{(1 + k_e)}$$

Example: One-period DDM valuation

Calculate the value of a stock that paid a $1 dividend last year, if next year's dividend will be 5% higher and the stock will sell for $13.45 at year-end. The required return is 13.2%.

Answer:

The next dividend is the current dividend increased by the estimated growth rate. In this case, we have:

$$D_1 = D_0 \times (1 + \text{dividend growth rate}) = \$1.00 \times (1 + 0.05) = \$1.05$$

The present value of the expected future cash flows is:

dividend: $\dfrac{\$1.05}{1.132} = \$0.93$ year-end price: $\dfrac{\$13.45}{1.132} = \$11.88$

The current value based on the investor's expectations is:

stock value = $0.93 + $11.88 = $12.81

Multiple-year holding period DDM. With a multiple-year holding period, we simply sum the present values of the estimated dividends over the holding period and the estimated terminal value.

For a two-year holding period, we have:

$$\text{value} = \frac{D_1}{(1 + k_e)} + \frac{D_2}{(1 + k_e)^2} + \frac{P_2}{(1 + k_e)^2}$$

Professor's Note: It is useful to think of the subscript t on dividends (D_t) and prices (P_t) as the end of period t. For example, in the preceding equation, P_2 is the price at the end of Year 2. Think of it as the selling price of a share, immediately after D_2 is received.

Example: Multiple-period DDM valuation

A stock recently paid a dividend of $1.00 which is expected to grow at 5% per year. The required rate of return of 13.2%. Calculate the value of this stock assuming that it will be priced at $14.12 two years from now.

Answer:

Find the PV of the future dividends:

$$D_1 : \frac{\$1.05}{1.132} = \$0.93$$

$$D_2 : \frac{\$1.05(1.05)}{(1.132)^2} = \frac{\$1.103}{1.2814} = \$0.86$$

PV of dividends = 0.93 + 0.86 = $1.79

Find the PV of the future price:

$$\frac{\$14.12}{(1.132)^2} = \$11.02$$

Add the present values. The current value based on the investor's expectations is $1.79 + $11.02 = $12.81.

The most general form of the DDM uses an infinite holding period because a corporation has an indefinite life. In an infinite-period DDM model, the present value of all expected future dividends is calculated and there is no explicit terminal value for the stock. In practice, as we will see, a terminal value can be calculated at a time in the future after which the growth rate of dividends is expected to be constant.

Free cash flow to equity (FCFE) is often used in discounted cash flow models instead of dividends because it represents the potential amount of cash that could be paid out to common shareholders. That is, FCFE reflects the firm's capacity to pay dividends. FCFE is also useful for firms that do not currently pay dividends.

FCFE is defined as the cash remaining after a firm meets all of its debt obligations and provides for the capital expenditures necessary to maintain existing assets and to purchase the new assets needed to support the assumed growth of the firm. In other words, it is the cash available to the firm's equity holders after a firm meets all of its other obligations. FCFE for a period is often calculated as:

> FCFE = net income + depreciation – increase in working capital – fixed capital investment (FCInv) – debt principal repayments + new debt issues

FCFE can also be calculated as:

> FCFE = cash flow from operations – FCInv + net borrowing

In the second formula, **net borrowing** is the increase in debt during the period (i.e., amount borrowed minus amount repaid) and is assumed to be available to shareholders. Fixed capital investment must be subtracted because the firm must invest in assets to sustain itself. FCFE is projected for future periods using the firm's financial statements.

Restating the general form of the DDM in terms of FCFE, we have:

$$V_0 = \sum_{t=1}^{\infty} \frac{FCFE_t}{(1 + k_e)^t}$$

Estimating the Required Return for Equity

The capital asset pricing model (CAPM) provides an estimate of the required rate of return (k_i) for security i as a function of its systematic risk (β_i), the risk-free rate (R_f), and the expected return on the market [$E(R_{mkt})$] as:

$$k_i = R_f + \beta_i[E(R_{mkt}) - R_f]$$

There is some controversy over whether the CAPM is the best model to calculate the required return on equity. Also, different analysts will likely use different inputs, so there is no single number that is correct.

 Professor's Note: The CAPM is discussed in detail in the Study Session on portfolio management.

Recall from the topic review of Cost of Capital that for firms with publicly traded debt, analysts often estimate the required return on the firm's common equity by adding a risk premium to the firm's current bond yield. If the firm does not have publicly traded debt, an analyst can add a larger risk premium to a government bond yield.

LOS 51.d: Calculate the intrinsic value of a non-callable, non-convertible preferred stock.

CFA® Program Curriculum, Volume 5, page 251

Preferred stock pays a dividend that is usually fixed and usually has an indefinite maturity. When the dividend is fixed and the stream of dividends is infinite, the infinite period dividend discount model reduces to a simple ratio:

$$\text{preferred stock value} = \frac{D_p}{\left(1 + k_p\right)^1} + \frac{D_p}{\left(1 + k_p\right)^2} + \ldots + \frac{D_p}{\left(1 + k_p\right)^x} = \frac{D_p}{k_p}$$

Example: Preferred stock valuation

A company's $100 par preferred stock pays a $5.00 annual dividend and has a required return of 8%. Calculate the value of the preferred stock.

Answer:

Value of the preferred stock: D_p / k_p = $5.00 / 0.08 = $62.50

In the previous example, if the dividends were paid semiannually and the preferred stock had a maturity of one year, we would use a formula similar to the one we examined earlier for common stock. Instead of the price, we would use the par value (*F*) paid by the firm. Instead of the required return on common, we would use the required return on preferred:

$$\text{value} = \frac{D_1}{\left(1 + \dfrac{k_p}{2}\right)} + \frac{D_2}{\left(1 + \dfrac{k_p}{2}\right)^2} + \frac{F_2}{\left(1 + \dfrac{k_p}{2}\right)^2}$$

With a 1-year maturity, there are two semiannual dividends of $2.50 remaining, and with a required semiannual return of 4% we have:

$$\text{value} = \frac{\$2.50}{(1 + 0.04)^1} + \frac{\$2.50}{(1 + 0.04)^2} + \frac{\$100}{(1 + 0.04)^2} = \$97.17$$

LOS 51.e: Calculate and interpret the intrinsic value of an equity security based on the Gordon (constant) growth dividend discount model or a two-stage dividend discount model, as appropriate.

CFA® Program Curriculum, Volume 5, page 254

The **Gordon growth model** (or **constant growth model**) assumes the annual growth rate of dividends, g_c, is constant. Hence, next period's dividend, D_1, is $D_0(1 + g_c)$, the second year's dividend, D_2, is $D_0(1 + g_c)^2$, and so on. The extended equation using this assumption gives the present value of the expected future dividends (V_0) as:

$$V_0 = \frac{D_0(1 + g_c)}{(1 + k_e)} + \frac{D_0(1 + g_c)^2}{(1 + k_e)^2} + \frac{D_0(1 + g_c)^3}{(1 + k_e)^3} + \ldots + \frac{D_0(1 + g_c)^\infty}{(1 + k_e)^\infty}$$

When the growth rate of dividends is constant, this equation simplifies to the Gordon (constant) growth model:

$$V_0 = \frac{D_0(1 + g_c)}{k_e - g_c} = \frac{D_1}{k_e - g_c}$$

Professor's Note: In much of the finance literature, you will see this model referred to as the constant growth DDM, infinite period DDM, or the Gordon growth model. Whatever you call it, memorize D_1 over (k minus g). Note that our valuation model for preferred stock is the same as the constant growth model with no growth (g = 0).

The assumptions of the Gordon growth model are:

- Dividends are the appropriate measure of shareholder wealth.
- The constant dividend growth rate, g_c, and required return on stock, k_e, are never expected to change.
- k_e must be greater than g_c. If not, the math will not work.

If any one of these assumptions is not met, the model is not appropriate.

> **Example: Gordon growth model valuation**
>
> Calculate the value of a stock that paid a $2 dividend last year, if dividends are expected to grow at 5% forever and the required return on equity is 12%.
>
> **Answer:**
>
> Determine D_1: $D_0(1 + g_c) = \$2(1.05) = \$2.10$
>
> Calculate the stock's value = $D_1 / (k_e - g_c)$
>
> $$= \$2.10 / (0.12 - 0.05)$$
> $$= \$30.00$$

Professor's Note: When doing stock valuation problems on the exam, watch for words like "forever," "infinitely," "indefinitely," "for the foreseeable future," and so on. This will tell you that the Gordon growth model should be used. Also watch for words like "just paid" or "recently paid." These will refer to the last dividend, D_0. Words like "will pay" or "is expected to pay" refer to D_1.

This example demonstrates that the stock's value is determined by the relationship between the investor's required rate of return on equity, k_e, and the projected growth rate of dividends, g_c:

- As the difference between k_e and g_c widens, the value of the stock falls.
- As the difference narrows, the value of the stock rises.
- Small changes in the difference between k_e and g_c can cause large changes in the stock's value.

Because the estimated stock value is very sensitive to the denominator, an analyst should calculate several different value estimates using a range of required returns and growth rates.

An analyst can also use the Gordon growth model to determine how much of the estimated stock value is due to dividend growth. To do this, assume the growth rate is zero and calculate a value. Then, subtract this value from the stock value estimated using a positive growth rate.

Example: Amount of estimated stock value due to dividend growth

Using the data from the previous example, calculate how much of the estimated stock value is due to dividend growth.

Answer:

The estimated stock value with a growth rate of zero is:

$$V_0 = D / k = \$2.00 / 0.12 = \$16.67$$

The amount of the estimated stock value due to estimated dividend growth is:

$$\$30.00 - \$16.67 = \$13.33$$

Estimating the Growth Rate in Dividends

To estimate the growth rate in dividends, the analyst can use three methods:

1. Use the historical growth in dividends for the firm.
2. Use the median industry dividend growth rate.
3. Estimate the sustainable growth rate.

©2012 Kaplan, Inc.

The **sustainable growth rate** is the rate at which equity, earnings, and dividends can continue to grow indefinitely assuming that ROE is constant, the dividend payout ratio is constant, and no new equity is sold.

sustainable growth = (1 – dividend payout ratio) × ROE

The quantity (1 – dividend payout ratio) is also referred to as the **retention rate**, the proportion of net income that is not paid out as dividends and goes to retained earnings, thus increasing equity.

Example: Sustainable growth rate

Green, Inc., is expected to pay dividends equal to 25% of earnings. Green's ROE is 21%. Calculate and interpret its sustainable growth rate.

Answer:

g = (1 – 0.25) × 21% = 15.75%

With long-run economic growth typically in the single digits, it is unlikely that a firm could sustain 15.75% growth forever. The analyst should also examine the growth rate for the industry and the firm's historical growth rate to determine whether the estimate is reasonable.

Some firms do not currently pay dividends but are expected to begin paying dividends at some point in the future. A firm may not currently pay a dividend because it is in financial distress and cannot afford to pay out cash or because the return the firm can earn by reinvesting cash is greater than what stockholders could expect to earn by investing dividends elsewhere.

For these firms, an analyst must estimate the amount and timing of the first dividend in order to use the Gordon growth model. Because these parameters are highly uncertain, the analyst should check the estimate from the Gordon growth model against estimates made using other models.

Example: A firm with no current dividend

A firm currently pays no dividend but is expected to pay a dividend at the end of Year 4. Year 4 earnings are expected to be $1.64, and the firm will maintain a payout ratio of 50%. Assuming a constant growth rate of 5% and a required rate of return of 10%, estimate the current value of this stock.

Answer:

The first step is to find the value of the stock at the end of Year 3. Remember, P_3 is the present value of dividends in Years 4 through infinity, calculated at the end of Year 3, one period *before* the first dividend is paid.

Calculate D_4, the estimate of the dividend that will be paid at the end of Year 4:

$$D_4 = \text{(dividend payout ratio)}(E_4) = (0.5)(1.64) = \$0.82$$

Apply the constant growth model to estimate V_3:

$$V_3 = D_4 / (k_e - g_c) = \$0.82 / (0.10 - 0.05) = \$16.40$$

The second step is to calculate the current value, V_0:

$$V_0 = 16.40 / 1.1^3 = \$12.32$$

Multistage Dividend Growth Models

A firm may temporarily experience a growth rate that exceeds the required rate of return on the firm's equity, but no firm can maintain this relationship indefinitely. A firm with an extremely high growth rate will attract competition, and its growth rate will eventually fall. We must assume the firm will return to a more sustainable rate of growth at some point in the future in order to calculate the present value of expected future dividends.

One way to value a dividend-paying firm that is experiencing temporarily high growth is to add the present values of dividends expected during the high-growth period to the present value of the constant growth value of the firm at the end of the high-growth period. This is referred to as the **multistage dividend discount model**.

$$\text{value} = \frac{D_1}{(1 + k_e)} + \frac{D_2}{(1 + k_e)^2} + ... + \frac{D_n}{(1 + k_e)^n} + \frac{P_n}{(1 + k_e)^n}$$

where $P_n = \dfrac{D_{n+1}}{k_e - g_c}$ is the terminal stock value, assuming that dividends at $t = n + 1$

and beyond grow at a constant rate of g_c.

Steps in using the multistage model:

- Determine the discount rate, k_e.
- Project the size and duration of the high initial dividend growth rate, g^*.
- Estimate dividends during the high-growth period.
- Estimate the constant growth rate at the end of the high-growth period, g_c.
- Estimate the first dividend that will grow at the constant rate.
- Use the constant growth value to calculate the stock value at the end of the high-growth period.
- Add the PVs of all dividends to the PV of the terminal value of the stock.

Example: Multistage growth

Consider a stock with dividends that are expected to grow at 20% per year for four years, after which they are expected to grow at 5% per year, indefinitely. The last dividend paid was $1.00, and k_e = 10%. Calculate the value of this stock using the multistage growth model.

Answer:

Calculate the dividends over the high-growth period:

$$D_1 = D_0(1 + g^*) = 1.00(1.20) = \$1.20$$

$$D_2 = D_1(1 + g^*) = 1.20(1.20) = 1.2^2 = \$1.44$$

$$D_3 = D_2(1 + g^*) = 1.44(1.20) = 1.2^3 = \$1.73$$

$$D_4 = D_3(1 + g^*) = 1.73(1.20) = 1.2^4 = \$2.08 \text{ (rounded up)}$$

Although we increase D_3 by the high growth rate of 20% to get D_4, D_4 will grow at the constant growth rate of 5% for the foreseeable future. This property of D_4 allows us to use the constant growth model formula with D_4 to get P_3, a time = 3 value for all the (infinite) dividends expected from time = 4 onward.

$$P_3 = \frac{D_4}{k_e - g_c} = \frac{2.08}{0.10 - 0.05} = 41.60$$

Finally, we can sum the present values of dividends 1, 2, and 3 and of P_3 to get the present value of all the expected future dividends during both the high- and constant growth periods:

$$\frac{1.20}{1.1} + \frac{1.44}{1.1^2} + \frac{1.73}{1.1^3} + \frac{41.60}{1.1^3} = \$34.84$$

Professor's Note: Many finance textbooks solve multiple stage growth problems like this one by using the first dividend that has grown at the constant long-term rate to calculate the terminal value, one period after the dividend we have used. Except for rounding, this results in the same current stock value. In fact, the constant growth model can be employed using any dividend during the assumed constant growth period.

A common mistake with multistage growth problems is to calculate the future value, P_3 in this example, and then to either forget to discount it back to the present or to discount over the number of periods until the constant growth dividend is paid (four in this example) rather than using the correct number of periods for discounting the constant growth value (three periods in the example). Don't make these mistakes because question writers like to present these common errors as answer choices.

LOS 51.f: Identify companies for which the constant growth or a multistage dividend discount model is appropriate.

CFA® Program Curriculum, Volume 5, page 258

The Gordon growth model uses a single constant growth rate of dividends and is most appropriate for valuing stable and mature, non-cyclical, dividend-paying firms.

For dividend-paying firms with dividends that are expected to grow rapidly, slowly, or erratically over some period, followed by constant dividend growth, some form of the multistage growth model should be employed. The important points are that dividends must be estimable and must grow at a constant rate after some initial period so that the constant growth model can be used to determine the terminal value of the stock. Thus, we can apply multistage dividend growth models to a firm with high current growth that will drop to a stable rate in the future or to a firm that is temporarily losing market share and growing slowly or getting smaller, as long as its growth is expected to stabilize to a constant rate at some point in the future.

One variant of a multistage growth model assumes that the firm has three stages of dividend growth, not just two. These three stages can be categorized as growth, transition, and maturity. A 3-stage model would be suitable for firms with an initial high growth rate, followed by a lower growth rate during a second, transitional period, followed by the constant growth rate in the long run, such as a young firm still in the high growth phase.

When a firm does not pay dividends, estimates of dividend payments some years in the future are highly speculative. In this case, and in any case where future dividends cannot be estimated with much confidence, valuation based on FCFE is appropriate as long as growth rates of earnings can be estimated. In other cases, valuation based on price multiples may be more appropriate.

LOS 51.g: Explain the rationale for using price multiples to value equity and distinguish between multiples based on comparables versus multiples based on fundamentals.

CFA® Program Curriculum, Volume 5, page 262

Because the dividend discount model is very sensitive to its inputs, many investors rely on other methods. In a **price multiple** approach, an analyst compares a stock's price multiple to a benchmark value based on an index, industry group of firms, or a peer group of firms within an industry. Common price multiples used for valuation include price-to-earnings, price-to-cash flow, price-to-sales, and price-to-book value ratios.

Price multiples are widely used by analysts and readily available in numerous media outlets. Price multiples are easily calculated and can be used in time series and cross-sectional comparisons. Many of these ratios have been shown to be useful for predicting stock returns, with low multiples associated with higher future returns.

A critique of price multiples is that they reflect only the past because historical (trailing) data are often used in the denominator. For this reason, many practitioners use forward (leading or prospective) values in the denominator (sales, book value, earnings, etc.). The use of projected values can result in much different ratios. An analyst should be sure to use price multiple calculations consistently across firms.

When we compare a price multiple, such as P/E, for a firm to those of other firms based on market prices, we are using **price multiples based on comparables**. By contrast, **price multiples based on fundamentals** tell us what a multiple should be based on some valuation model and therefore are not dependent on the current market prices of other companies to establish value.

LOS 51.h: Calculate and interpret the following multiples: price to earnings, price to an estimate of operating cash flow, price to sales, and price to book value.

CFA® Program Curriculum, Volume 5, page 262

Price multiples used for valuation include:

- **Price-earnings (P/E) ratio**: The P/E ratio is a firm's stock price divided by earnings per share and is widely used by analysts and cited in the press.
- **Price-sales (P/S) ratio**: The P/S ratio is a firm's stock price divided by sales per share.
- **Price-book value (P/B) ratio**: The P/B ratio is a firm's stock price divided by book value of equity per share.
- **Price-cash flow (P/CF) ratio**: The P/CF ratio is a firm's stock price divided by cash flow per share, where cash flow may be defined as operating cash flow or free cash flow.

Other multiples can be used that are industry specific. For example, in the cable television industry, stock market capitalization is compared to the number of subscribers.

Multiples Based on Fundamentals

To understand fundamental price multiples, consider the Gordon growth valuation model:

$$P_0 = \frac{D_1}{k - g}$$

If we divide both sides of the equation by next year's projected earnings, E_1, we get:

$\dfrac{P_0}{E_1} = \dfrac{D_1 / E_1}{k - g}$, which is the leading P/E for this stock if it is valued in the market

according to the constant growth DDM.

This P/E based on fundamentals is also referred to as a **justified P/E**. It is "justified" because, assuming we have the correct inputs for D_1, E_1, k_e, and g, the equation above will provide a P/E ratio that is based on the present value of the future cash flows. We refer to this as a *leading P/E ratio* because it is based on expected earnings next period, not on actual earnings for the previous period, which would produce a lagging or *trailing P/E ratio*.

One advantage of this approach is that it makes clear how the firm's P/E ratio should be related to its fundamentals. It illustrates that the P/E ratio is a function of:

- D_1 / E_1 = expected dividend payout ratio.
- k = required rate of return on the stock.
- g = expected constant growth rate of dividends.

> **Example: P/E based on fundamentals**
>
> A firm has an expected dividend payout ratio of 60%, a required rate of return of 11%, and an expected dividend growth rate of 5%. Calculate the firm's fundamental (justified) leading P/E ratio.
>
> **Answer:**
>
> expected P/E ratio: 0.6 / (0.11 – 0.05) = 10

The justified P/E ratio serves as a benchmark for the price at which the stock should trade. In the previous example, if the firm's actual P/E ratio (based on the market price and expected earnings) was 16, the stock would be considered overvalued. If the firm's market P/E ratio was 7, the stock would be considered undervalued.

P/E ratios based on fundamentals are very sensitive to the inputs (especially the denominator, k – g), so the analyst should use several different sets of inputs to indicate a range for the justified P/E.

Because we started with the equation for the constant growth DDM, the P/E ratio calculated in this way is the P/E ratio consistent with the constant growth DDM. We can see from the formula that, *other things equal*, the P/E ratio we have defined here will increase with (1) a higher dividend payout rate, (2) a higher growth rate, or (3) a lower required rate of return. So, if the subject firm has a higher dividend payout ratio, higher growth rate, and lower required return than its peers, a higher P/E ratio may be justified.

In practice, other things are not equal. An increase in the dividend payout ratio, for example, will reduce the firm's sustainable growth rate. While higher dividends will increase firm value, a lower growth rate will decrease firm value. This relationship is referred to as the **dividend displacement of earnings**. The net effect on firm value of increasing the dividend payout ratio is ambiguous. As intuition would suggest, firms cannot continually increase their P/Es or market values by increasing the dividend payout ratio. Otherwise, all firms would have 100% payout ratios.

 Professor's Note: Watch for the wording "other things equal" or "other variables unchanged" in any exam questions about the effect of changing one variable.

Example: Fundamental P/E ratio comparison

Holt Industries makes decorative items. The figures below are for Holt and its industry.

	Holt Industries	Industry Average
Dividend payout ratio	25%	16%
Sales growth	7.5%	3.9%
Total debt to equity	113%	68%

Which of these factors suggest a higher fundamental P/E ratio for Holt?

Answer:

- The higher dividend payout ratio supports Holt having a higher P/E ratio than the industry.
- Higher growth in sales suggests that Holt will be able to increase dividends at a faster rate, which supports Holt having a higher P/E ratio than the industry.
- The higher level of debt, however, indicates that Holt has higher risk and a higher required return on equity, which supports Holt having a lower P/E ratio than the industry.

Multiples Based on Comparables

Valuation based on price multiple comparables (or comps) involves using a price multiple to evaluate whether an asset is valued properly relative to a benchmark. Common benchmarks include the stock's historical average (a time series comparison) or similar stocks and industry averages (a cross-sectional comparison). Comparing firms within an industry is useful for analysts who are familiar with a particular industry. Price multiples are readily calculated and provided by many media outlets.

The economic principle guiding this method is the **law of one price**, which asserts that two identical assets should sell at the same price, or in this case, two comparable assets should have approximately the same multiple.

The analyst should be sure that any comparables used really are comparable. Price multiples may not be comparable across firms if the firms are different sizes, are in different industries, or will grow at different rates. Furthermore, using P/E ratios for cyclical firms is complicated due to their sensitivity to economic conditions. In this case, the P/S ratio may be favored over the P/E ratio because the sales are less volatile than earnings due to both operating and financial leverage.

The disadvantages of using price multiples based on comparables are (1) a stock may appear overvalued by the comparable method but undervalued by the fundamental method, or vice versa; (2) different accounting methods can result in price multiples that are not comparable across firms, especially internationally; and (3) price multiples for cyclical firms may be greatly affected by economic conditions at a given point in time.

Example: Valuation using comparables

The following figures are for Renee's Bakery. All figures except the stock price are in millions.

Fiscal Year-End	20X3	20X2	20X1
Total stockholder's equity	$55.60	$54.10	$52.60
Net revenues	$77.30	$73.60	$70.80
Net income	$3.20	$1.10	$0.40
Net cash flow from operations	$17.90	$15.20	$12.20
Stock price	$11.40	$14.40	$12.05
Shares outstanding	4.476	3.994	3.823

Calculate Renee's lagging P/E, P/CF, P/S, and P/B ratios. Judge whether the firm is undervalued or overvalued using the following relevant industry averages for 20X3 and the firm's historical trend.

Lagging Industry Ratios	20X3
Price-to-earnings	8.6
Price-to-cash flow	4.6
Price-to-sales	1.4
Price-to-book value	3.6

Answer:

To calculate the lagging price multiples, first divide the relevant financial statement items by the number of shares to get per-share amounts. Then, divide the stock price by this figure.

For example, for the P/S ratio for 20X3, divide net revenue (net sales) by the number of shares:

$$\frac{\text{sales}}{\text{number of shares}} = \frac{\$77.30}{4.476} = 17.270$$

Then, divide the stock price by sales per share:

$$\frac{P}{S} = \frac{\$11.40}{17.3} = 0.7$$

Using the net income for earnings, the net cash flow from operations for the cash flow, and stockholder's equity for book value, the ratios for Renee's Bakery are:

	20X3	20X2	20X1
P/E	15.9	52.3	115.2
P/CF	2.9	3.8	3.8
P/S	0.7	0.8	0.7
P/B	0.9	1.1	0.9

Comparing Renee's Bakery's ratios to the industry averages for 20X3, the price multiples are lower in all cases except for the P/E multiple. This cross-sectional evidence suggests that Renee's Bakery is undervalued.

The P/E ratio merits further investigation. Renee's Bakery may have a higher P/E because its earnings are depressed by high depreciation, interest expense, or taxes. Calculating the price-EBITDA ratio would provide an alternative measure that is unaffected by these expenses.

On a time series basis, the ratios are trending downward. This indicates that Renee's Bakery may be currently undervalued relative to its past valuations. We could also calculate average price multiples for the ratios over 20X1–20X3 as a benchmark for the current values:

Company average P/E 20X1–20X3	61.1
Company average P/CF 20X1–20X3	3.5
Company average P/S 20X1–20X3	0.7
Company average P/B 20X1–20X3	1.0

The current P/E, P/CF, and P/B ratios are lower than their 3-year averages. This indicates that Renee's Bakery may be currently undervalued. It also may be the case, however, that P/E ratios for the market as a whole have been decreasing over the period due to systematic factors.

LOS 51.i: Explain the use of enterprise value multiples in equity valuation and demonstrate the use of enterprise value multiples to estimate equity value.

CFA® Program Curriculum, Volume 5, page 271

Enterprise value (EV) measures total company value. EV can be viewed as what it would cost to acquire the firm:

EV = market value of common and preferred stock + market value of debt – cash and short-term investments

Cash and short-term investments are subtracted because an acquirer's cost for a firm would be decreased by the amount of the target's liquid assets. Although an acquirer assumes the firm's debt, it also receives the firm's cash and short-term investments. Enterprise value is appropriate when an analyst wants to compare the values of firms that have significant differences in capital structure.

EBITDA (earnings before interest, taxes, depreciation, and amortization are subtracted) is probably the most frequently used denominator for EV multiples; operating income can also be used. Because the numerator represents total company value, it should be compared to earnings of both debt and equity owners. An advantage of using EBITDA instead of net income is that EBITDA is usually positive even when earnings are not. When net income is negative, value multiples based on earnings are meaningless. A disadvantage of using EBITDA is that it often includes non-cash revenues and expenses.

A potential problem with using enterprise value is that the market value of a firm's debt is often not available. In this case, the analyst can use the market values of similar bonds or can use their book values. Book value, however, may not be a good estimate of market value if firm and market conditions have changed significantly since the bonds were issued.

Example: Calculating EV/EBITDA multiples

Daniel, Inc., is a manufacturer of small refrigerators and other appliances. The following figures are from Daniel's most recent financial statements except for the market value of long-term debt, which has been estimated from financial market data.

Stock price	$30.00
Shares outstanding	300,000
Market value of long-term debt	$800,000
Book value of long-term debt	$1,100,000
Book value of total debt	$2,600,000
Cash and marketable securities	$300,000
EBITDA	$1,200,000

Calculate the EV/EBITDA multiple.

©2012 Kaplan, Inc.

Answer:

First, we must estimate the market value of the firm's short-term debt and liabilities. To do so, subtract the book value of long-term debt from the book value of total debt: $2,600,000 – $1,100,000 = $1,500,000. This is the book value of the firm's short-term debt. We can assume the market value of these short-term items is close to their book value. (As we will see in the Study Session on fixed income valuation, the market values of debt instruments approach their face values as they get close to maturity.)

Add the market value of long-term debt to get the market value of total debt: $800,000 + $1,500,000 = $2,300,000.

The market value of equity is the stock price multiplied by the number of shares: $30 × 300,000 = $9,000,000.

The enterprise value of the firm is the sum of debt and equity minus cash: $2,300,000 + $9,000,000 – $300,000 = $11,000,000.

EV/EBITDA = $11,000,000 / $1,200,000 = 9.2.

If the competitor or industry average EV/EBITDA is above 9.2, Daniel is relatively undervalued. If the competitor or industry average EV/EBITDA is below 9.2, Daniel is relatively overvalued.

LOS 51.j: Explain asset-based valuation models and demonstrate the use of asset-based models to calculate equity value.

CFA® Program Curriculum, Volume 5, page 273

Our third category of valuation model is **asset-based models**, which are based on the idea that equity value is the market or fair value of assets minus the market or fair value of liabilities. Because market values of firm assets are usually difficult to obtain, the analyst typically starts with the balance sheet to determine the values of assets and liabilities. In most cases, market values are not equal to book values. Possible approaches to valuing assets are to value them at their depreciated values, inflation-adjusted depreciated values, or estimated replacement values.

Applying asset-based models is especially problematic for a firm that has a large amount of intangible assets, on or off the balance sheet. The effect of the loss of the current owners' talents and customer relationships on forward earnings may be quite difficult to measure. Analysts often consider asset-based model values as floor or minimum values when significant intangibles, such as business reputation, are involved. An analyst should consider supplementing an asset-based valuation with a more forward-looking valuation, such as one from a discounted cash flow model.

Asset-based model valuations are most reliable when the firm has primarily tangible short-term assets, assets with ready market values (e.g., financial or natural resource firms), or when the firm will cease to operate and is being liquidated. Asset-based models are often used to value private companies but may be increasingly useful for public firms as they move toward fair value reporting on the balance sheet.

Example: Using an asset-based model for a public firm

Williams Optical is a publicly traded firm. An analyst estimates that the market value of net fixed assets is 120% of book value. Liability and short-term asset market values are assumed to equal their book values. The firm has 2,000 shares outstanding.

Using the selected financial results in the table, calculate the value of the firm's net assets on a per-share basis.

Cash	$10,000
Accounts receivable	$20,000
Inventories	$50,000
Net fixed assets	$120,000
Total assets	$200,000
Accounts payable	$5,000
Notes payable	$30,000
Term loans	$45,000
Common stockholder equity	$120,000
Total assets	$200,000

Answer:

Estimate the market value of assets, adjusting the fixed assets for the analyst's estimates of their market values:

$10,000 + $20,000 + $50,000 + $120,000(1.20) = $224,000

Determine the market value of liabilities:

$5,000 + 30,000 + $45,000 = $80,000

Calculate the adjusted equity value:

$224,000 – $80,000 = $144,000

Calculate the adjusted equity value per share:

$144,000 / 2,000 = $72

LOS 51.k: Explain advantages and disadvantages of each category of valuation model.

CFA® Program Curriculum, Volume 5, page 257

Advantages of discounted cash flow models:

- They are based on the fundamental concept of discounted present value and are well grounded in finance theory.
- They are widely accepted in the analyst community.

Disadvantages of discounted cash flow models:

- Their inputs must be estimated.
- Value estimates are very sensitive to input values.

Advantages of comparable valuation using price multiples:

- Evidence that some price multiples are useful for predicting stock returns.
- Price multiples are widely used by analysts.
- Price multiples are readily available.
- They can be used in time series and cross-sectional comparisons.
- EV/EBITDA multiples are useful when comparing firm values independent of capital structure or when earnings are negative and the P/E ratio cannot be used.

Disadvantages of comparable valuation using price multiples:

- Lagging price multiples reflect the past.
- Price multiples may not be comparable across firms if the firms have different size, products, and growth.
- Price multiples for cyclical firms may be greatly affected by economic conditions at a given point in time.
- A stock may appear overvalued by the comparable method but undervalued by a fundamental method or vice versa.
- Different accounting methods can result in price multiples that are not comparable across firms, especially internationally.
- A negative denominator in a price multiple results in a meaningless ratio. The P/E ratio is especially susceptible to this problem.

Advantages of price multiple valuations based on fundamentals:

- They are based on theoretically sound valuation models.
- They correspond to widely accepted value metrics.

Disadvantage of price multiple valuations based on fundamentals:

- Price multiples based on fundamentals will be very sensitive to the inputs (especially the k – g denominator).

Advantages of asset-based models:

- They can provide floor values.
- They are most reliable when the firm has primarily tangible short-term assets, assets with ready market values, or when the firm is being liquidated.
- They are increasingly useful for valuing public firms that report fair values.

Disadvantages of asset-based models:

- Market values are often difficult to obtain.
- Market values are usually different than book values.
- They are inaccurate when a firm has a high proportion of intangible assets or future cash flows not reflected in asset values.
- Assets can be difficult to value during periods of hyperinflation.

KEY CONCEPTS

LOS 51.a

An asset is fairly valued if the market price is equal to its estimated intrinsic value, undervalued if the market price is less than its estimated value, and overvalued if the market price is greater than the estimated value.

For security valuation to be profitable, the security must be mispriced now and price must converge to intrinsic value over the investment horizon.

Securities that are followed by many investors are more likely to be fairly valued than securities that are neglected by analysts.

LOS 51.b

Discounted cash flow models estimate the present value of cash distributed to shareholders (dividend discount models) or the present value of cash available to shareholders after meeting capital expenditures and working capital expenses (free cash flow to equity models).

Multiplier models compare the stock price to earnings, sales, book value, or cash flow. Alternatively, enterprise value is compared to sales or EBITDA.

Asset-based models define a stock's value as the firm's total asset value minus liabilities and preferred stock, on a per-share basis.

LOS 51.c

The dividend discount model is based on the rationale that a corporation has an indefinite life, and a stock's value is the present value of its future cash dividends. The most general form of the model is:

$$V_0 = \sum_{t=1}^{\infty} \frac{D_t}{(1 + k_e)^t}$$

Free cash flow to equity (FCFE) can be used instead of dividends. FCFE is the cash remaining after a firm meets all of its debt obligations and provides for necessary capital expenditures. FCFE reflects the firm's capacity for dividends and is useful for firms that currently do not pay a dividend. By using FCFE, an analyst does not need to project the amount and timing of future dividends.

LOS 51.d

Preferred stock typically pays a fixed dividend and does not mature. It is valued as:

$$\text{preferred stock value} = \frac{D_p}{k_p}$$

LOS 51.e
The Gordon growth model assumes the growth rate in dividends is constant:

$$V_0 = \frac{D_1}{k_e - g_c}$$

The sustainable growth rate is the rate at which earnings and dividends can continue to grow indefinitely:

$$g = b \times ROE$$

where:
b = earnings retention rate = 1 – dividend payout rate
ROE = return on equity

A firm with high growth over some number of periods followed by a constant growth rate of dividends forever can be valued using a multistage model:

$$value = \frac{D_1}{(1+k_e)} + \frac{D_2}{(1+k_e)^2} + \ldots + \frac{D_n}{(1+k_e)^n} + \frac{P_n}{(1+k_e)^n}$$

where:

$$P_n = \frac{D_{n+1}}{k_e - g_c}$$

g_c = constant growth rate of dividends
n = number of periods of supernormal growth

LOS 51.f
The constant growth model is most appropriate for firms that pay dividends that grow at a constant rate, such as stable and mature firms or noncyclical firms such as utilities and food producers in mature markets.

A 2-stage DDM would be most appropriate for a firm with high current growth that will drop to a stable rate in the future, an older firm that is experiencing a temporary high growth phase, or an older firm with a market share that is decreasing but expected to stabilize.

A 3-stage model would be appropriate for a young firm still in a high growth phase.

LOS 51.g
The P/E ratio based on fundamentals is calculated as:

$$\frac{P_0}{E_1} = \frac{D_1 / E_1}{k - g}$$

If the subject firm has a higher dividend payout ratio, higher growth rate, and lower required return than its peers, it may be justified in having a higher P/E ratio.

Price multiples are widely used by analysts, are easily calculated and readily available, and can be used in time series and cross-sectional comparisons.

LOS 51.h

The price-earnings (P/E) ratio is a firm's stock price divided by earnings per share.

The price-sales (P/S) ratio is a firm's stock price divided by sales per share.

The price-book value (P/B) ratio is a firm's stock price divided by book value per share.

The price-cash flow (P/CF) ratio is a firm's stock price divided by cash flow per share. Cash flow may be defined as operating cash flow or free cash flow.

LOS 51.i

Enterprise value (EV) measures total company value:

> EV = market value of common and preferred stock + market value of debt − cash and short-term investments

EBITDA is frequently used as the denominator in EV multiples because EV represents total company value, and EBITDA represents earnings available to all investors.

LOS 51.j

Asset-based models value equity as the market or fair value of assets minus liabilities. These models are most appropriate when a firm's assets are largely tangible and have fair values that can be established easily.

LOS 51.k

Advantages of discounted cash flow models:
- Easy to calculate.
- Widely accepted in the analyst community.
- FCFE model is useful for firms that currently do not pay a dividend.
- Gordon growth model is useful for stable, mature, noncyclical firms.
- Multistage models can be used for firms with nonconstant growth.

Disadvantages of discounted cash flow models:
- Inputs must be forecast.
- Estimates are very sensitive to inputs.
- For the Gordon growth model specifically:
  - Very sensitive to the k − g denominator.
  - Required return on equity must be greater than the growth rate.
  - Required return on equity and growth rate must remain constant.
  - Firm must pay dividends.

Advantages of price multiples:
- Often useful for predicting stock returns.
- Widely used by analysts.
- Easily calculated and readily available.
- Can be used in time series and cross-sectional comparisons.
- EV/EBITDA multiples are useful when comparing firm values independent of capital structure or when earnings are negative and the P/E ratio cannot be used.

Disadvantages of price multiples:
- P/E ratio based on fundamentals will be very sensitive to the inputs.
- May not be comparable across firms, especially internationally.
- Multiples for cyclical firms may be greatly affected by economic conditions. P/E ratio may be especially inappropriate. (The P/S multiple may be more appropriate for cyclical firms.)
- A stock may appear overvalued by the comparable method but undervalued by the fundamental method or vice versa.
- Negative denominator results in a meaningless ratio; the P/E ratio is especially susceptible to this problem.
- A potential problem with EV/EBITDA multiples is that the market value of a firm's debt is often not available.

Advantages of asset-based models:
- Can provide floor values.
- Most reliable when the firm has mostly tangible short-term assets, assets with a ready market value, or when the firm is being liquidated.
- May be increasingly useful for valuing public firms if they report fair values.

Disadvantages of asset-based models:
- Market values of assets can be difficult to obtain and are usually different than book values.
- Inaccurate when a firm has a large amount of intangible assets or future cash flows not reflected in asset value.
- Asset values can be difficult to value during periods of hyperinflation.

CONCEPT CHECKERS

1. An analyst estimates a value of $45 for a stock with a market price of $50. The analyst is *most likely* to conclude that a stock is overvalued if:
   A. few analysts follow the stock and the analyst has less confidence in his model inputs.
   B. few analysts follow the stock and the analyst is confident in his model inputs.
   C. many analysts follow the stock and the analyst is confident in his model inputs.

2. An analyst estimates that a stock will pay a $2 dividend next year and that it will sell for $40 at year-end. If the required rate of return is 15%, what is the value of the stock?
   A. $33.54.
   B. $36.52.
   C. $43.95.

3. What would an investor be willing to pay for a share of preferred stock that pays an annual $7 dividend if the required return is 7.75%?
   A. $77.50.
   B. $87.50.
   C. $90.32.

4. The constant growth model requires which of the following?
   A. $g < k$.
   B. $g > k$.
   C. $g \neq k$.

5. What is the intrinsic value of a company's stock if dividends are expected to grow at 5%, the most recent dividend was $1, and investors' required rate of return for this stock is 10%?
   A. $20.00.
   B. $21.00.
   C. $22.05.

6. Next year's dividend is expected to be $2, $g = 7\%$, and $k = 12\%$. What is the stock's intrinsic value?
   A. $28.57.
   B. $40.00.
   C. $42.80.

7. The XX Company paid a $1 dividend in the most recent period. The company is expecting dividends to grow at a 6% rate into the future. What is the value of this stock if an investor requires a 15% rate of return on stocks of this risk class?
   A. $10.60.
   B. $11.11.
   C. $11.78.

8.   Assume that a stock is expected to pay dividends at the end of Year 1 and Year 2 of $1.25 and $1.56, respectively. Dividends are expected to grow at a 5% rate thereafter. Assuming that k_e is 11%, the value of the stock is *closest* to:
     A. $22.30.
     B. $23.42.
     C. $24.55.

9.   An analyst feels that Brown Company's earnings and dividends will grow at 25% for two years, after which growth will fall to a constant rate of 6%. If the projected discount rate is 10%, and Brown's most recently paid dividend was $1, the value of Brown's stock using the multistage dividend discount model is *closest* to:
     A. $31.25.
     B. $33.54.
     C. $36.65.

10. A firm has an expected dividend payout ratio of 60% and an expected future growth rate of 7%. What should the firm's fundamental price-to-earnings (P/E) ratio be if the required rate of return on stocks of this type is 15%?
     A.   5.0×.
     B.   7.5×.
     C.   10.0×.

11. Which of the following firms would *most likely* be appropriately valued using the constant growth DDM?
     A.   An auto manufacturer.
     B.   A producer of bread and snack foods.
     C.   A biotechnology firm in existence for two years.

12. Which of the following is *least likely* a rationale for using price multiples?
     A.   Price multiples are easily calculated.
     B.   The fundamental P/E ratio is insensitive to its inputs.
     C.   The use of forward values in the divisor provides an incorporation of the future.

13. Which of the following firms would *most appropriately* be valued using an asset-based model?
     A.   An energy exploration firm in financial distress that owns drilling rights for offshore areas.
     B.   A paper firm located in a country that is experiencing high inflation.
     C.   A software firm that invests heavily in research and development and frequently introduces new products.

ANSWERS – CONCEPT CHECKERS

1. **B** If the analyst is more confident of his input values, he is more likely to conclude that the security is overvalued. The market price is more likely to be correct for a security followed by many analysts and less likely correct when few analysts follow the security.

2. **B** ($40 + $2) / 1.15 = $36.52

3. **C** The share value is 7.0 / 0.0775 = $90.32.

4. **A** For the constant growth model, the constant growth rate (g) must be less than the required rate of return (k).

5. **B** Using the constant growth model, $1(1.05) / (0.10 − 0.05) = $21.00.

6. **B** Using the constant growth model, $2 / (0.12 − 0.07) = $40.00.

7. **C** Using the constant growth model, $1(1.06) / (0.15 − 0.06) = $11.78.

8. **C** ($1.25 / 1.11) + [1.56 / (0.11 − 0.05)] / 1.11 = $24.55.

9. **C** $1(1.25) / 1.1 + [$1(1.25)^2 / (0.10 − 0.06)] / 1.1 = $36.65.

10. **B** Using the earnings multiplier model, 0.6 / (0.15 − 0.07) = 7.5×.

11. **B** The constant growth DDM assumes that the dividend growth rate is constant. The most likely choice here is the bread and snack producer. Auto manufacturers are more likely to be cyclical than to experience constant growth. A biotechnology firm in existence for two years is unlikely to pay a dividend, and if it does, dividend growth is unlikely to be constant.

12. **B** The fundamental P/E ratio is sensitive to its inputs. It uses the DDM as its framework, and the denominator k − g in both has a large impact on the calculated P/E or stock value.

13. **A** The energy exploration firm would be most appropriately valued using an asset-based model. Its near-term cash flows are likely negative, so a forward-looking model is of limited use. Furthermore, it has valuable assets in the form of drilling rights that likely have a readily determined market value. The paper firm would likely not be appropriately valued using an asset-based model because high inflation makes the values of a firm's assets more difficult to estimate. An asset-based model would not be appropriate to value the software firm because the firm's value largely consists of internally developed intangible assets.

12 questions: 18 minutes

1. An investor purchased 550 shares of Akley common stock for $38,500 in a margin account and posted initial margin of 50%. The maintenance margin requirement is 35%. The price of Akley, below which the investor would get a margin call, is *closest* to:
    A. $45.00.
    B. $54.00.
    C. $59.50.

2. Adams owns 100 shares of Brikley stock, which is trading at $86 per share, and Brown is short 200 shares of Brikley. Adams wants to buy 100 more shares if the price rises to $90, and Brown wants to cover his short position and take profits if the price falls to $75. The orders Adams and Brown should enter to accomplish their stated objectives are:

	Adams	Brown
A.	Limit buy @ 90	Limit buy @ 75
B.	Limit buy @ 90	Stop buy @ 75
C.	Stop buy @ 90	Limit buy @ 75

3. Which of the factors that determine the intensity of industry competition is *most likely* to be affected by the presence of significant economies of scale?
    A. Threat of new entrants.
    B. Threat of substitute products.
    C. Bargaining power of suppliers.

4. Price-to-book value ratios are *most appropriate* for measuring the relative value of a:
    A. bank.
    B. manufacturing company.
    C. mature technology company.

5. An index of three non-dividend paying stocks is weighted by their book values of equity. After one year, the stock with the largest weight is down 15%, the next-largest is down 10%, and the smallest is down 5%. The total return of this index for the year is:
    A. less than the price return of the index.
    B. equal to the price return of the index.
    C. greater than the price return of the index.

6. Financial intermediaries that buy securities from and sell securities to investors are *best* described as:
    A. dealers.
    B. brokers.
    C. investment bankers.

7. Among the types of assets that trade in organized markets, asset-backed securities are *best* characterized as:
    A. real assets.
    B. equity securities.
    C. pooled investment vehicles.

8. Which of the following market indexes is likely to be reconstituted *most* frequently? An index that is designed to measure:
    A. real estate returns.
    B. growth stock prices.
    C. commercial paper yields.

9. Rogers Partners values stocks using a dividend discount model and the CAPM. Holding all other factors constant, which of the following is *least likely* to increase the estimated value of a stock?
    A. An increase in the next period's expected dividend.
    B. A decrease in the stock's systematic risk.
    C. A decrease in the expected growth rate of dividends.

10. Brandy Clark, CFA, has forecast that Aceler, Inc., will pay its first dividend two years from now in the amount of $1.25. For the following year she forecasts a dividend of $2.00 and expects dividends to increase at an average rate of 7% for the foreseeable future after that. If the risk-free rate is 4.5%, the market risk premium is 7.5%, and Aceler's beta is 0.9, Clark would estimate the current value of Aceler shares as being *closest* to:
    A. $37.
    B. $39.
    C. $47.

11. An arbitrageur buys a security on a European exchange, where it is quoted in euros, and simultaneously sells the same security on a U.S. exchange, where it is quoted in dollars. The security is *most likely* a:
    A. global registered share.
    B. global depository receipt.
    C. sponsored depository receipt.

12. Under what financial market conditions can active portfolio management outperform a passive index tracking strategy consistently over time? Active management:
    A. cannot outperform a passive strategy if markets are weak-form efficient.
    B. can outperform a passive strategy if markets are weak-form efficient but not semistrong-form efficient.
    C. can outperform a passive strategy if markets are semistrong-form efficient but not strong-form efficient.

SELF-TEST ANSWERS: EQUITY INVESTMENTS

1. **B** The price below which the investor would receive a margin call is:

$$\left(\frac{38,500}{550}\right)\left(\frac{1-0.5}{1-0.35}\right) = \$53.85$$

2. **C** Adams should enter a stop buy at 90, which will be executed only if the stock price rises to 90. Brown should enter a buy order with a limit at 75 because he wants to buy stock to close out his short position if he can purchase it at 75 (or less).

3. **A** Economies of scale represent a barrier to entry into an industry. Existing competitors are likely to be operating on a large scale that new entrants would find difficult and expensive to develop, reducing the threat of new entrants.

4. **A** Price-to-book value is an appropriate measure of relative value for firms that hold primarily liquid assets, such as banks. Manufacturing companies typically have a large proportion of fixed assets for which the book value (historical cost less depreciation) may be less relevant as a measure of their economic value. A mature technology company likely has valuable intangible assets, such as patents and human capital, that may not be reflected fully (or at all) on the balance sheet.

5. **B** Because the stocks in the index do not pay dividends, there is no difference between the price return and the total return, regardless of the weighting system used or the direction of price movement.

6. **A** Dealers maintain inventories of securities and buy them from and sell them to investors. Brokers do not trade directly with clients but find buyers for and sellers of securities to execute customer orders. Investment banks are primarily involved in assisting with the issuance of new securities.

7. **C** Asset-backed securities represent claims to a portion of a financial asset pool.

8. **C** An index of commercial paper yields needs to be reconstituted frequently because its constituent securities need to be replaced when they mature and commercial paper matures in 270 days or less. Indexes of growth stocks and real estate are likely to be reviewed periodically to confirm that their constituent assets still meet the qualifications to be included in the index.

9. **C** Other things equal, a decrease in the expected growth rate of dividends (g) will decrease the value of a stock estimated with the dividend discount model. Using the CAPM, a decrease in the stock's systematic risk would decrease the required return on equity and increase the present value of the future dividends.

10. **B** The required rate of return on Aceler shares is 4.5 + 0.9(7.5) = 11.25%.

    The dividend at t = 3, $2.00, is expected to grow at 7% for the foreseeable future so the DDM value of Aceler shares at t = 2 is 2 / (0.1125 − 0.07) = 47.06.

    The t = 0 value of the shares is (47.06 + 1.25) / 1.1125^2 = $39.03.

11. **A**   Global registered shares are identical shares of the same issuer that trade on multiple global exchanges in the local currencies.

12. **B**   One of the implications of market efficiency is that if markets are semistrong-form efficient, active portfolio management cannot consistently achieve abnormal risk-adjusted returns.

FORMULAS

$$NPV = CF_0 + \frac{CF_1}{(1+k)^1} + \frac{CF_2}{(1+k)^2} + ... + \frac{CF_n}{(1+k)^n} = \sum_{t=0}^{n} \frac{CF_t}{(1+k)^t}$$

$$IRR: 0 = CF_0 + \frac{CF_1}{(1+IRR)^1} + \frac{CF_2}{(1+IRR)^2} + \cdots + \frac{CF_n}{(1+IRR)^n} = \sum_{t=0}^{n} \frac{CF_t}{(1+IRR)^t}$$

$$payback\ period = full\ years\ until\ recovery + \frac{unrecovered\ cost\ at\ the\ beginning\ of\ the\ last\ year}{cash\ flow\ during\ the\ last\ year}$$

$$PI = \frac{PV\ of\ future\ cash\ flows}{CF_0} = 1 + \frac{NPV}{CF_0}$$

$WACC = (w_d)[k_d(1-t)] + (w_{ps})(k_{ps}) + (w_{ce})(k_{ce})$

after-tax cost of debt $= k_d(1-t)$

cost of preferred stock $= k_{ps} = D_{ps}/P$

cost of common equity:

$$k_{ce} = \frac{D_1}{P_0} + g$$

$k_{ce} = RFR + \beta[E(R_m) - RFR]$

$k_{ce} = $ bond yield + risk premium

unlevered asset beta:

project beta:

$$\beta_{ASSET} = \beta_{EQUITY}\left[\frac{1}{1+\left((1-t)\frac{D}{E}\right)}\right]$$

$$\beta_{PROJECT} = \beta_{ASSET}\left[1+\left((1-t)\frac{D}{E}\right)\right]$$

cost of common equity with a country risk premium:

$$k_{ce} = R_F + \beta\left[E(R_{MKT}) - R_F + CRP\right]$$

where:
CRP = country risk premium

$$CRP = \text{sovereign yield spread}\left(\frac{\text{annualized standard deviation of equity index of developing country}}{\text{annualized standard deviation of the developing country sovereign bond market in terms of the developed market currency}}\right)$$

where:
sovereign yield spread = difference between yields of government bonds in the developing country and Treasury bonds of similar maturities

$$\text{break point} = \frac{\text{amount of capital at which the component's cost of capital changes}}{\text{weight of the component in the capital structure}}$$

$$\text{degree of operating leverage} = \frac{Q(P-V)}{Q(P-V)-F} = \frac{\%\Delta EBIT}{\%\Delta\text{sales}}$$

$$\text{degree of financial leverage} = \frac{EBIT}{EBIT-I} = \frac{\%\Delta EPS}{\%\Delta EBIT}$$

$$\text{degree of total leverage} = DOL \times DFL = \frac{\%\Delta EPS}{\%\Delta\text{sales}}$$

$$\text{breakeven quantity of sales} = \frac{\text{fixed operating costs} + \text{fixed financing costs}}{\text{price} - \text{variable cost per unit}}$$

$$\text{operating breakeven quantity of sales} = \frac{\text{fixed operating costs}}{\text{price} - \text{variable cost per unit}}$$

$$\text{current ratio} = \frac{\text{current assets}}{\text{current liabilities}}$$

$$\text{quick ratio} = \frac{\text{cash} + \text{short-term marketable securities} + \text{receivables}}{\text{current liabilities}}$$

$$\text{receivables turnover} = \frac{\text{credit sales}}{\text{average receivables}}$$

$$\text{number of days of receivables} = \frac{365}{\text{receivables turnover}} = \frac{\text{average receivables}}{\text{average day's credit sales}}$$

$$\text{inventory turnover} = \frac{\text{cost of goods sold}}{\text{average inventory}}$$

$$\text{number of days of inventory} = \frac{365}{\text{inventory turnover}} = \frac{\text{average inventory}}{\text{average day's COGS}}$$

$$\text{payables turnover ratio} = \frac{\text{purchases}}{\text{average trade payables}}$$

$$\text{number of days of payables} = \frac{365}{\text{payables turnover ratio}} = \frac{\text{average payables}}{\text{average day's purchases}}$$

operating cycle = average days of inventory + average days of receivables

$$\text{cash conversion cycle} = \left(\begin{array}{c}\text{average days}\\\text{of receivables}\end{array}\right) + \left(\begin{array}{c}\text{average days}\\\text{of inventory}\end{array}\right) - \left(\begin{array}{c}\text{average days}\\\text{of payables}\end{array}\right)$$

$$\% \text{ discount} = \left(\frac{\text{face value} - \text{price}}{\text{face value}}\right)$$

$$\text{discount-basis yield} = \left(\frac{\text{face value} - \text{price}}{\text{face value}}\right)\left(\frac{360}{\text{days}}\right) = \% \text{ discount} \times \left(\frac{360}{\text{days}}\right)$$

$$\text{money market yield} = \left(\frac{\text{face value} - \text{price}}{\text{price}}\right)\left(\frac{360}{\text{days}}\right) = \text{holding period yield} \times \left(\frac{360}{\text{days}}\right)$$

$$\text{bond equivalent yield} = \left(\frac{\text{face value} - \text{price}}{\text{price}}\right)\left(\frac{365}{\text{days to maturity}}\right)$$

$$= \text{holding period yield} \times \left(\frac{365}{\text{days}}\right)$$

$$\text{cost of trade credit} = \left(1 + \frac{\% \text{ discount}}{1 - \% \text{ discount}}\right)^{\frac{365}{\text{days past discount}}} - 1$$

where:
days past discount = number of days after the end of the discount period

$$\text{holding period return} = \frac{\text{end-of-period value}}{\text{beginning-of-period value}} - 1 = \frac{P_t + Div_t}{P_0} - 1 = \frac{P_t - P_0 + Div_t}{P_0}$$

$$\text{arithmetic mean return} = \frac{(R_1 + R_2 + R_3 + \ldots + R_n)}{n}$$

$$\text{geometric mean return} = \sqrt[n]{(1 + R_1) \times (1 + R_2) \times (1 + R_3) \times \ldots \times (1 + R_n)} - 1$$

$$\text{population variance from historical data: } \sigma^2 = \frac{\sum_{t=1}^{T}(R_t - \mu)^2}{T}$$

$$\text{sample variance from historical data: } s^2 = \frac{\sum_{t=1}^{T}(R_t - \overline{R})^2}{T - 1}$$

$$\text{sample covariance from historical data: } Cov_{1,2} = \frac{\sum_{t=1}^{n}\left\{[R_{t,1} - \overline{R}_1][R_{t,2} - \overline{R}_2]\right\}}{n - 1}$$

$$\rho_{1,2} = \frac{Cov_{1,2}}{\sigma_1 \times \sigma_2}$$

standard deviation for a two-asset portfolio:

$$\sigma_p = \sqrt{w_1^2\sigma_1^2 + w_2^2\sigma_2^2 + 2w_1w_2\sigma_1\sigma_2\rho_{1,2}} \text{ or } \sqrt{w_1^2\sigma_1^2 + w_2^2\sigma_2^2 + 2w_1w_2Cov_{1,2}}$$

$$\text{equation of the CML: } E(R_P) = R_f + \left(\frac{E(R_M) - R_f}{\sigma_M}\right)\sigma_P$$

$$E(R_P) = R_f + (E(R_M) - R_f)\left(\frac{\sigma_P}{\sigma_M}\right)$$

total risk = systematic risk + unsystematic risk

$$\beta_i = \frac{Cov_{i,mkt}}{\sigma_{mkt}^2} = \rho_{i,mkt}\frac{\sigma_i}{\sigma_{mkt}}$$

capital asset pricing model (CAPM): $E(R_i) = RFR + \beta_i[E(R_{mkt}) - RFR]$

$$\text{margin call price} = P_0\left(\frac{1 - \text{initial margin}}{1 - \text{maintenance margin}}\right)$$

$$\text{price-weighted index} = \frac{\text{sum of stock prices}}{\text{number of stocks in index adjusted for splits}}$$

$$\text{market cap-weighted index} = \frac{\sum\left[(\text{price}_{today})(\text{number of shares outstanding})\right]}{\sum\left[(\text{price}_{base\ year})(\text{number of shares outstanding})\right]}$$

$$\times \text{ base year index value}$$

preferred stock valuation model: $P_0 = \dfrac{D_p}{k_p}$

one-period stock valuation model: $P_0 = \dfrac{D_1}{1 + k_e} + \dfrac{P_1}{1 + k_e}$

infinite period model: $P_0 = \dfrac{D_1}{k_e - g} = \dfrac{D_0 \times (1 + g)}{k_e - g}$

multistage model: $P_0 = \dfrac{D_1}{(1 + k_e)} + \dfrac{D_2}{(1 + k_e)^2} + ... + \dfrac{D_n}{(1 + k_e)^n} + \dfrac{P_n}{(1 + k_e)^n}$

where:

$P_n = \dfrac{D_{n+1}}{k_e - g_c}$, and D_{n+1} is a dividend that will grow

at the constant rate of g_c forever

earnings multiplier: $\dfrac{P_0}{E_1} = \dfrac{\dfrac{D_1}{E_1}}{k - g}$

expected growth rate: $g = (\text{retention rate})(\text{ROE})$

$$\text{trailing P/E} = \frac{\text{market price per share}}{\text{EPS over previous 12 months}}$$

$$\text{leading P/E} = \frac{\text{market price per share}}{\text{forecast EPS over next 12 months}}$$

$$\text{P/B ratio} = \frac{\text{market value of equity}}{\text{book value of equity}} = \frac{\text{market price per share}}{\text{book value per share}}$$

where:
book value of equity = common shareholders' equity
= (total assets – total liabilities) – preferred stock

$$\text{P/S ratio} = \frac{\text{market value of equity}}{\text{total sales}} = \frac{\text{market price per share}}{\text{sales per share}}$$

$$P/CF \text{ ratio} = \frac{\text{market value of equity}}{\text{cash flow}} = \frac{\text{market price per share}}{\text{cash flow per share}}$$

enterprise value = market value of common and preferred stock
  + market value of debt
  – cash and short-term investments

Index

©2012 Kaplan, Inc.

Notes

Notes

INCREASING PRODUCTIVITY IN FOODSERVICE

RAYMOND B. PEDDERSEN
ARTHUR C. AVERY
RUTH D. RICHARD
JAMES R. OSENTON
HARRY H. POPE

Jule Wilkinson, Editor

Published by
INSTITUTIONS/VOLUME FEEDING MAGAZINE
Chicago

Distributed by
Cahners Books, 89 Franklin St., Boston, Mass. 02110

ISBN 0-8436-0560-X

Library of Congress Catalog Card No. 73-84798

Printed in the United States of America

Table of Contents

List of Illustrations

Foreword

As the writers of this timely book make clear, productivity in the Hospitality Industry is a function of the quality of management. Any increase in productivity must start with improved management or, more correctly, with better managers.

But what is productivity? It is not, for instance, the same as *production*, which is the total amount of goods or services produced. Rather, *productivity* is the amount of goods and services produced *per unit* of input—and input can be labor, or capital, or both.

In the Hospitality Industry, both in foodservice and lodging, the most common productivity measure is output per man-hour of labor. Converted from "real" terms to dollar amounts, this measure becomes volume of sales per labor payroll-hour cost in dollars. These figures are normally readily available in our industry, and if for no reason other than relative ease of calculation, we shall probably continue to use output per man-hour as a standard measure of efficiency for many years to come.

But as we continue to grow, both in size and in sophistication, the Hospitality Industry must also recognize the shortcomings of this standard. For one thing, output per man-hour implies, quite incorrectly, that all productivity gains are the result of labor's efforts. In fact, an increase in output per man-hour means only that there has been an increase in the efficiency with which labor is utilized. It tells absolutely nothing about the source of the increased efficiency.

For another thing, there is no effective way in which changes in *quality* can be taken into consideration with this measure, unless we assume that quality changes are reflected accurately in changes in price. This is not a good assumption even in times of stabilized prices; it is probably not correct at all in times of wage and price inflation.

An additional shortcoming is that output per man-hour leaves out many of the human factors which in our industry make the difference between sales and non-sales, success and failure. Motivation is one of these; training is another. A highly motivated waitress, a highly trained cook or a highly motivated and trained career employee in any job from entry level to manager can produce much more. We all know this from experience and recent research backs us up. There is much more to efficiency than utilization of labor. Our employees are our most valuable (and valued) resource.

Finally, we share with all fast-growing service industries particular measurement difficulties, which arise from trying to count people as statistics. We have parallels to education, for example, which asks whether a teacher with a class of twenty-five students is half as productive as one with a class of fifty? How does one statistically measure the quality of a haircut (or a soufflé) or the productivity of a TV repairman (or a maitre d')?

If increasing productivity is the nation's "biggest undeveloped resource" (to quote *Business Week*), it is also the Hospitality Industry's biggest challenge. NRA President Richard J. Harman titled a recent speech "Productivity or Perish!" We must start now by finding out where we stand, using conventional measures in the knowledge that they are not sufficiently precise or complete for our industry. Then we must apply the industry's proven ability to innovate, from top management down throughout our organizations. Managers can start by: (1) finding out what motivates employees to do their best; (2) setting and communicating fair and agreed performance standards; and (3) organizing tasks and equipment to make it easy for employees to meet the standards set.

The challenge to the nation's number one employer, the Hospitality Industry, is clear.

Chester G. Hall, Jr., Ph.D.
Executive Vice President
National Institute for the
Foodservice Industry

Preface

"Productivity. . . in the Food Service Industry. . . is the measure or level of relative output or value obtained from combining and using available resources. . . in fulfillment of a feeding function."

"Here are some of the things greater productivity can do for you. . .

Maintain or improve quality of food and service

Stabilize or increase *profits*

Reduce and/or *control costs* more effectively

Simplify internal operations

Provide opportunity for more and better *salesmaking* activities

Permit Management to *MANAGE*—to plan, direct, control, improve, supervise, train develop and forecast."[1]

In the foodservice industry in recent years, increasing productivity has been like the weather: a subject frequently mentioned when groups got together but "What can you do about it?" There were always operators who refused to admit that low productivity had to be a fact of foodservice life and individually they began investigating tools and techniques and then putting together programs that succeeded in meeting or bettering productivity standards they had set in their own operations. These innovative actions combined to produce a variety of successful approaches.

It has been the intent of the Editor to gather and distill for this book the productivity know-how of five such foodservice industry leaders who are known for "thinking" in addition to long histories of "doing." Through their theories and their proven experience, the reader has the opportunity to learn new methods as well as sharpen old skills in the quest for better operations and higher productivity.

It soon became clear that the first step in a study of ways to increase productivity in foodservice requires understanding of what motivates today's workers. Raymond B. Peddersen, in his introductory overview of the schools of thought on management science and philosophies, briefs the positions of

[1]"Productivity Produces Profits," National Restaurant Association, May 1967.

scientific management and of the behavioral school on what makes workers want to improve their performance. Mr. Peddersen then takes a look at the basic organizational structure that is required to insure maximum productivity and reviews the personnel function and its contribution to affirmative employee attitudes.

Operation-tested methods are outlined for employee evaluations, especially difficult to make in foodservice operations since quantitative measures cannot always be taken. Alternate ways of measuring productivity are described with accompanying forms and charts that have been successfully used by operations in foodservice employee evaluation.

Since maximum worker productivity needs the basis of manager productivity, techniques for achieving full scale productivity are detailed for foodservice managers with a concluding section in which Mr. Peddersen suggests ways to prevent the organizational dry rot that can undermine a successful program.

In his chapter on Equipment Arrangement for Greater Worker Productivity, Arthur C. Avery explains the techniques for gathering man-machine relationship data; tells how to determine the most productive locations for work centers and equipment as well as the most effective arrangement of equipment within the centers. He gives further pointers on selecting equipment to save labor. The principles of efficient receiving, the potential of a central ingredient room and productivity factors affecting dishroom location are among other basics discussed.

In Task Planning, Ruth D. Richard starts with foodservice industry attitudes that have slowed task planning, then discusses the steps in task planning, the principles of motion economy and their application to equipment placement. Work areas are diagrammed and step-by-step photographs showing steps in task-planned preparation of salad ingredients, baked meat loaf and pizza clarify this successful method of improving employee output.

Ways in which application of The Stored Labor Concept can assure the substitution of productive periods for periods formerly considered "slack time" are reported by James Osenton who offers new applications of this concept. He urges a new look at daily activities for an answer to the questions: Who prepares what in slack time? What can be cooked ahead? What can be stored? Acting on the answers inevitably leads to higher levels of productivity.

Previously published studies[2] by Lendal Kotschevar on applying the principles of work simplification to foodservice operations are included since they remain an essential foundation for any attempt to increase productivity.

---

[2]Institutions Magazine, reprints no longer available.

The first step in devising a program of work simplification is understanding how to help workers use the least possible physical energy in performing their tasks. This is achieved by knowing how the body functions, how to conserve energy, and how to increase efficiency in performing a variety of physical tasks and so avoiding the tiredness that too frequently makes the worker accident-prone as well as non-productive.

Ways to make work easier in an individual operation are set forth in practical terms. Techniques for taking jobs apart and putting them back together in more trouble-free form are easy to follow. Charts and forms that offer assistance in job analysis are explained.

Even though day-to-day operations have achieved maximum efficiency through work simplification, there is still further potential for increased productivity. In his chapter on Convenience Foods, Disposables and Automation, Raymond B. Peddersen recommends the elimination of as many tasks as possible. Bases required for successful decision-making in these areas with operation-tested methods of selecting the best options and then introducing these elements offer proven guidelines to those seeking to streamline all jobs to the ultimate.

The keystone of all efforts undertaken to increase productivity, as pointed out by Harry H. Pope in his summary chapter, Utilization—Prerequisite to Increasing Productivity, is *full utilization of labor.* Since full utilization is only possible when standards of performance have been determined and communicated to workers, Pope points up the need for (1) further cooperative industry-wide effort on standard setting and (2) setting and meeting the operation's own standards while waiting for data from larger standard setting projects.

Throughout the text there are comprehensive illustrations, forms, charts, graphs and guides to clarify the text and add a visual link between authors and reader.

This book has been compiled not only as an aid to the operator who wishes to obtain a more productive foodservice but also for the student of foodservice who desires to become an effective foodservice operator. Those who read and *use* this book will be well on the way to effective, increasingly productive foodservice/lodging operations.

Jule Wilkinson, Editor

ABOUT THE AUTHORS

Raymond B. Peddersen—formerly director of food services, Hillside Hospital, Glen Oaks, N. Y. where he successfully incorporated convenience foods into an existing system; now, director of hospital food service systems, Chef's Orchid, Inc., Flushing, N. Y. *Affiliations:* American Society for Hospital Food Administrators, American Hospital Assn.; Food Services Executives Assn.; American Management Assn.; Conference on Productivity in Economic Research of the National Commission on Productivity.

Arthur C. Avery—Professor and director of Institutional Management Research, Purdue University, former director of food service research for the U. S. Navy, where many innovative equipment and layout ideas were developed. *Affiliations:* International Society of Food Service Consultants (past president); Society for Advancement of Food Service Research; Council on Hotel, Restaurant and Institutional Education.

Ruth D. Richard— director of food services, Rowland Unified School District, Rowland Heights, Calif. Designer of award-winning food service installation and recipient of Silver Plate Award from the National Restaurant Assn. *Affiliations:* American School Food Service Assn.; Food Service Executives Assn.; National Restaurant Assn.; Society for Nutrition Education; American Home Economics Assn.; Council on Hotel, Restaurant and Institutional Education.

James R. Osenton—director, Restaurant Trades Dept., L. H. Bates Vocational-Technical Institute, Tacoma, Wash. As an experienced executive chef, Osenton provides well tested systems of operation for his students. *Affiliations:* Food Service Executives Assn.; International Stewards and Caterers Assn.

Harry H. Pope—president, Pope's Catering Co., St. Louis, operating 11 public cafeterias, 3 foodservices offering varied fare for fast service, 3 retirement residence food services, 10 employee cafeterias and a number of franchise operations in the United States and Europe. Winner of the NRA's Golden Plate Award, Harry Pope also has interests in subsidiaries of the Moevenpick Restaurants in Switzerland as well as other interests in European foodservice operations. *Affiliations:* International Society of Food Service Consultants (charter member); International Food Service Management Guild (chairman); Society for the Advancement of Food Service Research; World Business Council; National Restaurant Assn., (for many years active in the Equipment Testing Committee).

1 Motivation and Foodservice Worker Productivity

Raymond B. Peddersen

INFORMATION on foodservice worker motivation and productivity is certainly more difficult for the professional foodservice manager to search out than is comparable information for the industrial manager. A scant quantity has been written on these subjects and certainly less is generally known about their significance in foodservice.

The true foodservice professional is looking for something better than "rules-of-thumb" or "seat-of-the-pants" decision-making processes. Rather, through the understanding and application of true motivation, he seeks ways to better organize his management processes to achieve high long-range productivity growth.

An understanding of motivation starts with a review of the research done by experts in this area. Such a review should familiarize the reader with motivation-maintenance theories; job satisfiers and job dissatisfiers; horizontal and vertical job enlargement; theory X and theory Y; scientific management; the behavioral school; authoritarian-exploitive; authoritarian-benevolent, consultive and participative management.

It is also important to analyze the factors involved in proper foodservice organization, basic research, administration of the personnel function, morale administration and production control.

As a logical progression from this basis in theory, some practical guides are presented to aid in increasing the productivity of the foodservice manager.

Because coverage of background information has been kept brief for reasons of space, an extensive list of readings on these and other subjects is covered at the end of the book.

MANAGEMENT SCIENCE
AND PHILOSOPHY

In many ways, the foodservice industry is barely at the beginning of its own "Industrial Revolution". The Industrial Revolution of 150 years ago was basically a transfer of skills from the hands of craftsmen to machines. The foodservice industry is today transferring skills from the hands of skilled craftsmen, the chefs, to the machines of the bulk processors.

With unarguable certainty, the *saucier* is being replaced by pre-processed fresh and frozen vegetables, the *chef* is being replaced by fully prepared entrees, the *waiter* is being replaced by the waitress, the *waitress* by the cafeteria or fast food counter aide, the *server* by the vending machine, the *executive chef* by the *food production manager.* As the volume of public feeding increases every day, the need for new technologies in foodservice management becomes increasingly urgent. Men are being replaced by machines for the first time in the history of our industry.

After too long a period when his low wages, in effect, subsidized the restaurant meals of the more fortunate, the foodservice worker is beginning to receive an adequate monetary return for his work. The impact of these higher wages upon our foodservice costs demands the development of higher foodservice worker productivity as an offset. Motivation is, on balance, the first step to higher productivity.

SCIENTIFIC MANAGEMENT

Scientific management is a broad term encompassing a wide variety of specific techniques which include, among others, human engineering, personnel administration, plant layout and design, time and motion study, production planning and wage incentives. These concerns, which may be said to fit under the topic of efficiency and production, have been closely studied in this century. The findings of these studies are briefly outlined here:

Frederick W. Taylor

The principal researcher in modern scientific management was Frederick W. Taylor. It was Taylor's philosophy that management should establish wide-ranging overall *daily goals* and that the laborer should be rewarded for achieving these goals but punished for not achieving the goals. Under the Taylor philosophy, production costs would soar. Taylor's answer to this problem was that, although labor costs would rise, production would rise at an even faster pace, thereby lowering the cost per unit of production. Twenty-six years of tests proved Taylor to be right.

Taylor's 4 principles of scientific management are the foundation of modern management thought:
  (1)   Workers should be scientifically selected, trained and placed in jobs which closely relate to each individual's capacity.
  (2)   The work to be done should be scientifically analyzed to reduce the physical effort needed to accomplish the worker's tasks.
  (3)   There should be close cooperation between the planner of the work and the worker.
  (4)   Management and labor should share equal responsibility in the accomplishment of the work.

The Gilbreths

Another significant quantity of research progress in scientific management was the result of the extensive work of Frank and Lillian Gilbreth. The Gilbreths were responsible for much of the early development of the methods now universally applied by industrial engineers. It was Frank Gilbreth who identified the basic unit of hand motion, "therbligs"*, with which all basic hand motion analysis is conducted. Many references, including several listed at the end of this book, are available on the topic of time and motion study of foodservice workers, so we will not explore the topic further. (Also see chapters 3 and 5.)

Of equal, if not greater importance than her husband's work with therbligs is the fact that Lillian Gilbreth introduced the behavioral concept. It was Lillian Gilbreth who widened the recognition, common today, that psychological factors affect industrial productivity.

*Gilbreth spelled (almost) backward is Therblig. Therbligs in foodservice are explained, in detail, in Chapter 5.

Hawthorne Experiment

The scientific approach would lead us to believe that altering environmental and/or physical factors in work will lead to higher productivity. This is not necessarily so, as demonstrated by a five-year experiment conducted at the Hawthorne works of the Western Electric Company.

In this experiment, a small group of workers was segregated in a special room away from the regular assembly lines. Between 1927 and 1932 the production and physical factors of their situation were, one at a time, continually changed. No matter how much more laborious—or less, that it seemed any change would make the work, it was found that *no individual change* affected productivity. Productivity increased steadily for the entire 5 years. Regardless of change, the rate of absence for all reasons was reduced by 80%, and absence because of illness was reduced by two-thirds.

The final analysis of the reason for the long term gain in productivity attributed it wholly to *human factors*. The human factors responsible were greater freedom, less strict supervision and the opportunity to vary the pace of the work.

Professional foodservice management should carefully consider these Hawthorne results. The lesson they teach is that in the *long run,* productivity is affected in a positive manner by a pleasant, free and happy working environment. When the basic working conditions of a physically adequate—preferably physically *pleasant*—foodservice facility are provided, then the psychological environment will be a prime determinant in motivation vis-a-vis productivity.

BEHAVIORAL SCHOOL

The behavioral approach to management and motivation centers on the human element. The behaviorists contend that interpersonal relationships are at the heart of getting things done through people.

Everything in foodservice depends upon interpersonal relationships. There is extensive human contact in every aspect of foodservice work. The theories explored below are at the core of the philosophies of foodservice operations that are enjoying *long range success* in motivated productivity gains.

Frederick Herzberg

Herzberg did an initial study of some 200 individuals which led him to the theory that there are some work factors that are human satisfiers and some that are human dissatisfiers. More than 30 studies have since been made to test Herzberg theories. Each test has proven the validity of his "Motivation-Maintenance" theories.

The Herzberg study may shock many foodservice operators, especially those who have assumed that the worker will be motivated to increase his production by means per se of company policy and administration, tighter supervision, higher salary, better interpersonal relations or better working conditions. According to Herzberg's findings, these assumptions are quite wrong.

Actually he finds the factors listed in the above paragraph to be *potential dissatisfiers* and not satisfiers or motivators. The potential dissatisfiers are all work factors which must be acceptable before management can attempt to motivate the worker.

If the foodservice manager wanted to have an *unhappy* work force, he could assure it by being arbitrary in decision making, unclear about policy, authoritarian in supervising; by paying a wage upon which the worker could not decently support his family, encouraging jealousies among the staff and providing working conditions that are uncomfortable. Doing these things, he could be certain that productivity would be low.

On the other hand, the foodservice operator who wishes to motivate his staff will learn from Herzberg that there are definite *satisfiers* which may be used to motivate. People are motivated to higher productivity via achievement, recognition, the work itself, responsibility and advancement. The worker who is given the opportunity to undertake difficult assignments, who has the freedom to use his imagination and ingenuity in doing the job, who has been encouraged to learn new skills and has the opportunity for promotion or to earn more money *as recognition for achievement* is the worker who will be motivated to higher productivity.

With this knowledge, the foodservice operator has the capability to maximize the satisfiers and minimize the dissatisfiers for his staff. On page 13 there is a formula that may be used to express the relationships of all work factors.

To provide a summary of Herzberg's findings, a list follows noting (1) the maintenance factors (or ways to hold workers' feelings at a constructive level), and (2) the satisfiers, i.e., motivating forces, that he has established.

Human relations programs, supervisory training, recreation facilities and wage and fringe benefits do not serve as motivators because they are potential dissatisfiers. However, if the maintenance factors are satisfactory, the atmosphere will be right for the motivators.

MAINTENANCE NEEDS

The physical environment provided for the worker must meet certain basic human requirements. The failure of management to provide such things as parking facilities, a lunchroom, clean restrooms, a low noise level and the proper lighting, ventilation and temperature control in the kitchen will reduce morale and productivity. The work layout, the type of equipment provided, the consistency of the work rules and the physical demands of the work must be at the best possible level if discontent is to be avoided. A kitchen which is hard to work in due to poor layout, poor equipment, improper temperature, lighting or poor location will detract from the potential productivity.

The failure to provide some type of clarification of the status of the worker will demoralize him. Every worker needs to have a title, location and set of privileges of his own. The working relationship between job classification groups should be formalized. Such seemingly small items as different hats, pants or coats for cooks vs. kitchenmen or busboys vs. dishwasher will re-enforce the security of the workers and help prevent trivial discontent due to status confusion.

The failure of management to allow, encourage, even boost such social gatherings as the employees may need to foster a feeling of goodwill amongst themselves may prove fatal to morale. By all means the foodservice manager must encourage car pools, a bowling team, softball games and outings. Employees should be allowed to take coffee breaks and lunch breaks as a group, wherever possible, so as to encourage pleasant social intercourse.

Every worker needs the basic tenets of security if he is to be content. Beyond the normal policies of seniority rights and a grievance precedure, the worker needs to know that he is fairly dealt with, that management is consistent in policy enforcement and that a friendly environment is assured. Who would want to go to work in the morning knowing he faces a hostile environment?

A sure-fire means of de-motivating workers is the failure to provide decent economic conditions. A wage upon which the worker can maintain a satisfactory living standard and the provision of insurance for illness, disability and pension are expected by employees. Provision of the good economic conditions for the employee is basic and, therefore, not a source for higher motivation.

Another basic maintenance need is proper orientation and on-going communication about the job and the company. Providing this information does not lead to higher motivation but does help stop discontent before it starts. The employee is entitled to job instruction, training films and access to in-house publications.

MAINTENANCE NEEDS

Physical
work layout
job demands
work rules
equipment
location
grounds
parking facilities
aesthetic lunch
   facilities
rest rooms
temperature
ventilation
lighting
noise

Social
work groups
coffee groups
lunch groups
social groups
office parties
ride pools
outings
sports
professional groups
interest groups

Status
job classification
title
furnishings
location
privileges
relationships
company status

Security
fairness
consistency
reassurance
friendliness
seniority rights
grievance procedure

Economic
wages and salaries
automatic increases
profit sharing
social security
workmen's compensation
disability insurance
unemployment compensation
retirement
paid leave
insurance
tuition
discounts

Orientation
job instruction
work rules
group meetings
shop talk
newspapers
bulletins
handbooks
letters
bulletin boards
grapevine

MOTIVATION NEEDS

Growth, Achievement
delegation
access to information
freedom to act
atmosphere of approval
merit increases
discretionary awards

Responsibility, Recognition
involvement
goal setting
planning
problem solving
work simplification
performance appraisal

The Job

company growth
promotions
transfers
rotations
education
memberships

Argyris Analysis

In his approach to motivation, Chris Argyris theorizes that traditional management fails to recognize the difference between the adult and the child. Argyris contends that industry often forces grown men and women to spend their entire work life suppressing their own brainpower in order to maintain systems that may or, more likely, may not be efficient. This is a situation encountered by many in traditional foodservice management.

It occurs because

(1) the foodservice organization is often quite inflexible, and

(2) the foodservice operator frequently fails to recognize the unintentional communication barriers that exist in his organization.

A look at Argyris' seven principal differences between child and adult should help the foodservice operator to recognize the all-too-common barriers to motivating higher productivity that may exist in his organization. These differences point up the importance of treating employees as purposeful adults. For the purposes of this discussion, an "adult" is a grown man or woman who has attained a state of maturity which enables him to distinguish right from wrong, to react to criticism in an objective manner and to weigh and value long term effects of actions over momentary pleasures. A "child" is a person who lacks the above stated qualities of an adult and who, moreover, is dependent upon the support of others to sustain even minor decisions.

In his analysis of the mature vs. the immature worker, Argyris states:

(1) Whereas children need close supervision, the adult is mature enough to handle trust. The adult does not need close supervision, what he needs is a clear indication of what is required of him and why.

(2) A child has few values but the adult has a clear set of values which are a product of his entire life experience. The adult will make any sacrifice, *even his job,* to defend his personal pride or sense of equity.

(3) The child is a learner and most of what he experiences is new. While the child may be fascinated by something and repeat the same simple tasks almost endlessly, the adult is bored by the endless repetition of one set of actions.

The endless repetition of some jobs in the foodservice industry (dish machine operators, potwashers) indicates that not all foodservice workers should be "mature" adults. Because a mature person may be hopelessly bored by repetitive jobs it may be advisable to hire child-like or immature people for such jobs if such jobs cannot be enlarged and enriched with other non-repetitious tasks or eliminated via automation.

(4) The child has few skills and limited creativity as compared to the mature adult. A child will consider a task to be done as something laborious whereas an adult may regard a task as a challenge to his skill and creativity.

(5) The child has a short memory and limited ability to see the future. The adult, as a result of long experience, is able to make judgments regarding the future that are based on his past experience. This means that the adult may be willing to make short term sacrifices where he sees the possibility of a long term gain.

(6) Children need close supervision if they are to form proper values and to assure their physical safety. An adult is capable of performing tasks, once properly instructed. Being bossed is a burden to an adult.

(7) The child's ego is being formed and, as such, is not easily bruised. The adult has a fully developed ego which must be recognized and dealt with.

Douglas McGregor

McGregor has made extensive studies of both management technique and workers' behavior. His analysis shows that excessive controls over workers serve to provoke uncooperativeness from those people for whom plans fail. Making the controls tighter only aggravates the situation.

Foodservice operators often make the mistake of *over-supervising workers,* requiring too many checks on production control and materials issue. The point of McGregor's analysis that food operators should act upon is that people seek responsibility as an avenue to fulfillment. If a worker is not given latitude and the opportunity to assume full authority and responsibility for his work, then supervision will continue to be a psychological burden for the worker and an economic burden for management.

The McGregor theories are known as Theory X and Theory Y.

Theory X is typical of the management attitude of foodservice operators who deem themselves essential to every daily activity in their operations. Such managers are probably insecure and their operations do need them.

The foodservice operators who follow the Theory Y school of management, however, seem to have smooth running operations even though they are rarely in on the daily activities in their operation. The Theory X people develop only short term effectiveness whereas the Theory Y people develop long range effectiveness through the development of self-sufficient workers.

Theory X holds that people are generally lazy, lacking in self-control and unable to think for themselves. The three major points of this theory are:

(1) Work is not a natural activity for men.

(2) Because work is not a natural activity, men must be compelled to work.

(3) Although compelled to work, men would prefer not to think.

Theory Y says that people develop definite attitudes towards work and are quite capable of being responsible and mature, if so treated. The manager who is willing to surrender traditional authority as fast as possible while meeting both management needs and worker desires will achieve a motivated and productive organization. The four characteristics of Theory Y are:

(1) Work is neither attractive nor unattractive to men and, therefore, men can learn either to like or to dislike work.

(2) All results of work and achievements of men must be measured, both on a short term and long term basis.

(3) People are capable of setting objectives and selecting goals for themselves and are self-motivated in the pursuit of those goals.

(4) People need fulfillment and, therefore, seek responsibility and the fulfillment it affords.

Finally, the McGregor analysis finds that financial rewards develop only skin-deep loyalties and exertions. This point parallels the motivation-maintenance theories, mentioned earlier, as to the effect of money on workers. The foodservice operator who expects productivity increases *solely* as a result of salary increases is going to be disappointed.

Rensis Likert

Likert, in his book, *The Human Organization,* seems to have come closest to outlining what all the possible management systems are. The characteristics of his definitions are listed on pp. 16-25.[1] Likert proposes four systems that are here designated:

(1) Authoritarian-Exploitive
(2) Authoritarian-Benevolent
(3) Consultive and
(4) Participative.

The *authoritarian-exploitive* manager is easy to find in the foodservice industry. He is the manager who uses fear and threats, who knows everything and needs no advice, is distrusted and distrustful. His organization is tightly controlled at the top and generally incapable of operating without the boss.

The *authoritarian-benevolent* manager is also common in our industry. Instead of treating his employees as slaves, he treats them as children, doling out rewards and punishment, occasionally admitting error, accepting advice in a paternalistic manner, condescending rather than confidence-building in his manner toward employees and, in fact, quite incapable of building their confidence. His organization is tightly controlled at the top but does offer a bit more freedom and self-reliance than the authoritarian-exploitive.

The *consultive* foodservice manager is marked by a genuine concern not only for his operation, which is also true of the above two types, but also for his employees. The consultive manager may use rewards and punishment but also involves employees in order to motivate them; he uses a broad range of knowledge besides his own; is trustful and trusted. The people in his organization are consulted about planning the work and, therefore, his organization runs well with or without his presence.

The *participative* manager shares authority and responsibility with his workers, whatever their position. His is a team effort where the participation of everyone is vital if goals are to be reached. His organization is self-sustaining and the accomplishment of their long term objectives is assured.

The operator checking through the list of characteristics of each system should take a look at those areas in which he wishes his foodservice organization were strong and compare them with the actual. He will have to answer two questions:

Is my system in need of a change?
Do I have the courage to do it?

Claude S. George, Jr.

In his book, *The History of Management Thought,* Claude S. George, Jr. proposes the following excellent schematic model of management. This for-

[1]From *The Human Organization: Its Management and Value* by Rensis Likert. Copyright, 1967, McGraw-Hill Book Company. Used with the permission of McGraw-Hill Book Company. No further reproduction authorized.

mula is a clear *visual* model of the interactions of people as related to management.[1]

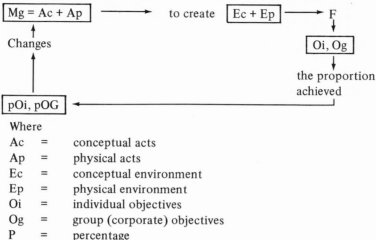

Where

Ac = conceptual acts
Ap = physical acts
Ec = conceptual environment
Ep = physical environment
Oi = individual objectives
Og = group (corporate) objectives
P = percentage

George states that . . . "managerial acts are functions of goals, and the effectiveness of these acts is in proportion to goal achievement". The actions of a manager, both physical and conceptual, change with the percentage of achievement attained. These management actions function so as to create a change in the environment, both physical and conceptual. If management actions result in 80% achievement of the company's goals and only 20% achievement of the employees' personal goals, then new management action must take place to alter the balance. Any and all management actions have an effect upon and with the individual and group objectives as well as the physical and the conceptual environment.

It is George's philosophy, in common with all the others studied in this section on the behavioral school, that management only gets things done through people. Therefore, management must be studied from the viewpoint of interpersonal relationships.

The works of the management researchers studied here all end in the conclusion that management centers on the human element. The foodservice operator and his employees are a very "human-contact intensive" group of people both in the kitchen and at the point of service. The operator must recognize this and give top priority to dealing with the human element, or he is not recognizing the true nature of his business. The ultimate result of

[1]Claude S. George, Jr. *The History of Management Thought,* © 1968, pp. 168-170. Reprinted by permission of Prentice-Hall, Inc., Englewood Cliffs, N. J.

the failure to deal effectively with the human element may be financial failure or, more pervasive, failure as a person—which can affect the lives of all
with whom he comes in contact.

Summary

In summarizing the above findings and relating them to foodservice operation, the author has drawn on his own experience in applying behavioral
concepts:

Foodservice is essentially a factory in that raw products are received,
the labor of men is added and a finished product is delivered to a customer.
There is a flow of people, a flow of things and finally a flow of people and
things.

It is the concern for people—their objectives, capacities, relationships,
motivations and satisfactions—which makes the difference between effective
and ineffective organizations.

While foodservice workers have made clear that they want money for
more than the basic maintenance needs, the money will not go for extra gro-
ceries but to answer those "desires of the heart," i.e. for a bigger slice of the
American dream. They want the large and small luxuries from which the so-
cially underprivileged foodservice worker has long been barred economically.

The foodservice worker who has been freed from the basic economic
and security anxieties has demonstrated that he will then spontaneously do
his best job.

*Management is not the manipulation of people; management is the
understanding of people*—their life styles, heart's desires and need for personal
fulfillment.

The horizontal enlargement of jobs, i.e., the addition of a variety of operations, is regarded as a frustrating addition or burden by the unskilled kitch-
en worker. In contrast, the vertical enlargement of jobs, i.e., the involvement
of employees in planning, organizing, inspecting and evaluating the work turns
out to be a motivator of employees and, as such, a positive influence upon
productivity levels. Foodservice workers have worked tirelessly to achieve
goals *they* helped set but often have balked at working vigorously toward goals
which have been dictated by management.

It takes courage on the part of management to introduce consultive
and/or participative management systems. It takes a long time for employees
to develop belief in the sincerity of a participative system implemented by
management. Employees who have worked *under* authoritarian managers
have good reason to expect that participative management is yet another form
of manipulation. When true trust has been won through continuing performance, then, and only then, can employees work *with* management as an opera-

tion team for the common goals of the foodservice organization and the people who work for it.

If the worker helps define the job and it is defined for him *only*, then he will treat that job as a possession with all the care and responsibility which he assumes for his other possessions.

Finally, the foodservice operator should make sure the employee knows what to do; that he is given every opportunity to plan and influence his job; that the employee is urged to be personally concerned with the evaluation of how well the job is performed.

Be careful to be consistent and concerned as a manager because experience has found that *participative management must be responsible management* if it is to benefit the organization and individual alike.

TABLE OF ORGANIZATIONAL AND PERFORMANCE

ORGANIZATIONAL VARIABLE	SYSTEM 1 AUTHORITARIAN EXPLOITIVE
1. Leadership processes used Extent to which superiors have confidence and trust in subordinates	Have no confidence and trust in subordinates
Extent to which superiors behave so that subordinates feel free to discuss important things about their jobs with their immediate superior	Subordinates do not feel at all free to discuss things about the job with their superior
Extent to which immediate superior in solving job problems generally tries to get subordinates' ideas and opinions and make constructive use of them	Seldom gets ideas and opinions of subordinates in solving job problems
2. Character of motivational forces Manner in which motives are used	Fear, threats, punishment and occasional rewards

CHARACTERISTICS OF DIFFERENT MANAGEMENT SYSTEMS

SYSTEM 2 AUTHORITARIAN BENEVOLENT	SYSTEM 3 CONSULTIVE	SYSTEM 4 PARTICIPATIVE
Have condescending confidence and trust such as master has to servant	Substantial but not complete confidence and trust; still wishes to keep control of decisions	Complete confidence and trust in all matters
Subordinates do not feel very free to discuss things about the job with their superior	Subordinates feel rather free to discuss things about the job with their superior	Subordinates feel completely free to discuss things about the job with their superior
Sometimes gets ideas and opinions of subordinates in solving job problems	Usually gets ideas and opinions and usually tries to make constructive use of them	Always gets ideas and opinions and always tries to make constructive use of them
Rewards, and some actual or potential punishment	Rewards, occasional punishment and some involvement	Economic rewards based on compensation system developed through participation; and involvement in setting goals, improving methods, appraising progress toward goals, etc.

(cont.)

TABLE OF ORGANIZATIONAL AND PERFORMANCE

ORGANIZATIONAL VARIABLE	SYSTEM 1 AUTHORITARIAN EXPLOITIVE
2. (continued) Amount of responsibility felt by each member of organization for achieving organization's goals	High levels of management feel responsibility; lower levels feel less; rank and file feel little and often welcome opportunity to defeat organization's goals
3. Character of communication process Amount of interaction and communication aimed at achieving organization's objectives	Very little
Direction of information below	Downward
Extent to which downward communications are accepted by subordinates	Viewed with great suspicion
Accuracy of upward communication via line	Tends to be inaccurate

CHARACTERISTICS OF DIFFERENT MANAGEMENT SYSTEMS (cont.)

SYSTEM 2	SYSTEM 3	SYSTEM 4
AUTHORITARIAN BENEVOLENT	**CONSULTIVE**	**PARTICIPATIVE**
Managerial personnel usually feel relatively little responsibility for achieving organization's goals	Substantial proportion of personnel, especially at high levels, feel responsibility and generally behave in ways to achieve the organization's goals	Personnel at all levels feel real responsibility for organization's goals and behave in ways to implement them
Little	Quite a bit	Much with both individuals and groups
Mostly downward	**Down and Up**	Down and Up, and with peers
May or may not be viewed with suspicion	Often accepted but at times viewed with suspicion; may or may not be openly questioned	Generally accepted but if not, openly and candidly questioned
Information that boss wants to hear flows; other information is restricted and filtered	Information that boss wants to hear flows; other information may be limited or cautiously given	Accurate

(cont.)

TABLE OF ORGANIZATIONAL AND PERFORMANCE

	SYSTEM 1
ORGANIZATIONAL VARIABLE	**AUTHORITARIAN EXPLOITIVE**
3. (continued) Psychological closeness of superiors to subordinates (i.e., how well does superior know and understand problems faced by subordinates?)	Has no knowledge or understanding of problems of subordinates
4. Character of interaction-influence process Amount and character of interaction	Little interaction and usually with some condescension by superiors
Amount of cooperative teamwork present	None
5. Character of decision-making process At what level in organization are decisions formally made	Bulk of decisions at top of organization
To what extent are decision makers aware of problems, particularly those at lower levels in the organization	Often are unaware or only partially aware

CHARACTERISTICS OF DIFFERENT MANAGEMENT SYSTEMS (cont.)

SYSTEM 2	SYSTEM 3	SYSTEM 4
AUTHORITARIAN BENEVOLENT	**CONSULTIVE**	**PARTICIPATIVE**
Has some knowledge and understanding of problems of subordinates	Knows and understands problems of subordinates quite well	Knows and understands problems of subordinates very well
Little interaction and usually with some condescension by superiors; fear and caution by subordinates	Moderate interaction, often with fair amount of confidence and trust	Extensive, friendly interaction with high degree of confidence
Relatively little	A moderate amount	Very substantial amount throughout the organization
Policy at top, many decisions within prescribed framework made at lower levels	Broad policy and general decisions at top, more specific decisions at lower levels	Decision making widely done throughout organization, although well integrated through linking process provided by over-lapping groups
Aware of some, unaware of others	Moderately aware of problems	Generally quite well aware of problems

(cont.)

TABLE OF ORGANIZATIONAL AND PERFORMANCE

ORGANIZATIONAL VARIABLE	SYSTEM 1 AUTHORITARIAN EXPLOITIVE
5. (continued) 　　Extent to which technical and professional knowledge is used in decision making	Used only if possessed at higher levels
To what extent are subordinates involved in decisions related to their work?	Not at all
Are decisions made at the best level in the organization so far as the motivational consequences (i.e., does the decision-making process help to create the necessary motivations in those persons who have to carry out the decisions)	Decision making contributes little or nothing to the motivation to implement the decision, usually yields adverse motivation
6. Character of goal setting or ordering 　　Manner in which usually done	Orders issued
Are there forces to accept, resist, or reject goals?	Goals are overtly accepted but are covertly resisted strongly

CHARACTERISTICS OF DIFFERENT MANAGEMENT SYSTEMS (cont.)

SYSTEM 2 AUTHORITARIAN BENEVOLENT	SYSTEM 3 CONSULTIVE	SYSTEM 4 PARTICIPATIVE
Much of what is available in higher and middle levels is used	Much of what is available in higher, middle and lower levels is used	Most of what is available anywhere within the organization is used
Never involved in decisions; occasionally consulted	Usually are consulted but ordinarily not involved in the decision making	Are involved fully in all decisions related to their work
Decision making contributes relatively little motivation	Some contribution by decision making to motivation to implement	Substantial contribution by decision-making processes to motivation to implement
Orders issued, opportunity to comment may or may not exist	Goals are set or orders issued after discussions with subordinate(s) of problems and planned action	Except in emergencies goals are usually established by means of group participation
Goals are overtly accepted but often covertly resisted to at least a moderate degree	Goals are overtly accepted but at times with some covert resistance	Goals are fully accepted both overtly and covertly

(cont.)

TABLE OF ORGANIZATIONAL AND PERFORMANCE

ORGANIZATIONAL VARIABLE	SYSTEM 1 AUTHORITARIAN EXPLOITIVE
7. Character of control processes Extent to which the review and control functions are concentrated	Highly concentrated in top management
Extent to which there is informal organization present and supporting or opposing goals of formal organization	Informal organization present and opposing goals of formal organization
Extent to which control data (e.g., accounting, productivity, cost, etc.) are used for self-guidance or group problem solving by managers and non-supervisory employees; or used by superiors in a punitive, policing manner	Used for policing and in punitive manner

CHARACTERISTICS OF DIFFERENT MANAGEMENT SYSTEMS (cont.)

SYSTEM 2	SYSTEM 3	SYSTEM 4
AUTHORITARIAN BENEVOLENT	**CONSULTIVE**	**PARTICIPATIVE**
Relatively highly concentrated, with some delegated control to middle and lower levels	Moderate downward delegation of review and control processes; lower as well as higher levels feel responsible	Quite widespread responsibility for review and control, with lower units at times imposing more rigorous reviews and tighter controls than top management
Information organization usually present and partially resisting goals	Information organization may be present, and may either support or partially resist goals of formal organization	Informal and formal organization are one and the same; hence, all social forces support efforts to achieve organization's goals
Used for policing coupled with reward and punishment, sometimes punitively; used somewhat for guidance but in accord with orders	**Largely used for** policing with emphasis usually on reward but with some punishment; used for guidance in accord with orders; some use also for self-guidance	**Used for self-guidance** and for coordinated problem solving and guidance; not used punitively

CREATING THE
FOODSERVICE ORGANIZATION

KNOWLEDGE of people and knowledge of food are not the only requisites for being a good foodservice manager. Perhaps the most misunderstood area of foodservice management is the nature of organization. In heavy industry, it is almost axiomatic that top management people can be as effective in one industry as in another; these people, for example, can switch fairly easily from automobiles to refrigerators. We all know of persons who have made such changes with great success.

This is possible because these men understand organization and, therefore, are able to create productive staffs through the selection of the proper technical people for each line position. The principles which work for the managers of thousands work equally well for the managers of hundreds, scores or dozens.

No matter how many good people one may have on the foodservice staff, that staff cannot produce unless good people are placed in organization juxtaposition for creation of productivity and motivation.

Organization Chart

The first thing that must be done is to work out a chart of organization. This is a task that must first be thought through carefully before the chart can be drawn up in final form. Several charts may have to be prepared before the one from which the organization will run is created. In discussing the work involved, four steps in organization chart preparation are outlined:

Chart 1 should be prepared to show the *formal organization* as it is today. Draw each reporting and cooperating line of function and/or authority as it is today. Do not be surprised at finding everybody reporting to the person at the top. This is a common organizational error and is discussed in greater detail later in this chapter.

Chart 2 should be prepared to show the reporting functions of the *informal organization*. Chart 2 is likely to be very different from Chart 1 because the formal organization rarely identifies the way the organization operates informally. Problems are often taken to a third cook or a cashier instead of a supervisor. If Chart 2 reveals that there are influential people in nonsupervisory positions in the foodservice operation, special care should be given to the cultivation and education of those people as they may be effective in supervisory and management positions.

Chart 3 should show the *ideal organization*. This chart can only be drawn after a careful functional analysis of the work that needs to be done. The individual preparing this chart will need to work separately with each member of the staff in determining the functions, duties and responsibilities that should be handled. In the ideal organization, there should be a minimum number of people reporting to each level of supervision.

The supervisory functions should make good common-sense. In the kitchen, there should be one person with overall authority and responsibility for food production. If the kitchen is large, there may be need for supervisors of hot food production and cold food production, each reporting to the person who bears the overall food production responsibility.

There should be a separate person in charge of sanitation. If necessary, there may be dishmachine room and porter supervisors reporting to the overall sanitation supervisor. The same common-sense rules apply to the supervision of waiters and waitresses, counter workers, distribution personnel, bookkeepers, dietitians and managers.

Here are some common errors in foodservice organizations which lead to chaotic, ineffective and unproductive operations.

(1) The number one person—the owner-operator, manager or foodservice director—has everyone, from dishmachine operator to chef, reporting directly to him. With so many functions to supervise, this boss must spend all of his time on today's problems and never really has time to plan, organize or direct the future of the operation.

(2) Waitresses are responsible to the cooks. This leads to fights, tears and poor service. Service personnel, such as waitresses, should report to a person with overall responsibility for dining room operations. Any difficulty the cooks have with the waitresses, or vice-versa, should be negotiated between the person who supervises the cooks and the person who supervises the wait-

resses. If a confrontation is necessary between a waitress and a cook, then it should be done in a quiet room over a cup of coffee. This will remove the "heat" from the situation.

(3) The chef or head cook supervises the kitchen porters. A chef is technically trained in the preparation of food. This does not mean that he is knowledgeable in the chemistry of cleaning products and sanitation techniques. Do not leave pathogenicity to someone untrained in pathogen control. Supervision of sanitation belongs to a sanitation supervisor who knows the values and dangers of procedures and chemicals. The chef and the sanitation supervisor should function at the same level in the organizational hierarchy and should cooperate closely in all matters relating to sanitary food production.

(4) Registered dietitians are used as kitchen supervisors or assembly supervisors. A dietitian, who has the valued resource of a formal therapeutics education, should not be under-utilized in a job which does not call upon her technical training. The therapeutic dietitian should be doing diet therapy and other related professional tasks and not be checking the assembly of trays.

Chart 3 will show clear lines of authority; will reflect an understanding of position functions; will reflect the correct use of specialized staff; will show an understudy for each key position to achieve fluid promotional lines.

Chart 4 should be the median between an overlay of Chart 1 and Chart 2 and the ideal situation which is Chart 3. It should represent the best of all three charts (to be put in effect at once). Chart 4 will show the reorganization of the lines of authority and, as such, will function as the operational stepping-stone between the present and the future. This interim chart (4) should enable the organization to function better immediately without creating large morale problems by a sudden change to the ideal chart (3).

Basic Research

Although it is impractical for any but the largest of foodservice organizations to maintain anything resembling a research staff, the basic research function cannot be ignored by even the smallest of foodservice organizations.

The effective operator makes it his business to allot regular hours for the review and reading of the business publications relating to his segment of the foodservice industry. Articles and advertisements of particular interest should be clipped and filed for future reference. Any employee who has the desire to read the publications should be given access to them. On several occasions, an employee, upon reading of a new product or technique in a trade magazine, has spontaneously suggested and/or implemented new and better operations because of what he has learned from the trade magazine.

Every operator should have a basic library of books on foodservice management, food preparation and production and related topics. The cost of a basic library is no great capital expense as it may be assembled at a cost of $200 to $500. Such a library gives the operator and his staff immediate access to most of the information needed by the organization, whether it be food cost control or the classic recipe for apricot brioches. These books should be loaned freely to line employees as they will often use them to improve their present work and prepare for future promotions.

Each foodservice organization is unique in and of itself. The customers served by the operation have a "group" or "mass" taste all their own; the foodservice staff at each operation has its own special character. Because of this, accurate long-term records of all major, as well as some of the minor, activities of the foodservice organization should be kept. Such records will not only serve as research material on which to base future activities of the organization, but also will provide for continuity when a change-over in management takes place.

Essential records which may be kept include:

inventories	costs per meal served—labor
quotation sheets	costs per meal served—direct
contracts	menu changes
receiving records	special functions held by whom;
quantity consumption by category	what costs
invoices	relative cost data comparison and mov-
production history	ing averages for specific time frames
major price changes	turnover statistics
meals served per man hour worked	break-even charts
check average charts	upward mobility histories chart
costs per meal served—food	projections vs. actual results charts

A good manager will rely on his operation's historical data as an indication of need for immediate change as well as a basis for determining long-term trends.

The Personnel Function

Careful handling and well thought-out procedures are essential to the administration of the personnel function in foodservice operations, since all too often high turnover, improperly or poorly trained workers, low morale and restless employees are traceable to the haphazard handling of the personnel function. The operator who tries singlehandedly to be all things to all phases of his operation makes the mistake of spreading himself too thin.

A recommended ratio is one full time personnel employee for each 125 to 150 in an operation. For a lesser number of employees, there should be a proportionate part-time assignment of a personnel person. The personnel employee should conduct the search, initial interviews, tests, job and benefit orientation and exit interviews for all employees. In addition to this, the personnel person should be involved in the health and safety programs and the administration of fringe benefits.

The success of an employer in providing motivation and inspiring high productivity starts the minute a prospective employee walks through the outside door. The person who does the initial interviewing must conduct a smooth and uninterrupted interview which results in an effective exchange of information—from the interviewer to the applicant—about the company and the job and—from the applicant to the interviewer—about his or her abilities and potentials.

The newly hired employee deserves a formalized introduction process and a training program which *trains.* Once at work, the *employee will judge* the operation and his chances for personal fulfillment during his first few days just as he *will be judged* by management during those days. Whether or not the employee stays with the operation is frequently determined by his experience during this introductory period.

In addition to overseeing the worker's job orientation, the personnel representative will thereafter try to keep potential employee dissatisfiers to a minimum; will provide systematic assistance in such matters as processing insurance claims and grievances.

He should also remind management when evaluations are due, where promotion lines should or should not be followed and where rewards for initiative are called for.

The foodservice operator should assure that his supervisory staff is personnel-minded and that every effort is made to be fair and just, not only in fact, but also in the *eyes of the workers.*

When all else has failed and an employee is leaving the operation, voluntarily or otherwise, then it is of crucial importance that an exit interview be conducted. The exit interviews will often turn up a pattern of operational problems which, if corrected, will halt the exit of more employees.

EMPLOYEE EVALUATIONS

EVALUATING non-professional employees in a manner which the employee can accept as being fair and just is a problem as old as our industry itself. The problem centers on the fact that service employees perform tasks which are difficult or impossible to measure in quantitative terms.

In the hospitality industry, the tasks performed are qualitative. The measures for these are primarily subjective rather than objective. A typist can be measured in terms of words-typed-per-minute; a stenographer can be measured in terms of letters-per-day, but how can the quality of a cashier's courtesy, a hostess' efficiency or a cook's food be measured in quantitative terms?

There has been much written and reported about the public's opinion that the quality of service in our hotels, restaurants and other institutions has severely declined. Only a fool would buy the argument that this is purely a result of employee apathy. Indeed apathy, if existent, starts at the top and winds its way down to the line employees.

There are many means of creating and maintaining high morale and the quality service which accompanies it. A fair and just system of evaluation is a primary ingredient of good operational management. An evaluation, such as explained below, can go a long way toward developing high morale and quality service.

GRADE SYSTEMS AND WAGES

Many foodservice operations have a grading system that places jobs of like difficulty or like skill needs at a specific grade. Each grade then has a number of graduated salary increment levels which are attained through either length of service or merit or a combination of both. Such a system is usually designed early in the growth of an organization as a means of establishing salary relationships among jobs.

What such a system really does, however, is give the manager an easy way out when employees confront him to ask for a raise. The manager can say, "This is the grade of job and this is the salary. I'm sorry, but that is the system." A grade system may be something for the manager to hide behind, a way to avoid coming clean and saying the honest thing, such as: "Look, you do an average job in an average way and do not merit a raise. If you work more diligently and devise better ways of doing your job then, and only then, will we discuss a salary adjustment."

Far better than a closely structured grade system is a grade system which is flexible. Instead of all waitress jobs being rated grade 2, there should be a rating range of grade 1, grade 2 and grade 3. The inexperienced may be hired at grade 1, the experienced at grade 2 and grade 3 may be reserved as a salary schedule for the truly superior performer.

To be sure, original or median salaries have to be set for all jobs. One excellent way of doing this is to separate the factors common to all jobs, i.e., mental demands, education required, effect of error, personal contact and general job conditions and assign weighted points to each factor. In this manner you can arrive at a weighted relative scale such as is shown below:

	Cashier	First Cook	Kitchen Porter
mental demands (weight 2)	60-120	60-120	10-20
education (weight 5)	40-200	60-300	10-100
effect of error (weight 3)	50-150	70-210	30-90
personal contact (weight 2)	50-100	20-40	5-10
gen. job conditions (weight 1)	30-30	70-70	120-120
Total	600	740	340

Regardless of how salaries are set, levels should be determined by the salary market in the area. Employees should be paid the highest salary the operator can afford to pay while earning a fair profit on his investment. The more an employee earns, the less he is going to be distracted by off-the-job problems. If a man cannot decently support his family and hold his head up at home, he cannot be fully productive at work or sincerely interested in the patron. The more he earns, the less likely he will be to steal, either directly or through the carelessness of error. The more he earns, the less likely it is that he will leave his job for higher pay. Remember that job turnover is costly: A new dishmachine operator may cost $200-$500 to train. A supervisor's resignation could ultimately cost a foodservice operation thousands of dollars.

PERFORMANCE MEASURES

Our industry still has a long way to go in the development of objective measures of quantitative performance. Just how many "average" covers should a fry cook be able to handle in an hour? In a shift? How many check-outs per cashier? How many pots per pot-washer? The list could go on and on.

There are "rules of thumb" for some areas, such as the number of square feet mopped per minute or seats per waitress, etc. But even in these instances, for a variety of reasons, allowances must be made; consequently, rules of thumb are often impossible to hold out as hard statistics.

In the absence of the development of reliable quantitative measures by the reliable scientific efforts of our hotel and restaurant schools, the individual operator must develop standards which reflect the labors of the better people in his organization. This will take some time but it should be possible to come down to about a half dozen reliable hard measures for each job. These will be the measurements used in the quantitative section of the evaluation form shown on page 35.

ANALYZING THE JOB AND JOB DESCRIPTIONS

As a first step, a brief list of factors common in varying degrees to every job should be developed. The four general factors listed on page 35 should be broken into component parts and listed on a single sheet. A separate sheet should be drawn up for each job.

Unless an analysis of a job is made *before* the job description is written, the description will be meaningless. *A job description which shows the actual functions of his job is a basic right of every employee.* An employee cannot be expected to do a job that is not clearly described nor should he be held accountable for an under-described job at the time of evaluation.

The well-written job description will take one of two forms. The duties will either be delineated by specific time periods or by the percentage of time to be spent at each task. The *specific time period* job description will apply to jobs which are primarily routine, such as dishmachine operation, while jobs of the cook, waitress or dietitian will probably be written with *time percentages*.

The other sections of the proper job description are common to all areas. The information required in all job descriptions includes: position; title; department; work area; hours per week; basic functions; regular and special duties and responsibilities; unique working conditions; qualifications for the job, i.e., education, experience, physical fitness; employees supervised; person supervised by; professional relationship; line of promotion and specific performance standards.

The more the employee is involved in the writing of his job description, the better it is likely to be. Rather than giving up a management right by asking the employee's help, management is showing the employee that his opinion on how the job should be done is respected.

At Hillside Hospital* Food Services Department, four broad categories of factors have been set by which an employee should be measured. These four broad areas have been further divided into fourteen sub-categories. These are listed on the facing page.

Using the fourteen factors, each job should be listed and weighted as shown on pp. 36-37. Just as everything in life is relative to something else, so every job in a kitchen is relative to the others. If the absence of a potwasher is more critical to the operation than that of a cook, then it must be so weighted. If getting along with the peer group is more important for first line supervisory personnel than for a sandwich girl, then that must be so weighted. This procedure of weighting factors, by order of importance for each job, establishes a fair basis for evaluation.

Evaluation Form

When the master sheet of factors has been completed with factors weighted for the job, the points earned by the holder of the job should be transferred to a simple, single sheet form. The front of this form, shown on p. 35, will give the point-factor analysis; the back of the form should allow for the employer's comments and suggestions as well as the employee's comments.

The Act of Evaluating

To help the employee understand just how he is being measured, the forms shown on pp. 40-42 were devised. Using these forms, the department head, the supervisor and the employee each evaluate the employee on the point scale. The employee's performance is considered acceptable when 75% of the points possible are awarded to him. More must be awarded for excellent performance and fewer points will indicate poor performance. As a special incentive, a small bonus or penalty is built into the dependability factors. Test scores never count more than 10% of the total possible.

The high-sounding score figures were used to give the employee the

---

*Now the Hillside Division of the Long Island Jewish-Hillside Medical Center, New Hyde Park, New York.

Job Title: 1st Cook   Position No. 620.9-3

Grade: 8

Evaluation Measures

%	Mix		Actual Points	Possible Points
	20	1. Attitude		
		(a) towards job		5
		(b) towards peers		10
		(c) towards supervisors		5
		Total		20
	20	2. Dependability		
		(a) absence record		5
		(b) lateness record		5
		(c) response to directions		10
		Total		20
	35	3. Production		
		(a) quality		15
		(b) quantity		15
		(c) test results		5
		Total		35
	25	4. Other Work Factors		
		(a) learning speed		3
		(b) mature judgment		3
		(c) initiative		4
		(d) adaptability		5
		(e) sanitation		10
		Total		25
		Grand Total		100

Score of 90 or above superior
Score of 70-89 acceptable
Score of 60-69 marginal
Score of 59 or below not acceptable

JOB	(Attitude)			(Dependability)				(Production)				(Other Factors)		
	Job	Peer	Supervisors	Absence	Lateness	Directions	Quality	Quantity	Tests	Learning	Judgment	Initiative	Adaptability	Sanitation
Chef	5	10	5	3	2	5	20	10	5	5	10	5	5	10
1st Cook	5	10	5	5	5	10	15	15	5	3	3	4	5	10
2nd Cook	5	5	5	8	4	8	10	12	8	5	5	10	5	10
3rd Cook	5	5	5	10	5	10	7	7	6	10	5	10	5	10
Counter/Supervisor	10	10	5	5	5	10	10	5	10	2	10	5	3	10
Kitchen/Counteraide	4	3	3	10	5	10	15	25	10	2	2	3	3	5
Porter/Potwasher	2	2	1	15	5	5	15	35	5	2	3	3	2	10
Cook Trainee	10	5	10	5	5	5	3	2	5	20	5	10	5	10
Dishroom/Supervisor	10	10	5	5	5	10	10	10	5	2	10	5	3	10

Position													
Dining/Dishroom Aide	10	2	3	2	3	5	25	10	10	5	10	5	5
Cashier	5	5	2	5	3	5	10	10	5	10	10	5	10
Salad/Sandwich Aide	5	2	3	3	2	10	20	20	10	5	10	3	3
Salad/Sandwich Supervisor	5	2	3	8	2	10	15	25	3	3	4	5	10
Foodservice Supervisor	5	5	15	15	10	3	5	7	10	5	5	5	5
DAU Supervisor	10	6	12	13	2	10	5	10	5	5	5	3	4
DAU Aide	10	6	12	13	3	10	5	10	5	5	5	3	3

chance to brag of an 88 score to his co-workers and/or family even though the employer and employee both know this represents only a high "acceptable" performance. Again, *personal dignity is upheld.*

The evaluation opinions of all three evaluators should be pooled and discussed over a cup of coffee in an area where the *employee* feels comfortable. *The boss' office is not the proper atmosphere for making an employee feel at ease and free to speak.* The evaluation session is a golden opportunity to clear the air and discuss future plans. Any resolution on the employee's part and suggestions for improvement on management's part should be written on the back of this form.

Experience has shown that the institution of less subjective formal evaluation procedures, like those described above, will help in raising morale, raising productivity, improving service and reducing turnover. When fair procedures are established, the rewards are certain to be great.

Morale

While the many means of creating morale through effective foodservice management have been outlined, these are additional factors to consider:

The foodservice manager who stands off from his employees may be in error. While undue familiarity with line employees is not recommended, employees should know what to expect from the foodservice manager. Comfortable employer-employee relations permit the employer/manager to demonstrate his understanding of employee problems.

Management should also offer the employee as many ancillary services, such as professional personal counseling, as possible. Music should be provided to ease nerves and add verve to productivity. An incentive program for cost saving and/or productivity-improving suggestions should be offered.

PRODUCTION CONTROL

The suggested readings on pp. 196 to 201 will provide specific instructions on setting up production control procedures. When production control systems have been established, then they *must be used.* Control procedures should be reviewed and re-evaluated at least once every 2 years. The test of a good control record is that it provides "up to the minute" information on the operation's productivity. Quantity controls are important, to be sure, but not nearly as important as quality controls.

Optimum production can only be achieved if the physical layout and human engineering of the operation are correct. If workers must endure an outdated physical plant, then see that wherever possible equipment is put on casters for ease of movement and flexibility of layout. This "human engineering" is explained in depth in Chapter 3.

PROBLEM SOLVING

There is no one ideal way to solve every problem but there is one method which comes close to being best in many situations. *Reduce every problem to its smallest components and put the difficult parts aside for further thought.* Each component of the problem will need a separate solution.

If the problem is in personnel, then train the employee to perform the proper function for each component of the problem area and follow up his performance until the procedure is perfected. After repeated experience with this training method, it is easy to measure human understanding.

THE EFFECTIVE MANAGER

The effective manager is oriented to the employee as much as he is to the physical aspects of his foodservice because he realizes that the end product is the result of the labors of men and women.

He creates an atmosphere of mutual respect, a friendly and congenial atmosphere in which every employee may easily merge the relationships of work and life.

He encourages employees in their individual goals because he realizes that there is no uniform pattern in personal "work-life" development.

He works to develop creativity in employees.

Access to the effective manager is easy and he listens well, giving moral support on a consistent basis.

The effective manager will take a risk but it is a calculated risk because he knows what needs to be done and the possible human alternatives in getting it done.

Last of all, the effective manager is a true V. I. P. because, to him, every employee is a V. I. P. and it is only through his employees that the effective manager achieves *his own* professional and personal fulfillment.

EVALUATION MEASURE CHECKLIST

This checklist is a means of making subjective measures more objective. This guide is to be used by the Director of Foodservices and the supervisor *with* the employee in making an evaluation.

1.   Attitude

A.   Towards Job

Are you interested in the work?
Do you stick to a job through completion?
Are you interested in the work of the department?
Have you made suggestions to improve and/or simplify your job or the department?

B.   Towards Peers

Are your relationships with fellow employees and hospital staff salutary?
Have you had many arguments with your peers? If so, whose fault?
Do you lend a helping hand to others when you have time?

C.   Towards Supervisors

Do you follow directions readily and cheerfully or do you resent being directed?
Are you open with your supervisor about work problems?

2.   Dependability

A.   Absence Record

How many days and times absent?
Did you follow departmental regulations in making notification? (No score if more than 12 days/8 absences during year, except for long term illness.) No score if you had any no-call absences other than a major emergency such as an automobile accident. No score for any unexcused absences.

B.   Punctuality

No score if late six or more times because of snowstorms, etc. No score if more than one hour late without call more than three times. Bonus of one point if never late without call.

C.   Response to Directions

Do you readily grasp new instructions?

Do you do assigned tasks immediately and completely?

Do you accept and follow the constructive suggestions offered by your superiors?

Do you remember the long term tasks and follow them to completion?

3.   Production

A.   Quality

Do you follow the qualitative measures outlined in your job description?

Do you produce the same quality of work consistently?

Do you always follow directions/recipes?

Do you make suggestions to your supervisors which could improve the quality of your work and the product?

Does the quality of your work change when you are under stress?

B.   Quantity

Do you produce as much satisfactory work as called for in your job description?

Do you produce more or less than your co-workers?

Do you do the same amount of work all the time?
If not, why?

C.   Test Results

Have you been taught the things you were asked on the test?

4.   Other Work Factors

A.   Learning Speed

Do you learn new tasks at the first or second instruction?

Do you remember the new procedure the next time you ask for clarification if you do not understand the instructions? If not, why not?

B.   Mature Judgment

Have you the opportunity to make judgments?

Are you "cool" when there is a crisis or when pressure is put upon you?

Have you made any wrong decisions?

Do you participate in department meetings?

C.   Initiative

Do you see to it that all routine tasks under your job description are completed properly and on time?

Do you correct a wrong situation when you see one?

Do you make constructive suggestions?

Do you help others when you have time?

D.   Adaptability

Do you resist change without thinking it over for both the good and the bad?

Do you readily adjust to a new work situation or new means of doing a task?

Do you adjust easily to the changes in your routine necessitated by an emergency situation?

E.   Sanitation

Are you clean in your personal habits and appearance?

Do you do your cleaning tasks completely and correctly in the kitchen?

FOODSERVICE MANAGER PRODUCTIVITY

THE FOODSERVICE organization cannot achieve maximum worker productivity until the foodservice manager learns to be productive.

To be successful, to be productive, a foodservice manager must enjoy his work. The tone of the operation is often an outgrowth of the tone of the foodservice manager. If the boss regards his work as a burden and a less-than-pleasant part of life, then it is reasonable to presume that his employees will come to regard work likewise. A person who runs an organization must *believe* in his work or his organization may well be doomed to failure.

A manager in foodservice has one of the last eclectic jobs left in this society. While others specialize in one area or another, the foodservice manager must achieve a level of competence in accounting, personnel, labor relations, industrial engineering, marketing and other disciplines.

The successful people in this business are those who learn to be self-starters; who are not afraid of long hours or crisis situations; who serve others for the love of it; who can achieve ego-gratification through their own recognition that their job is well done. Since there is nobody to pass out pats on the back to the foodservice manager, he must derive his satisfaction from the job itself.

Managing is all about planning, directing and controlling operations.

Planning means the setting of definite objectives. Broad objectives should be subdivided into manageable segments which are called goals. Realistic goal-accomplishment dates must be assigned and adhered to. (The last few pages of this chapter are devoted to a method for finding what amount of time is realistic.)   What objectives should a manager have?   Here is a list of management activities and of questions from which ideas and answers may flow:

Analysis of sales activities
Analysis of customer traffic information
Analysis of labor utilization
Analysis of materials utilization
Analysis of production activity
When and what should we rent or buy or lease
How much growth capital do we need?
For *whom*. . .are we trying to do *what*. . .with food and beverage services?
Is our physical plant appropriate?
Are external appearances satisfactory?
What can we do to increase the effectiveness of our promotion, advertising, internal merchandising and personal selling?
Are prices within range of acceptability for our types of customers?
Do we have enough people to operate efficiently—or too many?
What skills do we really need to have on-premise? Off-premise but available?
How can we upgrade and broaden skills needed through on-the-job training?
Can we schedule labor more effectively?
What labor pools can we tap?
Where can we tighten/improve our system of management direction, supervision and control? How? At what cost?
Do we have an adequate management information and control system?
What kind of quality image do we want?
How can we make eating more fun?
How can we make our services more convenient?
Analysis of: menu mix; financial management controls; manpower utilization; manpower recruitment, selection, training; equipment mix; physical layout; physical plant; production system; service system; sales-making system.[1]

Once a manager has developed objectives and goals he must work toward the accomplishment of those goals. This means setting aside a reasonable period of time from each working day, or a longer period from each work-

---

[1] "Productivity Produces Profits," National Restaurant Association, May, 1967.

ing week, which is to be devoted to the goal at hand. The operation which is in a continual state of crisis evidences the failure of management to allocate time and energy to fulfilling goals and objectives.

Various modes of measuring *results* are discussed in earlier chapters.

An excellent analysis of one area not dealt with in detail earlier in this book—forecasting—has been made by Richard K. Rodgers of Kelly Rodgers and Company of Chicago.[1] It is as follows:

"The sales or revenue forecast—This amount represents the number of sales dollars or revenue dollars which management expects to receive from providing foodservices in the coming financial period.

"The expense forecast—Here management computes fixed and variable costs based on different levels or amounts of sales/revenue dollars within the forthcoming financial period forecasted.

"The profit forecast—At various levels of sales dollar or revenue dollar production, and with accompanying expense loads at each level of activity, appropriate production of profit dollars should take place.

"Utilization of capital and cash flow forecasts—This forecast typically sets forth a program showing what kinds and amounts of capital will be required during the forthcoming fiscal period, as well as when that capital will be needed, and where best to obtain it. Sometimes the forecast also will cover return of investment (ROI) and return on capital employed (ROCE). With such a forecast on needs for capital, foodservice executives should not be surprised by regular or to-be-anticipated payout situations arising during the forecasted period. In addition, proper advance preparations can be made to have the capital available, and to arrange for it at the time needed, from the best source and at the most favorable rates.

"The Pro Forma forecast—This is an organized attempt to predict what will happen during the forecasted period in the area of revenues, expenses and profits, based on certain assumptions about what will happen within the business in the way of costs, transactions and other expenses. You could say that the Pro Forma is an arithmetical model of the forthcoming period, as it would look when presented in summary form, as if all the various forecasts had taken place. Then, at the close of the period, the Pro Forma can speed the process of comparing performance against plan in the various areas forecasted, and in determining what factors caused deviations from plan."

P. E. R. T.

The world moves fast and so does the technological advance in foodserv-

---

[1] Richard K. Rodgers, "Five Steps to Financial Strength," *Fast Food* (1/68).

ice. *Performance Evaluation and Review Technique* (P.E.R.T) is a method for determining just how long it should take to accomplish a job. By using a PERT chart to pre-plan a schedule or undertaking, the foodservice manager may avoid the crisis of delay which occurs when one activity (which depends upon the completion of another activity) is not completed. PERT points out the critical processes and, thereby, defeats emergencies. The foodservice manager should not be afraid of formulas and signs. What appears to the untrained eye to be higher mathematics or computer language is really just a simple form of shorthand. Mathematics uses symbols to take the place of lengthy explanations. If a person can understand the few symbols presented here, then he will be on to a relatively accurate means of determining how long it will take to accomplish a given task.

a = the *least* time it may take to do a given task
b = the *most* time it may take to do a given task
m = the most *likely* time it may take to do a given task

To calculate the most *probable* (allowable in the schedule) amount of time it will take to do a given task we use the following formula:

$$\frac{a + 4m + b}{6} =$$

Let us say, for instance, that we want to know how much time should be allowed to mop a heavily obstructed 1600 square foot institutional kitchen:

A sloppy, cursory job will take 20 minutes. a = 20 (minutes)*
An extremely thorough job will take 120 minutes. b = 120 (minutes)*
The job, done adequately, will most likely take 45 minutes.
m = 45 (minutes)*

Using the formula

$$\frac{a + 4m + 6}{6} =$$
$$\frac{20 + (4 \times 45) + 120}{6} =$$
$$\frac{20 + 180 + 120}{6} =$$
$$\frac{320}{6} =$$

53-1/3 minutes

Knowing that the most probable time to mop the floor is 53-1/3 minutes, we will allot that amount of time daily to that task.

---

*Derived from actual time study of cursory, thorough and adequate.

A few more symbols must now be learned:

t_e = activity time. The amount of time it takes from the start of a task to the completion of that task.

T_E = expected time. The amount of time elapsed at the completion of a task. In terms of the chart shown on p. 51, the difference between t_e and T_E is shown as "slack". The t_e for the "Spec typed" is 15 weeks, that is, there are 15 weeks of time allowed to do a job which should take 2 weeks (T_E). If the 2 week job is not completed by the end of the 15 week period, then the next step ("Let out bids") becomes delayed. So, T_E is how much time it *takes* to do a task but t_e is how much time is *available* to do the task.

T_L = least allowable time. This is the expected time minus the activity time ($T_E - t_e$).

Critical Path = the most time allowable to complete a task with the least time lag. In the example on p. 54, the Critical Path is shown by a heavy, solid line. This Critical Path line shows the time route to completion of the job with the least delay. If that Critical Path line followed any of the other lines in the chart, then the "time to completion" would be much longer.

◯ = Event. Something that is completed or something that must happen.

⟶ = Activity. This symbol denotes the t_e.

⤳◯ = Node. An Event which needs one or more activities before it can be completed.

◯⤙ = Burst. Activities which cannot be started without an Event.

On the next few pages is presented a set of objectives and a PERT for the planning of a foodservice management function—the merger of the food purchasing functions of two hospitals. This particular PERT was prepared by the author in two days time as a proposal to top management. For various reasons, which have nothing to do with this PERT, this plan was not activated. The important point is that the author, with no more knowledge of PERT than already presented here and with little post-high school mathematical education, is able to plan with PERT. If he can do it, you can do it.

OBJECTIVE:

To establish a joint food purchasing program between the two divisions of the Long Island Jewish-Hillside Medical Center for the mutual physical and financial benefit of each division and the total corporation.

OBJECTIVE:

Standardization of purchase specifications.

A series of meetings between the representatives of the foodservice departments should be conducted with the goal of maximum purchase specification standardization.

These standardization meetings should be conducted in an atmosphere of total cooperation and compromise as far as is possible without either division making sacrifice of overall food quality or production effectiveness.

OBJECTIVE:

Standardization of purchase cycle.

In order to obtain maximum purchasing effectiveness, through the power of the size of individual deliveries, the representatives should determine purchase and delivery dates which are identical as far as physical plant resources permit.

OBJECTIVE:

Development of purchase contracts.

The representatives of the foodservice department should prepare a listing of specific products which should be contracted to sole purveyors for the purposes of increasing quality control, simplifying receiving and accounting procedures.

OBJECTIVE:

Standardization of accounting systems.

In order to simplify and coordinate the purchase effectiveness of the inter-divisional food purchasing program the representatives should agree upon internal accounting procedures which will give accurate comparisons of the inter-divisional purchasing program, the individual purchasing programs which preceded the joint program and the JPC purchasing program.

OBJECTIVE:

The representatives of the materials management and foodservice departments should determine the feasibility of pooling storage resources as a means of increasing joint capacity and reducing both product cost and number of receipts. This study should also consider the feasibility and costs of inter-divisional food transfers.

OBJECTIVE:

Development of forms for physical and financial controls and ease of operation.

A.   The purchasing and foodservices departments should develop a printed requisition/order form for each category of non-contract food purchase. This form, for purposes of physical ease, should be coordinated with order/receiving/inventory/storage records of the respective foodservice departments.

B.   The purchasing department should develop forms and procedures for the quotation and ordering procedures.

C.   Accounting, purchasing and data processing should determine the feasibility of and forms for the computer storage and computer retrieval of food purchase and inventory and physical data.

D.   The accounting department should develop a "transfer journal voucher" for the purpose of simplifying the program of pooled storage and receiving operations.

E.   All the above forms should be designed with operating efficiency in mind. Accounting, purchasing, foodservices, data processing and materials management should each be reserved the right of veto over any or all forms.

OBJECTIVE:

To determine on or before November 1, 1972 the total annual financial impact of the inter-divisional food purchasing program in order to justify (a) the addition of personnel to either the purchasing or foodservices departments, (b) the purchase of specific equipment for the expansion of the storage and/or delivery systems or (c) the discontinuance of the inter-divisional food purchasing program.

A.   Method of Determination

(1) A chart of comparisons of each division's actual purchase prices for items of identical specification for the month of April, 1972 (T M 1).

(2) The month of September, 1972 (T M 2), should be the month in which the purchasing department should purchase, separately, pre-determined items for each division. Using the *Producers Price-Current* and JPC bids as price bases, a "plus-percentage" determination of prices paid will be entered upon a chart of comparison in the same form as (1) above.

(3) The month of October, 1972 (T M 3) should be the month in

which the purchasing department should purchase, jointly, the same items as it purchased, separately, in T M 2. A comparison chart as in (2) should be prepared.

(4) Using T M 1 consumption as the master base for determining percentage of consumption cost, the T M 2 and T M 3 comparison charts should be extended to show the *probable* annual purchase savings.

(5) Costs of pooled storage and inter-divisional transfers for the T M 3 period should be extended to show the *probable* annual cost impact.

(6) The difference between (4) and (5) above should be weighted *equally* with the opinions of the two foodservice directors regarding increased or decreased operations effectiveness in determining whether or not the inter-divisional food purchasing program should continue and expand beyond December 1, 1972.

OBJECTIVE:

To foster the understanding of and mutual cooperation between the two divisions in the development of future service sharing, each committee should complete a report of proceedings following each meeting. The secretary of the "master committee" should be charged with the safekeeping of these records for the purpose of the education of our successors and arbitration of disputes.

Explanation of this PERT

ASSUMES:

Both divisions have written specifications
Both divisions have consumption records
Crash imprinting of forms

FUNCTION	T_E	SLACK	WEEK NO.	CHART NO.	EVENT COMPLETED
1. Purchase Specifications					
	2	0	2	1 A	Compare specs and expense codes
	.2	0	2.2	1 B	Agree on specs that are identical
	1.8	0	4	1 C	Mediate differences
2. Purchase Cycle					
	2	19	2	2 A	Agree on purchase/delivery cycle
3. Purchase Contracts					
	2	15	6	3 A	Specs typed
	1	0	7	3 B	Let out bids
	4	15	11	3 C	Award contracts
4. Pool Storage Resources					
	2	9	2	4 A	Space study
	5	0	11	4 B	Usage study
	2	0	13	4 C	Cost analysis study
	2	0	15	4 D	Delivery study
	1	0	16	4 E	Equipment study
	1	0	17	4 F	Order equipment
	9	0	26	4 G	Equipment received

(cont.)

FUNCTION	T_E	SLACK	WEEK NO.	CHART NO.	EVENT COMPLETED
5. Inter-divisional Requisitions					
	0	0	15	5 A	Develop procedure
	2	0	17	5 B	Agree on expense billing
	2	0	19	5 C	Design form
	2	5	21	5 D	Return from printers
6. Purchase Order					
	0	0	15	6 A	Develop procedure
	2	0	17	6 B	Agreement with all departments
	2	0	19	6 C	Modify existing form
	2	0	21	6 D	Return from printers
7. Test Month I					
	0	0	21	8 A	T M 2 starts
	4	1	25	8 B	T M 2 finishes
	1	6	26	8 C	T M 2 chart prepared
8. Test Month II					
	0	0	21	8 A	T M 2 starts
	4	1	25	8 B	T M 2 finishes
	1	6	26	8 C	T M 2 chart prepared
9. Test Month III					
	0	0	26	9 A	T M 3 starts
	4	0	30	9 B	T M 3 finishes
	1	0	31	9 C	T M 3 chart prepared

10. Peripheral Operation Costs	0	0	15	10 A	p.o.c. data collected
	2	15	17	10 B	p.o.c. data compared
11. Calculation of Total Costs	1	0	32	11	All comparisons completed
12. Decision	1	0	33	12	Decision made to proceed or abandon purchasing project

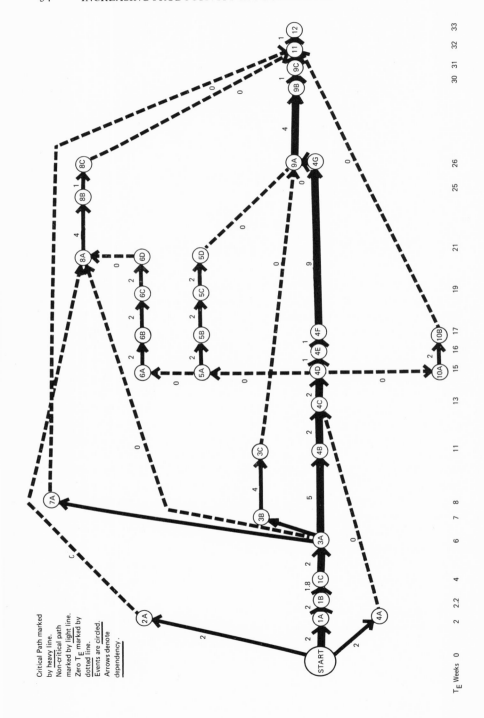

Critical Path marked
by heavy line.
Non-critical path
marked by light line.
Zero T_E marked by
dotted line.
Events are circled.
Arrows denote
dependency.

T_E Weeks 0   2   2.2   2   4   6   7   8   11   13   15   16   17   19   21   25   26   30 31   32 33

PREVENTING
ORGANIZATIONAL DRY ROT

THE PRECEDING five sections have explained much of the psychology of foodservice productivity and some of the methods to be applied in pursuit of an effective foodservice organization.

As a conclusion to this section of the book, some advice is offered on how to keep an organization effective once it has reached an effectiveness peak. John W. Gardner, former president of Carnegie Corporation and former Secretary of Health, Education and Welfare, wrote an exciting article entitled "How to Prevent Organizational Dry Rot" which is summarized here.[1]

"Like people and plants, organizations have a life cycle. They have a green and supple youth, a time of flourishing strength, and a gnarled old age . .

"But organizations differ from people and plants . . . An organization may go from youth to old age in two or three decades or it may last for centuries. More important, it may go through a period of stagnation and then revive. In short, decline is not inevitable. Organizations need not stagnate."

Mr. Gardner suggests nine rules for the prevention of organizational dry rot which are summarized here:

1. The organization must have an effective program for the recruitment and development of talent. People are the ultimate source of renewal.

2. The organization must be a hospitable environment for the individual.

3. The organization must have built-in provisions for self-criticism.

[1]Copyright © 1965, by Minneapolis Star and Tribune Co., Inc. Reprinted from the October, 1965 issue of Harper's Magazine by permission of the author.

4. The organization must have fluidity of internal structure. *Most organizations have a structure designed to solve problems that no longer exist.*

5. The organization must have an adequate system of internal communications.

6. The organization must have some means of combating the process by which men become prisoners of their procedures.

7. The organization must have some means of combating the vested interests that grow up in every human institution.

8. The organization capable of continuous renewal is interested in what it is going to become and not in what it has been.

9. Men have to believe their efforts as individuals will mean something for the whole organization and be recognized by the whole organization.

Summary

The management of a foodservice operation, whether commercial or institutional, is both a very simple task and a very complicated task. It is simple because good management is a matter of common sense being applied to every endeavor. It is easy to afford employees respect and dignity as individual human beings; it is easy to analyze job functions and create meaningful organization charts; it is easy to include the employee in the evaluation of his work; it is easy to create work flows which are functional; it is easy to make trade-offs in food and equipment sub-systems. All that is called for is the application of that which appears to make good sense.

The complicated part of good management comes under the heading of Murphy's Law: "That which can go wrong, will go wrong." The way to make Murphy's Law inoperative is the complicated matter of doing each simple, easy management task in the right way and at the right time. Every manager must develop his own sense of timing and be ready to back off, until another day, when things go very wrong. Employees must be involved in every stage of planning, development *and* implementation to prevent the simple from becoming complicated. This book and the ideabook scheduled for future publication are sources of inspiration and applicable operational suggestions but they cannot correct the problems of a manager who cannot or will not admit an error and use good common sense in correcting that error.

To be a manager who constantly increases productivity in foodservice you must keep an informal P.E.R.T. chart in your head, at all times, of what you want to do, when you want to do it, how you want to do it and the sensible way of getting it done. Complicated? Yes, but really rather simple when you break the job of management down into individual goals and the tasks that must be done to implement them. You *can* increase productivity!

2 Equipment Arrangement For Greater Worker Productivity

Arthur C. Avery

FOODSERVICE has long been the forgotten stepchild of industrial development in the United States. Thought of as a service industry, primarily, with its manufacturing functions minimized, foodservice has survived over the years by copious use of manpower. These workers are now in short supply, particularly skilled manpower, and wage demands are high as is resistance to higher food prices. So foodservice must look to making its available manpower more productive to keep prices down and yet to meet wage demands.

Making manpower more productive has been approached by some operators by purchasing more mechanical and automated equipment to do repetitious tasks. Others have traveled the route of convenience foods, where the factory applies the labor. A few have intensified training with good results. Some have worked at better worker motivation, incentive systems and work management and communications. However, few have followed the road of scientific kitchen arrangement based on principles similar to those used in laying out the modern factory. It can bring effective results in almost any kitchen.

Techniques for Gathering Man-Machine Relationship Data

In the factory, the industrial engineer seeks to arrange his machines so that those between which the greatest volume or weight of material travels are closest together. In foodservice, the weight of material moved between pieces of equipment or work stations is neither as important nor as expensive as the cost of the man having to make the movement. Thus in foodservice work study, it is probably better to follow the paths of the workers as they move about the kitchen than it is to follow the food. However, from the standpoint of food quality, it is desirable to have food move as little distance as possible from receiving to service, particularly after it is prepared.

To develop data on frequency of worker movement between pieces of equipment or work stations (for purposes of placing most-used combinations of equipment close together and in the most efficient arrangement), all of the workers using the area should be under study. In two or three days, a trained observer can watch the pattern of worker movement between pieces of equipment and between work stations or work centers and get a fairly good idea as to which are the most important relationships that should get prime consideration in placing equipment within the kitchen.

Another technique is to get three or four of the more observant and thoughtful kitchen workers—for example the kitchen supervisor, the first and second cooks and the salad supervisor—to put down their impressions as to the importance of the various work center and equipment relationships. By giving each of these opinions a numerical value and averaging them, a consensus can be obtained on, first, the work center and, second, the equipment relationships. (See Fig. 1 and 2 for work center relationships.) If the workers are observant and take the job seriously, fairly good data can be obtained.

The most definite data and the most expensive is obtained by trailing each worker through one to three representative days of kitchen work while recording his every movement between pieces of equipment and work stations. It saves time if one uses a code letter and number combination to record each piece of equipment rather than the descriptive words. (See Fig. 3.)

Cut Travel Costs of High-Pay Workers

Of course, it doesn't cost the same amount of money for each worker to travel a given distance. A $3,000 a year potwasher can take 100 steps for approximately half the cost of a $6,000 a year cook traveling the same distance. So, to put the travel of each into the proper importance perspective, the travel of the cooks should be multiplied by an importance factor of two. Usually, the lowest paid workers in the kitchen would be given a factor of one and, according to their salary rates, the importance factors of the other workers would go up proportionately.

Each worker's frequency of movement between each pair of equipment pieces multiplied by the distance in feet between the pieces, multiplied by the worker's importance factor, indicates the relative importance of the interaction to each individual. When these figures are totaled for all the workers and compared with other interaction pair totals, the relative importance to the business of each pair being close together is known.

Fig. 1—RELATIONSHIP CHART

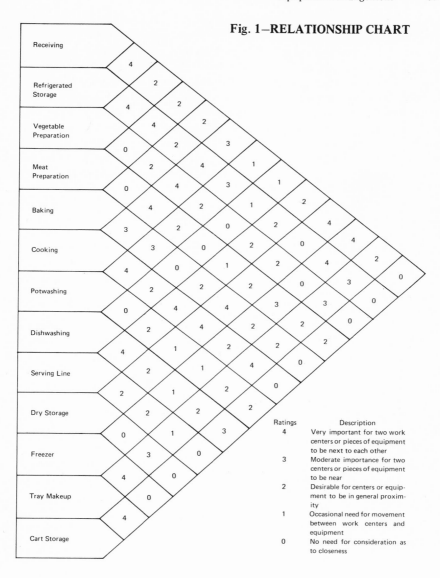

Ratings	Description
4	Very important for two work centers or pieces of equipment to be next to each other
3	Moderate importance for two centers or pieces of equipment to be near
2	Desirable for centers or equipment to be in general proximity
1	Occasional need for movement between work centers and equipment
0	No need for consideration as to closeness

Fig. 2—CONSENSUS RELATIONSHIP CHART

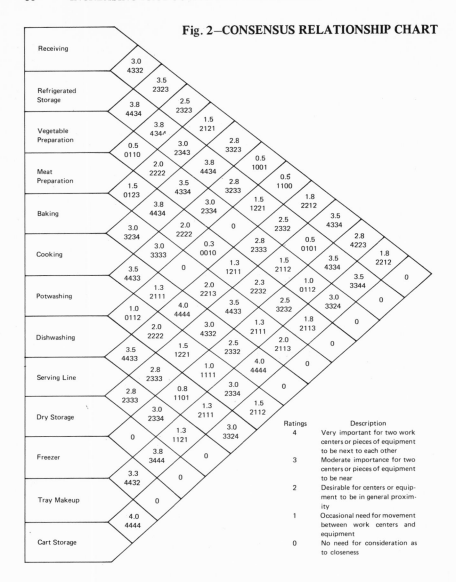

Ratings	Description
4	Very important for two work centers or pieces of equipment to be next to each other
3	Moderate importance for two centers or pieces of equipment to be near
2	Desirable for centers or equipment to be in general proximity
1	Occasional need for movement between work centers and equipment
0	No need for consideration as to closeness

Fig. 3—MAN-MACHINE INTERACTION STUDY FORM

Name Observer _A. C. A._   Date _9/26_   Time Start _5:00_

Name Observee _Cook A_   Time Stop _2:30_

                                                       Day No. Test _2_

Move to	*To Do*
T 2	Flour meat and arrange on pan
R 1	Take sheet pan of steak
Loc A	Get pan
HS 1	Wipe pan with towel
Griddle	Place pan
Pw	Take pots out so sheet pan can be washed
T 2	Take pans
DB 3	Throw cloth
T 1	Place utensil
Bench	Discuss beans being sorted
T 2	Wipe pans
Griddle	Place pans and grease
T 2	Flour steak and put on pan
R 1	Take prepared steak
Oven	Adjust controls, take pan
Griddle-Oven	Adjust racks in oven, place pan on range
Range	Grease sheet pan
Pw	Wash sheet pans
T 2	Wipe pans
Range	Grease pans
T 2	Place pan, four steaks, count
Pw	Wash hands
SR	Get small pan
T 2	Look at shipment, discuss, flour meat

For example, if Cook A with an importance factor of 3 (salary 3 times that of the potwasher) and Cook B (with an importance factor of 2) each took 100 10-ft. trips between the range and the can opener, and the potwasher (with an importance factor of 1) made 200 10-ft. trips between his sink and the can opener in the same period of time it would work out like this:

Range-Can Opener

Cook A   100 trips x 10 ft. x 3 importance factor = 3000 ft.
Cook B   100 trips x 10 ft. x 2 importance factor = 2000 ft.
                                    Total   5000 ft.

Sink-Can Opener

Potwasher   200 trips x 10 ft. x 1 importance factor = 2000 ft.

Thus, if the can opener is placed in the cook's area where they don't have to travel, and the potwasher now has to travel a maximum of 4000 ft., it would still mean a saving of the equivalent of 3000 ft. of travel overall. Whereas if the can opener were placed in the potwasher's sink area, it might mean an increase of the equivalent of 3000 ft. traveled.

Laying out or arranging the equipment of a kitchen from general observations and experience is the most commonly used technique. While it lacks objectivity and often overlooks important relationships, this method is better than designing on the basis of experience alone, as it has some operational basis.

In general, the designer or the owner decides where food will enter the kitchen and where it will leave to be served. He will join the two points with a line he calls the food flow line. This may be a long or short line, preferably the latter, and it may take many shapes—a straight line, a U shape, an L, an S or an oval—or it may split into several lines like a railroad switch yard. In most cases, the designer seeks to have each type of food move from receiving to service in a relatively uninterrupted line and with a minimum of back-and-forth movement or "back tracking." This sometimes becomes difficult, however, as the initial storage refrigerators are sometimes used for in-process materials as well. The designer has to determine if the worker time spent in back-tracking is less costly than having intermediate storage in the flow line.

A kitchen designer, foodservice consultant or food facilities consultant, as he is usually known, frequently first arranges the work centers in logical, production-based order along the food flow line, using the available space. Work centers are considered to be areas or groupings of equipment where one type of kitchen work is done or food is held. The usual order of work centers is:

Receiving—the area where food is accepted from the purveyor and is inspected and sorted. It is usually at an outside entrance or loading platform.

Storage—separate spaces where refrigerated and unrefrigerated foods and other supplies can be stored until needed. Storage for in-process or finished food is often known as "holding."

Preparation (sometimes called pre-preparation)—area where food is made ready for cooking. It frequently is composed of a vegetable preparation area, where salad preparation to varying degrees of completeness is carried out and vegetables are made ready for cooking, plus a meat preparation area where meats are cut up, trimmed and made cooking ready.

Holding—sometimes means a return of ready-to-cook foods to the same refrigerators from which they originally came but, where economically feasible, it means pass-through refrigerators between the preparation and cooking areas.

Cooking—area where most of the heat application takes place to make the food more easily consumed.

Bakery—may be part of the cooking area but in larger kitchens is a separate entity. While it is part of food flow, it doesn't have to be in the flow line as its product does not deteriorate rapidly and can be easily transported without damage. Unit is often placed to one side where it has ready access to both storage and potwashing areas.

Finished Holding—may be done in a large water-filled device called a bain marie but the modern method takes the form of hot and cold pass-through cabinets between the kitchen and the serving area. Cooking equipment, heated cabinets and refrigerators are used for this purpose also.

Service Area—the last link in the food flow line. It may take the form of a service station in the kitchen of a table service restaurant, a serving line in a cafeteria, a free flow serving center or even a rotating cafeteria line.

Dishwashing—while not in the food flow line, it is vital to the process to provide clean dinnerware when and where needed. In a table service restaurant, it is usual to locate dishwashing to the right of the point where the waiter enters the kitchen so that he can deposit his dishes before making up his order. In cafeterias, the dishroom is preferably close to the dining room exit. Or there is a conveyor at this location to carry the soiled dishes to the dishroom.

Potwashing—whether it be a mechanical potwasher or a compartmented sink for hand potwashing, the unit is located to one side of the food flow line where it can best support the work centers generating the greatest number of soiled pots, pans and utensils—generally the bakery, cooking and serving areas.

The outline above is actually an over-simplification of the way work centers are arranged along the food flow line. It seems to indicate that food flow is a straight line, and ideally it is if the main food flow line can be kept short.

However, the configuration of kitchen areas, obstructions and the locations of doors, windows, elevators and other equipment often alters what is ideal. Then the food flow line may become a zigzag, an L, a U or an S. The main things to remember are: Foods should, in general, progress in one direction; cross traffic should be held to a minimum, and work centers should be placed in logical locations close to the work centers with which they have the greatest interaction.

DETERMINING LOCATION OF WORK CENTERS AND EQUIPMENT

It was noted early in this chapter that there are 3 main techniques for determining the location of work centers and equipment within work centers— observation by a trained designer, consensus (opinions from a number of knowledgeable kitchen personnel) and a representative man-machine interaction study. The information presented to this point comes from the first two techniques and is what designers call experience-oriented. Some foodservice consultants have had so much designing experience that, given a certain number of persons to serve in a given serving period and by a given serving method, they can quickly whip up a standard kitchen layout to fit the space available.

However, kitchens designed this way are often wasteful of manpower as they do not take into consideration the real pattern of the workers' activities. To obtain this pattern, one must actually record the moves the worker makes between the pieces of equipment and work stations until a representative pattern indicates that for the average daily menu the workers move a certain number of times between each pair of pieces of equipment or work stations. By grouping the points into work centers, the movements between work centers can be ascertained.

What use does this information have? It can be used to determine relative location for both work centers and equipment within work centers. If there are a great number of interactions between the vegetable preparation area and cooking area, these two work centers should be placed close together in the kitchen plan. As one work center can be close to another anywhere in a circle (360 degrees) around it, there has to be another orientation, as well. This is orientation to the food flow line. If the cooking area is placed on the food flow line, then the vegetable preparation that usually occurs before cooking will be before it on the flow line but now will be oriented on the flow axis (see Fig. 4.)

If meat preparation has almost as many interactions with the cooking area as the vegetable preparation area and since it, too, immediately precedes cooking on the food flow line, it may be placed parallel to the vegetable pre-

Fig. 4—FOOD FLOW AND DISH FLOW IN KITCHEN OUTLINE

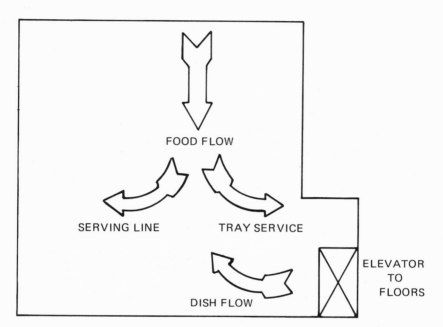

FOOD FLOW

SERVING LINE   TRAY SERVICE

DISH FLOW

ELEVATOR
TO
FLOORS

paration area. Potwashing may be used heavily both by vegetable preparation and by cooking. But instead of placing it in the food flow path, where it would only add to the distance the food would travel without acting to improve or change the food, it is placed to one side adjacent to the cooking area and the vegetable preparation area.

Plan Important Relationships First

To insure that the important relationships are given proper consideration, there is a simple technique for placing them in their best locations. First, the work center relationships are developed. Then the equipment arrangements within each work center are determined and adjusted for aisles, administrative decisions and space obstructional items. The procedure is as follows:

1. Taking the interaction data developed on pp. 58 and 60 (which is adjusted for the importance of the workers who are doing the interacting), the work center relationships are arranged in descending order of frequency of interaction. The top 10 to 20 percent are given "A" order of importance; the

next 10 to 20 percent are given "B" rating; the next 20 to 30 percent are given "C" rating, and the remainder "D" rating. ("D" rating relationships are often not considered in food facility planning.) The division points are usually made at natural break points or point separations and are not hard and fast. (See Table I.)

2. From the outline of the kitchen area to be laid out, sketch in the desired food flow line. It will extend, roughly, from the point where food enters the facility to the service area or areas.

3. Place the first "A" relationship in the form of circles on the line. These two circles are most often at the center, since the cooking area is usually part of the most important relationship, and it reacts with more work centers than any other. This pair is joined with four lines to denote their importance. The other relationships are similarly added, keeping in mind their usual order on the food flow line. The "B" importance relationships are then added. These are joined by three lines. Next are the "C" relationships, which are joined by two lines. Every effort should be made to avoid crossing "A" and "B" relationship lines and to minimize crossing "C" relationship lines. (See Fig. 5, p. 68.)

4. Calculate the area to be occupied by each work center. This is done by arranging scale templates of the equipment to go into each work center so they require the least space in the area arrangement. Scales of ¼-in. to the ft. or 1-in. to the ft. are best (scale means that 1/8, 1/4 or 1 in. on the paper equals 1 ft. in the kitchen).

In making these area determinations, be sure to allow aisle space—space equal to half an aisle where equipment is on one side of the aisle, and the whole aisle where equipment is on both sides. Arrangement is not too important, but including adequate table space is. (See Fig. 6, p. 69.)

5. These work center areas can be made into scale templates (shape doesn't matter at this point) and be substututed for the circles of Step 3.

6. The work center areas are then drawn into the available kitchen area in the relative positions as indicated in Steps 3 and 5. They may be altered in shape to fit but, if the work center size must be altered to include it all, equipment must be removed so that the work center is the necessary size. (See Fig. 7, p. 70.)

7. The procedure is repeated to arrange the equipment in each work center. When the equipment is being arranged, desired aisles must be kept in mind. Usually there should be one main aisle going through the kitchen and one secondary aisle. Neither should be on the main food flow line, as it is difficult for people to work in heavy traffic.

In designing by consensus as previously mentioned, all the important

TABLE I—BREAKDOWN OF INTERACTION TOTALS
INTO IMPORTANCE CATEGORIES

Work Center Pairs	Total Inter- actions	Importance Category
Tray service—production (cooking)	3533	A
Production—potwashing	1309	A
Tray service—refrigeration	1255	A
Tray service—tray cart storage	1068	A
Production—meat preparation	936	A
Production—refrigeration	854	A
BREAKPOINT		
Tray service—vegetable preparation	509	B
Meat preparation—potwashing	388	B
Dishwashing—tray service	386	B
Tray service—potwashing	381	B
BREAKPOINT		
Dishwashing—dumbwaiter and elevator	307	C
Meat preparation—refrigeration	301	C
Bakery—potwashing	292	C
Bakery—production	291	C
Production—dry storage (unrefrigerated)	280	C
Vegetable preparation—potwashing	239	C
Potwashing—dry storage (unrefrigerated)	222	C
Bakery—dry storage (unrefrigerated)	220	C
Vegetable preparation—refrigeration	199	C
Receiving—refrigeration	177	C
BREAKPOINT		

Fig. 5—WORK CENTER ACTIVITY-RELATIONSHIP DIAGRAM

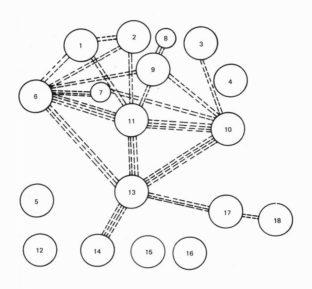

1. Storeroom	7. Meat Preparation	13. Tray Service
2. Bakery	8. Tray Service (Branch)	14. Tray Cart Storage
3. Receiving	9. Vegetable Preparation	15. Diet Kitchen Office
4. Freezer	10. Refrigeration	16. Storeroom (Branch)
5. Serving	11. Production (Cooking)	17. Dishwashing
6. Potwasher	12. Dietitian's Office	18. Dumbwaiter-Elevator

Fig. 6—DETERMINING WORK CENTER SIZE

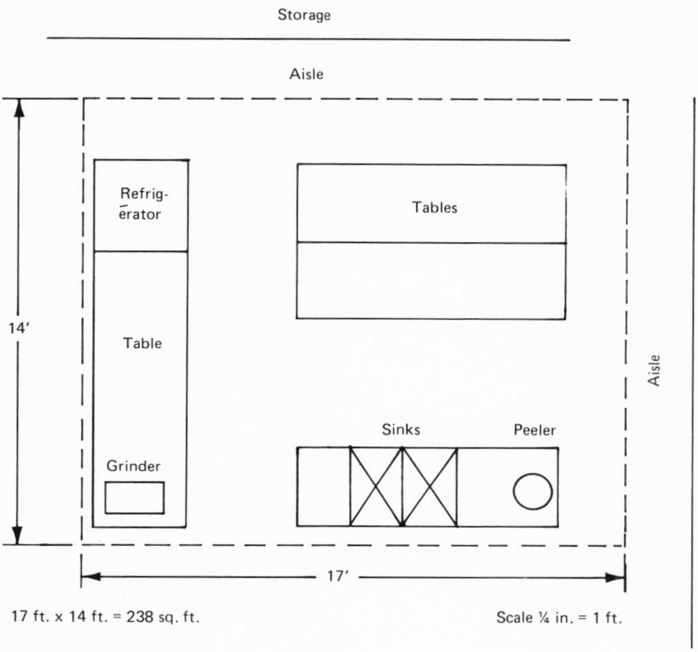

Storage

Aisle

Refrig-
erator

Tables

14′

Table

Aisle

Storage

Sinks   Peeler

Grinder

17′

17 ft. x 14 ft. = 238 sq. ft.   Scale ¼ in. = 1 ft.

relationships on which the raters are to determine relative importance are listed and then rated. These ratings are averaged and then listed in descending order of numerical averages in the same way frequency of interactions were listed in the procedure just discussed (See Table II, p. 71.) Then this list is broken down into importance categories and the remainder of the layout planning proceeds as in the procedure outline above.

Designing by use of interaction data requires 1 to 2 months to collect all the information, analyze it and develop the desired plan, but it comes close to providing the ultimate in kitchen efficiency. About the only way it can be improved is to study tasks of each worker and maximize the efficiency of doing them before making the interaction study . . . then incorporating the latest foodservice technology during the design phase.

With a little prior planning, designing by consensus can provide a kitchen layout plan in less than a day. However, it has the weakness that it is based on the memories and observations of the participants and is limited to their experiences. When the first atomic submarine was built, submarine commissary

Fig. 7–WORK CENTER AREA ACTIVITY-RELATIONSHIP DIAGRAM (ASSEMBLED)

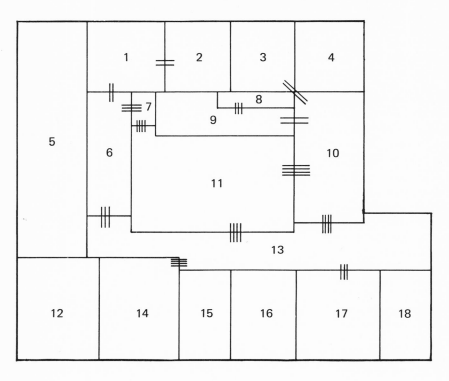

1. Storeroom
2. Bakery
3. Receiving
4. Freezer
5. Serving Line
6. Potwasher

7. Meat Preparation
8. Tray Service (Branch)
9. Vegetable Preparation
10. Refrigeration
11. Production (Cooking)
12. Dietitian's Office

13. Tray Service
14. Tray Cart Storage
15. Diet Kitchen Office
16. Storeroom (Branch)
17. Dishwashing
18. Dumbwaiter-Elevator

TABLE II–IMPORTANCE CATEGORY BREAKDOWN

Work Center Pairs	Consensus Rating	Category
Cooking and Serving Line	4	A
Cooking and Tray Makeup	4	A
Tray Makeup and Cart Storage	4	A
Refrigerator Storage and Vegetable Preparation	3.8	B
Refrigerator Storage and Meat Preparation	3.8	B
Refrigerator Storage and Cooking	3.8	B
Meat Preparation and Cooking	3.8	B
Dry Storage and Makeup	3.8	B
Dry Storage and Receiving	3.5	B
Refrigerated Storage and Freezer	3.5	B
Refrigerated Storage and Tray Makeup	3.5	B
Vegetable Preparation and Cooking	3.5	B
Dry Storage and Baking	3.5	B
Cooking and Potwashing	3.5	B
Serving Line and Dishwashing	3.5	B
Freezer and Tray Makeup	3.3	C
Refrigerated Storage and Receiving	3.0	C
Refrigerated Storage and Baking	3.0	C
Tray Makeup and Vegetable Preparation	3.0	C
Cooking and Baking	3.0	C
Baking and Potwashing	3.0	C
Dry Storage and Cooking	3.0	C

personnel were asked to plan the most modern and "way out" galley (kitchen) they could imagine. When completed, it looked much the same as all old submarine galleys, as this was the limit of the planners' experience. However, after the submarine galley was researched by using interaction studies, a most efficient and productive galley was developed. It was everything the submarine cook could desire.

The advantage of using the interaction data plus an optimizing step can be seen in a study made by the author on a hospital kitchen feeding 250 adults which was to be enlarged to feed 500. Each kitchen worker was studied for 6 days as he interacted with the kitchen equipment. There was a total of some 82,000 interactions and worker travel of some 114 miles.

After study of the interactions and application of optimizing techniques, the kitchen was enlarged to feed 500 people, yet the worker travel was decreased to 105 miles. An outside architect, using conventional design techniques, provided a plan that required 206 miles of travel to perform the same feeding operation.

Using the interaction data without the optimizing study would have produced a 500 meal kitchen that would have required 134 miles of travel to provide 6 days of meals. It was an improvement over the architect's plan but not as good as the interaction study plus optimizing.

Arrangement of Equipment within Work Centers

Much of the discussion concerning arrangement of work centers in the kitchen applies to the layout of equipment within work centers. In the work center, however, the food does not always flow in a straight line but follows a loop to one side or the other of the main food flow line. Ideally, work starts on the food as it enters the center and continues as it loops away and then back to the flow line. The last operation on the food may be at the point where it enters the next work center.

In some work centers, particularly those that are compact, the aisle of the work center may be parallel to the food flow line or even part of it unless it is the main traffic aisle of the kitchen. In this case, the work would flow down both sides of the aisle or, less desirably, zigzag back and forth.

In all of the above cases, the arrangement of the equipment within the work center would depend on the man-machine interaction data plus the flow of food within the work center. For example, in a meat cutting room one might plan to have a scale, two tables, garbage can, meat grinder, tenderizer, mechanical meat saw, sink and a pass-through refrigerator. The scale would probably be close to the entrance as it would be used first. Then there would be table no. A for initial work on the meat. If there were frequent interactions between the garbage can and table, the garbage can would be put beside, or under, the table. If the butcher frequently went to the sink to wash his knives, the sink might be put to one end of the table or, if frequent use were made of the meat saw in conjunction with the table, it might be placed at the end of table no. A.

If the meat used for tenderizing or grinding were normally taken to another table, then table B might be placed across the aisle from table A and the grinder and tenderizer placed on it—since the butcher has to have work space on both sides of each. The pass-through refrigerator would be at the exit of the work center to pass on the meat preparation center's finished products.

This example points up the pressing need to have tables where they are needed. Workers spend over 60% of their kitchen time at tables preparing food to use in equipment, but often these tables are not well located from the standpoint of worker efficiency, human engineering or supervision of cooking food.

The main reason for poor table placement has been the designer's (and often the owner's) desire to place only the cooking or heat and fume producing equipment under the ventilating hood in order to keep the hood at minimum size and cost. This has meant that the cook has had to face away from his cooking food at least 50% of the time, which can result in possible product failure. Also, the worker must necessarily travel back across an aisle to the table where he prepares his food for cooking and puts the cooked food when finished. Travel is excessive, and dripping in the aisle causes dangerous walking conditions.

In simplifying kitchen work, the cook is taught to arrange his preparation equipment so that he can proceed from left to right in the making-ready and cooking process. For example, in the cooking of veal cutlets, the cook would have, on a table to the left of the fryer and proceeding from left to right, the pan of cutlets, milk dip, draining colander and crumbs. Then would come the fry basket and the fryer and to the right of the fryer on a table would be the draining pan for the finished product. This confines all the drippage to tables, minimizes worker movement and allows the cook to watch his cooking product. (See Fig. 8, p. 74.)

The good designer spends a little more on immediate ventilating hood costs to save on future labor and product costs. He places tables beside the fryers, griddles, ranges, mixers and other similar cooking and labor-saving equipment. When the designer is reluctant to place tables beside steam-jacketed kettles, a substitute can be brackets that fit over the outside kettle edge to provide support for trays of ingredients and the serving pans into which the kettle contents may be dipped. Instead of 2 tables for each fryer, often 2 or 3

Fig. 8–VEAL CUTLET FRYING SETUP

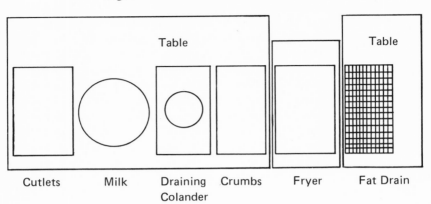

| Cutlets | Milk | Draining Colander | Crumbs | Fryer | Fat Drain |

fryers can be put together with one table on each side of the fryer bank. The tables can be made more valuable by placing 2-tier shelves over their backs to hold condiments, small pans, utensils and serving plates.

Some designers place a narrow cutting shelf in front of the griddles. While this is good for slicing sandwiches and small pieces of meat, it is not a good substitute for a table which will hold raw and cooked foods and various support utensils.

With front loading equipment like ovens, refrigerators, steamers and pressure cookers, the situation is different. To load from a table beside the equipment means that jerky back-and-forth movements are necessary, and if there is liquid in the pan, it may slosh on the worker and burn him. Thus, with front loading equipment, it is best to have a table close in front of the equipment for one-motion loading and unloading. It is less dangerous and the equipment is open for a shorter period of time. It is important that the aisles not be too wide. Ovens lose about one degree of temperature for each second they are open and it saves fuel and product to be able to close them quickly.

Table Working Heights Are Important

Some cooks bring portable tables or carts to place beside griddles, fryers, ranges and kettles as work spaces and in front of ovens, steamers, pressure cookers and refrigerators as landing places for pans of food. This narrows aisle space and presents obstacles to using adjacent equipment.

It is better to design tables with height-adjusting feet and, perhaps in many cases, to get them in 2 heights—one at 39 in. for women; one at 41 in. for men doing light hand work, and another at 36 in. for doing heavy work and working with table top equipment. People produce best when their work is just below elbow height.

Often forgotten in the design of kitchens is the location of working sinks and sources of water other than handwashing or potwashing sinks. There should be a sink and water source by the range to fill pots and provide a facility for draining pots. The mixer is often located remotely from a water source. Because of the frequency that water needs to be added to the mixer bowl, it should have its own water source or share an adjacent one. Oven, steamer, and pressure cooker pans often demand water and a ready supply should not be far from where it is needed. A sink should be available to drain pans in which foods have been cooked.

Right and Left Handed Storage

To keep expensive cooks from making frequent trips to the potwashing area with soiled pots and utensils, a few designers install soak and storage sinks at each point of major pot use. The low paid potwasher makes frequent trips to pick up the soiled accumulations from the sink and bring the clean ware back to the point of first use. By "point of first use" is meant the place where the clean pot, utensil or attachment is most often needed for use.

All too often a utensil rack will be placed near the potwasher and workers will come from all over the kitchen to get what they need. While even one trip is undesirable, many workers do not plan ahead and have to make many trips to the potrack in the preparation of a single recipe. To avoid this, some operators list all the equipment and materials needed for a given product on the recipe card, and the cook is encouraged to assemble all of his needs by use of a cart before starting work.

Most of the utensils and pans used in a given area should be stored in that area. Place utensils on shelves over the back of the work area with those used by the left hand being stored to the left and those used by the right hand stored on the right of the work area. For instance, a meat fork and hand grater may be on the left of the work area while spoons and knives should be on the right side.

Knives should be stored in a cleanable sheath to protect their sharp edges and the hands of groping workers. Pots and pans can be stored on shelves under the table top but not down as low as is commonly the rule. Sheet pans should be stored on a shelf not lower than 8 inches below the table top and the pot and roast pan shelf should be at knee height, or above.

Much time is wasted in chasing about the kitchen for inexpensive, frequently used items. The smart operator duplicates these items at each point of frequent use. Items that fall in this category are: salt, pepper, flour, sugar, scales, trash cans, can openers, sieves, steels and similar things.

Wheels are getting much more use than they once did. Workers are learning to consolidate loads and use a cart to carry them. Time and effort would be saved if the designer or operator would specify table-cart heights the same as those of the work tables so that heavy things can be slid, or rolled, from cart to table with a minimum of effort. Also, where the table cart is being used as a table, its height would be better for working.

Some mechanical equipment, which it is too expensive to duplicate, is needed in a number of locations in the kitchen. This calls for placing it on wheels so that it can be moved to the point where needed. If this is the case, care should be taken in specifying the cart style and height. It should be of a height that will bring the working surface just below elbow height. There should be support for the pan receiving the discharge of the device and a platform to hold the pan being used to load the device. If the equipment vibrates, it should have wheel locks or, as an even better solution, such equipment should have feet that drop down and raise the wheels off the floor.

Thought should be given to using conveyors wherever a considerable number of trips of the same general type and load are made. If there is a considerable frequency of travel, a conveyor can do the job more cheaply and in less time than a man can. Conveyors can be gravity or motorized; be supported on the floor, ceiling or wall, and be 1 way or 2 way. The top of the belt can bring food to a serving area, while the bottom of the belt can take the soiled dishes to the dishroom. More sophisticated conveyors can move both horizontally and vertically. Some can respond to a code on the load to unload it at a particular station.

The most frequent application of the conveyor in foodservice is to remove trays of soiled dishes from the dining room to some remote dishroom. A few industrial cafeterias have high stainless steel sides on the conveyor so that trays can be loaded 2 and 3 high in it. Thus it acts as a soiled dish storage; a small dishroom crew can be washing dishes far beyond the meal period. This is a boon for both industrial and school foodservice where the noon meal may be the only one but where it is desirable to give workers a reasonable day of work. This technique does have the limitation of somewhat higher-than-normal dish breakage; the use of strong plastic dishes can reduce this loss.

Reducing Size May Increase Efficiency

Reducing the size of the kitchen, in many cases, improves the productivity of the workers. The average kitchen worker spends 10% to 20% of his time in walking. At least half of this can be eliminated by proper planning of kitchen layout, thoughtful equipment selection and application of tested operational techniques.

In kitchen layout it has been stressed that those work centers and pieces of equipment between which there is the greatest amount of traffic should be located close together and arranged in the order of their most frequent inter-use while the food is proceeding from receiving to storage. Location of tables was emphasized as a travel reducer along with duplication of utensils, water, sinks and materials at most frequent points of use. Wheels and conveyors were advocated to reduce worker trips.

Aisle widths can be important, as well. In some military kitchens, aisles are as much as 14 ft. wide, while in some submarines they are but 18 to 24 in. wide. Both have disadvantages but the narrow aisles have one big advantage— the cook doesn't waste time walking. This has prompted some restaurants to make aisles 30 to 36 in. wide where the worker is the only one in the space and no one needs to travel behind him. Another 6 in. permits a worker to work on the other side of the aisle and 6 in. more permits passage of a man. A cart demands about 10 in. of room on each side of it for passage. These are minimum widths but an additional 6 in. more should be maximum. Aisles of these widths can be real man-savers.

EQUIPMENT SELECTION AND DESIGN FOR SAVING LABOR

The equipment selection and design can do much toward making the kitchen smaller and worker labor and travel less. Equipment that is unnecessarily large occupies space that has to be maintained, and it increases the clean-up load as well. When selecting this equipment, the operator or foodservice consultant often plans for the largest load that the operator can visualize even though it may occur only 2 or 3 times a year. This is wrong. One should plan equipment capacity to meet his daily needs and make other adjustments when 2 or 3 heavy loads a year occur. For these times he can plan for advanced preparation, buy foods with built-in preparation, lengthen the preparation or serving times or select a menu he *can* prepare in his equipment.

Equipment numbers can be reduced by using multi-purpose equipment, of which the fry pan or saute pan is a prime example. A properly selected fry-pan can substitute for a steam-jacketed kettle, a fryer, a griddle and, to a limited degree, an oven deck. In addition, it makes a fine egg poacher, storage for hot breads and a bainmarie. Thus, one of these of the proper capacity can replace at least three pieces of equipment retained for the heavy kettle, fryer or griddle meals, and do a number of other jobs besides.

The frypan has another attribute that one should look for in equipment. It will do two operations that follow each other and normally require that food be moved from one piece of equipment to another. For instance, it can brown off stew meat, swiss steaks or pot roast, have the fat drawn off and water added, and become a fast heating kettle. Or, one can blanch potatoes, drain off the water, add fat and have pan-fried potatoes without having to move them from one piece of equipment to another. Much time is spent in trasnferring food and, if it can be avoided, manpower is saved.

The more dependable the automatic controls one buys on his equipment, the more workers' time he saves and usually the less often product failure occurs. Automatic thermostats or temperature controls are well established for ovens, fryers, griddles and refrigerators. There are a few other locations where they are available and can be used to good advantage.

One of the most important of these is the steam-jacketed kettle where the rolling boil has been accepted as kettle temperature and the equipment is difficult to regulate for any other temperature except "off." The 185-degree simmer is easier on the texture of the food; saves leaching out many nutrients, and reduces the clouds of enervating steam that make kettle cooking onerous. It can be maintained by a simple control that senses the temperature of the kettle contents and regulates steam input to maintain the desired temperature of the product.

A similar device is available in range tops to sense the temperature in the center of the bottom of the pots and, consequently, the temperature of the kettle contents. Then electric current or gas is turned on or off to maintain a set temperature.

Versatility of Steam-Jacketed Kettles

Another labor and time saving function in some steam-jacketed kettles is cooling a product that has been kettle cooked without taking it to the refrigerator. The kettle can be built with a refrigerated coil around the exterior of the kettle liner, or existing kettles can be modified so that cold water can circulate in the steam jacket. This permits gelatin to harden, but its main advantage is to cool fatty meat sauces, stews and soups to where the fat rises and solidifies on the surface for easy skimming—to be followed then by reheating to the proper serving temperature. The refrigerated coil system facilitates making iced tea, iced coffee and flavored drinks without the possibly dangerous practice of using ice to cool them.

Steam-jacketed kettles often require that their seething contents be stirred with a wooden or metal paddle if the food is to cook evenly. This was always a hot, dangerous job. Now the motorized mixer-kettle stirs the contents of a steam-jacketed kettle to keep it heating evenly and, additionally, scrapes the sides of the kettle to improve heat transfer. These mixer-kettles come in all sizes.

In larger installations, another labor saver is the food pump that enables an operator to quickly fill numerous serving pans with the contents of steam-jacketed kettles. Today, pumps will pump everything from peanut butter to gravy, and they save much tiresome dipping and carrying.

To save themselves from constant surveillance and stirring of a kettle of spaghetti sauce being reduced in volume, a few cooks have learned to place it in a high-sided pan and set it in the 225°F.-controlled oven, where it bubbles away without any need of attention except to take it out when it is done. One should be sure the oven vent is open.

While somewhat sophisticated, a device that saves considerable time is the semi-automated water meter together with faucet opening solenoids. The cook punches buttons on the water meter to get the recipe-indicated gallonage. Then he flips a switch to open the faucet at the kettle he wants filled. Cooks will use this device when often they will not use a gallon measure, a marked rod or etched gallon-markings on the kettle interior. Couple this device with the steam-jacketed kettle temperature control and the cook can set the water meter and the temperature control to the desired temperature and go off to get the rest of his ingredients ready. When he returns, he has almost exactly the amount of water he needs at the temperature required.

Fryers take constant attention and considerable skill to ascertain when a frying product is properly cooked and then to remove it from the fryer. The advent of the fryer-basket lift-out device has made it possible to reduce tedious cook-waiting and frequent over cooking or under cooking. Many cooks fail to take full advantage of its features.

The experienced cook should determine the proper basket load by weight or volume. This means a load that will not drop the frying fat temperature below 300°F. and will recover the initial frying temperature by the completion of the frying cycle. The cook also determines the correct frying period for the load he has chosen and sets the mechanical timer. Then he can turn the job over to a less-skilled man, who needs only to know how to weigh or measure and to set the time for each cycle.

Controls Signal When Food Is Done

There are other fryer controls that seem almost human. One will fry a certain size of french-fried potato to a desired interior moisture level and then sound an alarm. A similar control cooks 2 to 24 fish squares to a predetermined internal temperature and then sounds an alarm. Both of these controls prevent product failure and permit an unskilled worker to do a good job of frying.

Determination of doneness of meats in oven roasting is not too difficult with the proper use of meat thermometers but their use does demand that the cook be in constant attendance. In most cases, it requires that the cook open the oven and draw out the pans of meat to read the thermometer. This means that the oven will drop approximately one degree in temperature for each second the oven is open. Some operators obviate the need for opening the oven by connecting the temperature-sensing meat probe to an exterior dial or fan thermometer by means of stainelss steel-covered wiring. However, the cook still has to be present.

Some operators have installed custom-made control systems where the meat thermometer is connected to an exterior-mounted control dial. The cook sets the control dial at the internal temperature which he wants the meat to reach. When the meat attains the set temperature, the thermometer pointer makes an electrical contact, shuts off the oven and sounds an alarm. The cook, who may be doing other work, then comes back to remove the cooked meat.

A further modification of this system has the automatic control allowing the oven temperature to drop to the internal temperature set for the meat and then maintaining it there—with or without moisture being added to the oven compartment to prevent moisture loss from the meat. With this control, the cook can remove the meat when he returns, or when he needs it, without the meat suffering loss of quality or yield.

PRINCIPLES OF EFFICIENT RECEIVING

In general, receiving is at the back door or at a street entrance to which trucks have ready access without blocking traffic. Large feeding operations have a dock at truck-body height, but most restaurants have the receiving floor just above street height. This necessitates handing down heavy boxes, crates, and bags weighing 100 lb. or more. To help with this situation, many places have skate-wheel or roller conveyors which lower the food and other materials from truck body to floor height. Large operations use lift-trucks for this purpose.

The average receiving work center will have a table for small packages so they do not have to be handled from floor height, and a stand-up desk where the people receiving can keep their records temporarily. There should be at least one platform scale and, if possible, a table-mounted scale for smaller items. Both should be direct reading with a minimum use of weights. Everything should be handled from receiving by truck, pallet or conveyor. The usual succession of equipment from truck toward storage is the unload conveyor, scale with desk beside it, table, trash can and cart.

Some operators have a vegetable sink and drainboards in the area to break down large deliveries of vegetables and meats into batch lots and remove all gross waste at receiving. As the product goes through preparation, it is handled in a cart which is similar to a supermarket cart but has 2 baskets. The lower shelves are left out of the walk-in refrigerators to accommodate these carts.

Storeroom Ideas and Arrangements

Proper design of the storerooms can do much toward reducing worker travel and making it more productive. Walk-in refrigerators should sit in or on the floor so that the floor level of the refrigerators is about 1 in. above floor level of the room. By use of a small ramp, carts can be wheeled in and out with ease. The ramp permits use of wheeled shelving that can be rolled to the receiving platform—to load foods as they are received—and then taken into the refrigerator for storage without further handling. Shelving on wheels also facilitates cleaning of the refrigerator interior.

In all storage, but particularly in walk-in refrigerators and non-refrigerated storage, many steps and much worker time can be saved by placing most-frequently used foods close to the door and on shelves between waist and eye height. It is also helpful to place most often-selected combinations of items close together. It is well to place large tags or identification plates where each product should go, not only to help the worker find the products but to show the storeroom clerk where the shelf refills should go. Most of the time the worker will go directly to the proper food location if it is located at the same place every time.

Another labor and utility saver is used where the walk-in refrigerator or freezer is close to a work center in which a reach-in refrigerator is desirable but not economically feasible. Outside-operating reach-in doors are placed in the walk-in refrigerator in position with interior shelving so that the refrigerator can be used as a reach-in for temporary storage of foodstuffs, and can also be used as storage for foods that will be drawn from stock throughout the day. Taking the day's ingredient list, the stockroom clerk enters the refrigerator or freezer and places the foods that will be used that day in front of the reach-in doors in the order they will be used. This saves constant and tiring opening of heavy walk-in refrigerator doors and the spilling out of large quantities of cold air.

It is imperative that reach-in refrigerators have adjustable shelves that can be regulated according to the height of the products they store. It is desirable, when most of the contents of one compartment will be moved at one time, to have all the shelving unitized and removable at one time to a cart. This allows prepared school lunch meals, and to some extent hospital meals handled as a bulk unit, to be moved to a reheat oven and then back to the cart again for transport to the serving area.

It is well to have reach-in refrigerator shelving that is below waist height as pull-out drawers or slide-out shelving so that the worker can see the contents without stooping low and moving the shelf contents.

Another small, but desirable idea to consider is to have refrigerator doors self-closing except when opened to the full-open position. This helps the worker with his hands full to deal with the door-closing situation. Sliding doors can be similarly self-closing. With walk-in refrigerators, the self-closing door feature is desirable. A door opener is similarly helpful. This may operate from breaking the beam of an electric eye or actuating a pressure plate or pushing a button. Most self-opening doors are sliding doors.

CENTRAL INGREDIENT ROOMS

Too little consideration is given to the use of central ingredient rooms. Without them, expensive cooks spend much time in walking to collect ingredients and performing the ingredient weighing and measuring operations. Weighing and measuring at the individual work stations require duplication of both the equipment to do the job and often the containers of spices used. The central ingredient room uses only one set of weighing and measuring equipment, uses spices before they lose their potency. Further, the salary of the person doing the job is much lower than the cook's. Better security is obtained if only one person is entering the storeroom.

The unrefrigerated storeroom used as a central ingredient room will have sets of scales—one to handle bulk packs in pounds and another to handle spices in hundredths of a pound or tenths of an ounce. Both should be mounted on a table 36 to 38 in. high with one or more shelves over its back for storage of partial containers of condiments and other foods. The table should be located next to the door. Under it should be stored bins of flour, sugar, salt, legumes and rice. The bins should have false bottoms in order to bring the contents close to waist height. Bins that go almost to the floor should not be used. The bins should be on wheels so that they can be pushed or pulled to that part of the storeroom where the refills are located.

At times, it saves on manpower to lose some of the storeroom security by dividing the storeroom between two locations. Non-refrigerated storerooms usually have two focal points. One supplies the bakery, cooking area, meat preparation area, vegetable and salad preparation area and possibly potwashing. The other supports the tray-making and serving line areas plus the dishwashing area. It is often good labor economics to have unrefrigerated storage for each of these major areas. In a similar way, it often saves to have refrigerated pass-throughs between the kitchen and service.

In the vegetable preparation area the vegetables are made ready for cooking. Many restaurants in high-cost labor areas now buy their vegetables ready to cook and their salad greens ready to portion.

VEGETABLE PREPARATION AREA

Those places that do peel their root vegetables use a left-to-right equipment setup. First comes a table or cart to hold the raw materials. Then comes the mechanical abrasion peeler, which opens onto a trimming table or sink. The table is better as it can be designed to hold the potatoes at approximately waist height to trim and cut them.

The trim receptacle should hang onto the side of the table; or it may be a can protruding from beneath the front edge of the table. Peels and trim should be drop delivered. From here, most operators use drop delivery to put the ready-to-cook vegetable in a colander or a steamer container sitting in an adjacent sink of cold water. Others use wheeled bins of water for this purpose. No sink bottom should be lower than 28 in. from the floor. If the vegetable has to be mechanically sliced, the slicing device should be on a low table so that it can be loaded at elbow height; the sliced vegetable will fall into a steamer or pressure cooker pan supported by the table under the device discharge. The device should have a tray to direct the food into the knives in bulk and not piece-by-piece.

Salad greens are washed and trimmed in double sinks—often the same ones used to trim the root vegetables. The same arrangement can do well. In a second sink, a colander or wire basket should be placed in the rinse water so that the greens do not have to be handled individually when they are lifted out. If the greens need to be machine cut, this device will come next in the order of equipment. If the cut greens come out of a discharge orifice or chute, a plastic bag should be tied over it to avoid rehandling the greens.

If individual salads are made up, tables should be provided to do this assembly-line fashion, with one worker carrying the ingredients and another worker using two hands to lay them on the plates. If individual salads are made to order, the salad maker should be established at a setup table with the ingredients arranged in a close semi-circle in front of him. (See Fig. 9, p. 84.) The most-used ingredients should be located close to center and the least used ingredients close to the extremities on each side. The ingredient holders should be placed so that their contents almost spill out and so they can be reached close to table height without going up and over a high pan edge. Workers should be trained to use both hands. Some operators find it best to place the ingredients in the order of use by both hands, proceeding from the front center to the sides.

Fig. 9–SALAD MAKING WORK AREA

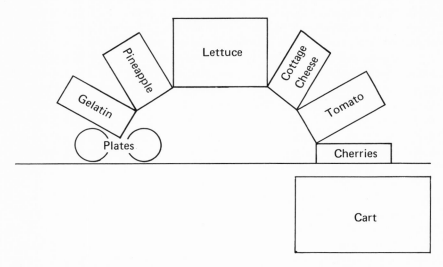

Individual salads can be handled on trays in a multishelved cart that can be wheeled into a refrigerated pass-through immediately behind the service area. Where possible, it is best to have the customer place the dressing on the salad or, failing this, have the service personnel do it immediately prior to service.

THE MEAT PREPARATION AREA

Although most meats today are delivered ready-to-cook, some operators like to cut their own meats and they pay a price for this service in space, equipment and the wages of a highly skilled butcher. This activity does not pay unless the butcher is so competent that he can get maximum usable yield from a carcass or primal cuts.

The meat preparation area should be set up as previously indicated, with the meat moving from left to right around the work loop. The scale should be close to table height at the entrance; the main cutting table should be next to it with a garbage can underneath. If this is the only table, the meat tenderizer and grinder, plus even a patty maker, may be on the table. The meat saw will be at the opposite end from the scale. If there is a second table, it should be across the aisle from the first. It should hold the table top devices and have work space on the sides of each piece of equipment. The pass-through refrigerator should be at the exit to the meat preparation area next to cooking.

COOKING AREA

Most of what has to be known about the cooking area has been noted in the general discussion on table and equipment *placement*. A point *not* mentioned was the placement of fryers, griddles and pressure cookers. These should be placed as close to the serving line as possible.

In some military and other installations (particularly fast food establishments), the griddles are placed in the serving lines with the fryers and pressure cooker immediately behind the line. This has several advantages. The first is that the cook can be in the service area assisting with this task. He can see those waiting to be served and load his cooking devices accordingly. Food quality is always at its highest and leftovers are minimal. Last, the cook is in a position to benefit from the remarks of his customers. The overall effect is to increase the value of demonstration cooking and both food costs and labor costs are decreased while food quality is increased.

The major disadvantage of the system is the need for a very efficient means of smoke and odor removal. The expense of this is more than offset by the advantages.

Some operators have the fryer, griddle and pressure cooker on wheels and have spaces where they may be used in the kitchen when desirable.

The main idea in good cooking center arrangement is to have the supplies of raw material, requisite condiments, utensils, pans, sinks and water, trash disposal, scales and slicers at the points where they are most needed and close to the equipment with which they have the greatest number of interactions.

DISHROOM LOCATION

The dishroom is often set up close to where the dishes enter the kitchens, although some operators use carts or conveyors to haul the dishes to a dishroom in the back of the establishment. As trays or boxes of dishes enter the dishroom, the silverware is placed in a silver soak-pan or sink, placed soiled end up in a cylinder or rack, or laid out flat in a rack. The glasses are often emptied and placed in tilted racks at chest or head height; cups and often bowls are similarly placed in racks designed for them.

As a rack is filled, it is pushed into the rack-type washing machine or placed on the pegs of a flight-type machine. The soiled plates are usually rinsed in a trough, plume or some other rinse and garbage grinder arrangement and are placed in a rack or between the pegs of the dishwasher. Some operators have one person clear the trays and dish (tote) boxes and stack the dishes, while another man loads the stacks into a rack or puts them into a flight-type machine.

The secret of a good dishroom arrangement is to have the tray clearing, pre-scraper and garbage disposer, racking facilities and machine loading so that they are in logical order. The worker should be able to use both hands with a minimum of stretching; actual loads should be light to carry and easy to slide. Having everything close to or slightly below elbow height is also desirable.

Dishrooms are notorious labor wasters. But because dishwashing personnel are low on the wage scale, the waste is often ignored. With a little prior planning of the dishroom layout and judicious use of conveyors, the dishroom staff can be cut in half and often reduced to one in all but peak-load situations.

Some do this with the carousel or merry-go-round continuous belt, rack-type dishwasher where either the waitresses put their own dishes in the racks, or 1 or 2 dishroom personnel do the job and another removes the clean dishes and stacks them in carts or dispensers. In slack times, one person can both load and unload. The problem with this arrangement is that it is difficult to get workers to wash their hands after loading the soiled dishes and before unloading the clean ones. A hand sink with foot-pedal operated faucets helps to encourage them to do so but, even so, constant supervision is needed.

Circle the Man with His Work

Larger flight-type machines can be operated by 1 to 3 persons if the soiled dish conveyor brings the dishes directly to the dishmachine operator and if he can clear the tray, pre-scrap and sort the flatware without moving and place the cups and glasses in inclined racks at shoulder height. He or his partner should be able to reach the pile of dishes and racks without traveling more than 1 or 2 steps and without stretching.

The secret is to group the work around the one doing it. One man should be able to unload if his dishcarts and dispensers can be brought up close to the end of the dishmachine. In slack times, one person can load the machine and then go down to the clean end and unload but, again, one has the question, "Has he washed his hands?" In some states, a wall must be erected between the soiled end and clean end of the dishwasher to prevent the dishmachine loader from running quickly to the clean end of the dishwasher to unload.

One of the problems with the rack type of machines is the return of the empty racks from the clean end to the loading end of the dishwasher. In one facility, the operator made 1900 trips in 6 days to get racks. The racks should not be carried, slid or thrown, but rather returned on their sides by an inclined roller conveyor. (An overhead carousel with hooks can be used instead.)

Another expedient is to use a side-loading and unloading narrow space rack-type machine. This can be done when the scrapping and loading table and the drying and unloading tables are parallel to each other and the ends of both cut across a wide soiled-tray belt conveyor with the soiled table being further from the conveyor load point. As the racks are unloaded, they can be placed on the conveyor to return to the soiled dish table for loading.

Another labor saver can be the sink used to soak the dishes and silverware that the dishwasher didn't get clean. If made portable, it can be stored under the clean dish table until loaded and then trundled over to the soiled dish table. It eliminates having to carry loads of dishes by hand from one table to the other.

If potwashing is done by hand, the main thought is to make it easier for the potwasher to do his job and reduce the number of times he handles each pot or utensil. There should be 3 sinks—a soak sink, a wash sink and a rinse sink. In the last 2, the tops of the sinks should be below elbow height and the bottoms no lower than the tip of the thumb when the arm hangs by the side. The top height of the soak sink is the same but the bottom can be 6 in. deeper than the other sinks. Workers should be cautioned not to throw hand utensils into it as they are too hard to find. As the potwasher, working from left to right, takes a pot from the soak sink, he washes it, rinses it and places it on a wheeled drain rack in one continuous operation. The rack is loaded from the top down and when loaded, is wheeled around the kitchen to place each work center's pots and utensils where they belong.

Summary

In summary, it is well to remember that the secret of designing kitchens for efficient manpower use encompasses:

(1) Grouping the tasks demanding skill around the workers having the skill.

(2) Placing the most-used combinations of equipment close together.

(3) Arranging them in the order of their most frequent interuse while proceeding along the food flow line from receiving to service.

(4) Insuring that men and women should do no work that machines can do more economically and efficiently.

(5) Consolidating loads and transporting them on wheels, whenever possible.

(6) Reducing fatigue-producing work and walking to a minimum.

All pictures illustrating this chapter on Task Planning were taken at the Ruth Richard Food Center, Rowland Unified School District, Rowland Heights, California. (Courtesy Southern California Gas Company).

3 Task Planning

Ruth D. Richard

TASK PLANNING and placement of equipment each has a tremendous effect on the productivity of employees within a foodservice facility. There is great evidence that in many foodservice operations far too little time has been given to these vital functions. A look at successful industrial operations, however, shows a different picture, for the majority of them have adopted a program of task analysis and work measurement. There has also been much emphasis placed upon industrial layouts and design of both equipment and facility.

Industrial operations differ widely from those in the foodservice industry in several distinct ways. One very important difference is that most of the products and services which this field offers cannot be "stockpiled." They are highly perishable and must be available upon the demand of the consumer.

Restaurants have peak periods each day when both service and product are in great demand, followed by intervals of little or no demand. Because of our work and social customs, the majority of people consume most of their food at three very clearly defined periods of the day. As the use of "convenience" foods, self service systems and more flexible work and school schedules increases, however, some of this rush hour pressure will be eased and a more even demand schedule will result.

Another factor establishing a difference between the foodservice industry and other industries is the variability of tasks which a single employee is involved in during his work period. Some employees in large operations may be involved with the same tasks for their entire work period, but for the most part foodservice employees will do many and varied tasks throughout each shift.

This should not be a deterrent to task planning and the establishment of efficient work procedures. The fact remains that while a worker may have many tasks to perform each day, these same tasks are ones that are likely to be repeated day after day, so there is a repetitive pattern to the work. As task analysis is employed and efficient work procedures established, management will discover that peak periods of demand will create far less havoc, and employees will be able to perform their duties without the tremendous physical and emotional pressures created formerly. At the same time, customers will appreciate the difference, not only in service but also in the atmosphere or climate of the establishment.

Progress Slow in Task Analysis and Measurement

Management in the foodservice industry has been reluctant to accept and apply task analysis and work measurement techniques. This may be partly due to the fact that in the past the availability of low cost labor made it unnecessary for the operator to be critically concerned about his labor cost and, consequently, he devoted the majority of his time to keeping *food* costs within the appropriate range.

Much emphasis has been placed upon food cost, and its control has been used as a criterion for judging the effectiveness of management. Productivity of foodservice employees normally tends to be high when volume of sales is high. During periods of high sales volume, then, labor productivity is high, and if food costs are controlled, profits should be good. So the need for concern over labor costs would tend to be less.

Another factor contributing to the absence of task planning in this field is the lack of understanding of the principles of motion economy and the benefits to be derived from their application. For many years foodservice employees have been placed in two classifications—those who were considered to be individually creative or talented and who developed their own systems, and those that were unskilled and provided merely another pair of hands to help with the work.

Define Tasks and Detail Steps

As the cost of wages and fringe benefits increases, however, management must find ways to develop work standards and methods of procedure to provide the necessary framework for all employees to work within to achieve maximum productivity. This indicates a great need for planning on the part of management, for it is management that must define the tasks to be done, develop written procedures, specify the equipment and provide for the areas in which the work will be accomplished. A thorough knowledge and understanding of motion economy and the application of the principles of motion economy are necessary as a background for this critical planning if optimum production is to be realized.

Still another factor contributing to the absence of task planning in food-service operations is the inability (or lack of concern) of those in management to define tasks and to detail the steps involved in performing those tasks. The majority of procedures are never put in writing; are never analyzed for effectiveness or efficiency, and are allowed to vary each time there is a change in personnel. Many times tasks that require the least amount of skill are never considered at all and chances are they are the ones that waste the most man-hours and in so doing increase labor costs appreciably.

Task planning is not an easy management function to perform in this field, because of the many variables affecting production. There are variables such as skill of workers, kinds of equipment, layout and design of facility and location, all affecting identical tasks in separate foodservice facilities. There are many variables, also, within an individual operation. Not only do workers vary in their skills, but food items, as grown, vary considerably and do not conform to standard specifications as do nuts and bolts produced by a machine. Seasons of the year greatly affect the kinds, quality and textures of some foods, altering the time necessary for handling and preparation.

Workers, as human beings, vary in their ability to perform work, and as they tire or are affected by personal problems they become less productive, thus creating a difference in the individual's rate of production throughout the day. The morale within the organization is a variable factor which can alter the results achieved from even the most effective system of task planning.

Controlling Labor Cost Is Challenge

Management must consider it a challenge to offset rising labor costs by seeking methods of reducing the number of employee hours needed to perform the tasks by increasing the productivity of those on the job. It is important that labor costs be given careful scrutiny and that satisfactory systems be developed to decrease or hold constant the percentage of dollar income being charged against labor. A knowledge of those factors which can determine labor cost is helpful. Ten specific methods of controlling the amount of labor needed are:

1. Limit menu items to those that require a minimum amount of labor.
2. Purchase fully processed foods that require no additional labor or require only that necessary to reconstitute the food.
3. Limit service to customers.

4.   Analyze work methods and establish effective work procedures for all tasks to be performed.
5.   Select labor saving equipment and schedule it for maximum use.
6.   Plan facility layout with efficient work centers and smooth production flow patterns.
7.   Set work standards and hire employees who are capable of meeting such standards. Compensate accordingly.
8.   Train and schedule all employees for efficient production.
9.   Limit number of employees to that necessary to perform the tasks.
10.   Supervise employees and guide them to maximum productivity.

In this chapter, we are concerned primarily with increasing productivity through task planning and proper placement of equipment.

Planning Is Prime Management Job

One of management's prime tasks is that of planning. Good *pre-planning* can spell success for a foodservice operation, while lack of it can cause failure.

The first step to take in planning is to establish objectives. In this instance, the overall objective is to increase productivity, thus lowering production and serving costs. As this is a very broad objective, it must be broken down into smaller objectives which, when reached, will all have a contributing effect towards accomplishing the main goal. Any one of the preceding 10 specific methods of controlling the amount of labor needed could become an objective.

Immediately after the objectives have been declared, a time line or time schedule should be developed. The success of planning is determined by the end result and far too often the desired result is never realized because a time schedule was either not made or was not adhered to. It is important to set a realistic time schedule which will be possible to maintain without undue pressure or opportunity for employees to lose interest or to lose sight of the objective.

Following the establishment of the time schedule, various methods of accomplishing the objectives should be analyzed and the proper ones selected. Workers should be selected to perform the necessary tasks, and a system of checks and evaluations should be decided upon. If the correct selections and decisions have been made throughout the procedure, it is most likely that objectives will be achieved.

Foodservice operators have achieved great success by following the first of the ten methods for controlling the amount of labor needed by merely limiting menu items to those that require a minimum amount of labor. It is generally found that in such operations the number of menu items is also limited to a minimal number.

Reckon Preparation Savings in Advance

Other operators have been successful by purchasing fully processed foods that require no additional labor or a very minimal amount of labor. Before deciding which menu items to purchase fully prepared, tests should be run to determine which products or dishes are of the quality desired and what the savings in labor will be. The one important factor here, if the primary reason for the purchase is to reduce labor costs, is to be certain that the product can be purchased at less total cost than the cost of producing it yourself. There are other advantages also for purchasing ready prepared foods, but they will not be discussed here.

There are various ways of limiting service to the patron as a means of controlling labor costs also, as is evidenced in the use of cafeteria and buffet service. Once the menu has been established, the decision made as to which foods will be prepared on location and what type of service will be performed, it is time to think of task planning and selection and placement of equipment. Following are the steps in the task planning process.

STEPS IN TASK PLANNING

1. Select the task to be planned; identify and describe it.
2. Determine the factors that affect the task.
   a. Raw materials—storage, accessibility, handling
   b. Process to be used
   c. Finished product desired
   d. Quantity to be produced
   e. Work area—tools and utensils
   f. Equipment necessary
   g. Employees needed—number and skill
   h. Location in relation to section and total layout
   i. Timing—amount of time, timing in relation to other products and service.
3. Establish the procedure—apply principles of motion economy as related to the use of the body.
4. Set up the work area.
   Apply the principles of motion economy—as related to the employee and the arrangement of the work place.
5. Evaluate the procedure, challenge it.
6. Establish revised procedure and test.

7.   Establish work performance criteria and standards.
8.   Supervise until steps in procedure become a habit.
9.   Check periodically to see if procedure is being followed and if there is a better way.

Select the Task

The most important and, frequently, the most difficult step in task planning is to identify and describe the task to be planned. For the person who is planning task procedures for the first time, it is wise to select a relatively simple task such as buttering bread; making sandwiches; breading meat, fish and poultry; assembling salads, or pre-dishing desserts.

When selecting a very complex task, it may be desirable to break it down into components and to develop a task procedure for each component. Whatever the task, a knowledge of the principles of motion economy and their application is of great significance if maximum productivity is to be the end result. If simple tasks are selected for planning initially, skill in applying the principles of motion economy can be developed.

The preceding tasks require few and simple procedures, as well as simple work areas. Simple application of these principles is given later in this chapter. No costly tools or equipment are needed in accomplishing the task of buttering bread if the quantity desired is not above 5000 to 6000 slices. This does not necessarily imply that when producing extremely large quantities of product, the task could not require considerable capital outlay for automated equipment. For example, the bread buttering task could be set up with a bread slicer, stacker and feeder, a buttering machine, a conveyor belt and an automated wrapper if the quantity and system warranted them. This would be a decision for management to make.

From Simple to Complex

After skill in task planning has been developed, more complicated and time-consuming projects should be undertaken. Select especially those tasks which cause bottlenecks in production or produce frustration for employees. Production and serving of a complete menu or of a menu item will only be as efficient or time-consuming as the slowest step of the process. Suppose, for example, a procedure that appears to be good has been written up and put into practice. After a shakedown it is found that one step is very time-consuming and is holding up the following steps. The total procedure is then ineffective.

All too frequently one slow process will be causing a bottleneck, affecting the productivity of workers, not only in that section but in others as well.

At times it may be difficult to detect where the trouble spots are if productivity is low for the entire operation. After gaining confidence by establishing simple task procedures in the beginning, it is then wise to select a task that is causing a bottleneck. In so doing, the results will usually be very rewarding, and employees will respond favorably upon viewing the obviously good results.

As inefficient task procedures are replaced with efficient ones, employee frustration will be reduced and work will be easier and less tiring. Productivity will be increased and labor costs per unit will be lowered.

It is of great importance to properly identify and describe the task selected for planning. Too often several tasks combined appear as one, and an attempt to set up procedures is difficult because of the complexity of work areas and actions involved. Tasks must be broken down into their simplest form before effective procedures can be established. Once fundamental procedures have been established for each task, it is often possible to simplify, combine or eliminate some steps or even entire procedures for more effective production.

Determine Factors That Affect the Task

Consideration must be given to the various factors which affect the performance of a task. In some instances it may be difficult to determine all such factors until a work system or procedure has been established and tested.

One factor influencing the performance of all food production tasks is the accessibility and storage of raw materials. It is important that all raw materials be readily accessible to the work area. All materials that are used daily should be stored close to the point of use and a system established that provides ease in handling or no handling at all—as is provided where water is piped to a spigot directly above a kettle or mixer.

Materials handling often accounts for the largest portion of labor costs related to production, as well as handling costs related to service. Handling of materials—which includes transporting and storage—does not add value to the product and should be kept to a minimum. A great portion of the majority of foodservice workers' time can be spent in materials handling if extreme care has not been taken in design of the facility to properly locate and arrange storage areas in conjunction with work areas and equipment. Production areas must be planned with serving areas also in mind to minimize handling of finished prepared product.

Labor costs are greatly affected by layout and often are initially determined on the drawing board. Therefore, it is of utmost importance that the proper steps be taken in the planning procedure and basic decisions be made before the layout is drawn. There will always be compromises that must be made in determining the layout, but if these are based upon the principles of motion economy, materials handling and good planning procedures, it will be possible to keep labor costs to a minimum and worker productivity high.

The Axiom of Materials Handling

The basic principle of materials handling is to move all foods, materials and supplies as little as possible, keeping distance traveled to a bare minimum. Materials should move through the facility in the shortest direct route possible and with little or no lateral or reverse direction. When size of facility warrants the use of mechanized materials handling equipment or when materials such as soiled dishes follow a fixed route repetitively, mechanized conveyors or lifts should be used. Machines, equipment, cabinets and like objects which are frequently moved from one section to another or from storage to in-use positions should be provided with wheels. All wheels should be of the proper size and construction to carry the weight and height of the maximum load they will carry.

Wherever possible, materials should be stored at the point of first use, and provisions should be made for easy and direct removal of scrap and trash. Tote boxes and other containers should be selected for easy handling, as well as sized properly for the job they will do. Ample aisle space should be allowed for whatever vehicle movement and traffic will be produced as materials are handled.

Factors that Affect Tasks

Another factor that affects the task is the determination of the process to be used in performing the task. The extent of the use of ready prepared or partially prepared food items greatly influences the type of process selected. The process defines the steps to be taken in producing the food so, therefore, it must be selected in the early stage of planning. This is not to say that the process may not be changed at a later date; should it be, the task procedure would also change. Menu items need to be listed one by one and the proposed method of processing determined for each. The type of organization and the size and layout of the facility will determine what processing methods will be used.

The finished product desired helps determine the process to be used and affects the task as well. Some food preparation tasks may be carried to completion in one work area, whereas others may not. The less a food item is delayed or transferred in the preparation process, the more efficient can be its production.

The quantity of a given menu item to be prepared is also a determining factor affecting task planning. The preparation procedure and even the process can be directly influenced by the quantity to be produced. It is conceivable to change from a total hand preparation process to a totally automated process as the quantity needs change or as food production becomes centralized.

Work areas should be arranged to allow space for the tools and utensils that will be needed to perform the task. If it is impossible to store them in the work area, mobile carts, dollies or cabinets should be provided for ease in assembling and conveying tools or utensils to the area or work center. Tasks requiring the use of the same tools or utensils should be assigned to the same area if the time schedule permits. Selecting the right location for a work area is extremely important also in increasing productivity of workers.

Another factor that affects task planning is the equipment available to perform the task. Many times limited funds, limited floor space or lack of adequate electrical power make it necessary to develop a task procedure which is somewhat less than efficient. It is important, however, to develop the system that will be the most productive within the limitations present.

Timers and automatic controls should be included on equipment wherever the budget will allow and when the expenditure is justifiable to increase worker productivity. Special equipment should be designed and fabricated whenever there is nothing available to serve the purpose for optimum efficiency and minimal use of labor. Equipment should be scheduled for maximum use and should be located for easy and safe operation. Provisions should be made for flexible use of equipment in performing more than one task.

How Many Persons? . . . Least Possible Number

The number of employees needed to perform a task greatly influences the task and the cost of performing the task. All tasks should be performed with the least number of employees necessary. Employees should be assigned according to their skills and the skills the task requires. If a foodservice worker with no specially developed skill can perform a task, don't assign a cook, a baker or other highly skilled employee to do it, unless it would be more economical to use a highly skilled person (as in a small operation) or unless the use of that person would avoid the need to hire an additional employee.

To maintain maximum productivity, select the proper location for each work area or work center within the total facility layout, as well as within the special section to which it is attached. The layout should provide for easy flow of raw materials from receiving, through storage, into preparation, through production and out into serving or shipping. The layout has a tremendous effect on task planning and the level of productivity achieved in a foodservice facility.

A factor that has been determined as affecting task planning is that of timing. Both the amount of time it takes to perform the task and the time at which production is scheduled in relation to other products and service must be considered. It may, at times, be necessary to delay the performance of a task or a portion of the task, while at other times it may be necessary to schedule the task far in advance of product need. An alternative is to produce menu items simultaneously in different work areas.

Establish Procedures

A large percentage of work done by foodservice employees is the handling of foods, tools and utensils. With the exception of a small amount of work done by equipment, the remainder is hand work. It is this hand work that consumes time and, therefore, every effort should be made to shorten the length of time needed to perform all tasks, thus increasing a worker's productivity per labor hour. The large amount of hand work required, and the fact that it has been considered to be individual in nature, has contributed to the slow acceptance of motion and time study principles by the industry.

Cost analysis should determine when labor saving equipment or pre-processed foods should be purchased to reduce hand labor. When it becomes economically sound to purchase a piece of equipment as a means of increasing worker productivity or eliminating work functions, this should be done. If ready-prepared foods are purchased to decrease labor costs, management must see that labor hours are reduced proportionately or that sales are increased sufficiently to provide the desired savings.

The basis for establishing defined procedures for all tasks performed in a foodservice operation is to increase workers' productivity by providing efficient work methods as opposed to allowing each employee to establish his own methods. Before attempting to work out methods and procedures, however, a thorough knowledge and understanding of the principles of motion economy should be acquired. Based upon the work done by Frank R. and Lillian Gilbreth as early as 1923, it was established that there are certain basic principles of motion economy and arrangement of equipment and work area that create increased worker productivity, while at the same time reducing employee fatigue. (See p. 4.) It is the observance of these principles in the task planning process that should conserve employee time and lower labor costs. Proper application of these principles has been found to increase worker productivity as much as 50% to 100% or more!

PRINCIPLES OF MOTION ECONOMY*

Use of the Human Body

1. The two hands should begin as well as complete their motions at the same time.
2. The two hands should not be idle at the same time except during rest periods.
3. Motions of the arms should be made in opposite and symmetrical directions, and should be made simultaneously.
4. Hand and body motions should be confined to the lowest classification with which it is possible to perform the work satisfactorily.
5. Momentum should be employed to assist the worker wherever possible, and it should be reduced to a minimum if it must be overcome by muscular effort.
6. Smooth continuous curved motions of the hands are preferable to straight-line motions involving sudden and sharp changes in directions.
7. Ballistic movements are faster, easier, and more accurate than restricted (fixation) or "controlled" movements.
8. Work should be arranged to permit easy and natural rhythm wherever possible.
9. Eye fixations should be as few and as close together as possible.

Arrangement of the Work Place

10. There should be a definite and fixed place for all tools and materials.
11. Tools, materials and controls should be located close to the point of use.
12. Gravity feed bins and containers should be used to deliver material close to the point of use.
13. Drop deliveries should be used wherever possible.
14. Materials and tools should be located to permit the best sequence of motions.
15. Provisions should be made for adequate conditions for seeing. Good illumination is the first requirement for satisfactory visual perception.
16. The height of the work place and the chair should preferably be arranged so that alternate sitting and standing at work are easily possible.
17. A chair of the type and height to permit good posture should be provided for every worker.

---

*Ralph M. Barnes, M. E., Ph. D., MOTION AND TIME STUDY, Design and Measurement of Work, Copyright © 1958. By permission of John Wiley and Sons, Inc.

The preceding principles of motion economy as related to the use of the human body are concerned primarily with hand and arm motions. They also are based upon the comfort of the worker while performing the task. The motions of both hands in opposite and symmetrical directions made simultaneously establish a natural rhythm for the worker. Employees should be instructed in the application of these hand and arm movements in such a manner that they will accept them.

Employees Will Help Planning

The planning of all work procedures should be done, if possible, with the cooperation and assistance of the employees who are closest to the work. Their suggestions should be listened to, evaluated and incorporated whenever possible. Productivity will be highest in those operations where employees take an active part in the planning and become involved and interested in maintaining or improving work measurement standards.

On the following pages are examples of work procedures based upon the principles of motion economy as related to the use of the human body, as well as to the work place. The procedures were developed by foodservice employees. They are simple, requiring no special equipment and having many applications for every type of foodservice operation where food is prepared.

A diagram of work area for pre-dishing salads or desserts into portion cups is shown in Fig. 10. A diagram of the work area for preparing filled sandwiches with lettuce is shown in Fig. 11, p. 102. Fig. 12, p. 103 gives a diagram, and work procedure for breading fish, meat or poultry. A suggested diagram of work area for assembling individual salads is given in Fig. 13, p. 104.

WORK AREA OR WORK CENTER

The design of work areas or work centers has a great effect on the efficiency of an operation. Work areas must be designed so the worker can comfortably reach the materials and utensils he needs to accomplish the work. The maximum length of a work center should be 6 ft. and the minimum width should be 8½ to 9 ft. A single work center may comprise an entire section in a small operation and many tasks may be performed within it. As the size and complexity of the operation increases, however, work centers will become more specialized and will grow in number.

As the volume of food increases, it may be necessary to establish more than one work center to accomplish a specified task or it may be necessary to divide the functions being performed by one worker and assign additional workers to the task. Each worker might perform a portion of the task rather than carrying through the total function.

Fig. 10–DIAGRAM OF WORK AREA FOR PRE-DISHING SALADS OR DESSERTS INTO PORTION CUPS

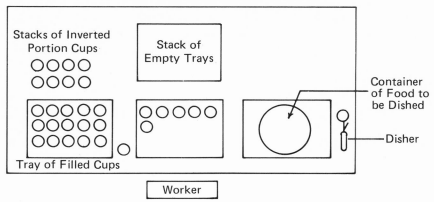

Set-up:

1. Place stack of empty trays at center back of table.

2. Lift top four trays and place directly in front of worker.

3. Place ice cream disher and container of food to be dished at right of worker.

4. Place the required number of portion cups in inverted stacks to the left of empty trays.

5. Bring one stack of inverted cups and place at left of small stack of trays, directly in front of worker.

Procedure:

1. With left hand pick up paper cup and turn right side up.

2. At the same time, with the right hand, scoop one serving of dessert into an ice cream disher of the correct size.

3. Bring filled disher over portion cup, invert and depress lever on disher with thumb of right hand to deposit food in cup.

4. With left hand place filled portion cup on tray beginning at top left corner, and as the left hand returns, pick up another portion cup. At the same time, with right hand, dip the disher into the pan to be filled for the next serving.

5. Work toward right and continue to work in this direction. Continue procedure until one tray is filled.

6. Take the filled tray from the stack and place on table. If filled trays are to be stacked, cover with sheet of precut wax paper. Place filled trays in mobile rack if filling a large number.

Fig. 11–DIAGRAM OF WORK AREA FOR PREPARING FILLED SANDWICHES WITH LETTUCE

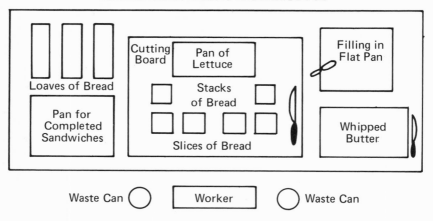

Set-up:

1. Arrange work area as shown in diagram.

2. Whipped butter is placed in a flat shallow pan. The butter must be of proper spreading consistency. A 6-in. spatula is used for spreading butter.

3. Place a *measured* amount of sandwich filling in flat pan, so that you know how many sandwiches should be spread from that quantity. This will be a guide to portion mixture accurately. Use a 3½-in. sandwich spreader.

4. Have lettuce washed, drained, and torn into pieces of the approximate size, or use shredded lettuce.

Procedure:

1. Unwrap bread by cutting paper across at center of loaf. Pick up a half loaf in each hand and place each with cut end down on bread board. Lift off wrapper and discard in the same motion.

2. Lift top two slices from each stack using both hands, place on board in front of stacks of bread, inverting top slice of each pair toward center.

3. Grasp spatula and draw the edge across butter evenly to accumulate enough butter for *four* slices of bread.

4. Spread the butter with one smooth motion for each slice.

5. Pick up enough sandwich filling on spreader for one sandwich.

6. Spread onto inside slice of one sandwich. Repeat for inside slice of second sandwich.

7. Bring forward two pieces of lettuce and place on filling on both sandwiches, using both hands at the same time.

8. Invert outside slices onto lettuce.

9. Using the bread knife, lift sandwich on the right onto the other and cut diagonally. Slide knife under stack of sandwiches, lift and deposit in pan.

Fig. 12–DIAGRAM OF WORK AREA FOR BREADING FISH, MEAT OR POULTRY

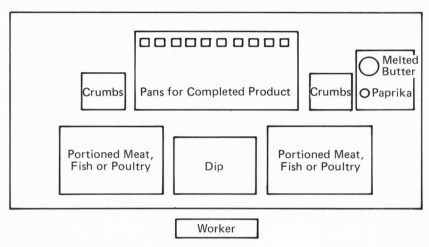

Arrangement of Work Area:

1. Place boxed frozen fish on trays in refrigerator overnight.

2. In morning, transfer trays of fish from refrigerator to work area. Use cart to transport large quantities of fish. Partially thawed fish is easier to handle than completely thawed fish.

3. Arrange work areas as shown in diagram. Dip-mixture will depend on desired product; may be milk; milk and egg; buttermilk; oil and lemon juice, etc.

Breading the Fish, Meat or Poultry:

1. Grease top pan of stack from shallow container of melted butter with a paper towel in each hand, using circular motions.

2. Grasp one portion of fish in each hand from pan directly in front of hand.

3. Dip into pan of dip-mixture with hands simultaneously.

4. Roll product in crumb seasoning mix, using both hands simultaneously.

5. Bring product to baking pan, filling pan from top center of pan to outer edge, completing the top row across pan.

6. Continue filling pan, starting at center and filling across to complete rows, using both hands simultaneously.

7. Sprinkle with paprika or other desired seasoning.

8. As pans are filled, place in rack to transport to oven.

Fig. 13–DIAGRAM OF WORK AREA FOR ASSEMBLING INDIVIDUAL SALADS

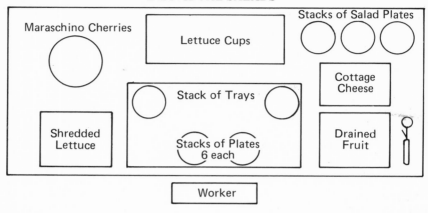

Set-up:

    1. Arrange work area as shown in diagram.
    2. Large bun pans will hold 12 6½-in. salad plates.
    3. Place on the stacked trays two sets of 6 salad plates.

Procedure:

    1. Using both hands at the same time, bring forward two lettuce cups and place them on the top plates of stacks on tray.
    2. With left hand pick up a small amount of shredded lettuce and bring to plate at the left while the right hand picks up a slice of pineapple, peach, or pear half.
    3. Place shredded lettuce in the lettuce cup, then put the piece of fruit on the shredded lettuce.
    4. Repeat Step 2 and Step 3 for plate on the right.
    5. With the right hand, fill scoop with cottage cheese, as the left hand reaches for a cherry.
    6. Bring the cottage cheese to the plate and place in center of fruit on the salad on the left. Place cherry on cottage cheese.
    7. Repeat Step 5 and Step 6 for plate on right.
    8. Lift completed salads from stacks of plates and place them at the far outside corner of the tray.
    9. Make the next two salads in the same way and place them in center space of back row.
    10. Continue until 12 salads are made. The last two plates will be in position.
    11. Remove tray from the stack and place in rack for refrigeration.
    12. Bring forward two more stacks of six plates from the stacks on the right and place on top tray. This procedure may be used whenever individual salads are to be made. Salad components should always be arranged in best sequence for assembling.

The work area should be designed for the worker to stand, with provisions made for sitting also. When a worker can alternate between standing and sitting positions, he is able to remain in the work area for longer periods of ·time without becoming fatigued. The height of the stool must be adjusted for the worker to the height of the work area and should be of the type that has adjustable height, back and foot rest. Different tasks require different height work surfaces and can vary from waist height to 3 to 4 in. below the elbow, depending on the nature of the work. Heavy work is most efficiently done at the lower level, while light hand work, using paring knife for example, would be done at the upper level.

Apply Motion Economy Principles

Work centers should be planned by applying the principles of motion economy, not only as they relate to the use of the human body, but also as they relate to the work place. After the correct height of the work surface has been determined, the normal and maximum work areas should be established. This is done by having the worker stand up to the edge of the counter in a working position. Keeping his arms against his sides down to the elbow and bending his right arm so that the lower arm is across his body parallel to the work surface, he makes a sweeping arc out over the table until his hand has made an 180 degree curve. This curve represents the boundary of his normal work area. (See Fig. 14.) He repeats, using the left arm. Where the two curves overlap, a smaller area is defined which is the best area for performing two-handed tasks.

If the worker swings his arms out from the shoulder in the same manner, the arcs define the maximum work area. (See Fig. 15, p. 106.) Most work should be performed within the normal work area with only occasional reaches into the maximum work area. For the most productive work the worker

Fig. 14—NORMAL WORK AREA

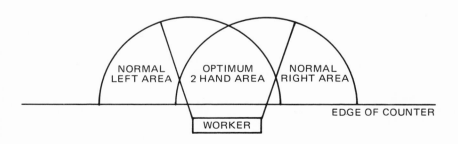

Fig. 15–MAXIMUM WORK AREA

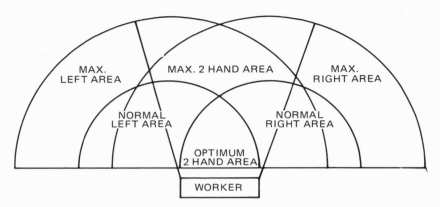

should not have to reach beyond his maximum work area nor should he have to travel back and forth.

To achieve the best work area, it is often necessary to move in mobile equipment and this should also be done whenever the number or supply of food items or utensils will not fit within the maximum work area on the work table. (See Fig. 16, p. 107.) It should also be kept in mind that these same areas are present in the vertical plane as well as the horizontal plane, a fact that equipment fabricators and designers do not often apply. (See Fig. 17, p. 108.)

Work areas should be designed to accommodate more than one task, if possible. Fig. 18, p. 109 shows a single work station which can accommodate many different tasks and could be used continually throughout the production and serving period as other pieces of mobile equipment are placed adjacent to the work counter. When mobile equipment is used in the serving line, it is possible to change the serving layout as the menu changes, thus creating efficient work areas for each serving period.

Good light and a pleasing climate are also necessary for good production and worker satisfaction. Well designed work centers promote good work and create good morale, while poorly designed areas produce inefficiency, fatigue and a negative attitude.

Evaluate, Challenge and Improve

Once the procedure has been determined, the work area established and a shakedown period has elapsed, it is time to make an evaluation. Be certain that workers assigned to perform the tasks have followed the steps that had been set up during the planning period. Alternate methods or arrangements

Fig. 16—SALAD ASSEMBLY

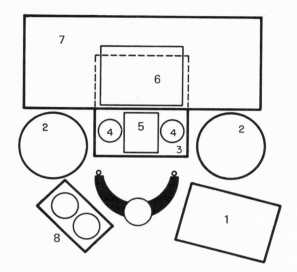

1. Mobile Rack
2. Salad Bowl w/Dolly
3. Pull-out Board
4. Bowls
5. Pan
6. 18- by 26-in. Pan
7. Table
8. Mobile Self-Leveling
   Dish Dispenser

Table (7) has been designed with an extension board (3) that pulls out and locks into place at the same level as the top of the table, making a continuous work surface. Salad bowls (2) with mobile stands are rolled up at each end of the pull-out board and well within the maximum work area. Salad bowls (4) or plates are stored in mobile self-leveling dish dispenser (8). The dispenser is placed in a convenient place for easy reach when all bowls on the table have been filled and placed on tray (6). Pan (5) is used to hold whatever garnish is used on salad.

When a tray has been filled, it is picked up and placed in mobile rack (1). When rack is filled, it can be moved to serving area or into walk-in refrigerator for storage. If kitchen does not have walk-in refrigeration space, roll-in refrigerators can be purchased and located convenient to work centers and serving area.

Fig. 17—HAMBURGER AND SANDWICH MAKING

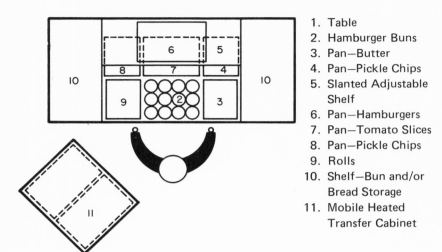

1. Table
2. Hamburger Buns
3. Pan—Butter
4. Pan—Pickle Chips
5. Slanted Adjustable Shelf
6. Pan—Hamburgers
7. Pan—Tomato Slices
8. Pan—Pickle Chips
9. Rolls
10. Shelf—Bun and/or Bread Storage
11. Mobile Heated Transfer Cabinet

For assembling hamburgers or other sandwiches made up of several different foods, a tier constructed work space is most efficient. Shelving (10, 5, 10) should be placed in an U-shape on top of the work table and within the maximum work area. The structure should be designed with adjustable shelves that can be easily set for the right height for the worker. They should also be designed so that they can be set at an angle with the back of the shelf higher than the front, thus producing a gravity feed situation.

A self-leveling pan or tray dispenser and a bread rack could be added to the above diagram to make a complete work center. Finished product, if hamburgers or other hot sandwich, can be placed directly into mobile heated transfer cart (11) and wheeled to point of service.

Fig. 18—ENCHILADAS

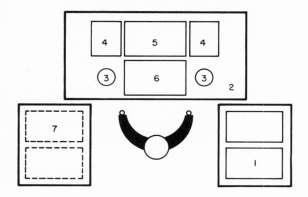

1. Mobile Pan Dispensing Unit
2. Table
3. Tortillas
4. Pan—Sauce
5. Pan w/Filling
6. Pan for Tortillas
7. Mobile Rack

This work center utilizes the benefits gained by mobile storage equipment. Mobile unit (1) is a pan dispensing unit that is stored under work table (2). It is pulled out when pans are needed and is placed in most efficient arrangement for the worker. When food has been served and pans are washed, this unit is wheeled to the pot and pan washing area to receive the clean pans. In a central kitchen operation, this pan dispenser would be placed in cart unloading area to receive clean pans coming back from satellite kitchens. When dispensing unit is filled, it would be returned to storage space beneath work table where it would remain until pans were again needed.

Mobile rack (7) receives pans of finished enchiladas where they will be stored until rack is moved to oven area for baking of the product.

of the work area have undoubtedly been thought of by the workers performing the task. The task should be taken a step at a time to see if any step can be eliminated, combined with another, simplified or changed in any way to increase productivity. Any changes made should be improvements based on the original principles of motion economy. All task procedures should be set up with a fixed review schedule so that productivity can be increased as improvements are made in technology, equipment and processing.

Establish Revised Procedure

If a review of a task shows that a revised procedure would increase productivity, the revised procedure should be worked out and tested. The new procedure should be written up with each step clearly defined for easy following. A simple layout should be included with the procedure so that no time is lost in setting up the work area. Whenever mobile equipment is used, it must be assigned to definite storage and in-use areas if efficient work centers are to be quickly assembled.

As new workers take over tasks, they can quickly become productive if written procedures and layouts are available to them. When establishing work centers for food preparation where recipes are involved, it is recommended that the work center diagram be placed on the back of the recipe card. The diagram should be accompanied by step-by-step directions for quick efficient assembly of the work center.

Work Performance Criteria

Management must establish work performance criteria for each task to be performed. Not only must the worker be given the task procedure and work area layout, but he must be told what is expected of him in the performance of the task. A work standard must be set and maintained for each task if maximum productivity is to be achieved. If work standards are not met, both the worker and the system should be checked out to see which needs to be changed.

It is possible to assign a worker to a task at which he will never become efficient. This should never be allowed to continue. Instead, an attempt should be made to reassign the worker where he can reach his maximum productivity. If the system proves to be inefficient, changes should be made in it. The location of the work area should be challenged also to ascertain if location within the facility is a hindrance.

Productivity of foodservice employees normally tends to be high when volume of sales is high. If, during periods of high sales volume, food costs are controlled and labor productivity is high, profits should be good. Every foodservice facility has a minimum work force that is necessary for basic operation. Each work force can efficiently prepare food and serve from a minimum number of customers up to a maximum number. It is to management's advantage, of course, to have employees serving a maximum number of meals per labor hour.

Productivity is usually measured by meals or other food items either produced or served, or both, per labor hour. For example, it takes three employees as a minimum crew to operate a facility. One of these employees works an 8-hour shift and the other two work 6-hour shifts, making a total of 20 labor hours. If they serve a minimum of 300 meals per day, their productivity would be measured as 15 meals per labor hour. The same crew can, if customers are available, prepare food for and serve 400 meals in the same length of time, thus increasing their productivity to 20 meals per labor hour. Volume of sales, then, is another factor which can influence the productivity of workers.

Supervision and Checking

All production and serving tasks must be continually supervised if standards are to be maintained. When a new worker begins a task, he should be closely supervised until following the steps in a given procedure becomes a habit with him. Even after this has been accomplished, a periodic check must be made to determine if the procedure is still being followed. A good worker will be constantly looking for ways to improve the task or the layout of the work area. The one basic thing to remember is there may be a better way of performing the task to increase productivity.

PLACEMENT OF EQUIPMENT

Placement of equipment is closely tied in with task performance as has been clearly shown on the preceding pages. It is impossible to set up a procedure for efficient production without considering the proper placement of equipment and necessary tools.

The placement of all fixed equipment and utility outlets for mobile equipment must be decided before the construction of the facility begins. Many hours must be spent in planning before a foodservice facility is ever put on the drawing board, for that is often the place where high labor costs and low employee productivity are established. To place the blame for this on any one member of the planning team would be unjust if qualified members representing the various areas of specialty have been selected to serve.

The planning team should consist primarily of persons representing ownership, management and architecture or design. These persons should be aided by the builder, food facilities engineer, materials and equipment manufacturers, employee operators and representatives of utility companies. A very important role should be given to the management person who understands the functions to be performed within the facility. Far too often this person is forced to take a subordinate role in the planning or is overlooked completely until it is too late.

For optimum productivity and minimal labor costs, the very size and shape of the building should be determined by the production and service functions which are to be performed in it. Repeatedly management is not consulted until the building has been basically designed, and sizes and shapes have been determined. Rarely are architects, designers and equipment representatives aware of the many specialized technical problems relating to food storage, preparation, production and service which must be accounted for in the planning process.

Management's Responsibility

Management must be prepared to take over the prime responsibility for selection of the proper equipment needed for the tasks to be performed. It is management that must determine what tasks are to be performed, who is involved, what equipment and utensils are needed, the amount of space needed and where this space should be allocated in the total facility layout. It is important also to allow for some flexibility, however, for as advancements are made in food processing, technology, equipment and systems, it will be necessary to take advantage of them if increased productivity is desired.

When, in advance of the building design, the management member of the team with the assistance of his employees has established tasks and task procedures, based upon motion and time study principles, a more efficient layout will be the result. It is, therefore, extremely important that the person who is thoroughly familiar with production and service play an important role in determining the layout.

In the general layout of the building the placement of equipment is of utmost importance, and many factors affecting productivity must be considered. One important factor is the flow of materials through the facility. All goods should be received in one area and go either into dry storage, refrigeration, freezer storage or directly into the kitchen to point of use. All storage areas must be readily accessible. Goods must flow from storage into the kitchen preparation areas, through production and on to holding areas or directly into serving or shipping.

After each task is planned and the location of its work area has been determined, these work areas must be grouped together to form sections or departments of the total production facility. Sections must be designed into the layout so that the proper flow of materials can be maintained. The layout must be planned also to avoid cross traffic and congestion.

Equipment must be placed where it can be easily operated and be extremely functional. In the event there is no existing equipment available to perform a particular task, existing equipment should be altered or new equipment designed to fit the task. In so doing, greater productivity and lower labor costs can be achieved. Capital outlay is a one-time expenditure which, in time, is written off, while labor is a continuing expense.

Equipment should be placed where it can receive maximum use by more than one section of the kitchen, if it is possible to do so without decreasing the rate of productivity. See Fig. 19, p. 114. The pot, pan and rack washer in this facility is strategically located convenient to the main cooking section and to the bakery. The tilting cooker-mixer, No. 4a, is located at the end of the cooking battery nearest the bakery so that it can be used by the bakers for pie filling, puddings, gelatin and dessert sauces, resulting in a substantial savings in equipment costs. The larger mixer, No. 38, is located within the bakery in an efficient flow pattern, but it is also convenient to the cooks if they have need for it.

All mobile equipment has a conveniently located storage space as well as designated floor space when in use. Bakery tables, No. 21 and No. 32, have electrical outlets mounted in the end nearest the walk-in bakery refrigerator and ample floor space has been left for mobile equipment such as the dough sheeter, No. 33, and cookie dropper, No. 39. Bakery table, No. 21, shows storage underneath for mobile self-leveling pan holders, and mobile bins, so that the necessary ingredients and pans can be stored at the point of use. There are many other examples of efficient placement of equipment which greatly increase the potential for high productivity.

Fig. 20, p. 115 shows how the placement of the vegetable preparation table and the cutter-dicer-slicer, No. 8, establishes a good flow pattern of raw product from the produce cooler to the salad, sandwich and main cooking sections. Prepared salad ingredients move from these two pieces of equipment directly to the food holding area. The mobile racks holding the salad ingredients are placed in roll-through refrigerator, No. 1 and are stored there until shipped out in food transport carts, No. 3. Lettuce and other sandwich ingredients move right across to the sandwich assembly line where they are incorporated into sandwiches. Sandwiches are stored in roll-in refrigerated cabinet, No. 6, until loaded and shipped out.

Vegetables used in cooking proceed to the cooking section where they are panned and processed. After the vegetables are processed, the pans are

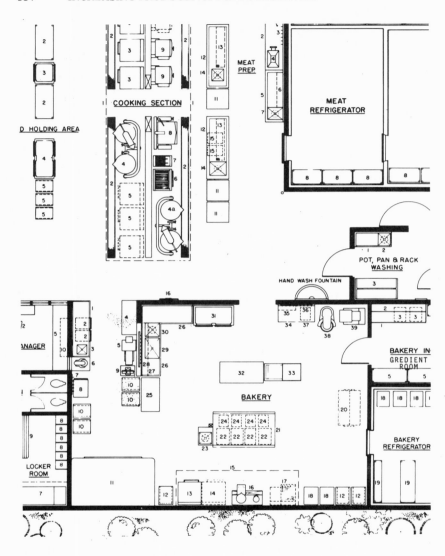

Fig. 19–*Partial floor plan of the Ruth Richard Food Center in the Rowland Unified School District, Rowland Heights, California. This central kitchen won an "Award of Special Distinction" in the 25th annual Institutions/VFM International Facility Design Program.*

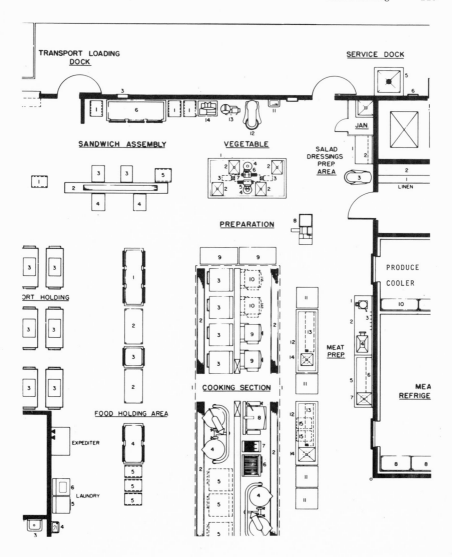

Fig. 20–*Partial floor plan of the Ruth Richard Food Center in the Rowland Unified School District, Rowland Heights, California.*

placed in racks and rolled into heated holding cabinets, No. 3 and No. 4, where they are held until loaded into transport carts for shipping. These are only a few examples of task planning and placement of equipment that facilitate a high rate of productivity within an operation.

Mobile Equipment in Work Centers

The advantages of using mobile equipment are many. One of the chief advantages of its use is the ease with which efficient work centers can be assembled. On the following pages are photographs which were taken to show, step-by-step, various tasks which were planned based upon the principles of motion economy as related to the use of the human body and to the work place. They also show how efficient work centers have been assembled by combining mobile equipment with stationary equipment. All of the work areas shown can be used for a variety of tasks by simply supplying other foodstuffs and perhaps other pieces of mobile equipment.

Another distinct advantage of mobility is provided by racks and carts which ease and simplify the task of materials handling. In this facility all of these mobile racks and carts are rolled into the pot, pan and rack washer to be washed and sanitized automatically.

The first task planning series of photographs, Fig. 21 to 24, pp. 117-119, show how the use of the specially designed vegetable preparation table becomes an efficient work area for many tasks. The second series, Fig. 25 to 28, pp. 120-123, gives the procedure and work areas for the preparation, baking and slicing of meat loaf.

In the third series of photographs, Fig. 29 to 40, pp. 124-134, the detailed preparation of pizza shows not only the efficient work centers, but also how two main production sections work together. The pizza task begins in the bakery with the preparation and sheeting of the dough and lining of the pans with dough. The dough-lined pans are then placed into mobile racks, which are rolled into walk-in refrigerators or into freezers, depending upon the time schedule. Wise planning places the dough preparation task into the work schedule in advance of the day the pizza is to be served. If it is to be served the following day, it will be refrigerated overnight. If the work load dictates that it be completed earlier, it is rolled into the freezer and held until final day of preparation.

The pizza product flows from the bakery into the main cooking section for the meat sauce, directly into the ovens, then the cutting station, into heated holding cabinets, through the cabinet and out the other side—where it is loaded into transport carts to be shipped to the schools. These are all examples of large quantity production, but efficient, highly productive systems can be planned for smaller operations also.

Good work flow and effective locations of equipment were made possible by the absence of columns or roof supports throughout the entire preparation, production and shipping areas. This design feature greatly assists the operation in maintaining a high rate of productivity. In this particular instance, the design was achieved at no additional construction cost.

Flexibility and Future Expansion Built In

Flexibility and expansion were built in by designing, into the layout, space requirements and utilities for future equipment. Many utilities were brought in from overhead, thus making it possible to change the location of the source of power or bring in a different source of power, if needed, should more efficient equipment be available at a later time. Budget permitting, this facility can be kept up-to-date as methods of food processing, serving and shipping change. Square footage can be added to the building by knocking out one wall, should it ever be determined that more space is needed.

Prior to the placement of equipment in this facility, many hours, days, weeks and months were devoted to planning. Menu was decided; basic use of ready-prepared foods was determined; production needs were established; production methods were determined; tasks were planned; procedures were described; equipment was selected and layout was made before the size and shape of the building were determined. In this manner a very efficient facility which is most effective in keeping labor cost to a minimum, resulted.

FRUIT AND SALAD PREPARATION
PROCEDURE AND WORK AREA

Fig. 21—*Specially designed vegetable preparation table. Apples served to elementary students are cut in half. Table is designed so that apples can be washed in one sink, (left of worker) brought up onto cutting board to be cut in half, and then slid off with knife blade into second sink containing an antioxidant (at right of worker), thus making use of several of the principles of motion economy.*

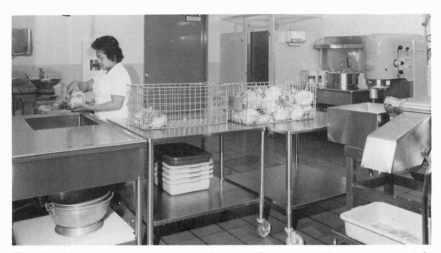

Fig. 22—*Modular mobile tables bridge over from vegetable preparation sink to cutter, dicer/slicer, strip cutter where salad ingredients and vegetables are cut to correct size.*

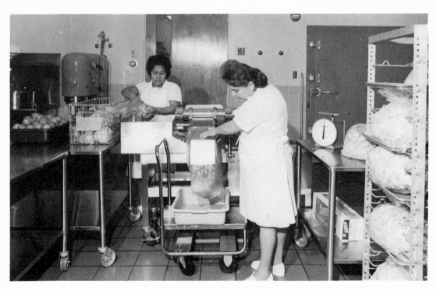

Fig. 23—*Two adjoining work centers augmented by additional mobile equipment provide area for efficient cutting and packaging systems for tossed green salad or cole slaw.*

Fig. 24—*Close-up of salad ingredient packaging. Plastic bags fill in seconds.*

MEAT LOAF PREPARATION
PROCEDURE AND WORK AREA

Fig. 25—*Ground meat and other ingredients are blended in the mixer when small quantities of meat loaf are needed. When larger quantities are required, ingredients are blended in the tilting mixer kettles.*

Fig. 26—*A modular mobile table has been used here to extend the fixed counter to form this meat loaf weighing and molding center. When pans are filled, they are placed in specially designed mobile racks sized for modular pans.*

Fig. 27—*Working from mobile rack that has been transferred from weighing and molding center, employee removes pans and loads convection oven.*

Fig. 28–*Baked meat loaf is loaded directly from oven into mobile racks for easy transfer to slicing center composed of a modular mobile table, a mobile slicer stand, a fixed counter and a mobile rack. The mobile racks, after loading, will be transferred to heated roll-through holding cabinet.*

PIZZA PREPARATION
PROCEDURE AND WORK AREA

Fig. 29—*Employee weighs dough for pizza. The use of mobile cart brings the working height to a correct and comfortable level. Dough filled mixer bowl on dolly was easily rolled into work center.*

Fig. 30–*Portioned dough is taken from pan in mobile rack and deposited into dough sheeter. Dough is sheeted in the correct size to fit 18- by 26-in. bun pans. After dough is stretched to conform to pan, the pan is placed in enclosed mobile rack for easy transfer into refrigerated storage.*

Fig. 31—*Spices are blended into ground pork as it browns preparatory to be-ing added to sauce. Modular mobile table provides efficient and convenient work space immediately adjacent to fixed equipment.*

Fig. 32—*View of assembly production line composed of modular mobile tables forming a bridge between mixer-kettle and convection ovens.*

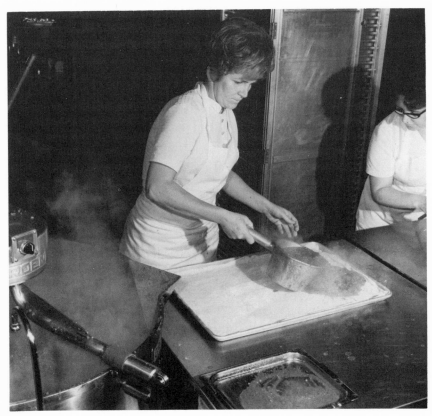

Fig. 33—*Employee ladles meat and sauce into dough lined pan at convenient working level. When funds are available, a food pump will be used in this process.*

Fig. 34—*As pans proceed down the assembly line, first worker applies chopped oregano and other spices to the pizza. The next employee, using both hands, sprinkles grated cheese over the product. Workers wear plastic gloves.*

Fig. 35—*Employee at end of assembly line picks up pan of pizza and places it into the convection oven. After pizza is baked, same employee removes it from the convection oven.*

Fig. 36–*Pizza is then placed into mobile rack which will be rolled to cutting station.*

Fig. 37—*Using efficient time-saving pizza cutter, employee portions pizza for serving. Use of cutter assures uniform servings.*

Fig. 38—*When all pizzas are cut, mobile rack is transferred into heated rollthrough cabinet for holding until loading time.*

Fig. 39—*Expeditor removes filled rack of pizza from opposite side of roll-through cabinet preparatory to loading transport carts.*

Fig. 40–*Mobile rack containing pizza is rolled adjacent to transport cart where pans are placed into enclosed carrier. Carrier has been mounted directly to cover of transport cart, thus enabling driver to take entire day's menu into serving kitchen in a single trip.*

4 The Stored Labor Concept

James R. Osenton

In a food factory, labor performs with maximum efficiency because everything is designed for the single purpose of producing food.

A foodservice establishment has a compound purpose. Its labor can't be totally specialized and its food preparation is less efficient than the factory. That is why, ordinarily, the use of pre-prepared or convenience foods lowers operating costs in foodservice establishments.

The product of the factory is purchased and placed on the shelf until needed. In a very real sense, the package represents the *stored labor* of the factory.

In a comparable way, the labor of the foodservice kitchen can also be placed on a shelf. The stored labor of the kitchen is not as efficient as the stored labor of the factory, *but it doesn't necessarily cost more.* It can cost *less,* obviously, if the wages of the kitchen worker are low enough to outbalance the greater efficiency of factory labor. That doesn't happen often.

What does happen—every day—is that kitchen labor has nothing productive to do at certain moments, yet must be paid for its time. The worker's effort at such a slack time can be considered free. Why not, therefore, "store it" until it's needed?

If you don't like the term "stored labor," think "advance preparation" instead. They mean almost the same thing.

Profitable use of the stored-labor concept requires three purposeful actions by management: (1) ascertaining whose time is slack at what periods; (2) planning menus in advance to reveal which foods will be needed, and

(3) understanding the preparation steps and storage capabilities of the items which will be pre-prepared.

Finding Out Where Slack Is

These statements require little explanation. As an example, you can ascertain who has slack time, when and how much by simple observation—merely by mingling with the workers.

Most of your stored labor will be applied to food pre-preparation, but not all. For instance, dishmachine operation should be scheduled so the attendant can perform other duties elsewhere part of the time. From personal observation, it has been noted that a large accumulation of dishware results in more breakage, cracked and chipped (and therefore unusable) dishes than can be justified by the few minutes of "stored labor" so gained.

Scrapping, stacking (and racking) rinsing, soaking dishes are the time-consuming factors. Running the machine takes little time. Sanitary storage routines are quickly accomplished by *properly trained* personnel.

There are two classifications of stored labor as applied to foods which are prepared or partly prepared in advance of need. One is for items cooked in gravy which require long cooking. Since meats and gravies, poultry dishes and stuffings are foods most often involved in Clostridium Perfringens*, held-over cooked foods should be stored at 45°F. or below and *thoroughly* reheated to boiling before serving. The second is for kitchen *mise en place* such as basic stocks, sauces and garnitures frequently used in daily food preparation and service. The expression "mise en place" now means *things* which are in place, but it is verbal in derivation and conjures up the action (labor) of preparing stocks and sauces and putting them where they will be needed at a future time. Again, stored labor.

Productive Use of Slack Time

Careful production scheduling of major cooking reduces kitchen preparation time when the kitchen is busiest and increases efficiency. After analyzing your menu and work schedules you will find there are many items on which advance production can be started during "downtime" or slack periods, and which can then be finished later as needed.

Changeover to the system can't be accomplished overnight. It takes orientation of personnel to the procedure; advance menu planning; recipe development; analysis of each step in food preparation; supervision of timing and purchasing of products to be delivered when needed for pre-preparation. Properly set up, the system will permit many tasks to be performed at times of convenience instead of emergency.

---

*Clostridium Perfringens (welchii) are bacteria that cause food poisoning.

Advance production of menu items should never be done to the detriment of today's production, except in cases where a double batch can be made and half can be saved for another meal. In such exceptions, it is noted that twice as much food certainly doesn't take twice as much labor and, consequently, efficiency is improved.

There are many entrees and other menu items which lend themselves to the stored-labor concept. Many require only supervision by the chef and utilize assistant cooks to their best advantage. Dishes which *don't* lend themselves to the concept are those which don't keep well or whose cooking time is such that advance production would be a duplication of work. Many of the items best suited for stored labor—items which can be very helpful in an unexpected rush and at times when the crew is reduced are listed in the following paragraphs.

Items such as stuffed cabbage rolls can be made during slack time and easily reheated when needed. This type of preparation can be done in stages. Cabbage leaves don't spoil if steamed off a day or so before the meat stuffing is made. Once they are made up they should be cooked off and stored in pans ready for reheating.

Always remember that stored moist foods are conducive to bacterial growth and foods to be held should be quick-chilled and refrigerated properly for a specified period only. Soaking the bread and cooking the onions for meat loaf, meat balls, salisbury steaks or meat dumplings in advance and then doing the finishing work later is a classic example of planned use of kitchen slack time.

Many component parts of menu items can be made as stored labor, with final assembly done later. For items prepared in advance as suggested here, be sure to detail length of time and proper temperature for safe storage as well as size of pan and depth of contents.

In analyzing the menu, consider everything which might affect the normal flow of production and service—banquets, special functions, available labor, holidays and days off. If meat loaf is on the menu for Tuesday and meat balls are scheduled for a club luncheon on Wednesday, both can be produced at once, with only one clean-up of the machine area. To insure that these items can be held safely, again length of time and size of pan should be specified to workers preparing them.

Balance Wage Rates with Productivity

The objective in utilization of slack kitchen time and stored labor is to keep a normal work level. Do not confuse motion with productivity—more handling increases a product's cost but not its value. The idea is to balance wage rates with productivity. Short, daily production meetings can outline the objective and "sell" the means to be taken.

The second category of stored labor, after pre-preparation of principal menu items, is what was previously referred to as *mise en place*. Building and replacing mise en place items is a continuous job. It should be done during slack kitchen time or when items like meat balls, meat and mushroom sauce, various soups, etc., are made in extra quantity. This is the true meaning of stored labor.

Ready for Peak Periods

You never need such mise en place items when you are not busy, but they must be ready for busy times to complete the service demanded during breakfast, lunch, dinner and special functions. Such items, however, may safely be held for not more than a day and safe storage methods must be in effect.

The second cook's mise en place items include basic brown and white stocks, au jus, consomme, chicken broth, veloutes, some finished sauces such as meat and mushroom, bordelaise, spanish, creole, depending on the menu. Also soups, garnitures, roux, glaces, chili con carne and such incidental items as chopped garlic, cooked onions and some special seasonings.

The fry cook's mise en place items for breakfast, luncheon, dinner and a la carte generally consists of diced cheese for omelettes, denver style mixes, various kinds of potatoes. He uses the second cook's items such as spanish sauce for omelettes. His daily menu dictates what he will need in the way of advance production: getting batters ready for hot cakes and waffles; cracking eggs for french toast. His main "props" are a clean griddle, clean fat in the french fryers, egg pans clean, daily garnishes ready.

Who Prepares What in Slack Time

The pantry mise en place includes everything needed which can be held, including dressings, cold sauces, garnitures, hard boiled eggs (be sure not to peel until just prior to use), some fruits and vegetables, salad greens, tomatoes, relishes and appetizers. Also lined up are cut lettuce, sandwich spreads, pickled beets, items for buffet service and, of course, clean cutting tools, boards and chilled plates.

The butcher and gardemanger's mise en place items are cold meats, fresh meat, fish, poultry, such mixtures as croquettes, forcemeats and stuffings, some stocks and sauces, mushrooms washed and ready for slicing. Every other station sends its left-over items to this station, and they are worked into following menus. His advance production is greater than other stations for each daily menu or special function. For example, if chicken a la king is on the menu, a worker in the garde manger dices the chicken, slices the mushrooms, green peppers and pimentos, getting them ready a day in advance. Meats are portioned and fish cut a day ahead also.

The vegetable cook's mise en place is merely his peeled vegetables such as onions, carrots, potatoes, cooked potatoes for hash browns, a potato croquette mixture for duchess, rosette potatoes, etc., plus having many cooked vegetables which can be made a day ahead ready for the daily menu items.

The bakery mise en place is in the form of various set doughs, fruits for pies, flour mixes, some batters, icings, fondants, egg yolks separated from whites, some pastries and pies made up and frozen, coloring and flavorings. These items are worked into daily advance production to fill the menu requirements.

The sous-chefs, banquet chefs and night chefs seldom require a build-up of mise en place items, since they work from the various stations which already have their items ready for regular service and scheduled banquets. Sometimes, of course, special functions require that extra ingredients be made ready. There must be close communication with all stations and departments for these persons to function properly.

Nonfoods Can Be Mise en Place

The storeroom and dining room mise en place requires housekeeping items, paper goods, glasses, napkins and stores. Most items are things required for daily service. Advance planning and work can prepare for special functions and extra services as well. The storeroom attendant fills daily requisitions to replace products in the kitchen cupboard.

The broiler cook's mise en place is limited to au jus, fancy butters, some garnitures and perhaps dressing mix or completed dressings for turkey. *Most of his preparation is done on a daily basis.* If he needs mushroom sauce, it is produced by the second cook. However, he does have an au jus pot on the back of his range, simmering from day to day.

We actually have more slack kitchen time than prime serving time, and it is during slack time that advance production should be taking place. Otherwise the slack time is just plain "wasted" time.

Napoleon, who hated wasted time, combined vast comprehension with directness of action. He never blundered into victory, but won his battles in his head before he won them on the field. So it is with kitchen work. We must observe, communicate and plan before we can accomplish our job of systematic, advance production.

Check over all the items that are prepared by the butcher and garde-manger and you will be amazed at how much duplicate work is being done—of how much unnecessary work is created by extra product handling. If you eliminate part of a job through advance preparation and stored labor, you *gain* something. If you create an extra job for anyone (even the potwasher), then how will he find time to help you when help is needed? Every step or motion you save improves your efficiency and permits you to accomplish more with less effort.

Analyze Job Descriptions

Job descriptions will have to be analyzed and, in many instances, changed to fit the concept of stored labor using slack time or the allied concept of making double batches in order to serve some and save some. Naturally, we may have some duplication, at first, where job descriptions or jurisdictions conflict. But, with a careful analysis of each job, conflicts can be resolved and responsibilities established with little confusion.

As an example, suppose you need 2 lb. of onions for meat loaf, 2 lb. for meat balls, 3 lb. for salisbury steaks, 10 lb. for onion gravy, 10 lb. for spaghetti sauce and 10 lb. for onion soup. In the daily menu analysis, plans should be made to ask the vegetable man to have 37 pounds of extra onions peeled, ready to be passed to the cooks for slicing and dicing during the kitchen downtime which can be anticipated.

For Napoleon, war was a game in which he exercised his arithmetic. It consisted of having more forces than the enemy at point of attack. His whole strategy was to attain this numerical dominance by endless maneuver, then to destroy the enemy's forces piece-by-piece. That is what we are doing with advance production planning using slack kitchen time to store our productive labor. When a station is being hit hardest and needs immediate help, we can provide it because we have already developed the means.

The Problem of No Shows

How long does it take to serve a steak banquet for 200? . . . Perhaps only 12 to 15 minutes, depending on facilities and organization. It takes much longer than that to get ready for the banquet. So the advance production in preparing for the function and the ability to shift crew are important. Instead of hiring extra kitchen help for a short shift, it is better and more economical to move your regular personnel to the area where help is needed. You can do this only when part of the labor has been stored in advance.

There is hardly a banquet in which the house isn't in danger of losing because of lack of organization, "no shows" and/or failure to have or take advantage of the stored labor which could have saved the day. We have records of attendance shortages ranging from 20% to 70%. Similar percentages of the prepared foods are wasted, since you can't save a dished-up cocktail or salad or a cooked steak.

Following is a list of actual shortages which occurred recently at a leading hotel:

Monday	Lunch . . . 16% short	Dinner . . . 31% short
Tuesday	Lunch . . . 21% short	Dinner . . . 17% short
Wednesday	Lunch . . . 51% short	Dinner . . . 70% short
Thursday	Lunch . . . 12% short	Dinner . . . 18% short
Friday	Lunch . . . 36% short	Dinner . . . 18% short
Saturday	Lunch . . . 34% short	Dinner . . . 16% short

Average shortages of 28% for both lunch and dinner lead us to think we must adopt a more realistic and conservative attitude toward banquets, an attitude which uses stored labor and shifting help to cover unexpected demands. The greater the number of people expected to attend a banquet, the greater is the average percentage of "no show." The following attendance percentages should be considered reliable:

Number expected	Average % shortage
25 to 75	10%
76 to 125	15%
126 to 200	20%
201 to 300	25%

This table coincides closely with what actually happens and should be a rule-of-thumb in catering any function. There is nothing more discouraging to management than to see food brought back to be thrown away, unless it is extra help standing idle. To avoid both, menus and work load should be so arranged as to use stored labor and shifted personnel.

Planning for the Biggest Days

Holidays like New Year's, Mother's Day, Easter, Thanksgiving and Christmas are often the biggest business days of the year. Every bit of stored labor that can be built up in advance—leaving the finishing to be done on the day needed—releases employees to be shifted to prime serving time.

When holiday menus are planned, analyzed and distributed in advance—so as to get stored labor started—you will find that fewer production people will be needed for finishing on *the* day. More help will be available to meet the demand of the dining room. Every station should have its advance production so lined up that extra help won't be required. It takes a close look at the kitchen operation with nothing left to chance, regardless of how small the detail may seem to be.

A kitchen operations log should be kept for banquets, special functions and especially big holidays. It should include the menu, weather, number prepared for and actually fed, special instructions to cooks, bakers and pantrymen. How much meat was used; amount of vegetables, potatoes, salads, dressings and garnitures. How many employees were required—cooks, helpers, dishmachine operators, cleanup men, and the hour they reported for work and when they finished.

The log should answer such questions as these: How much stored labor was used and did it fit the occasion? Were there any shortages and did any service suffer for lack of anything? Were all the stations properly lined up and efficiently manned? Was there any free time after the big rush; if yes, did advance production get started for the next day during that period of time?

What Can Be Cooked

Special days aside, what are the menu items suitable for the stored labor idea? The vegetable station's advance production can include carrots, peas, cauliflower, spinach, turnips. Special potatoes may be cut, sized or shaped for last-minute finishing. If fresh julienne of carrots is on tomorrow's menu, they may now be peeled, cut and stored in water. The pre-preparation time is much longer than the 4 minutes it will take to cook them, in small pots, tomorrow.

The second cook's station is a gold mine of stored labor products because of the many things within his scope which keep well for finishing when needed. Braised or baked short ribs, pot roast, oxjoints, beef hearts and bottom round are excellent for slack time preparation, but these items must be scheduled for use within a safe period.

The butcher can cut, trim and tie the meat a day or so before browning, then pass it to the second cook to be refrigerated until time for advance preparation at his convenience.

Basic white and brown stocks were mentioned as mise en place because they can be made in any convenient slack period. However, in a well-regulated kitchen they are generally made at the same time every day, and simmered long enough to extract the desired flavor from the meat, bones and vegetables. An acceptable, good formula for stock—brown or white—is 22 lb. bones, 3 lb.

meat trim and some vegetables cooked in a 20-gal. pot with 17 gal. of water added. Bring to a boil and simmer slowly overnight. It is strained in the morning through a china-cap; brought to a boil again; fat skimmed off; then strained through a cloth, held for use in soups, consomme, moistening roasts and general cooking. The basic brown stock is used for brown sauce, au jus and some soups.

What Can Be Stored

Browned beef, veal or lamb stew can be browned off at convenience in pans, in the oven or on the grill, seasoned and added to a pan of finely diced smothered onions. Add a little flour and stock, and cook together until tender. Remove from heat, refrigerate as short ribs or pot roast.

As many as a few hundred salisbury steaks can be grilled, refrigerated and *reheated for club luncheons when needed.* Coordination among the butcher, the fry cook and the second cook is important as the job involves all three. The butcher makes the steaks, the fry cook grills them and the second cook makes the brown onion gravy. The steaks can be heated in the gravy just before the luncheon. The idea is not to disturb the regular routine of work, but to coordinate and use the slack time of all three.

The salisbury steaks may be finished in mushroom sauce, spanish sauce or bordelaise sauce, as alternatives.

Baked creamed macaroni with cheddar cheese is a product which can be partly made in advance. The macaroni can be cooked the day before and the cheese diced. The dish can be finished in the morning in thin cream sauce, put in buttered pans, topped with diced cheese and baked until melted and bubbling. Extra macaroni can be cooked for salads and garnitures for soup.

Advance Preparation of Many Items

Noodles for pot roast can be cooked ahead and used when needed; the idea is to cook an extra amount for another service in the same operation.

Chicken drumsticks or turkey wings can be cooked while gravy or such sauces as mushroom, bordelaise, spanish or fricassee are being prepared separately. Each component should be refrigerated separately. To reheat, put poultry in pan, pour sauce over it, cover pan with foil and put in 400°F. oven for about 45 minutes, or until it bubbles and is heated through. To reheat noodles, drop in boiling water for a minute, drain, put in buttered pans, season with salt, pepper and a very slight pinch of nutmeg. If the entree is served with rice, the rice should be cooked the day of use.

An ideal stored labor menu specialty is chicken pot pie with vegetables, topped with a buttered crust. This can be made during slack time but it requires planning, since several persons are involved in the job—the butcher to cut the fowl, the vegetable cook for the vegetables, the second cook for the sauce, and the baker for the crust.

The most efficient way I have found to make chicken pot pies is to line up the deep casseroles, fill them all with, first, the cut chicken, then the vegetables, then the sauce, and pass them to the baker to be sealed with a pie crust. They should be baked off at intervals timed to meet the demand of the dining room. If they have been frozen, bake about 45 minutes like ordinary pie.

In preparing fresh brisket or short ribs the greatest time saving is obtained by blanching the meat the day before and finishing it the day needed. Blanching meat is plunging it into boiling water for a few minutes, then washing it in cold water. Serve with horseradish sauce in the style of a New England boiled dinner.

Partially Cook Today, Finish Tomorrow

For boiled beef stew or boiled Irish stew, cook the meat nearly done one day and finish the next day, adding the vegetables and potatoes to cook at the same time. These stews may also be completed with the cooked vegetables and potatoes added when the stew is being put on the serving line.

Baked spareribs are excellently made by lightly browning them off, cooking in a thin stock or sweet and sour marinade and finishing the next day. Just thicken the sauce and boil it to assure that it has reached a safe temperature.

Chili con carne is almost always made up during slack time, except when chili-burger is listed—in which case it is made in a large batch and part is stored.

We use cut-up turkey and have timed our methods for preparing it. Make a stock; add necks, wing tips and trim; simmer one hour; add wing sections; simmer 45 minutes; add thighs, drumsticks and breasts; simmer 45 minutes; take off heat; quick chill in freezer; then refrigerate.

The fry cooks have few items that can be advance produced beyond their mise en place items. If reuben sandwiches are on tomorrow's menu, they can be made up this evening and grilled to order. Fish batter is best if a couple of days old. Many garnitures are lined up ahead.

The pantry station has many regular mise en place items and is dependent upon advance production for all daily menu and banquet service. Many of the items are prepared in stages with final assembly and finishing in the morning when needed. Special dressings, some sauces, garnitures, trimmed lettuce, seafoods, such salads as chicken and tuna, hard boiled eggs, cheese spreads, pickled beets and some fruits and vegetables come within the scope of pre-preparation.

An advance study of menus is absolutely necessary to proper functioning. Some early production must be started days ahead for special events.

The butcher and gardemanger station is entirely dependent on advance production, as it sends most of its items to different stations for finishing. The station makes up croquettes, scrapple, poultry, fish, meat, cold meats, decorated items, hors d'oeuvres, aspics, buffet work and ice sculpture. It sends cooked meats, diced chicken, sliced mushrooms, sweetbreads and seafoods to various stations for lunch, dinner and a la carte service.

Ideas for Butcher and Baker

The bakers' advance production goes on every day as they always prepare or set doughs, some mixes, pastries, fruit fillers, made-up pies, icings, cakes, gelatin and some puddings. It's not unusual to see the bakers weighing dry ingredients for muffins, biscuits or other items to save time the following morning.

Basic sweet doughs are set for butterhorns in a 3-day cycle, using one and replacing it during the slack times. Butterhorns are made up sometimes in larger batches, with some frozen and later heated and iced as needed.

Canned apples and peach-apricot pies are set in advance to provide for the expansion of the type of tapioca that will be incorporated in the final makeup of these pies. After makeup, they are frozen and baked as needed. Baking frozen pies doesn't present any problem, since baking time is about the same as for freshly made-up pies.

Pumpkin pie filler, with its spices, sugar, eggs, butter and scalded milk, is set in the afternoons and made up when needed. Pumpkin and custard pie shells are rolled out in the afternoons and frozen. They bake off perfectly. This procedure saves a lot of time in the morning when so many things are being made to meet a luncheon deadline.

A simple advance preparation of fruit pie is made up with 30 lb. of frozen blackberries, 3 lb. of white syrup, 10 lb. of sugar and 2 lb. of flour. Stir in well and make up into pies to be frozen. This formula can also be used with frozen blueberries.

The following 3-use formula provides rhubarb sauce, and filler for both lattice-crust and deep-dish pies. Divide a 15 lb. box of rhubarb into 2 parts, 10 lb. in one and 5 lb. in the other. Put the 10 lb. on to cook with 3 lb. sugar, 1 oz. salt and 1 lb. white syrup. Bring to a boil for 1 minute and add 1½ lb. sugar, 1 lb. quick cooking tapioca and bring back to a boil. Take off the heat and add the remaining 5 lb. rhubarb and cool. It sets up beautifully.

In some operations a variety of cakes can be made in large numbers; some immediately iced and used, and others frozen. Wrap them in saran.

We control our cake baking and restrict it to slack time after the other morning production is completed.

We find that cup custards and tapioca pudding, like gelatin puddings, are best made in the afternoon and allowed to set overnight. Custards require quick chilling to the center of mass so put them in the freezer til proper interior temperature is reached, then transfer them to refrigeration.

When stored labor and slack time planning are accepted and management is constantly searching for places to apply these concepts, the increase in individual employee productivity can be impressive.

Summary

Napoleon understood his business. Here was a man who in each moment and emergency knew what to do next.

Few men have any "next." They live without plan; after each action they wait for an impulse from above. Do you have such persons working for your organization? If you suspect so, then there is justification for "mingling" to see that slack time is utilized, that labor is "stored" and that the jobs get done.

5 How to Apply Work Simplification To Foodservice *

GETTING the job done the easiest way is sure to appeal to workers. It should appeal to operators, too, when they realize that studies of worker performance show that workers produce only 53 per cent of their time on the job and rest or waste 47 per cent.

Making workers' time more nearly 100 per cent productive is the goal of the industrial engineers. They have made detailed studies of working efficiency and have come up with work simplification principles that can be easily and profitably applied in institutions.

Up to now the foodservice industry has made little use of work simplification. However, where it has been tried, it has been very successful since work simplification can be especially helpful in industries where a lot of hand work is done.

Where work simplification has been tried in institutions kitchens and dining spaces worker productivity has usually increased from 20 to 50 per cent. Recently one operation, after adopting a limited work simplification program in its kitchen, made many jobs easier and reduced its payroll costs by almost $35,000. This reduction in costs meant a drop in payroll costs from 35 to 27 per cent.

This same institution made a complete study of its dishwashing and pot and pan washing operations. As a result of this study it was recommended that a dishwasher just appearing on the market, more powerful than the aver-

*The material in this section is reprinted, with modifications, from a series of articles by Lendal H. Kotschevar, Ph. D. originally published in *Institutions Magazine*.

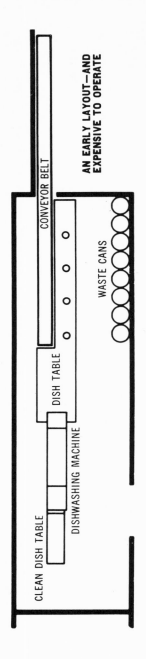

Fig. 41–*Dishes were handled 8 times per cycle in the old dishroom (above). This should be cut to 4 times in the new layout (below). Other features of the new dishroom: 2 water flushing waste troughs that feed into a pair of disposers; overhead rack designed to handle racks for personnel on either side of the belt; instead of 2 side-by-side belts, 1 wide belt. The extra soaking sink by the machine is for silverware that is missed at the first station.*

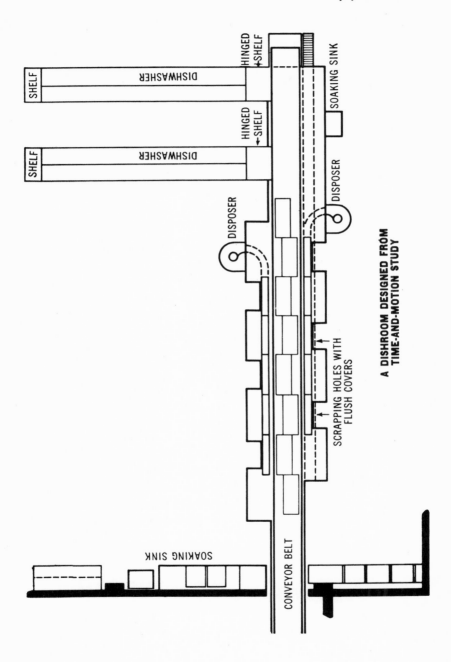

A DISHROOM DESIGNED FROM TIME-AND-MOTION STUDY

age, be purchased. The pot and pan unit was combined with the dishwashing unit. Jobs were replanned. The net result was that labor hours in a 7-day week were reduced from 576 to 320 and payroll costs were reduced from $1036.80 to $576. Work simplification in this case certainly paid off!

The industrial engineer knows how to plan work simplification, how to arrange tools, equipment, materials and workers in a job so that the workers achieve a high rate of production with a minimum expenditure of energy and time. He knows a great deal about how fatigue and rest affect production. The mechanics of the body are of interest to him and he knows there are ways to make work motions so they are easy; he knows also the limitations of the human body in doing work and in making motions.

Plan for Rest, Eliminate Waste

To simplify a job, the engineer must first break the job down so that productive motions are separated from waste or rest motions. He plans for rest, eliminates waste and then combines and rearranges the productive motions so that the job is simplified and done much more easily.

Of course, a lot of work simplification is plain common sense. Any alert person can watch a person doing a job, analyze the work, and usually come up with some suggestions for improving the job. It doesn't take a trained expert to do this. As a matter of fact, it is not difficult for an adept person to learn to use many of the tools that are used by industrial engineers in work simplification or in breaking down a job so that it can be done more easily.

If a worker is to maintain a high productive rate, three kinds of rest must be provided for him. First of all, the muscles of the body, like the heart muscles, must have small momentary fractions of rest between work motions. Too rapid a pace with no rest between motions tires the muscles and the quantity and the quality of the work accomplished drops.

Setting and maintaining the proper pace is extremely important in achieving satisfactory production. Work simplification teaches workers to work smarter, not harder, and speed-ups are not smart. A pace set so that the muscles of the body get momentary fractions of rest is the best pace. Workers also vary and so it is necessary to vary the productive pace according to the worker.

Second, after a sustained period of work, a worker tires, his energy reserves are depleted and short momentary flashes of rest are not enough for recovery. A longer period of rest is required to bring up the energy reserves so that the best productive pace can be maintained. It has been found that short breaks of 3 to 5 minutes taken during a shift eliminate fatigue and raise production.

Finally, workers also require sufficiently long periods of rest between shifts to rebuild their supply of energy. Workers cannot work long hours day after day without days off or vacations. If they do, their production drops.

Using this knowledge of rest and its effect on the body, the industrial engineer plans rest when he sets up a job. Wasteful rest is eliminated and only rest that overcomes fatigue is planned.

A knowledge of time is important too, for time is the measure of productivity. We hear the industrial engineer speak of a certain productive rate per hour. He is referring to the number of units produced either by one worker or by a group of workers in an hour, a shift, or some other specific period of time.

While it is not often realized, moving the body about takes a lot of energy. If a person weighs 150 pounds, that weight has to be moved if the body is to be moved. Try moving 150 pounds of flour! One hundred pounds is moved if the body trunk is moved, 15 pounds if it's the entire leg, 8 pounds if it's the lower leg or entire arm, 4 pounds if the lower arm, 1 pound if the hand, and 2 ounces if a finger. Think of how much weight one actually moves about if one moves about for five minutes waving his arms! The industrial engineer knows this and tries to eliminate movement in work and limit work motions to the simplest. It also takes time to move the body or any of its members. Some movements can be made more quickly than others. For instance, the finger can be moved twice as fast as the hand can be raised or three times as fast as the arm can be moved. The simpler motions are also more accurate. Thus, there are advantages in restricting motion in work and the industrial engineer knows it. That is why he tries to confine work to relatively restricted areas.

The Right Kind of Motions

The principles of motion economy state that work is easier and quicker to do if the two hands begin, as well as complete, work motions at the same time and if they are not idle at the same time except at rest periods. Motions which are ballistic, rhythmical, opposite, and symmetrical are easier and more accurate than fixed or controlled movements. Smooth continuous motions are preferred to zig-zag motions or straight line motions involving sudden and sharp changes in direction.

Placing all tools and materials in definite fixed places makes for easy work. These places should be close to and directly in front of the worker. Gravity or drop deliveries should be used to deliver materials closest to the point of use.

Furthermore, the location of foods and materials should be such that they are easily seen and grasped and are placed so they permit the best sequence of motions. Pre-positioning of tools and materials so they are within easy grasp saves time and effort.

Working conditions affect the ability of workers to work and can increase the difficulty of making motions. Good light, fresh air, comfortable seats, proper work heights, freedom from noise and many other things are essential if work is to be done economically and without undue effort.

A circular workplace assists greatly in gaining the advantages of the principles of motion economy through the placement of tools, materials, and equipment.

Sometimes this type of workplace is called an island type work center, but it is best to consider the worker as the island with the equipment, materials, and tools grouped about him. In designing such workplaces an attempt is made to reduce as much as possible the distances of reach. These distances are made to conform with what are known as the maximum and normal workplace areas.

If the distances a worker reaches with either hand are confined for the most part to the normal workplace area and if two-handed work is kept within the area where the two semi-circles for the normal reach overlap, the efficiency of the worker is increased.

At times it is difficult to confine work so one worker can reach all materials and tools. In such instances, and where the work is highly repetitious, assembly line methods can be used and work accomplished without violating normal and maximum working distances.

For the most part, workers in foodservice use the natural work habits they bring with them. Little or no attempt is made to train workers in gaining more efficient habits. In almost every kitchen and dining room in the country one will see, therefore, wasteful work habits. Eradicating these and encouraging workers to have more efficient habits will increase worker productivity and make jobs easier.

Because working conditions vary, each operation in developing a work simplification program must start with the general principles and then adapt them to the operation's specific needs.

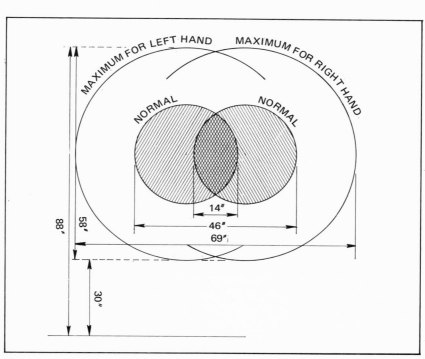

Fig. 42–*Chart indicates the maximum and normal workplace areas for a standing man (10 per cent less for a woman).*

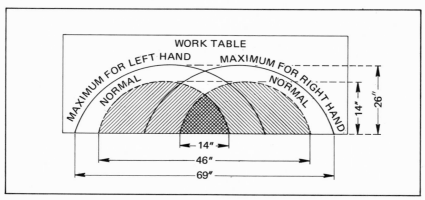

Fig. 43–*Chart indicates the maximum and normal workplace areas for a sitting man (10 per cent less for a woman).*

TECHNIQUES FOR
TAKING JOBS APART

IMPROVEMENTS in work simplification can only result if the complete job process is examined in detail—each step carefully analyzed by itself. To analyze a complete process, the process must be put down in detail in the order in which it is carried out. When this is done, it is possible to see what part of the work is contributing to actual production and what part is waste. When the job is rebuilt the wasteful parts can be eliminated and only the productive parts retained.

Breaking down a job and then rebuilding it can be a lot of fun. It's much like taking a toy or some mechanical gadget apart and then putting it together again in better shape than ever. Those who like crossword puzzles will like work simplification for there is much fitting of parts together to make the whole work. Of course, it all takes time, and it takes perseverance. Every detail of the job must be known and separated from the others. Actually, if a good job of analysis is done, the job process will have fewer secrets than a person rising from a psychoanalyst's couch!

An industrial engineer follows these steps in breaking down a job:

Select the job to be improved.

Break down the job in detail.

Question the job and each detail of the job.

Develop the new method.

Apply the new method.

1. To aid in *selecting a job to be improved,* consider that each job is made up of three parts: the *get ready* or the effort and time put into setting

up equipment, tools, or getting the materials with which to work; the *do* or the actual work accomplished; and the *put away* or the storage or clean-up following the *do*. The *get ready* and *put away* add to the cost but not the value of any product. Therefore, the more *do* that can be obtained for the *get ready* and *put away,* the lower the production cost.

If a baker makes 100 cinnamon rolls, the *get ready* and *put away* are about the same as for 1000 rolls. If he makes 1000 rolls and freezes 900 for later use, the production time per unit will be much less. A major source of work simplification, then, is elimination—elimination of *make ready* and *clean up.*

Start with a Troublesome Job

Pick a job that is giving you trouble, one where improvements will be most noted and appreciated. They may be "bottleneck jobs" or simply jobs that you know are taking too much time and effort, jobs that require a lot of walking or are obvious wastes of manpower. At a normal work pace, a worker will walk about 80 steps a minute or a little less than three miles an hour.

Recently a pedometer was put on a dinner cook where the storage units and work arrangements were poor. This cook walked over 3 miles in two hours. Her walking took up over half of her work time and it was estimated that at her hourly rate, her walking cost over $6.50 per work period. When the unit was reorganized and the work simplified, the cook's walking was reduced over half.

In another instance a dietitian wore a pedometer on a busy day. It was found that in an eight-hour shift she walked 9¾ miles. Because walking can be expensive, select jobs where there is a lot of walking going on. It's in these jobs that work simplification will achieve big savings.

2. *Breaking the job down in detail* has become pretty well standardized by industrial engineers. They ask many critical questions while at the same time evaluating the answers they receive. Each question is directed at uncovering a detail of how the job is done. The ultimate intent is to rearrange, simplify, eliminate, or combine certain motions to make the job easier. Hundreds of questions must be asked, for every detail of the job must be known. The person adept in work simplification must be as persistent and adroit with questions as a seven-year old.

3. In *making an analysis of a job* a few questions an industrial engineer might ask are: *What* is the purpose of the job? What are the steps? What does each step do? *Why* is it done? Is it necessary? *When* should it be done? *Who* should do it? Should it be done by a skilled person or can some unskilled per-

son do it as well? *Where* should it be done? *How* is the best way to do it? Will not some simpler method or mechanical device do the job as well? Would a change in layout or equipment and tools make the job easier?

The *what's, why's, when's, who's, where's* and *how's* of a job are most important and in asking these questions the analyst should be exhaustive and searching. Every aspect should be examined and studied. It is surprising how the inefficiencies and the productive parts of the job stand out after such questioning.

Ask the Right Questions

If a foodservice operator were making a similar analysis of the job of making a two-crust pie, some of the questions might be: *What* job is to be done? *Why* not shape the pie dough into two-ft. long rolls about 4-in. in diameter and pre-cut these rolls into discs weighing about 10 oz. each? This will reduce the time spent selecting the proper weight of dough used. Also, since it is already preshaped, it will permit easier rolling of the crust for the pan.

Why is the bottom crust trimmed, then the pie filled and the top crust put on and trimmed—couldn't both crusts be trimmed after the top crust is put on and thus save one motion? *Why* cut a fancy design in the top crust when one simple hole will do as well?

Who should open the canned apples—if the storeroom man opened the correct number of cans in the storeroom and dumped the contents in the mixing bowl, wouldn't valuable skilled time of the baker be saved?

Where should mixing bowl of apples be placed when pies are being filled? Putting it on a low stool to the right of the baker would make it easier to reach with the right hand and save valuable work table space by keeping it off the table where it is too high to reach into anyway.

How should the pies be filled—if a large dipper is used so that one dip will fill a pie, instead of having to dip several times with a smaller dipper, wouldn't time be saved? One will note that while the questions tear the job apart, possibilities for improving the job immediately follow. Better ways come up after every question. Almost before one realizes it, the new job shapes up in the questioner's mind. All that has to be done is to work it out on paper.

Job Determines Techniques to Use

4. To analyze the present job and *to develop the new method,* industrial engineers use various techniques and forms. The type of techniques used and the form used depend upon the job. Some jobs are relatively simple and do not require detailed study. However, some jobs have to be studied in minute detail; for instance, those jobs having few but highly repetitive motions.

Therefore, a multiple number of forms and techniques exist for analyzing old jobs and developing new.

Industrial engineers have also learned to use certain symbols or a sort of shorthand to indicate work that is done. They simplify the task of analyzing the job and building a better one. Experience has shown that all work can be broken down into certain classifications or main divisions of work and symbols have been developed to indicate them. These are:

○ Operation or accomplishment; something being changed; created, or added to.

→ Transportation; something moved from one place to another.

▢ Inspection; something checked or verified but not changed.

D Delay; something not progressing towards completion and remaining idle but not in storage.

▽ Storage; something retained in one place purposely awaiting further action.

These five symbols are used to break down a job into its main details. After they are placed on a work sheet in the order that each operation occurs, the analyst has what industrial engineers call a *flow process chart*. This gives the flow of the work as it is done.

Flow Process Chart Gives Complete Picture

A flow process chart can be made of a man at work, of materials being processed, or equipment at work or of a combination of any of these. Whatever is being charted, by glancing at the chart one can get a complete picture of the work as it is done. The operations or productive motions, transportations, inspections, delays, and storages are accurately shown.

A flow process chart is simple to prepare and is very useful in studying jobs where the worker or materials move about. Fig. 44 shows a flow process chart listing the details of mixing up a pie crust. Fig. 45 shows a revised or proposed method for this same work. Note that on the bottom of the flow process chart in Fig. 45 a summary of the number of operations and transportations, steps taken, feet traveled, and time used is given. Such a summary indicates the savings made by the new method. (See next page for Figs. 44-45.)

Fig. 44–BASIC CHART FORM   531216-02

Flow Process _____ Type of chart   Food Service ____ Department

Original or Present _____ Orig. or proposed   LHK _____ Chart by

Materials into Pie Crust ___ Subject charted   May 26, 1956 . Date Charted

Details	Division of Work	Steps	Feet	Time
1. Get mixing bowl	⟶	6	9	0:35
2. Weigh flour	◯	0	0	1:43
3. Secure shortening from storeroom	⟶	28	49	3:03
4. Weigh shortening	◯	0	0	2:22
5. Weigh salt	◯	0	0	1:11
6. Dump ingredients into bowl	◯	0	0	0:18
7. Set bowl on mixer	⟶	2	3½	0:18
8. Get mixing paddle	⟶	6	9	0:17
9. Put paddle on machine	◯	0	0	0:08
10. Start machine; blend ingredients	◯	0	0	3:12
11. Stop machine	◯	0	0	0:02
12. Get cold water at sink	⟶	4	7	0:29
13. Add water; start machine	◯	0	0	0:07
14. Blend ingredients	◯	0	0	0:40
15. Stop machine	◯	0	0	0:02
16. Remove paddle	◯	0	0	0:07
17. Take paddle to sink	⟶	4	7	0:14
18. Remove bowl and roll to table	◯⟶	7	13	0:18
19. Store scales and water measure	◯	7	13	0:20
Totals	13◯ 7⟶	64	110½	13:26

The easily prepared flow process chart simplifies the study of jobs where workers move about. Fig. 44 shows a flow process chart listing the detailed method of mixing a pie crust. Fig. 45 (facing page) is a similar chart containing at the bottom a summary of the number of operations and transactions, steps taken, feet traveled, time used for being studied.

Fig. 45—BASIC CHART FORM			531216-02	
Flow Process	Type of chart Food Service		Department	
Proposed	Orig. or proposed LHK		Chart by	
Materials into Pie Crust	Subject charted May 26, 1956		Date charted	

Details	Division of work	Steps	Feet	Time*
1. Get mixing bowl and paddle	⟶	6	9	0:39
2. Dump shortening, flour and salt which has been delivered preweighed by storeroom man	◯	0	0	0:19
3. Put mixing bowl on mixer	⟶	2	3½	0:18
4. Start machine; blend ingredients while blending get water at sink	◯⟶	4	7	3:16
5. Stop machine	◯	0	0	0:02
6. Add water	◯	0	0	0:07
7. Start machine; blend ingredients	◯	0	0	0:40
8. Stop machine	◯	0	0	0:03
9. Detach paddle and bowl	◯	4	7	0:24
10. Roll bowl to table	⟶	7	13	0:14
11. Paddle to sink	⟶	4	7	0:05
12. Scales and water measure stored	◯	7	13	0:20
	8 ◯ 5 ⟶	34	59½	6:08

Summary				
Item	Present	Proposed	Difference	
Operations	13	8	5	
Transportations	7	5	2	
Steps	64	34	30	
Distance (feet)	110½	59½	51	
Time (minutes)	13:26	6:08	7:18	
*minutes and seconds				

Flow charts are another means of analyzing a job and simplifying work. In these charts the worker's path of work is traced on a scale drawing. Flow charts are used when it is desirable to graphically portray distance values. Flow charts are usually made on scaled drawings of the work center. The drawing may be mounted on cardboard to give it firmness. Most frequently the scale of ¼ in. = 1 ft. is used. The surface area of the equipment in the work center is drawn in to scale. Then, the worker's path of work is traced on the chart. Excessive walking can be easily detected and if the job is revised, the savings made can be quickly compared.

How to Use a String Chart

Sometimes string charts are made; that is, string is used to trace the worker's path as he travels around the work center. First, a scale drawing of the work center is made and is mounted on cardboard to give it firmness. Then string is used to indicate the path of the worker. This is done by fastening the string around a brass paper fastener placed wherever the worker turns or stops. By unraveling the string the distance traveled by the worker is easily calculated since each ¼ in. of string equals one foot traveled by the worker. Comparisons of distances saved between the old and the new job are also quickly made by measuring the length of each string. Fig. 46 and 47 (facing page) show on a string chart the work delineated in Fig. 44 and 45 (pp. 158-59)

Because the eye is usually not quick enough to catch individual motions done in highly repetitive work, slow motion pictures are sometimes taken of a worker doing such work. Later the picture is run again and again and the worker's motions studied. First, the work done by one hand and then the work done by the other hand is recorded. If a timer or chronometer for giving elapsed time is used, the time used for each motion can also be recorded. If the chronometer has 100 equal divisions on its face and the hand travels around the face 20 times per minute, then each division on the face represents 1/2000 of a minute, and this fraction of time in work simplification is known as a "wink."

Because motion picture study of work usually breaks jobs down into greater detail than that given on the flow process chart, a set of symbols to show the more detailed motions is required. These motions symbols are called *therbligs* and in total represent every type of motion used in doing work.

Engineers use various symbols or use colored pencils to indicate the various therbligs but it is becoming more and more common to see therbligs

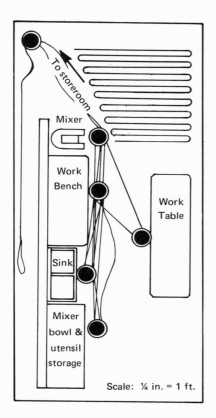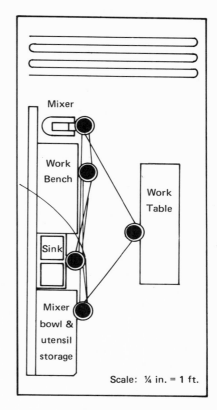

Fig. 46 and 47—*String charts may also be used to trace a worker's path as he travels around the work center. First, a scale drawing of the work center is made, then string is used to indicate the path of the worker. This is done by fastening string around a brass paper fastener wherever the worker turns or stops. When unraveled, the string can be measured to easily calculate distance traveled by the worker (¼ in. of string equals 1 ft. traveled by the worker). These two string charts show the work described in Fig. 44 and Fig. 45. Comparison of distances traveled is quickly made by measuring length of string.*

indicated by letter symbols. There are 17 therbligs. Their names, letter symbol, and definition follow:

THERBLIG	SYMBOL	DEFINITION
Search	Sh	The eyes or hands hunt for an object.
Select	St	A decision ending with the choice of an object.
Inspect	I	Examining and evaluating according to a standard.
Transport Empty	TE	The hand moving toward an object.
Grasp	G	Taking hold of an object.
Hold	H	A delay in grasp with no movement of the object.
Transport Loaded	TL	The object being moved.
Release Load	RL	Releasing the object.
Position	P	The object set into proper position for use.
Pre-position	PP	Setting into position for future operation.
Assemble	A	Joining two or more objects together.
Disassemble	DA	Separating two or more objects which are joined.
Use	U	Manipulating a tool or device to perform work.
Avoidable Delay	AD	Stopping the operation.
Unavoidable Delay	UD	Stopping the operation unavoidably.
Plan	Pn	Mental decision on procedure for action.
Rest	R	Cessation of work to overcome fatigue.

The use of these symbols is illustrated in Fig. 48 which shows excerpts of a film made of a worker trimming lettuce leaves for salad underliners. Fig. 49 is a film analysis of these motions. The chronometer is not shown. Sometimes engineers prefer to make from the film analysis record a chart showing the simultaneous motions being made by both hands. In this manner one can grasp the work being done and note the wasted motions. When such a chart is made it is called a *simultaneous motion chart* or a *simo-chart*. Fig. 50 shows a simo-chart for the worker cutting the lettuce leaves.

That the worker was working with only one hand while the other was idle or holding was not plainly evident while watching the worker nor from the film.

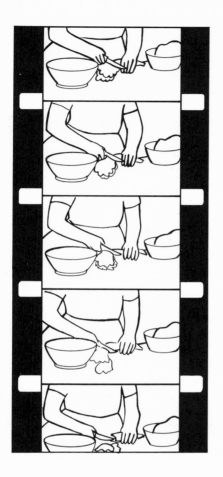

Fig. 48–*This film strip, used to "take a job apart," shows excerpts of a film made of a worker trimming lettuce leaves for salad underliners. It covers frames 5 to 12 as recorded on a film analysis chart, Fig. 49, p. 164. An alternate method of recording photographed motions for job analysis is the simultaneous motion chart, Fig. 50, p. 165.*

RECORD OF FILM ANALYSIS

Film number 52
Date filmed July 15
Analysis by LHK
Date 28 July

Operation Trimming lettuce
Operator Hefner
Part Name
Part No.

1 Sheet of 1
Dept. H. Economics
16 frames/sec.

Therblig symbol	Clock reading	Subtracted time (winks)	Left Hand Description	Therblig symbol	Clock reading	Subtracted time (winks)	Right Hand Description	Body number	Therblig symbol	Clock reading	Subtracted time (winks)	NOTES
TE		16	To bowl of lettuce	H		16	Holds knife					Frame 1
S		19	Selects lettuce leaf	H		19	Holds knife					not shown
TL		18	Carries lettuce leaf	H		18	Holds knife					Frame 2
P		27	Positions leaf for cutting	H		27	Holds knife					Frame 3
H		29	Holds leaf for cutting	TL		29	Moves knife to cutting position					Frame 4
H		210	Holds leaf for cutting	U		210	Trims off lettuce cups					Frames 5-12
G		17	Picks up waste lettuce	H		17	Holds knife					Frame 13
TL		21	Waste to garbage can	H		21	Holds knife					Frame 14
RL		8	Drops waste lettuce	H		8	Holds knife					Frame 15
TE		16	Returns to pick up	H		16	Holds knife					Frame 16
			lettuce cups to deposit									
			in bowl on left									

Fig. 49. *Motions filmed in strip, preceding page, were analyzed in this chart.*

However, when the motions were placed either on the film analysis record or the simo-chart, the idleness of the hand became immediately evident. Simo-charts have the advantage of graphically setting off waste motions from productive motions by showing such motions in black. The time lost by such motions is also very easily seen. When the job is simplified or improved and placed on another chart, comparisons of the improvement are easily made and evaluated.

SIMO-CHART

Method_____ Film No._____52_____

Operation__Trimming Lettuce_____ Operation No._____

Part No._____

Part Name_____ Chart No._____LHK_____

Operator_____Hefner_____ Date Charted_____

Left Hand Description	Symbol	Time	Total time in Sec.	Time	Symbol	Right Hand Description
To bowl of lettuce	TE	.50	.50	.50	H	Holds knife
Selects lettuce leaf	S	.60	1.10	.60	H	Holds knife
Carries lettuce leaf	TL	.60	1.70	.60	H	Holds knife
Positions leaf for cutting	P	.90	2.60	.90	H	Holds knife
Holds leaf for cutting	H	.90	3.50	.90	TL	Moves knife to cutting position
Holds leaf for cutting	H	2.10	5.60	2.10	U	Trims off lettuce cups
(continued)						(continued)

Fig. 50. *A simultaneous motion chart can also be used to record photographed motions.*

There are other ways of studying jobs and improving them. As an example, the use of a pedometer, previously mentioned, is very helpful in obtaining estimates of wasted motion and in indicating where detailed studies may be required. Industrial engineers also make use of cyclegraphs or place tiny lights on a worker's hands which trace the path used in making a motion.

It is also possible to set up a camera over a work center and fix the camera so that one frame per second is taken of work done in the unit instead of the usual 16 frames per second. In this manner the work done in an eight-hour work day can be compressed into a 20-minute film. Such a film is extremely helpful in indicating poor work habits and wasted motion of workers in a unit.

Whatever method is used, remember that the basis for the development of the new improved method of doing work will depend upon the results of the questions asked when breaking the job down into its details.

Change in Motion Sequence May Be Answer

Applying the question *why* to the question *what* tends to result in the elimination of details. The answers to *where, when,* and *who* along with *why* may lead to a combining of operations or motions or to the elimination of storages and transportations. Whenever two or more operations or motions are combined, they are often performed in the time formerly taken to do one or in even less time than that. The answers to these same questions may lead to further improvement in changing the sequence of motions and this may eliminate or combine previous motions.

After every elimination, combination, and change in sequence is made, the way in which the job is to be done can be revised. It is this process that will lead to the total over-all simplification of the job.

5. The last step is to apply the new method. It is necessary to review the new method to see that nothing has been omitted and that it is practical. Usually it is well to have the new method reviewed by someone else. A worker who must do the job is an excellent person to consult for he knows a great deal about the job. If possible, it is well to conduct a test or trial run of the new methods.

In applying the new method there are two important considerations that should not be overlooked: the technical and the individual. From the technical standpoint endeavor to determine whether the method will work and whether it will save effort and time. Will it affect other equally important questions? What will it cost? Will it result in a sufficiently large saving to warrant installation?

Consideration of the individuals involved in the job change is most important. It is essential when a new way of doing a job is offered to employees that it be easier and simpler than the old one. Otherwise they will be reluctant to accept it. Many employees will resent having to learn a new job and unless they see some advantage in it they will resist learning it.

Preparation for acceptance by employees of a work simplification program is very essential to its success. Employees will resist work simplification if it is used as a pretense for speed-up, to criticize their work methods, to eliminate jobs, to increase production without benefit to them, or when they are not consulted in advance as to the need for change or its purpose.

On the other hand, employees will cooperate—in fact, they will work to improve their jobs—when they are allowed to participate in the program and share in its benefits. Because most workers use natural habits learned earlier in life in doing their work, they have haphazard or wasteful methods. If it is to the advantage of the worker, he is usually glad to improve these.

All workers will be encouraged to change their work methods if they see they can make their jobs easier. It is a fact that workers who find their jobs easy like their jobs, that those workers who like their jobs stay on the job, and those workers who stay on their jobs make money for the operation.

Workers Like Easy Jobs Best

Perhaps the best way to approach work simplification in any institution is to think of work simplification as more of a philosophy than a technique. If workers can be induced to plan their work and to think about ways to simplify jobs while they are doing them, management may benefit more than if a formal program of work simplification is introduced abruptly and without previous worker acceptance having been developed.

Small savings here and there on a job may not be consequential when considered alone, but, in total over a day's work and among a number of workers, the result can be very significant. If such a philosophy is first introduced in the operation's kitchen and dining rooms, it becomes easy for workers to welcome more formal applications of work simplification. The workers will, as management already has, come to recognize that there is always a better way to do every job.

Management, having selected the techniques of taking jobs apart and rebuilding them most easily applied in their operation, will soon be cutting down on the 47 per cent of labor time that goes into waste motion and, at the same time, be building up employee morale by making work easy.

HOW TO HELP
WORKERS "WORK EASY"

KNOWING what makes workers tired—and doing something about it—can keep productivity high.

When a worker grows tired his production drops. For this reason it is essential to prevent fatigue if employees are to maintain a good rate of production during a shift. To prevent fatigue in a worker we need to know what makes him tired. We also want to know how being tired affects a worker's production.

Our bodies are machines. They consume fuel to create energy to do work just as an engine burns fuel to do work. In the human body the fuel used is a sugar called glucose; when this sugar burns in our bodies we develop heat and energy plus certain waste products such as carbonic acid, pyruvic acid, lactic acid, and others. When the body turns portions of fats or proteins into glucose, then waste products other than those from glucose also accumulate in the body.

The problem is to work just hard enough to allow the body to get rid of the waste products as they accumulate. If these burnt-out particles pile up in the body, that is, if we burn foods faster than we eliminate the waste products, we get tired. Some say the piled-up acids and other waste products cause a tired or an aching feeling in the muscles. Certainly, we know our muscles get sore after heavy exercise and they stiffen up, especially if we are not used to the exercise.

But the human body also differs from a machine. When an engine is stopped it ceases to use fuel, but not the human body. It has to keep running even though it is doing no work. The basic energy required to keep the body going when it is at complete rest is called the *basal* requirement. It is said to take about 1700 calories per day to keep the body of a man functioning when he is at complete rest.

When we work, energy over and above this basal requirement must be obtained to do the work. The harder we work the more fuel it takes. For instance, a man whose basal requirement is 70 calories per hour will use about 100 calories per hour while sitting still. If he works at a moderate rate he will require about three times this amount and if he carries a load upstairs it will take over 11 times his basal rate.

How to Conserve Energy

Frequently work which should require only a small amount of energy actually requires lots more and this is because a worker is wasteful of the energy he has or does the work improperly. A smart employee gets to know Mr. Less Effort for he is the fellow who can keep him from wasting "gas" and from making needless demands upon his fuel reserves.

ENERGY COST OF DOING WORK*

Activity	Calories required per hour by average man
Sleeping	65
Sitting at rest	100
Standing relaxed	105
Standing at attention	115
Singing	122
Dishwashing	144
Sweeping bare floor (38 strokes per minute)	169
Walking slowly (2.6 miles per hour)	200
Walking moderately (3.75 miles per hour)	300
Walking down stairs	364
Severe exercise	450
Walking very fast (5.3 miles per hour)	650
Walking upstairs	1100

*C. Sherman, *Chemistry of Food and Nutrition.* (New York: MacMillan Company, 1952), p. 180.

There is a maxim in work simplification which when followed cuts down consistently on the use of energy; it states:

> Never walk when you can stand.
> Never stand when you can sit.
> Never sit when you can lie;
> And be surprised how work hours fly.

Working with tense muscles rather than relaxed muscles increases the amount of energy required to do work. Workers should learn to use their muscles properly. Rhythmic, smooth motions take less energy than jerky motions or motions which stop and start suddenly. Earlier in this section the proper way to make motions in work was summarized under the principles of motion economy.

Hard work at a fast pace is wasteful of energy and causes rapid tiring of the worker. Over a period of time doing less at a steady rate produces more work than trying to do a lot with erratic bursts of speed. There is a saying which goes: "Life by the yard is apt to be hard, but life by the inch is more of a cinch." The turtle knew this when he won his well-known race with the hare.

Studies also show that workers at the end of a shift use more energy in doing their work than they do earlier in the day. Perhaps the muscles grow more tense and the worker has to exert more force upon his muscles to accomplish the work. Whatever it is, as the worker tires, his production drops. Under normal working conditions a worker should feel tired during about one-fifth of his shift and most of his tired feeling should occur at the end of the shift.

Some workers vary in their ability to produce according to the time of day. This may be because their blood sugar level is low at a particular time and they are, therefore, tired. Because of this some workers cannot get going in the morning but later in the day reach their peak and really accomplish something. Others start out like a house-a-fire but are burnt out by evening. These variations in production among workers are called diurnal variations. Most workers would prefer not to work at times when their ability to produce is low. This is important to remember in scheduling employees.

Value of Coffee Breaks

When a worker burns energy too quickly or gets tired at the end of a shift, a part of this tiredness may arise because he is running out of fuel. When this occurs, the blood sugar level drops—the gas tank runs dry—and he lacks fuel to create energy to do work. Rest allows the blood sugar level to rise and the fatigue goes away. We can raise the blood sugar level quickly by eating something sweet. That is why candy bar manufacturers talk about a "quick lift" from their product. Sugars are absorbed quickly into the blood stream thus raising the blood sugar level.

An interesting thing about the coffee break is that, besides providing rest which restores blood sugar, the caffeine in the coffee stimulates the liver to release stored glucose thus providing a quick shot of sugar that gives a "lift" and erases the feeling of tiredness. However, when the liver is stimulated by too much coffee it becomes fatigued and then we have what is known as the "coffee jitters," produced because the liver has exhausted its reserve supply.

All this is vital information to employers who wish to help their employees maintain good production rates. It points out the value of a short rest period in the shift just as the worker begins to tire. Furthermore, we realize, when we know these facts, how planning work ahead and developing smooth, flowing work habits can reduce fatigue and maintain production.

Plan Easy Work for End of Shift

We can be of assistance to workers in maintaining production by scheduling their easiest work near the end of a shift or at a time when their energy level is low. It is wise, for instance, to schedule cooks' preparation work, which can be done seated, toward the end of a shift and not at the beginning. It is wise also to schedule the filling of salt shakers, folding of napkins, and other work requiring less effort toward the end of a waitress' shift rather than at the beginning of it.

Some investigators think that fatigue is not as much a result of accumulated waste products in the body as it is a nervous reaction to work. Fatigue of this kind is thought to arise at the nerve endings, the synapses, or the place where one nerve ends and the other begins. It is thought that a worker gets tired because nerve impulses at this juncture have difficulty in being passed along to the next and so blocks occur. These blocks cause a loss of coordination and efficiency and thus work becomes difficult to do and production drops.

What Makes Workers Tired?

Boredom, monotony, dislike of a job, frustration, poorly planned work, and similar conditions can cause a worker to become tired on the job. Perhaps nerve blocks occur and that is why some easy jobs become very tiring to some people.

The production of workers will be higher where good working conditions exist. Good air—an air change about every 5 minutes—good light—about 20 to 40 foot candles—comfortable clothes, good floors, good colors, all relieve strain at work and assist in keeping up the productive rates of employees.

A quiet atmosphere and freedom from noise is important. Recently an air hammer had to be used to break out a cement wall in some kitchen construction. The work had to be done while the kitchen was in operation. It was noted that this constant hammering increased tension among the kitchen employees, a tension which increased as the days of hammering continued, and that production dropped among many of the employees as the tension increased. Production rose again when the hammering ceased.

Proper work heights are necessary if fatigue is to be minimized. For years work heights in kitchens have been 34 inches. Somehow or other this became a standard to which most equipment manufacturers adhered. However, it should never have been a standard. The work height should vary according to the work done and the body dimensions of the worker.

Wrong Working Heights Waste Energy

Poor work heights demand more energy from the worker. When one worker worked on a 31-in. table rather than a 34-in. table, the energy requirement rose over basal from 14 percent to 32 percent; the heartbeat increased over basal from 28 percent to 30 percent; breathing increased from 10 percent to 51 percent over basal, and the blood pressure increased from 2 percent to 21 percent over basal.

This is startling evidence of the extra work or energy required by an improper work height.

In another study a dishwasher washed dishes in a sink with a bottom 25.6 in. high, then in a sink with a bottom 29.4 in. high and finally in a sink with a bottom 33.5 in. high. The calories required per hour over basal were respectively 30, 24.4 and 20.3. Again, concrete evidence of the work required when work heights are not proper.

A work table on which beating or mixing occurs should be lower than one where hand work occurs. In certain sections of the country where workers in foodservices are larger and taller it has been found that hand work table heights are better at 28 in. In college dormitories, the beds for men are now 80 in. long instead of 72 in. long. Our boys are growing bigger and where these men work in the kitchens we have found a work height of 37 in. is a better height than the old 34 in. However, in the New York area and other areas where short, foreign-born workers predominate it has been found that work heights should be lower than 34 in.

For years sink manufacturers have been manufacturing sink bottoms too low for easy work by our workers. For the average woman lap boards about 26 in. off the floor make for easy work with the feet resting comfortably on the floor. At higher tables adjustable chairs should be used and the seat of the chair should be adjusted so that the forearm of the worker is on a level with the counter rim or table top. A foot rest should be provided about 16 in. below the seat and the width of the seat should be between 14 and 16 in. A back rest should be provided which supports the back fully. A full back rest is preferred by most workers.

Fig. 51—*Suitable chair for average woman employee has back rest and full-sized seat with footrest placed about 16 in. below seat.*

Fig. 52—*Worker has right kind of chair but has seat too near footrest which will cause fatigue.*

Fig. 53—*To find proper working height, have worker stand up next to table and press his hands down flat on the table top. If this can be done with arm fully extended but not stretched, work surface is right height for tester.*

Fig. 54—*To put work surface at right height for worker, a chopping block can be placed on too-low surface to bring work up to a comfortable position for the worker.*

In order to determine if a work table on which mixing, beating, or other such work will occur is correct for a worker, have the worker stand up next to the table and press his hands down flat on the table top. If this can be done with the arm fully extended but not stretched to the table then the height of the work surface is proper for that person.

Where a worker stands and works with small tools, pares vegetables for instance, the height of the work table should be about 4 in. below the worker's elbow. This allows the worker to stand and hold the arms naturally without having to lift the arms up higher or lower than necessary to do easy and accurate work.

Work simplification requires, among other things, a knowledge of body mechanics. Just as engineers are always trying to develop machines with more

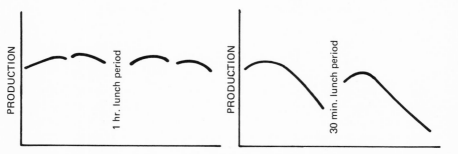

Production curve of kitchen worker working at a normal rate with two 10-min. coffee breaks during a shift.

Production curve of a worker doing heavy work but not at a fast pace drops toward end of shift when worker is tired.

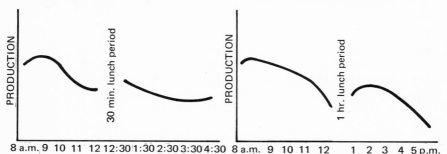

Production curve of a bored worker. Note how when worker sees end of shift approaching work production increases.

Production curve of a worker doing heavy work at a fairly rapid pace.

Fig. 55—*Production curves were recorded on these charts for four workers each in a different situation.*

reliable operation, those engaged in work simplification are always seeking methods of making the human machine operate more efficiently. For whether the machine is mechanical or human, the same principle applies, i.e., production is very closely related to efficiency.

Consider first of all the structure of the human machine. The weight of the body rests on the spine and the hips. In other words, the body is support-ed by an inverted "T." When the body is held erect, the weight is evenly dis-

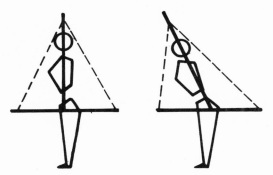

Fig. 56—*The head, chest and trunk of the body rest on an inverted "T" formed by the hips and spine. Correct posture insures that the weight will be evenly distributed over this "T." Poor posture will impose a heavier work load on some muscles, causing strain and fatigue.*

tributed over this "T," and very little energy is required to support the body. However, when the body bends out of line, then the weight is unevenly dis-tributed over this "T" and the muscles affected by additional weight must perform extra work to support it. Thus, as in the case of the worker who must bend too far over a work table or a sink, the carrying of extra weight adds tremendously to the energy required.

The more the body is kept in alignment, the less energy is required for performance of the task. Studies have shown that an employee who sits and works with poor posture will use more energy and become more quickly fatigued than one who stands and works with good posture.

Body fatigue due to the lifting, lowering and carrying of heavy objects also can be lessened. In lifting heavy loads it should be remembered that the leg muscles are stronger than those of the back. Therefore, the problem of lift-ing or lowering a load can be simplified if (1) the feet are firmly placed about 10 in. apart, (2) the bending is performed by the leg muscles while the back is kept straight, and (3) the object is firmly grasped and lifted slowly. The leg muscles also should do the bending while the load is slowly being lowered.

Fig. 57–*Three steps in good lifting: (1) place feet firmly 10 in. apart; (2) keep back straight and bend leg muscles; (3) grasp object firmly and lift slowly.*

Fig. 58–*The closer an object is to the fulcrum (triangle) of a lever, the better the balance. This is a good rule to remember when carrying loads—keep them close to the body.*

It is recommended that if the lifting is performed repetitively, weights be limited to 50 lbs. for men and 35 lbs. for women. This limitation actually makes it possible to lift more over an extended period of time than if heavier loads are lifted. One of the early experiments in work simplification showed that when men were given a smaller shovel with which to move coal, they shoveled greater quantities than when they used the larger tool provided by management.

When carrying a load it should be remembered that a weight held away from the body exerts a greater force than the same weight held close to the body. Therefore, when carrying a heavy load, it should be kept close to the body's center of gravity.

The weight of the body lifting a 50-lb. object is only of relative significance; the weight of the human being involved is important only from the viewpoint of the total amount of force available. The weight has nothing to do with the efficiency of that force.

The body acts as a lever, and the center of gravity of the body is like the fulcrum point of a lever. If a 50-lb. object is held 3 in. from the body, the units of energy necessary to move that force would be 12.5 ft-lb. If that same object is held 1 in. from the body, then the necessary force would be about 4.16 ft-lb.; a distance of 6 in. would require 25 ft-lb.

It is wise to have heavy loads lifted by two or more people. As in any operation which requires teamwork, one person should be appointed to give the signals so that all lift together. If the object to be carried is long, then the workers should be of about equal size and build and should walk out-of-step. This will prevent the weight from bouncing or shifting.

Heavy items should never be stacked more than 7 ft. high since even this height imposes a severe strain on workers as they lift weights over their heads. When lifting to shoulder height or above the head, body fatigue can be lessened if the load first is raised to waist level and then rested on a support. The grip can be changed at this point, and the knees bent to give added power for the final lift.

Momentum, when properly used, can assist greatly in making work easier. Watch a pair of professional piano movers and note what little effort they expend to move a heavy piano. Similarly, if a man uses a heavy mop to wash a floor, his work will be much easier if he will release the pressure on each swing as soon as the mop passes the center of his body. The momentum will carry the mop to the end of the swing, which is more efficient than if full pressure is applied on the mop until the end of the stroke. In the latter case, pressure must be used to stop the mop.

Workers who lift chairs and stack them on tables prior to a floor washing operation can perform this task much more easily if they take advantage of the momentum generated in the original lift. Also swinging a chair with an arc-like movement makes this task less fatiguing. The employee should stand directly behind the chair and place his left hand at the top left back of the chair. With counterclockwise motion, he swings the chair to the right and immediately places his right hand on the left rung or base. He then takes one step

Fig. 59—*Proper way of carrying long objects requires teamwork as demonstrated above. Long objects should be carried over the shoulder with the front end held as high as possible to keep it from striking other employees.*

Fig. 60—*Position 1 (left) shows worker's left hand on the top left back of chair with right hand ready to grip rung. Position 2 (right) shows chair properly inverted.*

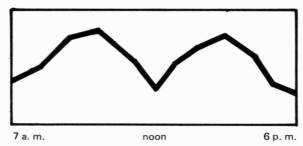

7 a. m.   noon   6 p. m.

Fig. 61—*Data compiled by the National Safety Council indicates that there is a sharp rise in accident probability 3 hours after starting time and 3 hours after the noonday break. This substantiates the author's statement that tired workers are accident-prone workers. Monotony and fatigue can be alleviated by work breaks.*

forward and places the new upside down chair on the table.

In this case the lifting should be done from the waist and abdominal areas rather than the shoulders. This, in combination with a rhythmic swinging motion, will enable an average employee to set up 20 to 25 chairs a minute.

Generally it can be said that rocking a barrel, swinging a sack—getting things in motion before lifting—are tricks of the trade for a professional mover who knows how to utilize momentum to make work easier.

Frequently it is easier to pull or push loads than it is to lift and carry them into place. Placing a very heavy object on a broom and pulling it is much easier than carrying the load. If a load is to be pushed, the worker should stand away from the item so that body weight can be used to assist in this job. If the worker stands close to the object to be pushed, the muscles alone will have to do all the work.

The tired worker is the accident-prone worker. As important as working properly is permitting the worker to take a rest period. This also increases the efficiency of the human body and will lessen the chances of accidents. Statistics show that the maximum period of accident occurrence is three hours after starting and three hours after the noonday meal. The harder the work the earlier this period occurs. Statistics also show that one injury out of every four occurs from the handling of material.

For the easiest, most efficient way to handle and move heavy loads, it would be well to keep this principle in mind—using headwork before footwork frequently saves time, energy and tempers.

IMPROVED UTILIZATION OF LABOR

Have I a good layout for efficient flow of work? Work centers?

Do I have a good training program for employees—teaching them good work habits and assisting in setting up and planning their work?

Is each employee doing the job for which he is skilled?

Am I eliminating all services and work which does not add value to the product?

Could I use more self-service?

Do I plan menu items which involve the least work?

Do I plan my scheduling, etc. to best utilize labor?

Do my employees plan their work so that it is done with efficiency?

---

6 Convenience Foods Disposables Automation

Raymond B. Peddersen

WORK SIMPLIFICATION assures the most effective day-to-day operation for a foodservice organization. Because the more details that need to be handled and the more people there are in the operation, the more likely it is that things will go wrong, every job should be reduced to its basic components. Once reduced, as many of the tasks as possible should be eliminated from the job through the use of *disposables, convenience foods and automated equipment.*

CONVENIENCE FOODS

There are many types of convenience food products available for foodservice operations. To a certain degree the range of products that can be used is limited by geographical location. However, there is no problem anywhere with the utilization of frozen products as there are, at this printing, in excess of 100 companies in national distribution of frozen foods.

The problem in setting up for use of convenience products comes with the short-term shelf-life refrigerated foods, such as prepared salads and desserts. However, a good convenience program will utilize prepared foods for all aspects of service.

Each operator needs convenience products for different reasons. Those in the large cities have an abundant potential labor force, *but* it is an expensive one. The small city and rural operator has the problem of *not* having a large pool of potential workers, regardless of how much he can afford to pay.

Thus, the metropolitan operator needs convenience foods to reduce his labor costs and the non-metropolitan operator needs convenience foods to fill the gap between his actual labor supply and his production needs.

In embarking upon a convenience program, there are three ways to operate. By far the most preferable way, although it is only practical for the high volume user, is the following:

Option 1—Tailored Convenience Foods

Standardize all recipe cards for hand-prepared items, not only as to products but also, when possible, as to specific quality and type of ingredients per USDA specifications.

Calculate, from production records, the annual number of portions needed and the maximum number of portions for which storage space for a single shipment is available. Take these requirements to the nearest two or three producers of convenience foods and take bids on their production—by the processing method preferred by the operator—of these convenience products. This takes care of a lot of the problems that have to be solved when convenience foods are purchased without reference to storage problems.

One problem is packaging size; few of the companies in national distribution package products in like packages. Even fewer foodservice operators agree on ideal packaging size. That is, the slow-paced commercial cafeteria or public restaurant may well prefer the very few portions that can be packed in a shallow half pan because their steam tables empty slowly. But the fast service, high volume operator—such as the hospital or airline food conveyor belt or the college or in-plant foodservice—may well prefer a large number of portions packed in a full-size, deep pan.

By specifying his own package, the operator can tailor the best type of reconstitution for the specific product with his specific kitchen facilities, be they conventional or modern. A hospital, with microwave ovens on the floor stations, will find convenience products delivered in the frozen state perfectly acceptable. However, where a high volume must be served in a short period of time, a more shallow package would be required for reconstitution in a convection oven.

If there is enough refrigeration area at controlled temperatures and conventional ovens are to be used for reconstitution, a bulk pack that can be reheated from the refrigerated state after a long defrost cycle may be preferred. Having the product packed to specification guarantees a product consistent with the tastes of the particular clientele.

Among the minimum standards which users agree on for convenience products are pathogenicity, nutritional content, shelf-life and accuracy of the manufacturer's claims regarding the number of portions per container. The standards should be applied to the new frozen, dehydro-frozen, freeze-dried, chilled or concentrated items that appear on the market almost daily.

The manufacturers and purveyors have special problems that operators do not have. Chicken cordon bleu, veal marsala, stuffed cabbage or codfish cakes are prepared differently in the various regions of the country. What passes for good clam chowder in San Diego may not pass muster anywhere near the Charles River in Boston.

Option 2—General Marketplace

When a foodservice is *not* big enough to have its own convenience food manufactured, the operator may enter the general marketplace.

The major shortcoming of convenience packaging is the failure of designers to communicate information about the contents and their use to the average unskilled kitchen employee. There are usually no receiving specifications on boxes to guide the receiver in examining the product for damage during transportation. There is no mention of dangerous temperature zones or shelf-life.

The advertising logo occupies the primary container space although this space should be allocated to instructions. Sometimes, instructions are placed on the bottom of the box—which means the worker may have to damage the product to read the instructions. Instruction copy is confusing. Few companies provide line drawings. Those manufacturers who publish product description sheets or merchandising brochures or more importantly, nutritional breakdowns, generally make them available "upon request only." Such data sheets should be included with each case.

Instructions should cover the following subjects: storage, including specific and numerical temperature figures, not the oblique "room temperature" or "freezing;" method of removal from master container; number and size of portions; alternate uses of product and handling of leftovers; alternate preparation methods and service equipment that can be used, and appropriate warnings.

The instruction language should be clearly organized; it should be short, simple, with instructions illustrated and, certainly today, bilingual.

Option 3—Make-Your-Own

In this approach, often called the "ready-foods" system, the operation manufactures and freezes its own convenience foods. This system utilizes forced down-time to have bulk quantities of foods prepared, packaged and frozen. In on-premises preparation of convenience foods, there are certain factors that must be carefully studied.

Regardless of how an operator meets his convenience food requirements, whether he buys from the outside or has convenience items produced in his kitchen, he is left with the complicated business of reconstitution.

When food is removed from the freezer, it must be carefully handled. The various types of food must be reconstituted in different manners. The only rule which always applies is, "Never defrost at room temperature." A tempering box, such as the Foster Re-con, is suggested for use as first stage reconstituting equipment. In such a box, most foods can be brought safely to the refrigerated state in under 24 hours. Some foods should be cooked and/or reconstituted right from the frozen state at low oven temperatures.

Tempering Foods, Crucial Step

Whatever is done about tempering foods, it must be done carefully. Foods thawed slowly over two or three days generally retain more stability and "eat" better than those thawed quickly. A tempering box can cause a burning of exposed surfaces while the middle remains frozen. Microwave reconstitution of frozen foods, if not properly done, can cause the food to lose its natural mass and thus become soft and mushy.

There is no doubt that a properly adjusted forced-air convection oven does an effective job in terms of load, efficiency and cost in reconstituting frozen, convenience foods.

In using microwave ovens care must be taken to adjust heating times depending on the thickness or shape of the products, improper timing can produce a steamed or ozone flavor in meat. Microwave ovens make their greatest contribution when used to bring cooked and/or refrigerated foods to serving temperatures. New combination convection-microwave ovens, if used properly, should offer an answer to many problems.

All of the above methods generally may be referred to as dry heat reconstitution.

Pressurized steamers, pressurized fryers and open fryers are effective, even if slow, methods of food reconstitution and/or cooking.

Another area of importance is the serving temperature. What holds true for freshly prepared foods applies equally to convenience foods. Hot food *must* be served hot and cold food *must* be served cold. Any variance from this rule may prove disastrous for the palatability, pathogenicity and nutritional value of food. While we know the facts of heat loss for liquids, new data is needed on the time requirements of all common foods as related to specific states and mass in order to set standards for reheating and for holding abilities during service.

The possibilities convenience foods offer in increasing productivity are almost limitless. Typically, a new kitchen planned for total convenience food usage takes only 1/3 as much space and capital as a conventional kitchen. Labor requirements may be reduced by as much as 80%, although a reduction of 40% to 60% is more common.

Almost every entree conceivable is available in a full convenience form. The preparation of these dishes ranges in quality from unsatisfactory to the best of haute cuisine. Soups and sauces of every variety are available. Sauced and seasoned vegetables are usually of very high quality. Cakes, pies and fancy pastries abound in the marketplace.

Although it may be difficult to purchase pre-prepared salad plates, it is possible to buy all fresh vegetables and fruits already peeled, chopped, diced, sliced or in any form needed for salad preparation. All salad mixtures including potato salad, cole slaw, macaroni salad, lobster salad and tunafish salad are readily available. Puddings and gelatins of high quality are available.

Gradual Modification Often Best

A foodservice operation may not be ready for a total convenience system and/or new equipment. Most operations are not. Where this is so, it is advisable to gradually modify conventional systems when and where possible. If an operation still butchers its meat, labor can be effectively reduced by purchasing meat prefabricated to the specifications of the *Meat Buyer's Guides* of the National Association of Meat Purveyors. Instead of operating a bake shop, labor can be eliminated through the purchase of commercial fresh or frozen bread goods.

Hillside Hospital Foodservice has devised an objective scale for rating products on their subjective values. The form, Fig. 62A, top of following page is an individual product rating chart. Pre-prepared products are rated against in-house prepared products on six-inter-related yet individual quality factors. The closer to 0 a product scores, the better it is for replacing the hand-prepared product. The goal is to equal the house product, not necessarily replace it.

The form, Fig. 63, on the following page measures the cost, in terms of labor dollars, of the on-premise product as compared with the tested convenience product. Such cards are kept for future reference. The important data on these cards is transferred to a card which records similar data on various manufacturers' samples of a particular product. This card is shown on p. 187.

When an adequate number of samples have been tested, a decision based on comparative quality, cost and time savings can be made. In this manner, it is possible to test products over an extended period of time without requiring a sophisticated research staff in the kitchen.

A list of man-minutes saved by using a selected product should be kept

CONVENIENCE COMPARISON RATING CHART

Product _____

Co.	Qual. Points	100 Portion Cost.	M M Savings	Test Date

Selection   Comments

Date   New Recipe Card No.

Fig. 62—*Data from individual cost cards can be transferred to this form for review.*

by the labor task analyst. Lists should be kept of cold products which are to be used by salad girls and of hot items prepared by cooks, and the minutes that can be saved through purchase rather than preparation of each product should be recorded. When a position becomes vacant and the time saved by using convenience foods in that work area is roughly equal in man-minutes to the output of the newly vacated position, the operator should leave the job empty and substitute use of the convenience products on the list.

These three simple forms are quickly filled in and may prevent mistakes which are costly in terms of customer satisfaction as well as money. This system, if used as outlined, should keep budget-oriented operations from cost overruns.

DISPOSABLES

The question of whether to use permanent ware or disposables is an item of discussion, often heated, wherever foodservice operators gather.

Before a move to (or from) disposable serviceware is made, there are several areas which need careful consideration.

Operating and labor costs are usually the area of first consideration.

Convenience Product Rating against   Date:_____
Hillside Hospital Product

Product _____ Packed by_____

Portion Size_____ Cost per portion _____

	-2 N.G.	-1 OK—	0 Same	+1 OK+	+2 Better	Comment
Color						
Sauce (Aroma)						
Sauce (Taste)						
Filler (Aroma)						
Filler (Taste)						
Seasoning (General)						
Total						
÷ 6=						

Cost per 100 portions

Man Minutes	Hillside Hospital Product	_____Product
Rec. and Storage		
Preparation		
Garnish and Display		
Difference x $.10		

Food Cost $ $

Recipe No. _____ as of   /   /

Diff.

+ or —

Fig. 63– *This form was designed for use as an individual product rating chart.*

The sensible formula for calculating these costs is as follows:

(a) Permanent ware

P = per meal served cost of permanent ware

$P = (mhw_1.wg.p) + (E_1 + d + v + r_1 + g_1 + i_1) \div m$

Where:

mhw_1 = annual number of man hours worked in warewashing and garbage disposal

wg = average hourly wage

p = percentage of time spent actually working at warewashing

E_1 = 10% of dishmachine's original cost (amortization + repairs)

d = annual detergent expense

v = utilities expense (50% of detergent expense)

r_1 = annual china replacement expense

i_1 = interest (8% of total value dishwashing equipment and minimum stock level of serviceware)

g_1 = garbage bags + hauling or incinerating cost

m = annual meals served

(b) Disposable ware

D = per meal served cost of disposable ware

D = $(mhw_2.wg.p) + (E_2 + r_2 = g_2 = i_2) \div m$

where (additionally):

mhw_2 = your estimate of the man hours need for disposable ware-handling (probably 20%-30% of permanent ware)

E_2 = 10% of original cost of disposal equipment ($3,000-$10,000 for compactors)

r_2 = annual expenditure needed for disposable ware + same percentage for loss as with china replacement

g_2 = garbage bags + hauling or incinerating cost (2-3 times what it is for g_1)

Quite aside from the cost aspect, the physical impact of disposable serviceware must also be considered. Will the customer accept it? Most institutions have found customer acceptance directly related to the quality of disposable ware used. Will disposables increase or decrease your heat retention? Sanitation? Can you incinerate in your area? Is compacted or pulped garbage allowed in your city?

As stated earlier, the simplification of a foodservice operation through the elimination of labor serves to reduce the complexities of operating and thereby provide less chance for error. The use of disposables wherever they can be economically justified can help to simplify a foodservice operation.

AUTOMATED EQUIPMENT

There are many types of equipment which may be utilized to de-intensify the labor aspects of foodservice operations. The degree to which automated equipment is taken for granted by Americans and Canadians is brought home forcibly by descriptions of recently visited kitchens in the hotels and institutions of the Iron Curtain countries. Slicing machines, vegetable peelers, choppers, mixers and warewashing equipment, behind the "Curtain," are often non-existent or of the type of design of our earliest models. Now that salaries for foodservice workers have caught up with the productivity gains (via equipment) of the past 40 years, new areas of automation must be developed.

At the point of purchase, automation makes its first contribution to foodservice operations through pre-printed forms and group contracts, central suppliers and data-phones. Purchasing time has been reduced by as much as 80%, without forfeiture of buying power, through the use of these labor-saving innovations.

At the point of receipt, the use of conveyors, pallets, fork lifts and rolling racks should be standard. However, the amount of hand and back labor still in use in foodservice storeroom and refrigerated goods handling is surprising. Heavy industry has many lessons to teach foodservice operations about the substitution of machines for manual labor.

In preparation areas, many tasks have been automated. Automatic-carriage slicers which stack the sliced food are a must to free hands for other jobs. Vertical or horizontal chopper-mixers reduce preparation time from hours to seconds. Potwashing machines reduce the physical labor in that area by 50% and more. Convection ovens reduce cooking time by one-third, often eliminating the need for a full half-shift of cooks. Electronic and quartz ovens reduce cooking time even more drastically. The use of sharp freezing, blast freezing and nitrogen freezing make greater utilization of personnel possible.

There is a machine that washes, dries and sorts silverware. There is a fully automatic dishroom that does not require an operator. There are automated and computerized tray assembly lines that can reduce hospital tray assembly crews by one-half to two-thirds. An automated machine now available needs only one operator to broil, roast, bake or fry massive quantities of food. Automated carts, monorails and conveyors can whisk food and supplies around and operate without need of human assistance.

There is mechanized assistance or replacement for nearly every food-service task. When management problems have been identified, it is not difficult to compare and evaluate the relative values of labor intensive equipment vs. automated systems. When this is done, productivity gains will exceed capital expenditures to an impressive degree.

Summary

The motivating of human beings, discussed earlier in this book, is the long term mode of increasing productivity in foodservice. The short term gains which, incidentally, last through the long term, are made through the use of convenience foods, disposable serviceware and automated equipment.

We have discussed the various means of evaluating the cost effectiveness of convenience foods against making foods in the "house." Every operation calls for its own mixture of on-site and off-site preparation; there is no magic formula. The overriding message is that all of the various areas of impact upon the foodservice operation must be considered when evaluating and/or implementing convenience food products.

Disposable serviceware can and does have its advantages. The exciting new materials, new colors, new patterns available make disposables more and more acceptable every year. Use of the formula supplied in this chapter, along with some keen insight into the operation's customer preferences should provide the answer to the "use/wash—use/throw-away" question.

Automated equipment can save minutes and it can save hours. The purpose of automation in foodservice equipment is to make food production more uniform while using fewer labor dollars.

All three of these management tools, convenience foods, disposable serviceware and automated equipment serve the very major purpose of eliminating labor hours while making the job itself more humane. Foodservice is people; and people like to be proud of their work. Using modernized foods, serviceware and equipment will help employees to take pride in their work and, thereby, increase productivity.

7 Utilization— Prerequisite to Increasing Productivity

Harry H. Pope

This book has presented several valid techniques for improving productivity. Raymond B. Peddersen's section describes how a sound organizational structure and modern personnel techniques affect productivity. Arthur C. Avery tells how productivity can be improved by using scientific principles to establish a more effective relationship between various pieces of equipment.

Ruth D. Richard's approach to productivity is through establishment of work centers based on analysis of the tasks to be performed. Chef James Osenton's solution to the productivity problem lies in planning of production. Raymond Peddersen has a further chapter describing how convenience foods, disposables and automation can be used to improve productivity.

Each of these approaches to increased productivity is valid, but the reader should be aware that *none of the methods will increase productivity unless management can achieve full utilization of labor.*

The foodservice industry has had a poor record of labor utilization. Much of a foodservice employee's time is spent in *"waiting," "watching,"* or *"coasting"*; these are the main symptoms of under-utilization.

"Waiting" is easy to detect as it involves inactivity.

"Watching" may be accompanied by some useless action, such as shaking the handle of the basket in which the chicken is frying.

"Coasting" can be detected by comparing actual labor output with a fair standard.

Made aware of these symptoms, alert management can quickly discover areas where utilization can be improved. When suppliers appreciate the fact that full utilization is the key to productivity, they can design their products to overcome under-utilization.

Any decision to purchase equipment, devices or products which are designed to increase efficiency should be based on the answer to the question, "How can the purchase improve utilization of labor?"

Throughout the foodservice industry, we encounter an attitude of skepticism toward the modern equipment and convenience foods which are designed to increase productivity. If the suppliers can help foodservice operators achieve full utilization of labor and, thereby, realize the efficiencies which are obtainable through equipment and convenience foods, the suppliers will have less trouble overcoming the skepticism and can actually improve their sales.

Foodservice operators must make sure that equipment, devices and products are being used to full potential of efficiency. For example, when permanent-press napkins, placemats or tablecloths are used, these items can be washed and dried in automatic equipment which can be installed where the equipment can be controlled by existing staff. This arrangement is more efficient than installing a separate laundry department, where it will be necessary to have special employees who will be waiting and watching while the machines do the work.

A job is usually an arbitrary set of tasks and should be subject to change at any time. But, one of the problems in providing alternate duties, or switching employees to different jobs in order to achieve greater utilization, is the natural resistance of employees to change. The usual reaction of the employee is to say, "You've got me doing two people's work." Management has to be ready for such a reaction by being able to explain why increased productivity is in the interest of the employee.

An effective argument for introducing methods that will increase the American worker's productivity—and one that today's workers are familiar with—is the need for American products to be able to compete in world markets. To keep the American standard of living at the desired level requires the improvement in productivity that will keep America's products competitive.

Workers are increasingly determined to have jobs that are interesting. When full utilization is made of worker time, a greater variety of activities can be included in the job description. A forceful argument can be made that the job that encompasses a variety of tasks is more interesting and more of a continuing challenge than the job that is narrowed to one or a very few tasks.

It should always be made clear to the employee that the basic standard for employees remains the same: "We only ask an hour's work for an hour's pay."

Also effective in explaining to employees why productivity must be improved is to point out the constant pressure for increased wages. Employees who try to resist changes should be asked whether they would also resist the change in wages which has been the pattern for over thirty years.

Another question also frequently raised is: "How can utilization be improved when union rules define jobs?" Here again, there is a need for clear thinking, logical explanations and hard selling by management. Recently, a union representative said, "If management spent more time negotiating for better work rules, rather than negotiating to hold down wages, unions would not be a barrier to increased productivity. In fact, the long-term goal of the union is the same goal of any enlightened employer: to improve wages through increasing productivity."

In most foodservice operations it is easy to find examples of Parkinson's Law: "Work expands to fill the amount of time available." Therefore, when

---

HOW FAILURE TO UTILIZE CAN RESULT IN FAILURE TO IMPROVE PRODUCTIVITY

In a restaurant which served 100 guests for lunch, one employee, working at a sink, washed all the glasses, china, and silverware. To increase efficiency, the restaurant operator installed a single tank dishwashing machine. Later, he was advised to install a conveyor type machine to save the work of opening doors and pushing the racks through. Still later, the restaurant operator replaced the conveyor type with a flight type machine, to eliminate the work of handling racks. After all these improvements at the company's expense, how much labor was saved? The restaurant is still using one employee to wash the tableware for 100 customers. True, the employee's work has been made easier and time has been saved. But the time has been saved for the employee— not for the restaurant!

---

application of the techniques suggested by the authors of this book results in newly-saved time, it is essential to have a plan that will utilize the time that has been saved.

One way to utilize newly available time is to provide alternate duties to be substituted for those no longer needed. For example, when a dishwashing machine replaces hand washing of dishes, the dishwasher can be assigned to additional duties such as porter work; or, small automatic laundry machines can be installed in the dishwashing area, so that the washing of no-iron linens can be part of the work performed in the department.

When the installation of automatic machinery makes the dishwashing department more efficient, it may be possible to postpone the washing of tableware until after most of the guests have been served, when service people can be transferred to the dishwashing department.

This concept of delaying work is related to James Osenton's concept that "Prime Time" and "Slack Time" have different values. "Prime Time," the busy time when guests are being served, should be utilized in the most profitable ways, ways that can maximize sales. Work which can be performed in advance, or work which can be postponed, should be scheduled for the "Slack Time."

If we can agree that Prime Time labor is more valuable than Slack Time labor, then a foodservice operation can often justify doing work which could otherwise only be avoided through use of convenience products, for this work can be done in Slack Time. The cook's Slack Time can be used to make and freeze breads, pies, soups, and entrees, which otherwise might have been purchased ready prepared. Salad greens purchased pre-cut can be replaced, at lower cost, with greens cut on the premises. Waitresses can put condiments into souffle cups, instead of using pre-portioned condiments. Crackers can be wrapped by hand instead of buying crackers already wrapped. An analysis of such tasks will show how costs can be lowered. It is a fact that many of these tasks can be handled without any additional labor, simply by using up some of the idle time which seems to exist in all foodservice operations.

It has been my experience that it costs nothing for most cafeterias to wrap silverware in napkins, rather than to present loose silver on a self-service basis. If a cafeteria has an adequate quantity of extra silverware, the manager can usually find plenty of idle time available for wrapping the silverware.

By having an adequate inventory of dishes and glassware, the foodservice operator can usually avoid having all tableware washed during Prime Time. Instead, the operation can concentrate on stacking the soiled ware during the meal period, and the washing can be done later.

One of the most important ways to increase productivity is to set standards. Just as standards have been responsible for the improved performance in athletic competition, standards can improve productivity in foodservice. Standards show what is possible, and encourage people to improve.

Standards can be set for overall performance. In this case the standard of "sales per labor/hour", or "meals per labor/hour" can be used. Tabulation of "sales per labor/hour" statistics and the distribution of the comparative statistics to various units of one foodservice chain has resulted in a 40% improvement in productivity in less than two years! This kind of improvement has been accomplished with no significant change in layout, equipment or methods. Simply by showing managers what could be done, and encouraging their competitive spirit, managers have been able to find many ways to eliminate idle time and achieve greater utilization.

In a like manner, the development and distribution of departmental productivity statistics has helped improve productivity.

Standards are needed for tasks in order to encourage better performance by individuals. For example, in a cafeteria a fair standard for wrapping silver is six sets per minute. If an employee is made aware of the standard, it is not difficult to get the employee to meet or better the standard. If no standard is communicated to the employee, the productivity may be one-half or one-third as much.

Trade associations, suppliers, and operators should work together to exchange information on standards. The foodservice industry needs more statistics on labor requirements, and the work output available from modern equipment and products.

If, through greater efficiency, we can hold down menu prices, more people will eat meals away from home. Greater utilization and greater efficiency will follow greater sales volume, and the process will be self-generating. These are exciting and challenging times in the foodservice industry—times that call for creative thinking and plenty of attention to details.

The successful approach to increasing productivity must recognize that the real key to efficiency is *productivity*, but the basis of productivity is *utilization*. *Standards* measure the value of methods and products designed to increase productivity. Meshing these three assures development of a maximum productivity rate.

Bibliography and Suggested Readings

American Frozen Food Institute. *Frozen Food Pack Statistics.* Washington, D. C.: American Frozen Food Institute, 1970.

American School Food Service Association. *Improvement of Personnel Through Testing, Interviewing, Orienting, Training and Evaluating, Part II.* Presented at ASFSA Convention. Detroit, Michigan, August 6, 1969.

Argyris, Chris. *Understanding Organizational Behavior.* Homewood, Ill.: Dorsey Press, 1960.

Avery, Arthur C. "Work Design and Food Service Systems." *Journal of The American Dietetic Association,* (August, 1967).

Bangs, E. O.; Christensen, H.; Pope, H. H.; Whyte, Wm. F.; Welch, J. M. "Improving Employee Productivity." *The Cornell Hotel and Restaurant Administration Quarterly,* (May, 1969), pp. 56-86, 109-13.

Barnes, Ralph M. *Motion and Time Study: Design and Measurement of Work.* New York: John Wiley and Sons, 1958.

Benge, Eugene J. "A Management Effectiveness Index." *Advanced Management,* (August, 1962), pp. 12-15.

Blau, P. and Scott, W. *Formal Organizations.* San Francisco: Chandler, 1962.

Brodner, J.; Carlson, H. M.; and Maschal, H. T., eds. *Profitable Food And Beverage Operation,* rev. ed. New York: Ahrens, 1966.

Brusk, Edward C. *Human Relations for Management.* New York: Harper and Bros., 1956.

California State Department of Education, Bureau of Food Services. *Work Improvement, A Course for School Food Service Personnel.* Sacramento, Calif.: State Department of Education, 1967.

Carpenter, Russ, ed. "Make or Buy." *Volume Feeding Management,* (May, 1970), pp. 3-5, 8-9, 12-13, 16-17, 20-22.

Coffman, James P. *The High Payroll—Low Profit Syndrome.* Chicago: Medalist Publications, Inc., 1970.

"Convenience Foods." *Volume Feeding Management,* (September, 1968), pp. 35-58.

"Convenience Foods 3rd Annual Report." *Volume Feeding Management,* (September, 1969), pp. 30-60.

"Convenience Foods: The Operator Speaks." *Volume Feeding Management,* (December, 1967), pp. 35-42.

"Convenience Revolution in U. S. Eating Habits." *Fast Food,* (May, 1969), pp. 62, 64, 66.

Culinary Institute of America. *Introduction to Professional Food Service.* Chicago: Institutions Magazine, 1968.

Dale, Ernest. *Organization.* New York: American Management Association, 1967.

Dana, A. W.; Kotschevar, L. H.; and Pope, H. H. "A Seminar on Labor Utilization." *Food Management In Hospitals and Nursing Homes,* n. d., pp. 17-27.

"Designing the Kitchen to Fit the Menu." *Food Service Magazine,* (March 3, 1965), pp. 69-72.

Donaldson, Beatrice. "The Future in Food Administration." *Journal of The American Dietetic Association,* (May, 1965), pp. 357-60.

Drucker, Peter F. *The Practice of Management.* New York: Harper and Bros., 1954.

Dungan, Avalon L. and Lacey, Stephen E. "Convenience Foods—What Are They? How Are They Utilized?" *The Cornell Hotel and Restaurant Administration Quarterly,* (August, 1969).

"Dynamics of Systems Dialogue." *Food Services Marketing, 34, 11,* (November, 1972), pp. 52-67.

Elliott, T.; Lassiter, Wm. E.; Galione, J.; Gibson, P. B.; O'Malley, P. L.; Pope, H. H.; Clark, Jr., W. F.; Warner, M.; Camp, Wm. T.; Rorke, N.; White, E. C.; and the Editors. "How to Make Restaurant Work Worthwhile." *Fast Food Magazine,* (October, 1967), pp. 1-64.

Fisk, Mary L.; Hart, Katherine M.; and Miller, Grace A. "Long-Range Planning for Food Service Layouts." *Journal of the American Dietetic Association,* (June, 1963), pp. 489-95.

Flory, C. D., ed. *Managers for Tomorrow.* New York: The New American Library, 1965.

　　　　　Managing Through Insight. New York: The New American Library, 1968.

"Food Service Equipment: The Present State of the Art." *Volume Feeding Management,* (May, 1969), pp. 27-45.

Gardner, John W. "How to Prevent Organization Dry Rot." *Harper's Magazine,* (October, 1965).

Gellerman, Saul W. *Motivation and Productivity.* New York: American Management Association, 1963.

　　　　　The Management of Human Relations. New York: Holt, Rinehart and Winston, 1966.

George, Jr., Claude S. *The History of Management Thought.* Englewood Cliffs, N. J.: Prentice-Hall, 1968.

Gilbreth, Frank B. *Primer of Scientific Management.* New York: D. Van Nostrand Co., 1912.

Gilbreth, L. M. *The Psychology of Management.* New York: Sturgis and Walton Co., 1914.

Ginzberg, Eli and Reilly, E. W. *Effecting Change in Large Organizations.* New York: Columbia University Press, 1957.

Gray, Evelyn M. and Donaldson, Beatrice. "Costs and Rate of Labor Turnover in a Hospital Dietary Department." *Journal of The American Dietetic Association,* (March, 1967), pp. 191-95.

Heinemeyer, Jane M. "Keeping Hot Foods Hot." *Hospitals,* (February 2, 1972), pp. 83-86.

Herzberg, F. et al. *Job Attitudes: Review of Research and Opinion.* Pittsburg: Psychological Services of Pittsburg, 1957.

        ; Mausner, B.;   and Snyderman, B. B.   *The Motivation to Work.* New York: John Wiley and Sons, 1959.

Higgens, Carter C. "The Organization Chart: Its Theory and Practice." *Management Review,* (October, 1956), pp. 889-93.

Hoff, Margaret Hodgson. "Traditional Equipment: Answer to Convenience Foods." *Cooking for Profit,* (April, 1969), pp. 34, 36, 38, 41.

Hysen, Paul. "Ready Foods May Provide Ready Savings." *Modern Hospital,* (June, 1971).

Institution Management Laboratory of the Department of Foods and Nutrition. *Methodology for Work Sampling: Productivity of Dietary Personnel.* Department of Foods and Nutrition, University of Wisconsin. Madison, Wisc., 1967.

Jay, Anthony. *Management and Machiavelli.* New York: Holt, Rinehart and Winston, 1967.

Josephson, Matthew. *Union House, Union Bar.* New York: Random House, 1956.

Kotschevar, Lendal H. *Food Service for the Extended Care Facility.* Boston: Institutions/VF Magazine/Cahners Books, 1973.

Kotschevar, Lendal H. and Terrell, M. E. *Food Service Planning: Layout and Equipment.* New York: John Wiley and Sons, 1961.

        How to Select and Care for Serviceware, Textiles, Cleaning Compounds. Chicago: Institutions Magazine, 1969.

Landsberger, H. *Hawthorne Revisited.* Ithaca: Cornell University Press, 1958.

Leskovec, Ernest W. "A Guide for Discussing the Performance Appraisal." *Personnel Journal,* (March, 1967), pp. 150-52.

Levenstein, Aaron. *Motivating People to Work.* New York: Training, Research and Special Studies Division, 1967.

Likert, Rensis. *The Human Organization: Its Management and Value.* New

York: McGraw-Hill, 1967.

Lipscomp, Mary and Donaldson, Beatrice. "How Well Do Directors of Dietetics Fulfill Managerial Responsibilities." *Journal of The American Dietetic Association,* (September, 1964), pp. 218-24.

Lundberg, Donald E. and Armatas, James P. *The Management of People in Hotels, Restaurants and Clubs.* Dubuque, Iowa: Wm. C. Brown Company, 1955.

Maier, N. and Hages, J. J. *Creative Management.* New York: John Wiley and Sons, 1962.

Mannini, Walter. "Disposable Ware for Food Service." *The Cornell Hotel and Restaurant Administration Quarterly,* (May, 1968), pp. 69-71.

Miller, Edmund, ed. *Profitable Cafeteria Operation.* New York: Ahrens, 1966.

Marrow, A. J.; Bowers, D. G.; and Seashore, S. E. *Strategies of Organizational Change.* New York: Harper and Row, 1967.

McFarland, Palton E. *Management Principles and Practices.* New York: MacMillan, 1958.

McGregor, Douglas. *The Human Side of Enterprise.* New York: McGraw Hill, 1960.

Mogensen, A. H. *Work Simplification Programs.* Lake Placid, New York: Work Simplification Conference, 1953.

Montag, Geraldine M.; McKinley, Marjorie M.; and Kleinschmidt, Arthur C. "Production Costs: Labor-Saving Equipment vs. Non-Machine Methods." *Journal of The American Dietetic Association,* (October, 1967).

National Association of Meat Purveyors. *Meat Buyers Guide to Portion Controlled Meat Cuts.* Chicago: N.A.M.P., 1967.

Peddersen, Raymond B. "How a Special Spice System Can Spark Success for Health Care Services." *Food Service Marketing,* 34, 9 (September, 1972) pp. 40, 42.

"Rather Fight than Switch?" *Hospitals: Journal of the American Hospital Association,* 46, 19 (October 16, 1972) pp. 132-138.

"Snap-On Concepts to Brighten Your Menu Fare." *Food Service Marketing,* 35, 4 (April, 1973) pp. 68, 70.

"The Convenience Conversion at Hillside Hospital, Glen Oaks, New York." *Food Service Magazine,* (February, 1972), pp. 53, 60-61.

"The Evolutionary Approach to the Implementation of a Health Care Feeding System." *Systems Impact: The Food Service Industry of the 70's.* Chicago: The Institutional Food Editorial Council, 1972, pp. P1-P9.

"Three Keys to Better Food Service." *Health Institution Purchasing,* (May, 1972), pp. 23-27.

Peter, L. J. and Hall, R. *The Peter Principle.* New York: William Morrow and Co., 1969.

Pinckard, Ch. P. "Automated Dishwashing Streamlines the Scullery." *The Cornell Hotel and Restaurant Administration Quarterly,* (May, 1968), pp. 125-32.

"Productivity Produces Profits." *National Restaurant Association,* (May, 1967).

Quam, Mary E.; Fitzsimmons, Cleo; and Godfrey, Ruth L. "Ready-Prepared vs. Conventionally Prepared Foods." *Journal of The American Dietetic Association,* (March, 1967), pp. 196-200.

Richard, Ruth D. and Garvey, Donald P. *Work Methods and Equipment.* Presented at American School Food Service Association. Las Vegas, Nevada, (August, 1968).

Rodgers, Richard K. "Five Steps to Financial Strength." *Fast Food,* January, 1968).
    "Sharpen Your Short-Range Planning." *Fast Food,* (May, 1968), pp. 68-72.
    "Systems Solutions in Four Dimensions." *Food Service Magazine,* (May, 1970), pp. 40-46.

Ross, Lynn Nannen. *Work Simplification in Food Service: Individualized Instruction.* Ames, Iowa: The Iowa State University Press, 1972.

Rothenbuhler, Ervin F. and Bartscht, Karl G. "Determining Dietary Staff in Hospitals—Methodology." *Journal of The American Dietetic Association,* (July, 1955), pp. 25-28.

Sayles, C. I. and MacLennon, H. A. "The Application of Mass Production to a la Carte Food Service Using Prepared-to-Order Food." *Research Report No. 16—The Cornell Hotel and Restaurant Administration Quarterly,* (February, 1968).

Smalley, H. E. and Freeman, J. R. *Hospital Industrial Engineering.* New York: Reinhold, 1966.

Stevenson, Eugene H. "What Is An Informative Label?" *Journal of The American Dietetic Association,* (April, 1968), pp. 304-07.

Stokes, John W. *How to Manage a Restaurant or Institutional Food Service.* Dubuque, Iowa: Wm. C. Brown, 1970.

Taylor, Frederick W. *Principles of Scientific Management.* New York: Harper and Bros., 1911.

Terrell, Margaret E. "New Features in Institutional Equipment." *Journal of The American Dietetic Association,* (May, 1965), pp. 374-78.

"Third Annual Single Service Survey: What You Don't Know Can Hurt You." *Institutions/Volume Feeding,* (March 15, 1972), pp. 61-68.

Thorner, Marvin. *Convenience and Fast Food Handbook,* Westport, Conn.: A.V.I., 1973.

"Throw-Away World." *Institutions,* (April, 1969), pp. 20, 24.

Tiffen, J. and McCormick, E. J. *Industrial Psychology,* Chap. 8. Englewood Cliffs, N. J.: Prentice Hall, 1958.

Wallace, Dorothy E. "Defining Salary Classes and Wage Ranges." *Hospitals,* (September 6, 1963), pp. 38-72, 218.

Ward, A. F.; Clark, C.; Kiino, H. M.; Pollard, D. M.; and Verzi, M. A. "Permanent Versus Disposable Service Ware in Hospitals." *Hospitals,* (March 1, 1972), pp. 144-45, 148, 150-51.

Wilkinson, Jule. *Storage Specifics.* Chicago, Ill.: Institutions Magazine, 1969.

The Finishing Kitchen. Chicago, Ill.: Institutions Magazine, 1969.

The Complete Book of Cooking Equipment. Boston: Institutions/Volume Feeding Magazine/Cahners Books, 1972.

Witzky, Herbert K. *Practical Hotel-Motel Cost Reduction Handbook.* New York: Ahrens, 1970.

Modern Hotel-Motel Management Methods. New York: Ahrens, 1964.

Work Simplification. Burbank, Calif.: Lockheed Aircraft Corporation, 1943.

Wortman, Max S. *Critical Issues in Labor: Text and Readings.* Toronto: Collier–MacMillan Canada, Ltd., 1969.

Whyte, William F. *Human Relations in the Restaurant Industry.* New York: McGraw-Hill, 1948.

Money and Motivation. New York: Harper and Bros., 1956.

Zander, A. F. *Performance Appraisals.* Ann Arbor: Foundation for Research on Human Behavior, 1963.

Index